MW00785117

SESSUE HAYAKAWA

A JOHN HOPE FRANKLIN CENTER BOOK

SESSUE HAYAKAWA

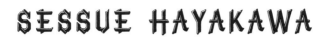

Silent Cinema and Transnational Stardom

DAISUKE MIYAO

DUKE UNIVERSITY PRESS

Durham & London 2007

© 2007 Duke University Press
All rights reserved

Printed in the United States of America
on acid-free paper ∞

Designed by Jennifer Hill
Typeset in Scala by Tseng Information Systems, Inc.
Library of Congress Cataloging-in-Publication Data
appear on the last printed page of this book.

In memory of Mitsunori Miyao and Makoto and Kyoko Shibasaki

CONTENTS

ILLUSTRATIONS

ABBREVIATIONS

EH: Exhibitor's Herald

ETR: Exhibitor's Trade Review

MPN: Motion Picture News

MPW: Moving Picture World

NYDM: New York Dramatic Mirror

SHE: Sessue Hayakawa: Locke Collection Envelope 659,
*New York Public Library for the Performing Arts,
Robinson Locke Collection*

SHS: Sessue Hayakawa: *Scrapbook,*
*New York Public Library for the Performing Arts,
Robinson Locke Collection*

ACKNOWLEDGMENTS

The completion of this book was enabled by numerous individuals and institutions that offered generous support. The bulk of this project was done while I was a graduate student at the Department of Cinema Studies at New York University, which provided a tremendously supportive environment. First, I want to thank Robert Sklar, who kindly and patiently managed to transform me from a naïve Japanese student who knew very little about the practice of cinema studies into a slightly more articulate scholar. I thank Zhang Zhen, who has been enthusiastic about my project from the very beginning. Without her inspiration, insights, and friendship it would have taken me forever to complete this book. I am very much obliged to William G. Simon for making my life in New York so much easier than it would have been if he had not been around. Without his clear-sighted reading and commenting, this project would have never come into existence as a book. Mitsuhiro Yoshimoto's work has always been a great model of scholarship on Japanese cinema. Charles Affron has taught me the appreciation of various melodramas, including literature, opera, and films, and shared a love of silent movie stars with me. Thanks to Richard Allen, the late William K. Everson, Ed Guerrero, Antonia Lant, Toby Miller, Robert Stam, and Chris Strayaar for their advice at various stages of this project. I must also thank the dissertation group, particularly Heather McMillan and Augusta Lee Palmer. They were willing to read all of my chapters at various stages, give me valuable comments, questions, and ideas, and even polish my English expressions, all without any complaint. Their friendship, generosity, intelligence, and sense of humor have always encouraged me.

My project involved extensive transnational research in the United States, Japan, and Europe, and I have been very fortunate to be assisted by many institutions in this regard. I thank above all Charles Silver at the Museum of Modern Art Film Study Center in New York and Okajima Hisashi at the National Film Center of the Museum of Modern Art in Tokyo. Our friendships started in 1993 when the National Film Center had a film series entitled "American Films—The Little Known," and Charles gave an opening lecture.

That was the series in which I saw Sessue Hayakawa's silent films for the first time, and those films laid a beautiful spell on me.

I also thank Kyoko Hirano at the Japan Society Film Center; Koike Akira, Okada Yoshiko, Sakano Yuka, Waji Yukiko, and staff members at the Kawakita Memorial Film Institute, who made it possible for me to read many early Japanese film magazines within short periods of time; Saiki Tomonori, Okada Hidenori, and Tsuneishi Fumiko at the National Film Center; Aoki Kazunori at the Chikura Town Office; Moriwaki Kiyotaka and staff members at the Museum of Kyoto; Madeline F. Matz and Brian Taves at the Library of Congress Motion Picture, Broadcasting, and Recorded Sound Division; Barbara Hall at the Margaret Herrick Library of the Center for Motion Picture Academy; Jennifer Tobias and Steven Higgins at the Museum of Modern Art; Ronny Temme at the Nederlands Filmmuseum; Edward Comstock at the University of Southern California Film-Television Library; Toshiko McCallum and Marie Masumoto at Hirasaki National Resource Center of the Japanese American National Museum; Russ Taylor at Brigham Young University's Harold B. Lee Library; Richard Andress at the New York State Archives Cultural Education Center; Ann Harris at the Study Center of the Department of Cinema Studies at New York University; Edith Kramer, Mona Nagai, Jason Sanders, Nancy Goldman, and Stephen Gong at the Pacific Film Archive; and John Mhiripiri and Shannon McLaclan at the Anthology Film Archive. I have also benefited greatly from my visits to Cinemateca Portuguesa, the New York Public Library for Performing Arts, the University of California, Los Angeles Department of Special Collections, the Theater Museum at Waseda University, the National Diet Library, Shochiku Otani Library, and the Library of Sociology and Media Studies at the University of Tokyo. Thanks to Pat Padua and John Harris for their assistance in obtaining illustrations.

The Freeman Postdoctoral Fellowship in Expanding East Asian Studies at Columbia University and the Mellon Postdoctoral Fellowship in Humanities at the University of California, Berkeley, provided me with precious time to complete this book. More importantly, thanks to these fellowships, I was able to have wonderful opportunities to talk profoundly about my project with Carol Gluck, Heidi Johnson, Paul Anderer, Richard Peña, and the colleagues of ExEAS at Columbia (Kenji, Si, T.J., and Bill, in particular); as well as Linda Williams, Alan Tansman, Paula Varsano, Kristen Whissel, Miryam Sas, Tony Kaes, Kaja Silverman, and the colleagues of Film Studies and East Asian Languages and Cultures at the University of California, Berkeley. I also received financial support from the Ito Foundation for International Education Exchange, Rotary International, and the Matsushita Foundation.

Among many friends, colleagues, and mentors on both sides of the Pacific who have provided invaluable professional and emotional support, I would like to particularly thank Chris Arnold, Cari Beauchamp, Joanne Bernardi, John Boccellari, David Bordwell, Barbara Brooks, Christy Burks, John Whiteclay Chambers II, Doi Shigeru, Ebina Suezumi, Fujiki Hideaki, Fujita Fumiko, Kathryn Fuller-Seeley, Funatsu Akiko, Will Gardner, Tom Gunning (I really appreciate his extremely valuable and encouraging advice at various stages), Elise Hansen, Hasumi Shigehiko (without his writings and lectures on cinema, I would never have started thinking seriously about the subject), Sumiko Higashi, Hirobe Izumi, the late Yuji Ichioka, David Jaffee, Sergei K. Kapterev (my fellow "cinemania"), Alex Keller, Kido Yoshiyuki, Kinoshita Chika, Donald Kirihara, Kitamura Hiroshi, Kitano Keisuke, Richard Koszarski, Kotani Mari, Kurita Toyomichi (who was supposed to be the director of photography for Oshima Nagisa's unrealized film on Sessue Hayakawa, *Hollywood Zen*), James Latham, Hyung-sook Lee, Maeda Koichi, Gina Marchetti, Masuda Hikaru, Matsuura Hisaki, Keiko I. McDonald, Mizuno Sachiko, Livia Monnet, Murakami Yumiko, Nogami Hideyuki, Ochi Toshio, Okada Mariko, Onishi Naoki, Abé Markus Nornes, Oshio Kazuto, Misa Oyama, Michael Raine, Paula Ratzsky, Donald Richie, Saito Ayako, Shinogi Naoko, Takagi Noritsune, Deborah A. Thomas, Mitsuyo Wada Marciano, Gregory Waller, Yamaguchi Masaaki, Uzawa Yoshiko, Yomota Inuhiko, Yoneyama Hiroshi, Yoneyama Miho, and Yoshida Kiju. I also thank enthusiastic audiences of my talks at the University of Oregon, Berkeley Film Seminar, Weatherhead East Asian Institute at Columbia University, Kinema Club, West Virginia University International Conference, Hawaii International Conference in Humanities, the Society for Cinema and Media Studies, and the Association for Asian Studies.

Mari Yoshihara deserves a separate paragraph of special thanks. Mari has been not only my intellectual and professional mentor but also a precious friend since my sophomore year at the University of Tokyo. It is impossible for me to think of being in academia without her guidance and friendship.

I would like to sincerely thank Nishimura Taro, Matsumoto Toshio, Tatsumi Takayuki, and the Faculty of Letters at Keio University; Notoji Masako, Kunishige Junji, Kamei Shunsuke, Shimada Taro, Shinkawa Kenzaburo, Takita Yoshiko, Sato Yoshiaki, Shibata Motoyuki, Hayashi Fumiyo, Endo Yasuo,

Uchino Tadashi, and the Faculty of American Studies at the University of Tokyo, Komaba, for their tremendous generosity.

Special thanks go to my editor at Duke University Press, Ken Wissoker, who has done an amazingly thorough and insightful job. I thank Katharine Baker and Courtney Berger as well for patiently guiding me through the book's production. I appreciate the extensive and extremely helpful comments and suggestions by anonymous readers for Duke University Press.

This book is dedicated to Sessue Hayakawa's family and relatives. Hayakawa Tokuko and the late Hayakawa Yukio in Los Angeles, and Hayakawa Masahiko in Chikura, generously showed me many personal photos and letters of Hayakawa Sesshu and Aoki Tsuruko, and shared many episodes of their family lives. Meeting with them has surely made this project more intimate to me.

I would like to thank my colleagues at the University of Oregon for their extreme kindness and generosity: Steven Brown and Alisa Freedman in Japanese Literature and Film, Maram Epstein in Asian Studies, Steve Durrant and Marjorie Woollacott in East Asian Languages and Literatures, and Mike Aronson, Sangita Gopal, and Kathleen Karlyn in Film Studies.

I am very grateful to my parents, Miyao Shunsuke and Masami, from the bottom of my heart for always believing in me. I am also very grateful to Akagi Sadao and Kimiko.

Finally, very, very special thanks go to Yoko and Dica, the loves of my life.

INTRODUCTION

Sessue Hayakawa. The greatest movie star in this century. . . White women were willing to give themselves to a Japanese man. . . . When Sessue was getting out of his limousine in front of a theater of a premiere showing, he grimaced a little because there was a puddle. Then, dozens of female fans surrounding his car fell over one another to spread their fur coats at his feet. . . . Valentino was very popular, too, but I think Sessue's popularity was greater. . . . Never again will there be a star like Sessue.

— MIYATAKE TOYO

These words of Miyatake Toyo, the renowned Japanese photographer in Los Angeles in the early 1900s, are astonishing because many popular audiences of cinema remember the Japanese actor Sessue Hayakawa (1886–1973) for his Oscar-nominated role as a frowning Japanese military officer in *The Bridge on the River Kwai* (David Lean, 1957). No matter how exaggerated Miyatake's words, they indicate that Hayakawa was very popular among white female audiences in the United States, in spite of his Japanese nationality. A film trade journal, *Wid's Daily*, stated in 1919 that Hayakawa had "a particularly large following among women" by the late 1910s.[1] A Japanese film magazine, *Katsudo Zasshi*, noted in 1922 that Hayakawa had "a mouth that all women love. When he opens his mouth and shows his crystal-like teeth, he becomes very attractive."[2] That is, Hayakawa had the status of a "matinee idol," whose career was "perceived as depending upon female fans."[3] Hayakawa himself was once quoted by an American journalist as saying, "My crientele [sic] is women. They rike [sic] me to be strong and violent."[4]

In 1917, a film fan magazine, *Motion Picture*, published a letter from a female fan addressed to Hayakawa:

O land of quaint and fascinating people,
Here's to thy son, who plays so well his art
That we take side with him in each creation,
Tho villain, friend or lover be that part.
Quiet he is, and smiles but very seldom,
Unerring in his mastery of the art;
The silent drama speaks in every picture–
When Sessue comes he leads, whate'er the part.

KATE MAY YOUNG, 842 W. 63d St., Seattle, Wash.[5]

This poem, especially the line "Tho villain, friend or lover be that part," indicates a (supposedly white) female fan's enthusiastic but ambivalent fascination with the actor from Japan, despite the fact that Hayakawa's attraction was obviously difficult for her to define. Was he villainous and evil? Was he an alien monster? Was he an example of the yellow peril, the pseudo-scientific discourse of the time among middle-class Americans who feared a Japanese imperialistic invasion of the United States? In Cecil B. DeMille's acclaimed film *The Cheat* (1915), Hayakawa was a sensationally villainous Japanese man. Was he friendly and gentle? Was he the representation of the American melting pot? Was he the model minority in American society? In his star vehicles that followed *The Cheat*, Hayakawa frequently played a Japanese or Asian immigrant hero who was eager to assimilate himself to American culture. Or, was he a good lover? In his star vehicles, Hayakawa's Asian hero often sacrificed himself for a white American woman whom he loved. Yet, in the end, his ethnicity often prevented him from being united with the one he loved. Did he become cruel when his wish was not fulfilled? Did he become erotic, instead, and seduce the woman he loved? What about Hayakawa himself as a person? Was he a villain, friend, or lover in early Hollywood and in American society as a whole? Was he an ideal, or lovable, product as an ideally Orientalized film star at the very beginning of the star system? Was he a villainous alien rebel against the emerging film industry with his unprecedented star image and his extraordinary acting skills? Was he an outsider of the industry and eventually excluded from it? Was he a representative of Japan who strategically embodied exotic Japaneseness for foreign viewers in order to secure a position in international political and economic relations? Or, was he a friendly Westernized Asian immigrant, a representative of Japanese immigrants who are willing to adapt to American society? No matter how difficult it was to define Hayakawa's star image, according to the film critic DeWitt

Bodeen, "the effect of Hayakawa on American women was even more electric than Valentino's. It involved fiercer tones of masochism as well as a latent female urge to experience sex with a beautiful but savage man of another race."[6] Both ethnic matinee idols, Hayakawa (in the 1910s to the early 1920s) and Rudolph Valentino (in the 1920s), redefined the imagery of a masculine star in new ways that appealed to female fans. The (in)famous Valentino cult was created in the 1920s via female-oriented media in consumer culture, such as women's magazines, fan magazines, plays, and popular literature, which were widely accessible to a broad segment of the female population.[7] The feminine quality of Valentino's star image could have had a subversive effect against "the socially imposed dominance-submission hierarchy of gender roles, dissolving subject-object dichotomies into erotic reciprocity."[8] Hayakawa's star image, which seemed to combine masculinity and femininity, and its tremendous success preceded the Valentino cult.

In the mid-1910s, Hayakawa suddenly emerged at the very beginning of the star system in Hollywood and rapidly became a superstar. As early as May 1916, only five months after *The Cheat* was released, Hayakawa was ranked number one in the *Chicago Tribune* popular star contests.[9] In 1917, the Madison Theater at Broadway and Grand Circus Park in Detroit juxtaposed Hayakawa in *The Call of the East* (George Melford, 1917) with other big stars, Charlie Chaplin (*The Adventurer*) and William S. Hart (*Double Crossed*), in its advertisement of "A Mammoth Triple Feature Program" (see fig. 1). Hayakawa had thus by 1917 achieved star status equal to that of Chaplin and Hart.[10]

Hayakawa's popularity was not limited to the United States. In Germany, in 1920, the critic Claire Goll named Hayakawa as one of the three "American" actors "most famous and most celebrated throughout the world," along with Douglas Fairbanks Sr. and Charlie Chaplin. Goll describes how sensational Hayakawa was to German audiences: "Wholly spiritual is the great Japanese actor, Sessue Hayakawa. He knows no trivial little feelings, but only primal sensation. One finds no trace here of an art sullied by civilization. When he portrays sorrow, his pain is of ancient dimensions. When he plays the lover, his smile has the grace and aroma of lotus and cherry blossoms. As the avenger, his body explodes in exotic wilderness. Whoever sees him knows everything about Japan, everything of the beauty of the mystical East."[11] In Russia, in 1922, Sergei Yutkevich and Sergei Eisenstein named Hayakawa as one of the "wonderful actors" in America, with William S. Hart, Mary Pickford, Douglas Fairbanks, Roscoe Arbuckle, and Charlie Chaplin.[12]

1 *A triple billing featuring Charlie Chaplin, William S. Hart, and Sessue Hayakawa, at the Madison Theater, Detroit.* Motion Picture News 16.20 (17 November 1917): 3435.

French audiences were even more enthusiastic. The drama critic Louis Delluc named Hayakawa and Charlie Chaplin, "whatever film they appear in," as "two expressions of beauty" and "the two masterpieces."[13] In *Le Film,* on 6 August 1917, Delluc wrote:

> Of Hayakawa, one can say nothing: he is a phenomenon. Explanations here are out of place. . . . Once more I am not speaking of talent. I consider a certain kind of actor, especially him, as a natural force and his face as a poetic work whose reason for being does not concern me when my avidity for beauty finds there expected chord or reflection. . . . It is not his cat-like, implacable cruelty, his mysterious brutality, his hatred of anyone who resists, or his contempt for anyone who submits; that is not what impresses us, and yet that is all we can talk about. . . . And especially his strangely drawn smile of childlike ferocity, not really the ferocity of a puma or jaguar, for then it would no longer be ferocity. The beauty of Sessue Hayakawa is painful. Few things in the cinema reveal to us, as the lights and silence of this mask do, that there really are *alone* beings. I well believe that all lonely people, and they are numerous, will discover their own resourceless despair in the intimate melancholy of this savage Hayakawa.[14]

Cecil Sorel, a renowned actress of the time, also praised Hayakawa's acting and compared it to classic arts: "Silence is the sum total of the emotions. Leonardo da Vinci expressed this in his 'Joconde,' Michelangelo in his 'Pensur,' and, in our day, in my own realm of the arts, . . . the Japanese, Sessue Hayakawa, condenses in his oblique gaze a whole inner tumult too great for expression."[15]

Delluc's claim (and Sorel's comparison between Hayakawa's acting and premodern arts) could be located within the primitivist dichotomy between the civilized West and the premodern East. Delluc insisted that Hayakawa's "beauty" came from "his race and virile style" and connected his "beauty" and acting skill with "a natural force." He even called Hayakawa "childlike" and "savage."[16] Yet, no matter how deeply French intellectuals' views on Hayakawa resided in primitivism and Orientalism, the impact of Hayakawa upon the French film culture was tremendous. Hayakawa's acting style inspired French intellectuals to develop the concept of *photogenie*, the unique aesthetic qualities that motion picture photography brings to the subject it films. The *photogenie* later became a significant theoretical basis of the French impressionist movement, filmmaking that "displayed a fascination with pictorial beauty and an interest in intense psychological exploration."[17]

Even when Hayakawa lost his popularity in the United States in the 1920s, French audiences enthusiastically embraced Hayakawa and made his French debut film *La Bataille* (*The Danger Line*, E. E. Violet, 1923), critically and financially successful. In April of the same year, 1923, when Hayakawa's star vehicle *The Swamp* (Colin Campbell, 1921) was released in France as *Le Devin du faubourg* [The neighborhood fortune-teller], the renowned film director René Clair, famous for his fantasy films, such as *Paris qui dort* (*The Crazy Ray*, 1924), and his experimental work, *Entr'acte* (1925), passionately praised Hayakawa:

> Everyone knows Sessue Hayakawa's talent, that powerful sobriety he revealed to us in *The Cheat*. Here Bessie Love seems to be inspired by him and worthy of that inspiration. Her frightened eyes, her curt gestures, her sad pout, remind us of the best moments of Lillian Gish. . . . That is where the cinema seems to me to have some advantage over the theater. . . . The expression of a silent face, taken in isolation, can be as beautiful appearing in a bad film as in a masterpiece. Working with mediocre and false material, actors like Sessue Hayakawa and Bessie Love are able to evoke beauty and truth.[18]

Consequently, Hayakawa even stayed in France throughout the period of World War II.

The popularity of Hayakawa is remarkable when one considers the fact that there were some popular non-Caucasian actors and actresses in the silent era, but they had mostly supporting roles as foils for white leading characters. From the early days in Hollywood, even when major characters were supposed to be Asians, Caucasian stars usually played the roles and displayed artificial Asian features ("yellow face"). Hayakawa was the one and only non-Caucasian star of the period. Hayakawa's stardom occupied an extraordinarily unique space in the racial and cultural map of early Hollywood. A Paramount Pictures ad in film trade journals in June 1917 noted that "Sessue Hayakawa has brought to the American motion picture the mysterious, the magic and mystic of Japan. No foreign-born actor of a generation has won so many admirers as this brilliant young Japanese, whose interpretations of the problems of the Oriental in Occidental lands has given him a unique place in the motion picture firmament."[19] Hayakawa was one of the first and most unusual stars of silent cinema.

Hayakawa's stardom was all the more astonishing because it went against the sociopolitical discourse of the time on Japan and the Japanese people. The period from the 1910s to the 1920s witnessed the rapid increase of anti-Japanese sentiment in the United States along with a xenophobic atmosphere, especially after World War I. Starting in the Pacific states, anti-Japanese movements developed against Japan's growing military and political power. Such anti-Japanese feelings were crystallized in the movements against immigrants from Japan. In 1920, the Japanese Exclusion League of California was organized. In November 1922, the Federal Supreme Court's *Ozawa v. United States* decision legally defined Japanese people as "aliens ineligible for citizenship" and denied naturalization to Japanese people.[20] Then, in 1924, the new immigration act passed by the U.S. Congress prohibited the entry of "aliens ineligible for citizenship," thus targeting Japanese immigrants. It is incredible that Hayakawa, in spite of his Japanese nationality, became a superstar under such sociopolitical conditions.

Simultaneously, however, the popularity of Hayakawa seemed to go along with that of Japanese culture. Alongside Japan's rapid sociopolitical and military modernization, Japan's image of cultural refinement, especially in the form of *Japonisme*, the European vogue in art and style, fascinated American women. Since the late nineteenth century, the penetration of Japanese goods into the American market brought about a "Japan craze."[21] Japanese art and culture were not only considered exotic but also high art because they were imports of European vogue. Especially after the Centennial Exhibition of 1876 in Philadelphia and the other international exhibitions that followed, where many Americans made their first contact with Japanese art and culture, high-class Japanese art and culture became gradually popularized among those of the middle class and fitted to their taste. In 1910, for instance, *Moving Picture World*, a film trade journal, remarked on the popularity of Japanese objects among "the American people": "The affection of the American people for the Japanese, then, springs from the fact that there is a sentimental link between the two nations. . . . Japanese art, Japanese life and Japanese costumes appeal to the occidental mind for many reasons. The grace, the charm, the poetry of Japan never fail to please us of the West. . . . We love our America, but oh you Japan!!!!"[22] Because of his Japanese nationality, Hayakawa had the potential to portray an image of cultural refinement that fascinated many Americans. Hayakawa's worldwide stardom thus existed in the midst of the dual identity that Japanese people were gaining in international political and cultural relations.

Even though it was unique and extremely complex, the career of Hayakawa has barely received critical attention in film history and was almost completely ignored in star studies. Books on the general history of film rarely mention Hayakawa. There are only a few studies focusing on his career, but most of them are speculative. Was Hayakawa's career so bizarre and paradoxical that it has been untouchable and hidden in a Pandora's box?

In these limited numbers of writings on Hayakawa, he has largely been described as a screen villain. Almost all of the obituaries of Hayakawa in November 1973 called him a villain, most likely because of his role as a ruthless Japanese officer in *The Bridge on the River Kwai* and his sensational image in *The Cheat*, in which Hayakawa's character brands a white woman's naked shoulder. For instance, the *New York Post* stated, "He [Hayakawa] was noted for his silent screen roles as a sinister Oriental during a bygone era of stereotypes."[23] However, his roles and his star image in silent films were not limited to only one category but were surprisingly varied and ambivalent.

How was Hayakawa able to become a movie star in the second decade of the twentieth century? How did early Hollywood studios construct Hayakawa's stardom in their formative period as an industry? What did Hayakawa think of his star image? How did the audiences in the United States, in Japan, and in Europe respond to Hayakawa's star image? The study of "early cinema," not only as a period term (approximately between 1895 and 1917 in the United States and Europe) but also as a critical category (films as well as media intertexts, industry, and market), emphasizes the practice of exhibition in film culture as well as that of production. In particular, it highlights the experience of early cinema in its intimate relation to a wide range of social and cultural practices, such as the vaudeville theater, the amusement park, shopping arcades, and so forth, to envisage the cinema in a broader landscape of modern life in the street and in the theater, in the city and in the country, and, as the historian Zhen Zhang insists, "in the West as well as in many other parts of the world."[24] Both at the stages of production and exhibition, Hayakawa's stardom in early cinema was entangled with many contradictory issues around gender, sexuality, race, ethnicity, class, and nation, which were spread in the complex network of social and cultural practices and experiences in modern life in the United States, Europe, and Japan.

In his influential work in star studies, Richard Dyer writes that all stars embody a tension, or a paradox. Dyer defines a star as a "structured polysemy" and explains the term as "the finite multiplicity of meanings and affects they [stars] embody and the attempt to structure them so that some meanings and affects are foregrounded and others masked or displaced." Dyer believes that a star, as a "real" individual "existence" in the world, succeeds in reconciling the contradictions through "magical synthesis."[25]

Yet, was Hayakawa a "real" individual "existence" in the world who succeeded in reconciling such various contradictions through "magical synthesis"? Hayakawa's career in silent cinema reveals that stardom is not a stable form of synthesis but an ongoing process of negotiation, a transnational negotiation in particular. This process of cross-cultural negotiation sometimes synthetically reconciles contradictions of images, but in many cases, especially in global contexts, it often enhances the contradictions. Cinema has been a transnational cultural form from the early period of its history. As the film scholar Miriam Hansen argues, "To write the international history of classical American cinema, therefore, is a matter of tracing not just its mechanisms of standardization and hegemony but also the diversity of ways in which this cinema was translated and reconfigured in both local and translocal contexts of reception."[26] Hayakawa's stardom had different meanings and modes of reception in different geographical and historical sites. It did not necessarily own a synthetic power over various contradictions but kept maintaining ambivalences.

Hayakawa's star image was initially formed in the early period of the American film industry. Then, Hayakawa's stardom was appropriated and articulated within various and contradictory political, ideological, and cultural contexts in the United States, Japan, and Europe during the period of public circulation. Hayakawa's stardom was the site of an infinite struggle between white American (and European) cultural domination and Japanese (and European) cultural resistance for control of representations of Japan. Hayakawa himself struggled within the Hollywood film industry that produced his films, while at the same time his stardom was rearticulated in a continuous cross-cultural dialogue in distribution and exhibition. Thus, there was a transnational war of images in Hayakawa's star persona among Hayakawa himself, the filmmakers, and the various audiences.

First, what was the mechanism that initially formed Hayakawa's stardom at the point of production in the United States? In the mid- to late 1910s, the Hollywood film industry was facing two interrelated structural transformations: the move toward production efficiency and the emergence of the star system. The star system exploited acting personalities as commodities with specific images in order to enhance audiences' horizon of expectations in a rationalized manner. Simultaneously, the Hollywood film industry was moving toward the refinement of motion pictures in order to appeal to broader middle-class audiences.[27] How did the Hollywood film industry create Hayakawa's star persona at the very beginning of the star system in accordance with the middle-class discourse?

The Jesse L. Lasky Feature Play Company devised a specific strategy as to how to publicize and promote Hayakawa's films and control Hayakawa's star image. What Lasky exploited most was Japan's movable middle-ground position in a racial and cultural hierarchy. The image of Japan was caught between the white and the nonwhite, between "uniformity" and "difference," and "between the pull of modernization and the antiquity of native traditions" in a racial and cultural hierarchy in American middle-class discourse in the late nineteenth century and the early twentieth.[28]

Between the Japanese victory over Russia in 1905 and the U.S. Supreme Court's *Ozawa v. United States* decision in 1922, a certain discourse existed that culturally and racially differentiated the Japanese from other nonwhites. The popularity of *Japonisme* and Japan's rapid sociopolitical and military modernization and Westernization served to picture Japanese culture as "more advanced" than other "primitive" or "exotic" ones, and, simultaneously, the Japanese race as "closer" to Caucasian. Thus, racial imagery and sociocultural imagery went hand in hand in the case of Japan in the early twentieth century.

Japanese art was regarded as echoing the ancient Greeks through its embodiment of an eternal, universal "spirit of antique time."[29] William Elliot Griffis, in his article in *North American Review* in 1913, juxtaposed the Japanese people, who "transformed their imported Buddhism as well as their exotic politics and social ideals," with the Greeks, who "transfused the simple, spiritual ethics of Jesus into an elaborate theology," and the Romans, who "turned it into an ecclesiastical discipline." Griffis continued: "It is as unscientific to call the Japanese 'Mongolians' as to say that Englishmen are Jutes or that Americans are Angles. . . . Their [Japanese] history, language, ethnology, physiology, religion, culture, tastes, habits, and psychology show that instead of being 'Mongolians' they are the most un-Mongolian people in Asia. There is very little Chinese blood in the Japanese composite and no connection between languages. Physically the two peoples are at many points astonishingly unlike."[30]

This movable middle-ground positioning of Japan in the racial and cultural hierarchy was most typically observed in the world's fairs of the late nineteenth century and the early twentieth, where careful racial and cultural classifications were visually presented to naturalize imperialist thoughts. Especially in the World's Columbian Exposition of 1893, which was held in Chicago, Japan was placed at an "ambivalent and twisted" position between the "civilized" European countries and the other "primitive" cultures.[31] The fair's hierarchical concept that connected culture and race was most symbolically visualized by the dichotomized layout of the fair ground: the White City, rows of white colossal monuments based on Greek and Roman classicism, where the modern technologies, products, and arts of European and North American nations were exhibited, and the subordinating adjacent Midway Plaisance, where "primitive" peoples and cultures were displayed for exotic entertainment.[32]

The Japanese exhibit, Ho-o-den, or the Phoenix Hall, was located on the Wooded Island in the Lagoon, a small piece of land near the Fine Arts Building in the White City, in spite of the exotic display of Japanese culture that was obviously different from Greek and Roman classicism or the technological products of the European and North American nations. The racial and cultural position of Japan, located not in the Midway Plaisance, not within but near the White City, typified the middle position between the "civilized" nations and the "primitive" regions.

According to the official guidebook of the exhibition, "Recognizing the radical differences between Japanese art and that of the western world, the authorities of the Art Department of the Columbian Exposition did not bind Japanese art exhibitors to the rigid classification established for other nations, but urged that the exhibit be made thoroughly national in character—exactly such an exhibit as would be formed under a classification devised for an art exhibition to be held in Japan."[33] The American studies scholar Mari Yoshihara argues that this passage suggests "the authorities' recognition of Japanese arts as having high enough standards to be included among those of western civilizations, while, at the same time, containing it in a separate space which allowed for a distance between it and its western counterparts."[34] Even when the American people recognized Japan's cultural adherence to the Western standard of refinement in its art and craftwork, they simultaneously had a "thirst for exotica" and were unwilling to give Japan more than honorary white racial status.

The Japanese government, however, self-consciously utilized this movable middle-ground status in the racial and cultural hierarchy in order to secure its position in international relations rather than trying to show a modernized and therefore Westernized sociopolitical and cultural status.[35] The Western recognition of the beauty of Japanese art had an important impact on the formation of Japanese national identity.[36] Japan chose to display not the modernized Japan of the present but the traditional, classical artifacts from Japan's past because it was "well aware of the Western gaze which valorized the 'authentic' artifacts from the Oriental past."[37] At the same time, Japan "longed to learn and appropriate the Western vision for itself, gazing at its own neighbors with imperial and colonial eyes."[38] Positioning itself in a middle ground between Europe and America on the one hand and Asia on the other, Japan was voluntarily, as well as involuntarily, trapped in the middle of a Eurocentric evolutionary ladder in the racial and cultural hierarchy.[39]

Japan's movable middle-ground position in a racial and cultural hierarchy also had to do with legal racialization of Asians in the late nineteenth century and the early twentieth. While Hayakawa was achieving superstardom, racial inassimilability of Asians was gradually but steadily being legalized. In an ongoing process, Asians were gradually categorized as "nonwhite" through various acts of Asian exclusion until the 1940s, for the purposes of American national formation and for the "construction of whiteness" and "a homogenous citizenry."[40] The sequence of laws in 1882, 1917, 1924, and 1934 that excluded immigrants from China, India, Japan, and the Philippines consistently racialized each national origin group as "nonwhite." Following the Chinese precedent, the legal racialization of Japanese as nonwhite "aliens ineligible for citizenship" was completed by the 1922 Ozawa case. Yet, until the early 1920s, Japanese people were not legally racialized and defined as "nonwhite" by immigration laws. Japanese people had been able to move around in the middle ground of a racial hierarchy until the early 1920s.

Hayakawa's star image, initially formed at the Lasky Company, strongly fit into the popular imaginary and legal movable middle-ground position of Japan in this racial and cultural hierarchy. Particularly, Hayakawa's image, which positioned him in the middle ground, was visualized with regard to the ideological structure of Americanism. Under the conditions of rapid industrialization, urbanization, and increased immigration, middle-class Americans prompted the nationwide "Americanization Movement." Hollywood studios made Hayakawa's star image symbolize successful assimilation into Euro-American culture. Through his display of the American way of life, Hayakawa became a representative of the model minority in the ethnically and culturally heterogeneous society who attained success in a legitimate industry without threatening the current sociopolitical and economic system or the middle-class sense of values.

In his star vehicles, Hayakawa's characters become sympathetic because they try to reform their traditional lifestyles to fit into the American way of life and to obey American laws and follow American customs. Or, they become heroic when they sacrifice themselves for white American women and maintain the patriarchal family system. In magazine articles, Hayakawa's lifestyle was publicized as being Americanized on the one hand, and the uniqueness of Hayakawa as a Japanese actor was emphasized on the other. Yet, this Japaneseness of Hayakawa was safely domesticated within the American middle-class cultural discourse on Japan. The embodiment of *Japonisme*, with its "civilized" high-art connotations, was considered valuable for product differentiation in the star system and effectively connected Hayakawa's star image to the refined cultural image that was appropriate for middle-class audiences. Thus, Hayakawa's star image was formed as a complex mixture of Americanization and Japaneseness: the middle ground between "civilized" white and "primitive" nonwhite, between "West" and "East."

Second, what was the mechanism of the rearticulation of Hayakawa's star image in transnational contexts? Lasky fit Hayakawa's Japanese star image strategically within a certain standard for the imagination of middle-class American audiences. Yet, Japanese spectators both in the United States and in Japan had ambivalent attitudes toward Hayakawa's stardom, an achievement "made in the U.S.A." They were often dismayed by the result and protested against Hayakawa's representation of Japan often in the light of authenticity. They criticized Hayakawa for appearing in anti-Japanese films that were considered as distorting actual Japanese national and cultural characteristics. They called Hayakawa *hi-kokumin*, an insult to the nation, or a national traitor.

At the same time, they praised Hayakawa for his star image, which had a universal appeal well beyond Japanese cultural boundaries. Japanese immigrants in the United States, who had been challenging anti-Japanese movements, tried to utilize Hayakawa's stardom in Japanese immigrants' identity politics. Across the Pacific, Japanese intellectuals and government officials, who were also enthusiastic viewers of foreign films, tried to reconstruct Hayakawa's stardom for their own political or nationalist concerns. They highly valued Hayakawa's films for their popularity in international markets and nationalistically praised Hayakawa as an ideal representative of the Japanese people. They even called Hayakawa the "Ambassador of the nation."[41] Since the 1860s, the Japanese government had adopted a modernization policy. Particularly after World War I, Japan tried to participate in world politics and economies as a modern nation. In the course of this effort, Hayakawa's American stardom was incorporated into Japan's modernity in a complicated manner. For instance, two completely different ways of appreciating Hayakawa's acting style simultaneously came to exist. In one case, a Japanese film magazine that praised Hayakawa's acting style for its fully utilized pantomimic gestures and facial expressions simultaneously acclaimed Hayakawa's "lack of moving facial muscle to tell tragic love stories with his two Eastern eyes," simply translating articles from American film magazines and accepting their views.[42] While Hayakawa's acting style was highly valued for its Americanized aspect, the rather stereotypical view of Japanese culture that was observed, or fictionalized, by American filmmakers and audiences also became an integral part of the Japanese reception of Hayakawa's stardom.

Thus, Hayakawa's stardom functioned as a site of transnational conflicts and negotiations, especially between the United States and Japan. It appeared in a continuing process of cross-cultural dialogue among filmmakers, various audiences, and the actor himself. During the period from the 1910s to the 1920s, Hollywood became a global center of film production and promotion. However, in the context of the globalization of film culture, Hayakawa's stardom was formed, consumed, and reconfigured in diverse ways within the struggle to define and control the cultural, racial, and national images of Japan on the part of white America and within the setting of Japanese cultural resistance. Not only did Hayakawa embody American stereotypical depictions of Japanese people, as well as represent a model minority who was successfully assimilated into American society, he also led Japanese spectators to question, "What is Japanese?" Hayakawa's transnational stardom revealed the volatile intersections between the Japanese and (white) American cultures.

The phenomenon of Sessue Hayakawa's stardom emerged suddenly. In late December 1915, a film made at the Jesse L. Lasky Feature Play Company and a Japanese actor in it shocked film spectators in the United States, Europe, and Japan. The film was *The Cheat*. The actor was Sessue Hayakawa. Chapter 1 of this book describes how Hayakawa became an overnight sensation through his fully stereotypical screen image of a Japanese man in *The Cheat*. Chapter 2 then goes back in time and discusses Hayakawa's pre-superstar roles in films about Japan and Japanese people made at the New York Motion Picture Company (NYMPC) under the renowned producer Thomas H. Ince in 1914–15. What was the nature of the cultural discourses toward Japan when Hayakawa entered the film business? Key terms will be Japanese Taste, the middle-class fascination with Japanese artifacts and culture, and the yellow peril, the middle-class fear of Japanese imperialist expansion and Japanese immigrants.

Ince was making films with Japanese subjects, which had certain popularity among American audiences who appreciated other cultural forms with the same subjects: novels, opera, and theatrical dramas. Chapter 2 analyzes Hayakawa's debut film *O Mimi San* (Reginald Barker, 1914) with regard to the discourse of Japanese Taste and in reference to the intertext of *The Mikado, or The Town of Titipu*, a popular light opera with Japanese subjects. Then, chapter 3 examines how *The Wrath of the Gods* (Barker, 1914), one of the first big spectacular productions, or sensational feature films, uses melodramatic imagination to construct an archetypal narrative between East and West and how Japanese actors were exploited in such a film made in early Hollywood. Chapter 4 analyzes *The Typhoon* (Barker, 1914) in reference to the relationship between the discourse of the yellow peril and the spy film genre, one of the first popular film genres in which Japan was a favorite subject matter. Chapter 5 discusses Hayakawa's Native American films in terms of the issues of racial masquerade and racial hierarchy.

Part 2 of this book deals with the strategy of the Jesse L. Lasky Feature Play Company to form Hayakawa's stardom. How did the early Hollywood film industry invest its stars with images that were fraught with certain sociopolitical and cultural conditions? How did Lasky draw out Hayakawa's own screen persona from the mere cultural stereotypic roles of Japanese people in order to establish Hayakawa's star status? Lasky took a double-barreled strategy that would make Hayakawa heroic, sympathetic, and assimilated enough to become a star while keeping his nonwhite persona safely distanced from white middle-class Americans.

Lasky had roughly four strategies to form Hayakawa's stardom. First, Lasky emphasized the Americanized characteristics of Hayakawa's (and his characters') personas (obedience to American laws, assimilation to the American way of life, and so forth). Second, in Hayakawa's star vehicles, Lasky resorted to melodramatic structure, the clear distinction between good and evil, and the motif of self-sacrifice for white women and white American families. Third, Lasky fully utilized the political conditions of World War I, the allied relationship between the United States and Japan in particular. Fourth, Lasky made clear the aspect of refinement in Hayakawa's image, especially his embodying of Japanese Taste, typified by his acting skill and manifested in his performances. All these tactics were mainly meant to heighten Hayakawa's (and his characters') racial and cultural status beyond that of other nonwhites to the middle-ground position, but not necessarily to equal that of white American characters.

Examining Lasky's strategy of Americanizing Hayakawa's star image, chapter 6 traces the ephemeral discourses of white patriarchal hegemony in American culture and illuminates how the representational means—the film culture—maintained and consolidated dominant sociopolitical and cultural discourses. This chapter reveals the ideological structure of an American pluralism that mobilized a sense of shared American community and shows that films made in Hollywood at that time functioned as a means of maintaining crucial cultural myths about American assimilative capacities.

With a close textual analysis of *Forbidden Paths* (Robert T. Thornby, 1917), chapter 7 examines the melodramatic structure and thematic motif of self-sacrifice in Hayakawa's star vehicles. The motif of self-sacrifice marked Hayakawa's characters as the moral center of the narrative and at the same time depicted them as ultimately inassimilable to white American society.

Chapter 8 turns to Hayakawa's villainous roles. In *The Soul of Kura San*

(Edward J. LeSaint, 1916) and *The Call of the East* (George H. Melford, 1917), Lasky provided Hayakawa with sympathetic and moralistic victim roles despite his villainy.

Chapter 9 discusses the influence of World War I upon Hayakawa's star image. Lasky integrated the allied situation between Japan and the United States after the latter's declaration of participation in World War I into Hayakawa's star vehicles.

Chapter 10 demonstrates how Hayakawa's lifestyle was publicized in fan magazines as overtly Americanized, while the uniqueness of Hayakawa as a Japanese actor was emphasized at the same time. Hayakawa's Japaneseness was codified within the middle-class discourse of Japanese Taste, which effectively connected Hayakawa's star image to the refined cultural image.

In 1918, when his contract with Lasky expired, Hayakawa established his own production company, the Haworth Pictures Corporation. Part 3 of this book documents the establishment of Haworth; this period marked the clear beginning of a triangular conflict in Hayakawa's stardom, consisting of a war of images. In this war there were three elements: cultural stereotypes of Japan versus Hayakawa's star image, which had been formed and popularized at Lasky, versus the identity politics Hayakawa took on as a Japanese entrepreneur at his own company. Part 3 traces how Hayakawa struggled with the horizon of expectations in regard to his star image, not only from American audiences but also from the newly founded film distribution company Robertson-Cole.

An Americanized Japanese image was so successfully created for Hayakawa at Lasky that it set up an entrenched assumption about Hayakawa's star persona. Yet, reactions from Japanese spectators made Hayakawa realize the need to re-create, or at least to adjust, his star image by balancing his already established star image for American audiences with his reputation among Japanese spectators both in the United States and in Japan. Hayakawa understood the relationship among his national identity, his cinematized cultural stereotype, and his star image, as well as how the market encoded his racial and cultural identity in the form of marketing, reviews, and audience reception. As a result, Hayakawa had to negotiate between the star image created by Lasky to appeal to American audiences and a more realistic image of Japanese people. The demands of authenticity from both American and Japanese audiences suggest the contradictions and slippage between the American stereotypical image of Japan, the "real" self-image of Japan, and the actual condition of Japan at a certain historical moment. One of the criteria that

Hayakawa had to use at Haworth was not to represent the reality of Japan at that time, but to conform to the ideal image that Japanese immigrants in the United States and Japanese spectators liked to convey of Japan.

Hayakawa's attempt to reconstitute his star image at Haworth was a product of "triple consciousness." W. E. B. Du Bois uses the concept of "double consciousness" regarding African American people's self image and identity politics: "always looking at one's self through the eyes of others."[43] Part 3 demonstrates that there were at least two "other" groups that influenced the course that Haworth would take when Hayakawa re-created his own star image, in addition to Hayakawa himself: American audiences and Japanese spectators.

Chapter 11 analyzes the first two films made at Haworth: *His Birthright* (William Worthington, 1918), a feature film, and *Banzai* (1918), a short promotional film for the Liberty Loan Campaign during World War I, in order to examine Hayakawa's intended direction at his own company.

Chapter 12 illustrates the continuous negotiation between Hayakawa and Robertson-Cole, which ended up depriving Hayakawa of his authority over his star image, through a close analysis of three of Hayakawa's star vehicles, *The Dragon Painter* (Worthington, 1919), *The Tong Man* (Worthington, 1919), and *An Arabian Knight* (Charles Swickard, 1920).

Not only at Lasky but also at Robertson-Cole, legitimate acting was the essential element of Hayakawa's stardom. What distinguishes Hayakawa as an actor from his co-stars? Chapter 13 focuses on the actual quality of Hayakawa's acting and examines the status of Hayakawa within the trend of acting styles in the early Hollywood film industry.

Hayakawa's popularity declined under the nativist conditions in the United States in the early 1920s. Hayakawa's farewell to the American film industry resulted from this change of social discourse on race and immigrants, particularly on Japan. Chapter 14 documents the final days of Hayakawa's stardom in Hollywood.

Hayakawa's American-made star image evoked different meanings in Japanese communities in the United States and in Japan. In the United States, Japanese audiences used Hayakawa's image for the purpose of constructing their identity politics; in Japan, audiences wanted to regard Hayakawa's image as an affirmation of Japan's modernization policy. Part 4 of this book examines these multiple modes of reception of Hayakawa's stardom from a cross-cultural perspective.

Chapter 15 first examines how Japanese communities in the United States, which were fighting against the nativist anti-Japanese movement in the United States, reacted to Hayakawa's stardom. Then, this chapter illustrates how Japanese spectators responded to Hayakawa's American stardom. Japanese reception of Hayakawa's stardom had a complicated relationship with the issues of nationalism, Americanization, and modernization. Japanese spectators, especially intellectuals, intensely felt the need for modernization of Japanese cinema, but their attitudes were extremely ambivalent toward Americanization and nationalism with regard to the representation of Japan in mainstream media. *Jun'eigageki undo*, or the Pure Film Movement, the intellectual attempt to modernize Japanese cinema (not only the practice of production but also that of exhibition) by way of adopting Western film culture, was a tension-ridden process of negotiating between cosmopolitanism, which regarded film as a potential "universal language" or visual Esperanto, and nationalism.[44] This tension had a huge impact upon the Japanese reception of Hayakawa's stardom and vice versa: Hayakawa's star image also enhanced this tension.

Hayakawa's standardized star image and the ambivalent modes of reception of it continued in his post-stardom career in the era of talking pictures. Examining *La Bataille, Daughter of the Dragon* (Lloyd Corrigan, 1931), *Atarshiki tsuchi* (*Die Tochter des Samurai*, Arnold Fanck and Itami Mansaku, 1937), *Tokyo Joe* (Stuart Heisler, 1949), *Three Came Home* (Jean Negulesco, 1950), and *The Bridge on the River Kwai*, among others, the epilogue discusses the relationship between the lingering star image of Hayakawa, its reception, and the issues of nation and nationalism in Japan and in the United States.

ONE

Emperor, Buddhist, Spy, or Indian

The Pre-Star Period of Sessue Hayakawa (1914–15)

A STAR IS BORN

The Transnational Success

of *The Cheat* and Its Race

and Gender Politics

O n December 13, 1915, a film titled *The Cheat*, produced at the Jesse L. Lasky Feature Play Company, directed by Cecil B. DeMille, and starring Fannie Ward, a renowned stage actress in New York and London, was released in the United States.[1] *The Cheat* soon achieved big box office success[2] and opened a gate for the Japanese actor Sessue Hayakawa to become a "full-fledged star."[3] Before the success of *The Cheat*, Hayakawa had already appeared in many films, but it was *The Cheat* that paved the way for him to achieve superstardom.

In *The Cheat*, a rich Japanese art dealer on Long Island, Hishuru Tori (Sessue Hayakawa), offers money to Edith Hardy (Fannie Ward), a white middle-class woman, who has invested money from the Red Cross Fund and eventually lost it, in exchange for her body. When Edith tries to return his money after her husband's success in the stock market, Tori assaults her and brutally brands his mark on her shoulder. However, Edith fights back and shoots Tori in the shoulder. Knowing everything, Edith's husband decides to be arrested on a charge of attempted murder in order to save her name. During the trial, Edith confesses the truth, and the excited court audience attacks Tori in the end.

Not very many reviewers and audiences were impressed by the film's leading actress. What fascinated them most was the supporting Japanese actor, Sessue Hayakawa. The *New York Times* insisted, "Miss Ward might learn something to help her fulfill her destiny as a great tragedienne of the screen by observing the man who acted the Japanese villain in her picture."[4] *Variety* agreed: "The work of Sessue Hayakawa is so far above the acting of Miss Ward and Jack Dean that he really should be the star in the billing for the film."[5]

Moving Picture World (MPW) noted that Hayakawa had "a prominent role" in *The Cheat* and added, "It is rumored he is soon to be starred by the Lasky Company in a big feature production."[6] Sessue Hayakawa thus became an overnight sensation to the moviegoers in America.

Cecil B. DeMille, the director of the film, recalled later that *The Cheat* was "Sessue Hayakawa's first giant stride on the road that made him within two years the peer of such contemporary bright stars as Douglas Fairbanks, William S. Hart, and Mary Pickford."[7] The *New Orleans Times* in February 1916 reported how prominent Hayakawa was after the release of *The Cheat*: "Undoubtedly the greatest success ever scored by a Japanese actor on [sic] American moving pictures was that of Sessue Hayakawa in the Lasky-Paramount production of "The Cheat," and so strong an impression thot [sic] make on New Orleans spectators that when the Japanese appeared for the moment on the screen in the part of a valet in "Temptation," at the Crescent, a murmur of recognition such as we have never known to greet any other player went through the audience—a most sincere tribute."[8] Similarly, *Wid's Films and Film Folk Independent Criticisms of Features* pointed out that Hayakawa was used in an inappropriate way in a minor role in *Temptation* (Cecil B. DeMille, 30 December 1915), the film that was released right after *The Cheat*: "Our Jap friend, of 'The Cheat' fame, is brought in for a very small 'valet' part at the finish. I think this is wrong. That boy is too big and too clever to be shoved into such films to do a small bit. It hits you in the eye like it would be to see Blanche Sweet come into the film as a maid."[9]

The Lasky Company dared not miss this opportunity. Right before the release of *The Cheat*, the studio head, Jesse L. Lasky, praised *The Cheat* as "one of the very best" films ever made, even though his claim should have contained a promotional intention. He said he was "so impressed by his [Hayakawa's] performance" that he "immediately signed him for a long term" contract.[10] After the box office success of *The Cheat*, the company came to recognize Hayakawa as its new potential moneymaker and to undertake a specific strategy to establish, publicize, and promote his star image.

Motion Picture News (MPN) reported on 15 April 1916: "Partly in response to the hundreds of requests from exhibitors and photoplay goers all over the United States, the Jesse L. Lasky Feature Play Company announces that it will present as a star early in May the well-known Japanese screen player, Sessue Hayakawa, in a photoplay production entitled 'Alien Souls.' Hayakawa's work in 'The Cheat,' in which he appeared in leading support of Fannie

Ward, stamped him immediately as a proficient figure in motion pictures."[11] Lasky spent five months before releasing the first star vehicle for Hayakawa, *Alien Souls* (Frank Reicher, 3 May 1916). This long five-month gap indicates the extent of Lasky's well-prepared publicity for the company's new star. When *Alien Souls* was finally released, reviews of the film appeared in various local papers such as the *New York Sun, Philadelphia Telegraph, Detroit News, Evening Wisconsin, Louisville Times, Springfield Mirror, Cleveland Daily, Atlanta Constitution, Los Angeles Examiner, Chicago Tribune, Toledo Blade,* and *Washington Star*, and they unanimously called Hayakawa a "star." After *Alien Souls*, Hayakawa's star vehicles were released in approximately two-month cycles.

But stardom has more than a national perspective, and Hayakawa, like Charlie Chaplin, was one of the first stars whose international reputation forms an essential part of his story. American spectators were not the only ones who were immensely impressed by Hayakawa in *The Cheat*. Hayakawa's performance was sensationally received in Europe and in Japan.[12] In France, when *The Cheat* opened at the Omnia Pathé Cinema in Paris in the summer of 1916, French intellectuals were "dumbfounded" by Hayakawa and the innovative aesthetics of *The Cheat*.[13] On 3 June 1918, the drama critic Louis Delluc claimed, "No one actually wanted to see anything in it [*The Cheat*] except the Japanese. . . . [The film] inspired nothing but pro-Japanese polemic."[14] In *Excelsior*, on 7 August 1916, the renowned poet, novelist, and essayist Colette reported, in an excited tone, on the impact of Hayakawa's performance in *The Cheat* on many artists:

In Paris this week, a movie theater has become an art school. A film and two of its principal actors are showing us what surprising innovations, what emotion, what natural and well-designed lighting can add to cinematic fiction. Every evening, writers, painters, composers, and dramatists come and come again to sit, contemplate, and comment in low voices, like pupils. To the genius of an oriental actor is added that of a director probably without equal. . . . We cry "Miracle!" . . . Is it only a combination of felicitous effects that brings us to this film and keeps us there? Or is it the more profound and less clear pleasure of seeing the crude ciné groping toward perfection, the pleasure of divining what the future of the cinema must be when its makers will want that future . . . ? . . . This Asiatic artist whose powerful immobility is eloquence itself. Let our aspiring ciné-actors go to see how, when his face is mute, his hand carries on the flow of his thought. Let them take to heart the menace and disdain in a motion of his eyebrow and how, in that his life is running out with his blood, without shuddering, without convulsively grimacing, with merely the progressive petrifaction of his Buddha's mask and the ecstatic darkening of his eyes.[15]

As mentioned in the introduction, Hayakawa's acting, which Delluc and Colette fervently described, inspired certain French intellectuals to generate a concept, *photogenie*, the unique aesthetic qualities that motion picture photography brings to the subject it films. For them, the concept of *photogenie* was the basis of a new idea of film as a unique art form, thus Hayakawa of a new form of acting. According to Delluc, using the camera and the screen, *photogenie* changes "real" into something else without eliminating the "realness" and makes people "see ordinary things as they had never been before."[16] It is a mystical and theoretically incoherent concept due to the fact that *photogenie* is "designed to account for that which is inarticulable, that which exceeds language and hence points to the very essence of cinematic specificity."[17] Yet, such a theorist as Delluc believed that the cinema would give viewers access to a realm beyond everyday experience and show them the souls of people and the essence of objects. The concept of *photogenie* later became a significant theoretical basis of the French impressionist film movement, filmmaking that "displayed a fascination with pictorial beauty and an interest in intense psychological exploration."[18] As a result, by 1921, French intellectuals achieved a consensus that *The Cheat*'s "revelation actually initiated the greater French public's education about the cinema."[19]

This enthusiastic reception of Hayakawa in France had a certain connection to the popularity of Madame Sadayakko, a Japanese actress. Sadayakko, who was in fact the aunt of Hayakawa's wife, Tsuru Aoki, was sponsored by the popular dancer Loie Fuller in the 1900 Exposition in Paris, together with her husband Kawakami Otojiro, who tried to modernize Japanese theater by dissociating it from the dominant world of kabuki and pleasure quarters. Sadayakko's geisha dance and act of dying and Kawakami's act of hara-kiri, which were in fact added at the request of Fuller, were sensationally received not only by the popular audience, but by some intellectuals and artists, including the renowned sculptor Auguste Rodin. Moreover, their acts were captured by a motion picture camera, which was another sensational form of entertainment at the Paris Exposition. After the Kawakami troupe returned to Japan, even Japanese-style dresses became fashionable in Paris. They were called "Yacco" style because Sadayakko always wore a kimono at parties. Sadayakko's fame was such that Guerlain introduced a perfume called "Yacco."[20]

Without Sadayakko, Kawakami, and Aoki, Hayakawa would never have entered the film business. In 1899, when Aoki was eleven, she went to the United States as a part of the Kawakami troupe. It was the first time a Japanese theater troupe had toured in the United States.[21] Aoki stayed in the United States as an adopted daughter of Aoki Toshio (Hyosai), an artist in San Francisco, and later, after Aoki Toshio died, of Louise Scher, a journalist at the *Los Angeles Examiner*. Aoki started her film career much earlier than Hayakawa and quite possibly introduced him to an influential producer in early Hollywood, Thomas H. Ince.

In 1925, the filmmakers Henri Fescourt and Jean-Louis Bouquet dated "the origins of the cinema around 1915–1916, with the appearance of the first good American films," and stated that "the most striking was *The Cheat*."[22] In 1937, Marcel L'Herbier remade *The Cheat*, entitled *Forfaiture*, using Hayakawa in the role of a Mongolian prince who attracts a French engineer's wife and entraps her using her gambling debts.[23] The images behind the opening credits of *Forfaiture*, a compilation of notable scenes with Hayakawa from *The Cheat*, clearly indicate the immense popularity of Hayakawa and *The Cheat* in France. *Forfaiture* thus presupposed the viewers' knowledge of the original.

Moreover, *Excelsior*, on 28 August 1917, reported that *The Cheat* was about to be staged as an opera. André de Lorde of the Théâtre du Grand Guignol and Paul Milliet wrote a music drama based on *The Cheat*, for which Camille Erlanger wrote the music. The opera, entitled *La Forfaiture*, was in fact produced by the Opéra-Comique in 1921, after Erlanger's death, and became the first opera to be based on a motion picture scenario, even though the opera was not successful and played only three times.[24] Colette's reaction to this announcement of the stage production of *The Cheat*, written in a conversation style, indicates how highly she valued Hayakawa's eloquent performance. Colette's insight even predicts Hayakawa's future, his loss of popularity after talking pictures arrived:

"And who will play it? Have they already found people worthy of taking over for Hayakawa and Fannie Ward?"

"Ah . . . that's the difficulty. What do you think of Mary Garden for the role played by Fannie Ward?"

"Mary Garden would be fine. And the Japanese?"

The friend of film leaned forward, with an anxious face: "The Japanese, the Japanese . . ."

He looked at me steadily.

"It's strange," he said, "the Japanese . . . I don't conceive of that role, you understand, as being sung. Or, let's say there'd be very little singing. One would need a great artist capable of mime. Gesture, stage presence . . . Very little voice. No vocal effects, no melodic phrases. Everything in *recitative*. But silence, you understand, above all, silence. Jean Périer, perhaps . . ."

"Of course. Besides"—I insinuated with a poisonous sweetness—"really, the Japanese has nothing to say in the story."

"That's quite right. My opinion exactly. He has nothing to say. The first, the glare, that's the whole role. I see so clearly what's needed. I can see it as if I were there."

"I think you were there. Wait, one moment, I have an idea. Supposing that the Japanese, in your opera, were made evil, seductive, and . . . mute?"

"Mute?"

"Mute. As mute as a screen. He could, by mime, make himself understood just as easily—perhaps better—and then . . ."

"I've got it, I've got it!" the friend of film cried. "We'll get Hayakawa to create the role in the opera!"

"I hoped you'd say that."

"Magnificent! Magnificent! That takes a weight off me . . . It's foolish, perhaps, but the idea of hearing the role of the Japanese sung . . . and even that of the woman, if it comes to that, in the great scene, the struggle between Fannie Ward and Hayakawa, I can't yet imagine how they would exchange the lines 'Be Mine!' 'No, never!' 'You swore it!' 'Pity, pity! Oh, the villain—!' and so on."

"I share your apprehension. One could, though, get around the difficulty with those cries . . ."

"How?"

"One could arrange, for example, a silent scene, very rapid, in the style of that lovely scene in the film . . ."

"Of course . . ."

". . . and since the scene would be silent, there wouldn't be any difficulty in having it played by Fannie Ward . . ."[25]

Hayakawa's performance in *The Cheat* was sensationally received by Japanese spectators, too. However, the tone of the Japanese reception was not as favorable as that of the American and French ones. Japanese communities in the United States severely protested *The Cheat*, insisting that the Japanese character in the film was depicted unfavorably. On 23 December 1915, right after *The Cheat* was released at the Tally Theater in Los Angeles, the *Rafu Shimpo*, a Japanese newspaper in Los Angeles, started a campaign against the film. Hayakawa wrote in his autobiography, "Recalling my experiences in making this picture [*The Cheat*] brings to mind the opposition my playing the role of the villainous Japanese stirred among those of my nationality in Los Angeles and throughout the country after the film was released. For portraying the heavy, as screen villains are called, as a Japanese, I was indignantly accused of casting a slur on my nationality."[26]

The *Rafu Shimpo* criticized *The Cheat* by insisting that the film "distorted the truth of Japanese people" and would "cause anti-Japanese movements." A report in the *Rafu Shimpo* noted, "The film depicts Japanese people as outrageously evil. . . . This film would have a bad influence on people, living in places where there are not so many Japanese. They would come to think that the Japanese people are extremely savage. The film destroys the truth of the Japanese race. It is unforgivable for Japanese actors to appear in such a film, even for money."[27]

Another report in the paper similarly stated,

> The issue of Japanese exclusion is a big problem not just between the U.S. and Japan, but in the world. The intellectuals in both the U.S. and in Japan have made every effort to solve this problem. Our people in the U.S. have experienced many troubles and hardships, and 60 million Japanese people have been extremely patient, in order to solve this problem. Under such conditions, how could Hayakawa, despite his blood of Japanese race, shamelessly appear in an anti-Japanese film, which leaves an impression of extremely evil Japanese? You, traitor to your country!! . . . The Japanese Embassy should do something to prevent this film from being exhibited.[28]

The *Rafu Shimpo* reported many incidents in which Japanese people were attacked by "white bad boys" after the release of *The Cheat*. A report noted, "Bad boys, who were crowded in front of the Tally Theater [where *The Cheat* was being played] and crying out anti-Japanese words, lynched a Japanese noodle shop owner, who came out of the theater, as Hayakawa was lynched in the courtroom scene." The report concluded, "the influence of the anti-Japanese film is doubtless."[29]

As a response to these serious criticisms against his character, Hayakawa had to quickly publish a note of apology in the *Rafu Shimpo* on 29 December. He wrote, "Sincere Notice: It is regrettable that the film *The Cheat*, which was exhibited at the Tally Theater on Broadway in Los Angeles, unintentionally offended the feelings of the Japanese people in the U.S. From now on, I will be very careful not to do harm to Japanese communities."[30]

Yet, the campaign against *The Cheat* continued after Hayakawa's apology. In February 1916, members of the Japanese Association of Southern California filed a protest against the showing of *The Cheat* with the Los Angeles City Council. The *Rafu Shimpo* reported almost every day until March 1916 the news about the Japanese Association's effort to ban *The Cheat* from playing in theaters. As a result, when *The Cheat* was re-released in 1918 because of popular demand, Hayakawa's character's nationality was changed from Japanese to Burmese in order not to excite anti-Japanese sentiment because Japan and the United States were allies during World War I. In the re-release version, which is the only version now extant, Hayakawa's Japanese character became a Burmese ivory king, Haka Arakau, by a change in intertitles.

Across the Pacific, in Japan, after *The Cheat* caused the anti-exhibition campaign in Japanese communities in the United States, Hayakawa's name was widely reported in newspapers and magazines for the first time. Hayakawa was scandalously introduced to Japanese spectators as a person who was recklessly enhancing anti-Japanese sentiment in the United States. Hayakawa was called "a cooperator in anti-Japanese propaganda films like *The Typhoon* and *The Cheat*." He was labeled as a "traitor" for appearing in such "insults to the nation."[31] The Japanese film magazine *Katsudo no Sekai* criticized Hayakawa's Japanese character in *The Cheat* as "a slave of carnal desire" and called Hayakawa an "unforgivable national traitor."[32] *The Cheat* was not released in Japan in the 1910s. It was imported in 1923 but never had a chance to be released.[33] Lasky and Paramount, the producer and the distributor of *The Cheat* in the United States, did not have a distribution branch in Japan at that time, which was the direct reason that most of Hayakawa's films did not come to Japan until 1918, when Hayakawa established Haworth Pictures Corporation, his own production company.[34] Yet, at the same time, there was no enthusiastic request for Hayakawa's films in Japan because they were considered too shameful to Japanese audiences.[35] As a result, for several years, Hayakawa had an extremely notorious reputation among Japanese spectators who knew him in name only. Okina Kyuin, a novelist and journalist who spent eighteen years in the United States, from 1907–24, wrote in 1930, "He [Hayakawa] made his way into the world with the success of *The Cheat*, but at the same time, he was cursed by the Japanese people with the success of *The Cheat*."[36] Thus, the success of *The Cheat* and Hayakawa's performance in the film had a huge transnational impact, positive and negative, in the history of cinema, and in the history of the sociopolitical relationship between the United States and Japan as well.

Hayakawa had appeared in many films with Japanese subject matter before *The Cheat* at the New York Motion Picture Company (NYMPC) and some others at Lasky. Yet, these films did not provide Hayakawa with as tremendous and sensational a success as *The Cheat*. Thomas H. Ince, the managing director at the NYMPC, never publicized Hayakawa as his star. What was different about *The Cheat*? What made Hayakawa stand out as a potential American star?

Thematically, most of the films in which Hayakawa appeared before *The Cheat* were set in faraway lands. In these films, Japanese people were objects to be looked at, but not people for American audiences to encounter in everyday life. Japan existed outside of the American domestic sphere. This image of Japan as a faraway land to be looked at in these early films was rooted in the nineteenth-century illustrated travel lecture, which was "a predominant form of magic lantern entertainment in America."[37] Such popular lecturers as John L. Stoddard and E. Burton Holmes, who actually spent five months in Japan in 1892, often talked about Japan and its people and drew mainly middle-class audiences. In contrast, in *The Cheat*, the Japanese man actually lives among white middle-class Americans.

There were actual human encounters between Japanese men and white American women in the middle-class domestic sphere in the Pacific states by the 1910s. Many male Japanese immigrants, who had entered the United States since the 1880s, were hired as domestic servants or valets. In contrast to Japanese art, which had been brought into the middle-class domestic sphere for the purpose of refining the home, Japanese immigrants, working as helping hands in the houses of white families, were often seen as a threat. The historian Robert G. Lee claims that the employment of the male Japanese servant to do "women's work" destabilized the gendered nature of labor. According to Lee, Japanese domestic servants were often regarded as a "third sex," which is "an alternative or imagined sexuality that was potentially subversive and disruptive to the emergent heterosexual and monoracial orthodoxy."[38] Japanese people, as opposed to Japanese art, could create threatening desires across race (multiracial), sex (homoerotic), and class and disturb conventional gender roles. Japanese in the middle-class American domestic sphere thus occupied an ambiguous middle-ground position between refined objects and threatening (human) subjects.

In fact, many tragic incidents were reported as a result of encounters between white women and Japanese men in the American domestic sphere. According to a report in the *Rafu Shimpo*, a married white woman named Mabel Smith shot to death Iguchi Eitaro, her Japanese lover, in July 1915.[39] The report noted, "Smith's husband knew the Japanese man as a nice guy. . . . During their three-year love affair, the Japanese man bought her clothes, and so forth. . . . The white woman got jealous when she heard that the Japanese man dated another woman. . . . The woman shot Iguchi when she thought he attacked her. . . . She said she killed Iguchi out of jealousy first, but she testified that she shot Iguchi to defend herself from him, who attacked her and her husband."[40] As in *The Cheat*, the white woman was declared not guilty on the grounds of self-defense.

In another case, a Japanese employee, Matsuno Shinkichi, was arrested because it was said that he threatened a white housewife with a pistol in order to rape her. The *Rafu Shimpo* reported, "The truth was . . . the housewife liked Matsuno very much and gave him extra money and her handkerchief, etc. Matsuno behaved carefully for a year because he had decided to marry a Japanese woman from Japan as soon as possible. One day, she woke up Matsuno in the middle of the night and took his hand and led him to the front door to check whether it was locked. The same thing happened the next day, and it is impossible to report here what kind of relationship they began to have then."[41]

The cases of Iguchi and Matsuno resembled that in *The Cheat*. They were tragic love affairs between married white women and rich Japanese men or Japanese servants. The white women were attracted to Japanese men and eventually destroyed them. Since these cases were reported when the *Rafu Shimpo* was conducting its campaign against *The Cheat*, the affinities of the situations stood out. *The Cheat* surely exploited such encounters between white American middle-class women and Japanese immigrants in the domestic sphere.

Hayakawa's rise as a prominent figure in *The Cheat* and the formation of his star image after *The Cheat* had a close relationship to these encounters. When the popular American cultural and racial imagination of Japan was connected to the discourse of the American middle-class domestic sphere, especially to that of gender politics, a strong momentum for Hayakawa's stardom was born.

More specifically, a white woman's sexual and economic transgression is metaphorically and metonymically expressed in the form of Japanese Taste and the yellow peril in *The Cheat*. The film historian Sumiko Higashi argues,

"The threat of sexual difference, represented by the demands of the 'new woman' . . . in a materialistic consumer culture, is displaced onto ethnic difference" in *The Cheat*.[42] Japanese objets d'art and the Japanese art dealer played by Hayakawa function as racialized rhetoric of consumption and the New Woman.

Historically, Japanese Taste and the yellow peril co-existed and formed ambivalent popular discourses on Japan in the early twentieth century. They were not simply antithetical but intersected in a complicated manner, especially in the middle-class domestic sphere. Japanese Taste in the middle-class home symbolized the fact that the gendered construction of the middle-class domestic sphere was extended to the turn-of-the-century racial paradigm.

Japanese Taste was the use of Japanese motifs, decorative style, and objects in the Western home with "congeries of attributes: physical, philosophical, moral, and educational" from the late 1870s.[43] Japan was first articulated in the American imagination through its arts, goods, and culture that were accepted favorably in accordance with the middle-class discourse on arts and the home.

After the forceful "opening" of Japan to the West in 1853 following the arrival of a U.S. naval squadron under the command of Commodore Matthew Perry, commerce between the United States and Japan was established. In the exchange, American male intellectuals, who were hired by the Japanese government to teach and consult in many areas, became the first "Japanologists," introducing Japanese culture to Americans. Many Japanologists were upper-class men from New England, such as Edward Sylvester Morse, who collected thousands of Japanese vernacular tools and daily objects, and Ernest F. Fenollosa, who became a curator at the Boston Museum of Fine Arts, who brought their knowledge about Japan to Americans as high culture.[44] In the 1870s Japanese goods penetrated American markets, following the European vogue of *Japonisme* in art and style. Because Japanese culture, art, and design were introduced by upper-class men or imported as European vogue, they were considered high art in the beginning.

After the Centennial Exhibition of 1876, when many middle-class Americans encountered Japanese art for the first time, upscale Japanese Taste became gradually popularized. The first height of Japanese Taste came in the 1885–89 period, when the number of publications on the social trend was peaking in popular magazines. Lafcadio Hearn, the most influential writer to interpret Japanese culture for genteel society, published a number of works in *Harper's Magazine* and others and introduced Japanese culture in the form of artifacts, architecture, natural scenery, religious beliefs, folk tales, and so forth, to middle-class female readers.

In this middle-class notion of Japanese Taste, Japanese art, design, and culture were nostalgically regarded as premodern and primitive and highly valued as an alternative or an antithesis to the modernity that was threatening the concept of Victorian morality.[45] Compared with Western "progress" in art, the painter John La Farge claimed in 1893, the "simplicity of attitude" of Japanese painters was that of "children."[46] Their childlike simplicity was an attribute of inherent sincerity, and, in terms of the Christian desire to reach heaven, was more expedient than extreme erudition and modern, scientific technique.

More specifically, Japanese Taste came to reflect "an exemplum of middle-class women's desire to carry out moral reforms in their own households and to present their families and themselves favorably to the public," and Japanese art was considered to incorporate "a number of moral and spiritual qualities."[47] In the industrialization, mechanization, urbanization, and the development of materialism in the 1880s, a wide range of magazines mainly targeted for women discussed the roles of both home and women in terms of their moral influence on the family. The cult of domesticity, or the idea of home as an agent of "Christian nurture," was propounded in such magazine articles. Home became regarded as a place that would provide physical shelter and artistic and general education for the whole family in order to contain the deepening contradictions between the new urban life and the older ideals of community, family, and social order.[48]

Japanese art was used in Christian homes to enhance morality, purity, and good taste, but the use was only justifiable by its evocative relationship between nature and religion in the imagination of the American middle class. That is, in the American domestic sphere, Japan was located in a middle-ground position in a cultural hierarchy: morally and artistically refined on the one hand, and premodern and primitive on the other.

Together with Japanese Taste, there was another discourse on Japan in the popular American imagination in the early twentieth century: the one that viewed Japan as a modernizing nation, often with the image of a political and economic threat. In such a view, Japan's modernization was a fanatical ultra-nationalistic patriotism in service to its emperor, and the Japanese were thus ultimately different from other Western modernized nations. Alfred T. Mahan, a captain of the U.S. Navy and an influential writer on American foreign policy, had a high estimation of Japan's "remarkable capacity and diligence in the appropriation and application of European ways." At the same time, Mahan insisted that ultimately Japan is "Asiatic," and "it must . . . be recognized and candidly accepted that difference of race characteristics . . . entails corresponding temporary divergence of ideal and of action, with consequent liability to misunderstanding, or even collision."[49]

American people largely admired Japan's fast-paced modernization, which had occurred since its "opening" to the West. However, especially after the Russo-Japanese War of 1904–5, when Japan's military power became obvious, anti-Japanese sentiment developed in the Pacific states, where the number of Japanese immigrants was steadily increasing.[50] Japanese immigrants became regarded as a threat because Japanese immigration was seen in the light of Japanese military power. Together with the specter of Japanese immigration, the fear of Japanese expansion into China, where the U.S. government had substantial interests, or a Japanese invasion of the mainland United States or the Philippines and Hawaii, which had come under American control, appeared.

Yellow journalism spread the discourse of the yellow peril in sensational articles and books.[51] In February 1905, a series of articles that regarded Japanese immigration as the "problem of the day" appeared in the *San Francisco Chronicle*. The *Chronicle* stated that Japanese immigrants would pose "a threat to American working men, American women, schoolchildren and the white race in general" because they were unable or unwilling to assimilate to the Anglo-American way of life.[52] Valentine Stuart McClatchy, an anti-Japanese agitator in San Francisco, called Japanese immigrants an "incoming yellow tide."[53] Jack London, who went to Asia as a journalist during the Russo-Japanese War, expressed his fear of Japan's expansion in his essay "Yellow Peril" (1904). The laboring classes in the Pacific states came to believe that Japanese immigrants achieved their working opportunities unfairly or dishonorably and formed the Asiatic Exclusion League in May 1905.

Except for those who were living in the Pacific states and facing immigrants from Asia in their daily lives, Japan's threat was still an ambiguous issue, not yet seen as a serious "peril." The number of Japanese residents in the United States was still limited, and the economic threat from Japanese immigrants was not yet a nationally perceived problem. Even President Theodore Roosevelt, although he recognized the potential conflict between Japan and the United States over control of the Pacific, was irritated by the activities of the anti-Japanese agitators on the West Coast. Yet, the term "yellow peril" gradually came to appear in such magazines for middle-class readers as the *Nation, Outlook,* and the *North American Review.*

In accordance with such popular discourses of the period, the narrative of *The Cheat* emphasizes the double-edged images of Japan, Japanese Taste, and the yellow peril from the very beginning and connects them to the ambivalent conception of consumerism in the middle-class American home, refinement and over-consumption. The first two scenes introduce the twofold image of the Japanese art dealer, Hishuru Tori. While the first scene implies Tori's threatening and primitive characteristics, the second scene shows how the same Japanese man looks Americanized and assimilated to American high society on the surface. The second scene also emphasizes that the Japanese man attracts a white woman by his refined and luxurious lifestyle.

The first shot of *The Cheat* after the title and credits is a medium shot of Tori in extremely low-key lighting. He is wearing a black Japanesque robe and a serious facial expression. Seated at his desk against a completely black backdrop, he brands a small objet d'art with his symbol mark (*torii,* a Japanese word meaning a shrine gate), using an iron poker from an Asian-style brass brazier. A line of smoke ominously rises from the brazier. He turns off the light with a satisfied expression and puts a lattice cover on the brazier. The glow of the brazier casts shadows of cross stripes on his face as though horrifying makeup has created a sinister mask.

The Cheat is famous for its innovative Rembrandt-like extreme low-key lighting effects that bathe characters in darkness but for a single source of illumination from the side. The film historian Lea Jacobs argues that in the DeMille films in 1915–16 "lighting is quite baldly used to create striking pictures which punctuate and heighten dramatic situations" and those films were "actually much *more* careful to motivate and integrate effects lighting than later classical filmmakers would be and than DeMille himself would be by the late teens."[54] In the opening shot in *The Cheat,* these lighting effects clearly enhance Tori's ominous and possibly villainous characteristics. Since this scene is directly followed by a medium shot of Richard Hardy (Jack Dean), a New York stockbroker, similarly seated at his desk but in uniform lighting, the effect of the low-key lighting in the first shot is emphasized. This scene clearly visualizes the ethnic and personality differences between Tori and the ordinary American gentleman.

While the introductory shot of Richard has a direct diegetic relationship with the following scene, the temporal connection between the shot of Tori in this opening and the next scene remains ambiguous. In the next scene Richard calls his wife, Edith, from the same office of the opening scene to scold her about her overconsumption. In contrast, the opening shot of Tori branding an object remains outside of the linear temporality of the narrative. It is unclear when this act of Tori's happens: Did it happen long before the actual story of *The Cheat* takes place? Does it happen in the middle of the story? Or is this simply Tori's habit? In either case, the temporal relationship between the first shot of Tori and the incidents in the narrative of *The Cheat* stays unclear. As a result, the major function of the first shot becomes to provide Tori with an innate ominous characteristic.

In the original script, however, Tori is located in the actual narrative temporality. In this script, Tori is first introduced as "One of Long Island's Smart Set in smart American flannels" just "reading magazine or newspaper, and smoking."[55] When his servant in Japanese kimono comes in and hands him a hat, he "looks at watch—smiles—and rises to go" to pick up Edith. Yet, there is a handwritten note in pencil, added in a margin, that reads "Scene dyed Red, Black Drop, brazier of branding" and "his face shown in light from coals."[56] Because of the change in the script, Tori's mysterious foreign nature is located in an atemporal and archetypal space in the film version.

In contrast, the following scene adopts an entirely different lighting technique and a costume strategy in order to emphasize the other characteristics of Tori: his apparent Americanized quality. In this scene, Tori is depicted as a person who has been assimilated into Long Island high society. Wearing a white duster, cap, casual tweed suit, and bow tie, Tori comes into the frame driving an expensive high-powered roadster in the flat high-key lighting of daytime. He is about to escort Richard's wife, Edith, to the Red Cross Fund Bazaar. He jauntily runs up the steps. When he enters Edith's room, he shakes hands with her and gives her a relaxed smile. In the script, in this scene, Tori gets angry when Edith tells him that Richard objects to her extravagance and to her seeing him. According to the script, Tori thinks he "would like to wring [Edith's] husband's neck." However, in the film, Tori's anger is not displayed on the screen. A handwritten note in the script crosses out this display of Tori's anger in order to emphasize Tori's cheerful, gentle, and restrained nature in this particular scene.

On their way back from the Red Cross Bazaar, Tori opens the door of his car for Edith, and when Edith stumbles, he gently helps her to get up. In the script, "for just a second he holds her close—Edith is confused," and "Tori abruptly lets Edith go—as if coming to himself and bows—deeply respectful—Edith holds out her hand to Tori, striving to be at ease." However, on the screen Edith does not show any confusion. With his gentle behavior, Tori looks well assimilated into the American way of life.

In addition to their differences of ethnicity and personality, another significant difference between the two gentlemen, Tori and Richard, is implied in this second scene. Tori does not have to work during the day, while Edith's husband, a typical middle-class American, is working in the stock market. Tori appears in the main narrative right after Richard blames Edith for her expenditure on luxuries. As soon as Tori hears Edith say "He's [Richard is] forcing me to give up everything," he replies, "Can't I help? No one need know." This line, which tempts Edith to the forbidden pleasure of overconsumption, is the first line spoken by Tori in *The Cheat*. The rich Japanese art collector is the man who can satisfy her desire for leisure and luxuries. Thus, the narrative of *The Cheat* connects a white woman and a Japanese man within the American domestic sphere via the transgressive attraction of leisure and consumption.

In reality, both consumerism and Japanese Taste had twofold meanings and functions in middle-class families. Therein lay a paradoxical situation of American modernization. On the one hand, there was an economic structure based on consumerism, and on the other hand, there were social values based on traditional Puritan ethics about productive and restrained behavior, which were linked with Victorian morality. In order to satisfy both of these imperatives, middle-class women had to spend money in order to display genteel status but to spend within reason and on appropriate objects for their families and for the consumerist economy. According to the film scholar Janet Staiger, "Women were important in the expansion of consumption into the realm of pleasure and leisure," and, simultaneously, a woman was "articulating the status of her family" by her dress, belongings, and furniture in the home; this became considered to be part of a woman's job.[57] During the period of the popularity of Japanese Taste among middle-class Americans, the collection of Asian art was an integral part of these women's assertions of their social positions both as cultural leaders and as New Women.[58] Japanese art and culture were recognized as having refined standards and high moral values that could be incorporated by Western civilizations and into the domestic sphere, while at the same time they should be financially and spatially contained in order not to threaten the image of Western gentility they projected.

Edith's words to Richard, when she is criticized for her expenditures, appropriately summarize middle-class women's new role of "conspicuous consumption," purchasing expensive clothes and exotic Asian objects to express her family's social status to other people. She says, "I must have new gowns for the Red Cross affairs." As a treasurer of the Red Cross Fund, Edith's voluntary charity work also symbolizes the "conspicuous leisure" of her upper middle-class life. In 1899 Thorstein Veblen published *The Theory of the Leisure Class*, based on his observation of late-nineteenth-century American society. Veblen argued that the wealthier an individual the more able he is—and the more necessary it is—to adopt an affluent lifestyle, with a strong emphasis on waste, to demonstrate to others an ability to consume time and goods in nonproductive ways ("conspicuous leisure" and "conspicuous consumption"). This is because the ostentatious display of goods and services that are both expensive and highly valued by others provides the individual with a path to social prestige in any society, which recognizes wealth as a major determinant by which status is conferred. Furthermore, according to Veblen there comes a point on the economic scale, as the social order descends, where the husband must work to support his family and so he passes the responsibility for conspicuous leisure to his wife. Similarly, if the husband is obliged to forego conspicuous expenditure then the responsibility for maintaining a socially "decent" level of conspicuous consumption to maintain an "expected" standard of living falls on the wife.[59]

Despite the fact that his assumptions and conclusions were empirically unfounded or unproven, Veblen's views on conspicuous consumption in American society went largely unchallenged and were accepted as the basis to condemn ostentatious economic display as a social evil in the United States in the years leading up to World War I.[60] *The Cheat*'s characterization of Edith as a conspicuous consumer and the eventual restriction of her behavior should be located in this context of the theorization and condemnation of conspicuous consumption. Edith, as a wealthy middle-class wife, is required to have conspicuous leisure and consumption, of Japanese Taste, in particular, in order to display the expected standard of living, but to have them at a socially decent level. Edith, as a New Woman, is expected to reconcile her consumer desire and sexual freedom with traditional obligations to her family and society.[61]

Richard himself understands the necessity of his wife's "conspicuous" behavior for generating and maintaining the appearance of the appropriate middle-class family life. Therefore, he cannot respond to Edith's words, "If you want me to give up my friends and social position—well—I won't." Richard is not mad at her spending itself. He is irritated because Edith is on the verge of overconsumption and about to lose the respectability of their middle-class family life.

Throughout its narrative, *The Cheat* substitutes and enhances a fear of overconsumption with a fear of racial hybrids.[62] The film's melodramatic binary structure attributes the cause of Edith's overconsumption to the racially and culturally inassimilable and threatening Japanese man. Edith's words to Tori, "My husband objects to my extravagance—and you," not only explicitly indicate that Japanese Taste is an integral part of her behaviors of consumption but also imply Edith's possible sexual transgression. The Japanese man is not only the rich art collector who brings refined products of Japanese Taste to her home but is also a consumable object himself in her domestic space. Tori's luxurious costume and belongings, including his beautiful car, and his words "Can't I help? No one need know," function in the narrative as a tempting but threatening voice of overconsumption and implicit miscegenation. Eventually, the white American man controls the white woman's overconsumption by regulating the nonwhite man's economic and sexual transgression.

The scene at Tori's low-key lighted Japanesque shoji room during the evening of the Red Cross Ball clearly connects the threat of overconsumption and the fear of miscegenation. The shoji room, with its proliferation of Japanese objects, not only represents Tori's luxurious lifestyle, which Edith appreciates, but also functions to reinforce Tori's ultimately inassimilable Japanese cultural and racial traits.

The contrast between the shoji room where Tori and Edith enjoy looking at Japanese objects and the main room where the ball is held is particularly emphasized in the script. While the main room is a "gorgeous combination of modern luxury and oriental beauty— *Not* typically Japanese as is the *Shoji* Room," the shoji room is "the typically Japanese room" with "Shoji Doors," "The Shrine of Buddha," a "gold screen," a "tall black vase full of cherry blossoms," and a "brazier of coals with small branding iron."[63] When Edith finds a brand of Tori's seal on the bottom of a small wooden statue of Buddha in the room, Tori demonstrates how to brand and explains to Edith, "That means it belongs to me." Edith gets "confused," according to the script, or even looks frightened on the screen and retreats back into the rear of the room toward the shrine of Buddha. She "tries to throw confusion off by laughing lightly."

Yet, Tori remains at the table for a while with a poker in his hands and his expression shows he has something on his mind. Here, for the first time since the introductory shot, the strong Rembrandt-like sidelight emphasizes the contrast of light and shadow on Tori's face, even though, at this point, Tori does not obviously show his villainous characteristics in his gestures or in his facial expressions.

Right after this, Edith's friend tells her that her stock investment using the Red Cross money has failed. When Edith faints, Tori kneels beside her, turns off the light, carries her out of the room, and hides in a dark corridor behind a shoji. In the off-screen light and the blue toning that imitate the moonlight, Edith's skin looks strikingly white. There, Tori steals a kiss. The sense of stealing is more emphasized on the screen, especially in the low-key lighting effects, than in the script and makes the scene more threatening.[64] The scene is much more romantically described in the script than on the screen. In the script, Tori brings the unconscious Edith to a bench in the garden, and "struck with her beauty and helplessness," he kisses her.

When Edith becomes conscious, she is scared by the thought of a newspaper headline, "EXTRA! SOCIETY WOMAN STEALS RED CROSS FUND," which is visually shown on the screen in double exposure. Tori leans closer to Edith and offers her money "if she will come to him," as the script is written, even though the intertitles on the screen never clearly state the line nor the details of their agreement. An intertitle states, "Do you agree?" before Tori signs his ten thousand dollar check for Edith and adds, "Tomorrow" after Tori hands the check to her. Here, *The Cheat* becomes a horrifying narrative of a fallen woman becoming a white slave under Asian despotism (see fig. 2).

The horror of miscegenation as a result of transgressive consumption reaches its height in the following scene after the intertitle declares, "The Cheat." The day after the ball, Edith comes back to Tori's place to return the money. Declaring that "You can't buy me off," Tori tries to assault her. He tears her clothes, grabs her hair, and throws her face forward onto the desk. In a close-up, Tori with the branding iron comes closer and closer to Edith's bare shoulder, and the iron almost reaches the white flesh. The lighting from the brazier casts ominous shadows on Tori's face and creates a horrifying expression. The branding itself is completed off screen, but the smoke comes up from off screen in front of Tori, who is grimacing with a tightly closed mouth.[65] His expression looks like a kabuki actor's exaggerated and temporally static face before entering his climactic violent act, *mie*, circling his head once, opening his eyes wide, raising his eyebrows, and glaring fiercely. The

2 *A still from* The Cheat.

strongly contrastive makeup that emphasizes Tori's black eyebrows, slanted eyes, and red lips reminds viewers of a special makeup technique of kabuki actors who play violent acts (*kumadori*) that suggests extremes of hatred or anger.

Moreover, in this scene, Tori wears a Japanese-style dressing gown over his Western-style evening dress, white tie, and tuxedo shirt. Even though he wears the gown over his shirt, it serves to represent his Japanese traits that are hidden behind the Westernized surface. The script emphasizes the "oriental" atmosphere surrounding Tori in this scene. Tori is "standing under big oriental light over table" and "another lantern remains lighted over shoji door leading outside." Tori's property—the gown, the poker, the brazier, the shoji, the Japanese garden that Edith has to pass through, and the Japanese servants—all change from attractive consumable objets d'art of Japanese Taste into dangerous weapons and an ominous backdrop for the eruption of Tori's hidden threat. Thus, the horrifying action of this scene is achieved by emphasizing the Japanese traits that exploit the makeup and the facial expression of kabuki and the "oriental" costume and objects. In this sense, Tori is the "cheat" who has hidden his Japaneseness under his disguise of a Westernized gentleman.

Yet, Edith is also the "cheat." She breaks her promise with him. Economically speaking, she should keep the promise, even if the promise is that she will be Tori's mistress. At the same time, Edith is about to deceive her husband. Morally speaking, Edith should stay faithful to her husband.

Eventually, the narrative of *The Cheat* represses the two "cheats," the heroine and the villainous Asian male, simultaneously under white American patriarchal control. First, Tori is a vehicle for white male desire. In their relationships with Edith, Richard and Tori become juxtaposed as masculine counterparts. When Tori attacks Edith, he is a victimizer. Tori's brutal way of treating Edith may be seen as the repressed desire of white men who have apparently become too civilized. With the contract and the branding, Edith is even treated as an object by Tori.

However, by the end of the film, Tori also turns into a victim of white male dominant society. Throughout the narrative of *The Cheat*, Tori is juxtaposed with Edith, the white woman, both visually and thematically, and portrayed as an effeminate character.[66] Even though Tori is a man, he does not find his place among men but among women. In the scene at the Red Cross Bazaar, Tori mingles only with women. The extreme long establishing shot of the bazaar and the following long shots show that Tori is introduced to other Red Cross women, surrounded by them, and chats cheerfully with them.

The pursuit of consumption connects Edith and Tori more fully. First, their elaborate costumes indicate the similarities between them. Edith appears in a striped coat, and Tori wears a striped shirt. The striped design may imply their twofold characteristics, refinement on the surface and hidden desire beneath. Then the two flirt in Tori's Japanesque shoji room, sharing the experience of admiring a woman's gorgeous kimono and looking at exquisite small objects on a table and a statue of Buddha seated before an incense burner releasing puffs of smoke into the air. Edith does not hide her happy excitement when she sees those objects. Tori offers the kimono to Edith, even though Edith refuses it after some hesitation. Tori playfully shakes a potted cherry and its blossom petals rain down on Edith. As Sumiko Higashi points out, this scene in the shoji room juxtaposes Edith and Tori as if they were two window shoppers at "a site replicating exotic displays in department stores," or two New Women, playing around in consumer culture.[67]

The branding sequence in the shoji room clearly emphasizes the visual equivalence between Tori and Edith. As Higashi points out, Edith is branded off screen and Edith shoots Tori off screen after his branding of her. Both lie diagonally on the tatami mat clutching their left shoulders in high angle shots.[68] We see the brand on Edith's left shoulder, and the shot wound on Tori's left shoulder. Each leans on the shoji while staggering with pain.

Eventually, both Tori and Edith come under white American patriarchal control. At the beginning of the twentieth century, with the increased participation of the New Woman in the suffrage, reform, and anti-imperialist movements and the increased presence of women and immigrants in the workplace and the spheres of commercialized leisure, white masculinity's privileged grip on political legitimacy, cultural authority, and social control appeared to loosen. *The Cheat* participated in "the discursive construction of a rejuvenated white masculinity that was manufactured in response to, and at the expense of . . . the new woman" and Japanese masculinity.[69] This is symbolically displayed in the final courtroom scene of the film. After Edith confesses what really happened at Tori's shoji room to the all-white male jury, the excited crowd, which previously included both men and women, becomes all white male.[70] Tori is arrested in the courtroom, surrounded by the mostly white male spectators. At the end of the scene, the white middle-class American husband embraces his penitent wife. The final shot of the film symbolizes the white woman's reintegration into the white male patriarchy. In a symbolical remarriage, Edith walks down the aisle of the courtroom, tightly embraced and protected by Richard. Edith's sexual and consumerist desires become "contained within the institutional framework of middle-class marriage and the family" and "the Victorian ideal of womanhood."[71]

Yet, as the courtroom scene indicates, no matter how similar Edith and Tori are, the narrative of *The Cheat* eventually makes an invidious distinction between the white woman and the Japanese man. The problem of female overconsumption in a white middle-class family is cleverly replaced in the end by the threat of the inassimilable Japanese. The morality tale of the attraction and threat of overconsumption is concluded in the form of the protection of the white middle-class family from transgressive foreignness by the white male. In order to defend the white woman and incorporate her into the American patriarchal system, the narrative of *The Cheat* puts all the blame on the Japanese man and excludes him from American society. An intertitle, "East is East and West is West and never the Twain shall meet," which is placed right before the final courtroom scene, clearly indicates the difference between the white woman and the Japanese man. At the climax of *The Cheat* the discourse of consumerism is finally differentiated from that of Japanese Taste, and the latter is overridden by the discourse of the yellow peril.

The largest difference between Tori and Edith is that Tori has almost no opportunity to speak out in court while Edith can speak out to make up for her mistake. In melodrama, in which muteness is a signal feature according to the literary critic Peter Brooks, the breaking of silence is a climactic declaration of personal identity and the confrontation of villainy.[72] Moreover, Janet Staiger argues, "For the middle class talk was becoming vital to protect the class from infringements upon its boundaries and to regulate the behavior of the New Woman and the New Man."[73] Edith experiences a conversion from an inappropriate New Woman, who has indulged in overconsumption, to a proper middle-class wife when she chooses to talk in the courtroom. Speaking up in the courtroom, she declares her personal identity and confronts the villain who embodies the peril of overconsumption and sexual transgression. Her expenditure, her overconsumption, and her improper entry into the world of men are forgiven because of her devoted public act of speech in the interest of her family.

In contrast, Tori is not allowed to speak up about what happened; he cannot tell the court about Edith's immoral conduct, which was tantamount to prostitution. No one questions why Edith was attacked. Edith does not take the heat for assault charges despite Tori's actions. Literally, the already concluded case is dismissed after Edith's nonofficial testimony without even a cross-examination of Tori.

Tori is not even permitted to express his emotion. The script gives eloquent expression to Tori's feelings, such that he smiles "with satisfaction" when Richard testifies that he shot Tori and that he "registers pleasure" at the verdict. Additionally, he shows "surprise and dissatisfaction" when Edith starts to talk. However, on the screen, Tori remains a speechless and emotionless object, despite several close-ups—sometimes irised—being inserted during the courtroom scene. Since there are no intertitles following those close-ups, Tori's emotion stays unexplained and much more ambiguous than Edith's. Tori sneers slightly only once during the trial when Richard testifies that he shot Tori and Edith. Also, he changes his expression slightly when Edith starts her desperate confession. Both of these changes in Tori's expression are so slight that they are not eloquent gestures that convey his entire thought or emotion, whereas Edith speaks out loudly with her exaggerated gestures: running to the judge with extended arms, wide open mouth, and eyes full of tears. Tori's emotionless facial expression and sardonic slight smile restrict him to the mere stereotypical image of Japanese despotism, rather than allow him to be a human being with psychological depth. Tori is given no opportunity to talk and no chance to deviate from an evil persona of a melodramatic villain.

In comparison, a film dealing archetypally with an all-American identity, such as Frank Capra's *Mr. Deeds Goes to Town* (1936), relies on the hero finally breaking his silence and speaking in public. Deeds's (Gary Cooper) willingness to speak, to express desire, comes in response to the woman's (Jean Arthur) courtroom declaration of her thought under cross-examination. Stanley Cavell calls the film "the comedy of equality and reciprocity" because Arthur's character grants Deeds "his wish to rescue, to be active, to take deeds upon himself, earning his name; as he grants her wish to her."[74] In contrast, we can call *The Cheat* a tragedy of inequality and non-mutuality because Edith never grants Tori his desperate wish to be active and to regain his reputation.

In the end, Tori is attacked by the dominantly male audience in the courtroom and bleeds from his mouth. The crowd yells, "Lynch him! Lynch him!" Historically, lynching was a punishment meted out to Negro men who had or were believed to have had sexual relations with white women. Tori turns into a stereotypical representation of the oversexualized nonwhite (racialized) male, a unidimensional villain because of his skin color, and a mere tool for the reunification of a white American patriarchal family. *The Cheat* thus integrated middle-class American discourses on family, gender, and race with American people's popular and stereotypical views of Japan. *Photoplay* called *The Cheat* "a melodrama so rational, so full of incisive character touches, racial truths."[75] Hayakawa's character embodied the popular twofold cultural and ethnic images of Japan, the refinement of Japanese Taste and the threat of the yellow peril, within a domestic melodrama that eventually supported white American patriarchy.

Contradictorily, although Hayakawa's lack of affect may silence him as a character in *The Cheat*, it opens up big potentiality for him to become a star. With his refined and villainous, apparently Americanized and ultimately inassimilable, role in *The Cheat*, Hayakawa vividly impressed the public consciousness. This ambivalent coexistence of refinement (Japanese Taste) and threat (the yellow peril), Americanization and Japaneseness, which is eventually controlled under the white patriarchy, became an essential core of Hayakawa's star image. Even in 1920, a review of *An Arabian Knight* (Charles

Swickard, 22 August 1920), a Hayakawa star vehicle, noted, "Whenever we hear of Sessue Hayakawa we think of 'The Cheat,' a five-reel production made about five years ago and to this day considered as the best example of photodramatic work ever presented on any screen. . . . And whenever we think of 'The Cheat' we think of Sessue Hayakawa because he was, in a big measure, instrumental in making 'The Cheat' the excellent production that it was."[76]

No matter how sensational Hayakawa's role in *The Cheat* was, it was not a result of Lasky's careful star-making plan. It was rather an accident. Hayakawa was only one of the supporting actors for Lasky. Hayakawa was originally engaged by Lasky in March 1915 to support Ina Clare with an "important" role.[77] Yet, Clare ended up making her debut on screen in a comedy, *Wild Geese Chase* (June 1915), in which there was no role for Hayakawa. Instead, Hayakawa appeared in several supporting roles for Blanche Sweet before being chosen to support Ward in *The Cheat*.

Lasky was recruiting such renowned theatrical figures as David Belasco, a Broadway producer, and William DeMille, Cecil's brother and a celebrated playwright, and such famous stage actors as Clare, Ward, and the opera singer Geraldine Farrar to "upgrade" cinema for respectable middle-class audiences.[78] According to Higashi, Lasky was "prescient in developing a strategy to legitimate cinema for 'better' audiences and to appeal as well to the aspiring masses by demonstrating the intertextuality of cultural forms as spectacle in genteel society."[79] Lasky modeled films after stage productions already deemed part of so-called highbrow culture for middle- and upper-class consumption and exploited "the affinity between stage and screen in order to acquire cultural legitimacy during an era of progressive reform."[80]

Lasky cast Hayakawa to support these famous stage actresses for a specific reason. The company was particularly interested in Japanese Taste in cinema for its prestigious value to middle-class audiences. Lasky planned to produce a film of *The Darling of the Gods*, which originally opened on Broadway on 3 December 1902, and became a hit.[81] Lasky also wanted Belasco to come to California to supervise the filming of his plays, including "probably *Madame Butterfly*."[82] To Lasky, the Japanese actor Hayakawa was the perfect fit for these productions with Japanese subjects. Hayakawa and his image of embodying Japanese Taste were to enhance the legitimate quality of the company's films. The NYMPC, which first used Hayakawa and other Japanese people to make films with Japanese subjects, had publicized that Hayakawa had a background in the Japanese theatrical arts. In reality, Hayakawa did not have any theatrical career in Japan, but the promotional biography made by the NYMPC was persuasive enough for the studio producers at Lasky to hire him to support renowned stage actresses.

Not only Lasky, but also Paramount Pictures Corporation, which distributed the Lasky films, was interested in films with Japanese subjects for their prestige status for middle-class audiences. One article in Paramount's own promotional magazine stated, "Lafcadio Hearn's wonderful word-paintings are like memorial pictures done with the golden brush of a master on panels of ivory, and he is only one of many who have contributed to our joy and interest in that Land of the Lotus Flower. Prominent among the ceremonies, feasts and celebrations which have become known to us through books and the drama and lately through motion pictures, in the Japanese play 'The Typhoon,' as representative of the social and religious habits of that people of the distant Empire of the Northern Pacific, none is more appealing and beautiful than the feast of Nobori No Sekku."[83] Paramount even distributed a NYPMC film with Japanese subjects, The Typhoon (Reginald Barker, 8 October 1914), even though the Mutual Film Corporation usually distributed NYMPC films.[84]

However strongly Lasky and Paramount were interested in the prestige status of the films with Japanese subjects, they did not consider making a star out of Hayakawa before the success of The Cheat. Before The Cheat, Hayakawa only played small roles like those of Japanese spies disguised as valets waiting for an opportunity to lay hands on valuable documents and to violently murder people in After Five (Oscar Apfel and Cecil B. DeMille, 28 January 1915) and The Clue (James Neill and Frank Reicher [credited as Frank Reichert], 8 July 1915). He also played a villainous Chinese "hop joint proprietor" who lures the innocent Blanche Sweet into opium addiction in a labyrinth-like den in San Francisco's Chinatown that is filled with stereotypically vicious Chinese faces in The Secret Sin (Frank Reicher, 21 October 1915). The New York Dramatic Mirror (NYDM) juxtaposed Hayakawa with other "Celestial actors."[85] Variety even spelled his name incorrectly, "Succo Hayakawa," and possibly considered his ethnicity to be Italian in its review of After Five.[86] These mistakes in trade journals indicate that Hayakawa was regarded as just another nonwhite supporting actor even in his early work with Lasky.

The Cheat was merely another film for Hayakawa to play a supporting Japanese character. Not only does the opening title of The Cheat feature Fannie Ward as the star of the film, but all of the advertisements of the film in trade

2296   THE MOVING PICTURE WORLD   December 25, 1915

PARAMOUNT

Jesse L. Lasky
presents
FANNIE WARD
In the sensational photo drama
"THE CHEAT"
by Hector Turnbull
Produced by Cecil B. DeMille

"Fannie Ward, the star, will in this picture, take her place as one of
the few great emotional actresses of the screen. I doubt if her
remarkable performance in 'The Cheat' has ever been surpassed."
— From a letter by Jesse L. Lasky
to W. W. Hodkinson, president of
Paramount Pictures Corporation.

Released through Paramount Pictures Corporation,
DECEMBER 13th

JESSE L. LASKY
120 WEST 41 ST STREET
JESSE L. LASKY Pres.   SAMUEL GOLDFISH

3   *An ad for* The Cheat. Moving Picture World *26.14 (25 December 1915): 2296.*

journals before the film's release also treated Ward as the star, while they almost completely neglected Hayakawa (see fig. 3).

In spite of the fact that Jesse L. Lasky praised Hayakawa's performance in
The Cheat before its release, he did not think of Hayakawa's potentiality of
becoming a star at that point. Lasky did not say that he would produce star
vehicles for Hayakawa.[87] When another film with Hayakawa in a supporting role as a Japanese valet, *Temptation*, starring the famous opera singer
Geraldine Farrar, was released right after *The Cheat*, there was almost no publicity about his minor appearance in it.[88] Lasky and Paramount recognized
Hayakawa as their potential star only when *The Cheat* achieved a huge box
office success and the popular recognition of Hayakawa became sensational;
at this point their attempts to make Hayakawa their star finally started (see
fig. 4).

As the forerunners of the star system in early Hollywood, Lasky and Paramount carefully prepared for Hayakawa's first star vehicle and planned how

4   *Portraits of Sessue Hayakawa and other popular film stars of 1916.*
Motion Picture News 14.16 (21 October 1916): 2545.

they should promote Hayakawa as a star. When *Alien Souls* (Frank Reicher, 11 May 1916) was finally released after a five-month gap, Hayakawa was no longer simply a capable supporting performer with a Japanese cultural stereotype. He became a star of the Famous Players-Lasky Corporation and Paramount Pictures Corporation.[89] After *Alien Souls*, fifteen star vehicles were made for Hayakawa at Famous Players-Lasky and distributed by Paramount between 1916 and 1918.[90] When *The Cheat* was re-released in 1918, not Ward but Hayakawa was publicized in trade journals as the star of the film.

In order to establish Hayakawa's star status, Lasky attempted to distinguish Hayakawa's own screen persona from the more pedestrian cultural stereotype roles accorded to Japanese people. Lasky also needed to carefully adjust his star image from the sensationally villainous one in *The Cheat* to a more appropriate but equally attractive one for middle-class audiences. Yet, before discussing Lasky's strategy in detail, I would like to go back in time a little and examine Hayakawa's film career before *The Cheat*. Before the success of *The Cheat* and before contracting with Lasky, Hayakawa appeared in many films at the NYMPC that stereotypically depicted Japan and its people. Hayakawa also played similarly stereotypical non-Japanese roles. What kind of stereotypes did the cinematic images of Japan, and other nonwhite cultures, contain, from which Lasky drew to distinguish Hayakawa's star image?

SCREEN DEBUT

O Mimi San, or *The Mikado*
in Picturesque Japan

Although *The Cheat* launched Sessue Hayakawa's stardom, Hayakawa had appeared in numerous films before *The Cheat.* According to studio publicity of the NYMPC and the Jesse L. Lasky Feature Play Company, Hayakawa had had acting experience in Japan even before his film career. Furthermore, Hayakawa's autobiography indicates that he was very popular at a theater in Los Angeles's Little Tokyo, where he played in dramas, including an adaptation of Tokutomi Roka's *Hototogisu* [The nightingale]. In his book, Hayakawa claimed that he started his film career as a star from the very beginning, with a high salary for *The Typhoon,* a feature production at the NYMPC.[1]

In reality, Hayakawa did not have any acting experience in Japan. He did not come to the United States to go into the film business, either. Hayakawa was never invited into the Hollywood film industry as a star. Hayakawa's entry into the film business happened accidentally under the distinct sociopolitical conditions of Japan and the cultural conditions of the United States in the early twentieth century.

Hayakawa, the son of a rich Japanese fisherman in Chiba prefecture, came to the United States in 1907. The main reason was that his elder brother, Oto-jiro, and other temporary immigrants from his hometown, Nanaura village, had been engaged in abalone fishing in California since the turn of the century. From the 1868 Meiji Reconstruction onward, the Japanese government had been addressing a plan for enhancing national prosperity and defense and had been supporting the modernization of fisheries in order to obtain foreign currency. The government subsidized Kotani Gennosuke and Kotani Chujiro from Nagao village in Chiba prefecture to help them engage in abalone fishing in California. Hayakawa's parents asked the Kotani brothers to manage Hayakawa's trip to America. With their support, Hayakawa was able to enroll in the Home-Study Department of the University of Chicago in 1908 to study political economy. In Hayakawa's passport, it is written that the purpose of his U.S. visit is "to study."[2]

After he left the University of Chicago, he struggled to survive as a temporary immigrant. Hayakawa was a dishwasher and a waiter at a restaurant, an ice cream vendor (1911), and a factory worker at a Mexican company in the United States (1911). According to his autobiography, after he left the University of Chicago, he appeared in theatrical dramas for Japanese immigrants in Little Tokyo in Los Angeles with Fujita Toyo's company. Even though Hayakawa insisted that he had been interested in theatrical dramas, joining Fujita's company seemed to be just one of his temporary jobs.[3]

While Hayakawa was performing in theatrical plays, Thomas H. Ince, the managing director of the NYMPC, happened to see one such play and hired him for his films. Ince recognized that films with Japanese subjects had a certain appeal to Caucasian audiences, especially those who were open to trying to experience the East and were attracted to Japanese Taste, and he had been looking for Japanese actors and extras. On 12 December 1913, *Variety* reported that the NYMPC would produce a series of five films about Japan starring the Japanese actress Tsuru Aoki, who had already appeared in Fred Mace's comedy films and a Majestic film, *The Oath of O'Tsuru San* (28 October 1913).[4] Two weeks later, the NYDM reported that a Japanese village was under construction at Inceville, the NYMPC studio in the Santa Ynez Canyon between Santa Monica and Malibu, named after Ince.[5] Ince was possibly persuaded by Aoki, Hayakawa's future wife, to see the plays in which Hayakawa appeared in Little Tokyo and eventually hired him to use in his films about Japan, but never as his star.[6] According to a letter that Hayakawa sent to his brother, he was not hired as an actor by the NYMPC but as a screenplay writer, who earned 300 dollars a month.[7]

According to the release record of the NYMPC, the first of Ince's "Japanese film" series was *O Mimi San* (Reginald Barker, 5 February 1914).[8] This two-reel short film seemed to be Sessue Hayakawa's debut film. In 1919, Hayakawa admitted that his first film was called *O Mimi San*, even though he decided not to mention this film later in any interviews or writings, probably because only Aoki was regarded as the prominent actor among the Japanese performers in the NYMPC at that point.[9] Then, what was his role in this film?

The MPW called *O Mimi San* a "picturesque Japanese number."[10] It is noteworthy that MPW used the term "picturesque" and a music metaphor, a "number," to describe *O Mimi San* because it indicates the film's ambivalent quality (authentic but stereotypical) and its intertextual relationship with *The Mikado, or The Town of Titipu* (1885), a popular light opera.

Using the term "picturesque," reviews in trade journals praised the "authenticity" and the "perfect atmosphere" of Japan that were depicted in *O Mimi San*. The "picturesque" was an anthropological notion that prevailed at that time. Sara Suleri claims that the "picturesque" was meant to catalog the distant in a discourse of "an unhinged aestheticism that veils and sequesters questions of colonial culpability."[11] The emphasis in the notion of the picturesque was on detailed images in order to achieve verisimilitude. The presupposition was that the essence of the picturesque imagery of the subordinate country was waiting to be recorded by the more civilized people of the West.

At the end of the nineteenth century and the beginning of the twentieth in the United States, as a response to the vast consumer culture and industrialization, a "culture of authenticity" was shaped by an intellectual elite and spread its influence beyond its core.[12] The historian T. J. Jackson Lears argues that the "feeling of overcivilization" in the industrialized and urbanized consumer culture of America by the 1880s led the "educated bourgeoisie" to feel that life had become "curiously unreal." In order "to experience 'real life' in all its intensity" for "alternatives to modern unreality," they turned to quests for "authentic" experience.[13]

This pursuit for authenticity acted hand-in-hand with nostalgia for premodern work. Japanese Taste among middle-class Americans' domestic sphere was one such example. With the help of such pseudo-scientific theories as social Darwinism and eugenics, which had been widely influential in the United States since the mid-nineteenth century, the nonwhite culture was nostalgically linked to premodern innocence or idyllic ruralness.

Striving for authenticity, show business developed the commercialization of authenticity in the form of films about the "Other." Informed by earlier representational practices such as travel novels, postcards, and the world's fair exhibits, commercial producers made early films featuring nonwhite peoples mainly for popular audiences in nickelodeons. Cinema functioned as an ideal apparatus to prepare audiences to encounter the real "Other." In cinema, the "Others" did not need to be exhibited outside their own environment as they were in the world's fairs. With movie cameras, they could be "authentically pictured" in their native place doing daily things.

Japan and the Japanese people were popular subjects for early films. *The American Film Institute Catalog 1893–1910* lists ninety-four films under the category "Japan and Japanese," and the *1911–1920* volume lists forty-three films under the categories of "Japan" and "Japanese."[14] Gregory Waller has identified over one hundred films noted in the pages of the MPW between 1909 and 1915 that were "distributed in the United States and that took Japan as their subject or setting and/or featured characters identified as Japanese."[15] The MPW noted already in 1910 how popular Japan was in early American cinema: "The affection of the American people for the Japanese, then, springs from the fact that there is a sentimental link between the two nations. The film makers take advantage of that sentiment. . . . Japanese art, Japanese life and Japanese costumes appeal to the occidental mind for many reasons. The grace, the charm, the poetry of Japan never fail to please us of the West. . . . We love our America, but oh you Japan!!!!"[16]

Ince took advantage of the popularity of films with Japanese subjects and the cultural conditions leaning toward these "authentic" experiences. He expected performers from the "Japanese race" to play Japanese roles in order to achieve the authentic representation of their culture, at a time when it was unusual to cast Asian actors in major roles in films; Caucasian actors usually played the parts. Actors from a certain race were considered to represent their cultural traits most appropriately because biological race was regarded as the determinant of personal characteristics or cultural traits.

At the same time, Ince thought that using Japanese subjects and Japanese actors could help the refinement and bourgeoisization of cinema for the newly cultivated middle-class audiences, who were interested in Japanese Taste. The success of the English operetta *The Mikado, or The Town of Titipu*, one of the typical works of *Japonisme*, which had been written and composed by William S. Gilbert and Sir Arthur Sullivan, and the popularity of the *Madame Butterfly* narrative (novel, play, opera; 1898–), which had an influence on strengthening the popular imagination about Japan among middle-class American audiences, were persuasive enough for Ince to produce films about Japan.

In the United States, *The Mikado* was first performed with the original cast in 1885, and it ran for 430 performances in New York. Then, the touring companies went across the country and "produced a rage for Japanese art and for things Japanese throughout Canada and the United States."[17] Under the influence of the popularity of *The Mikado*, many plays set in Japan appeared, including David Belasco's *Madame Butterfly* (1900). Even Japanese plays, including kabuki and *shinpa* (modern play), were played in several cities and appealed to middle-class audiences. In such cultural circumstances, films with Japanese subjects could be received as refined art forms.

O Mimi San pursues authenticity by using Japanese actors and by depicting Japanese sets and objects. The film displays such Japanese objects as gardens, scrolls, shoji, swords, torii (a shrine gate), costumes, and houses in considerable detail. Simultaneously, the pursuit of authenticity in *O Mimi San* is structured within the popular imagination or the cultural stereotype of Japan as premodern, atemporal, and ahistorical. *O Mimi San* has a close intertextual relationship with the narrative and visual imagery of *The Mikado*. What such narratives with Japanese subjects as *The Mikado* and *Madame Butterfly* emphasize most is archetypal dichotomies between civilized and primitive, urban and rural, modern and premodern, and Western and Eastern. With the wide popularity of these stories and limited access to more diverse narratives of Japan, there was no reason to doubt the representational authenticity of the archetypal narrative about Japan among American audiences.

The story of *O Mimi San* is set in Japan at a certain historical period when a shogun ruled the country. The shogun betroths his eldest son, Yorotomo (Hayakawa), to Sadan San (Mildred Harris), the daughter of the prime minister. Yorotomo's younger brother, Togowawa, who wants to succeed in the shogunate, conspires against the shogun and Yorotomo. Yorotomo becomes a political refugee, disguises himself as an ordinary man, and hides in the countryside. There, he falls in love with O Mimi San (Tsuru Aoki), a daughter of a gardener. But when the political conspiracy against him is resolved, he has to give up his love. Togowawa is captured, and the shogun orders him to commit hara-kiri, the samurai style of suicide. However, the shogun has a heart attack and Yorotomo has to go back and succeed in the position of shogun. Yorotomo then marries the prime minister's daughter.[18]

From the very beginning, *O Mimi San* is filled with images that are in accordance with the notion of the "picturesque." The film opens with a long shot of a room with a small platform, on which the shogun, Yorotomo, Sadan San, and Yorotomo's younger brother, Togowawa, are sitting close together. The old shogun staggers and leaves the room accompanied by Yorotomo, Togowawa, and the prime minister. They go to the shogun's private tatami room. Both rooms are ornamented with detailed Japanese objects, including vases and flowers, to simulate a Japanese domestic space. However, many of the details are incorrect. The platform is three high steps up from the tatami floor, but it is set too high. Usually, the platform is just one low step up from the tatami floor. Yorotomo's hairstyle tries to simulate an authentic *chyonmage*, the traditional Japanese style, although the bald part is too narrow and the topknot is too far back. Even though the stripe design of Yorotomo's kimono is too unusual, and his *haori*, the Japanese overgarment, is too long and looks like a white Western cloak, Yorotomo's costume, and those of the others, try faithfully to follow the design of the Japanese kimono. Even the family crests appear on the costumes, although they should not be on the chest and sleeves of the kimonos. The shogun has makeup that imitates *kumadori*, a special makeup for kabuki actors. Moreover, "Yorotomo" and "Togowawa" are improper for actual Japanese names, but they still sound Japanese and resonate historically, since they appear to derive from the names of actual shoguns, Minamoto-no Yoritomo in the twelfth century and Tokugawa Ieyasu in the seventeenth century.

The narrative of *O Mimi San* articulates these detailed images as premodern. O Mimi San is characterized as an embodiment of an idyllic maiden, displaying primitive innocence and pure love. Yorotomo, coming from the urban center, "discovers" her when he is cheerfully taking a walk in nature. First, O Mimi San is shown only in Yorotomo's point-of-view shots. She does not realize she is captured in his gaze. O Mimi San, in a kimono, cheerfully and in childlike fashion, runs out of a gate made of bamboo. At this point, Yorotomo functions almost as a Western gaze that records premodern lives in the Japanese countryside.

The following medium close-up of the pair sitting under a tree emphasizes an idyllic atmosphere and the pure love between Yorotomo and O Mimi San. O Mimi San plays a Japanese-style guitar and sings at the side of Yorotomo. When Yorotomo tries to take her hand, she stops playing the music, looks down shyly, and smiles. This depiction of the relationship between Yorotomo and O Mimi San fits perfectly with M. M. Bakhtin's articulation of "the love idyll" in the history of literature in the West. In "the love idyll," Bakhtin argues, the "utterly conventional simplicity of life in the bosom of nature is opposed to social conventions, complexity and the disjunctions of everyday private life; life here is abstracted into a love that is completely sublimated."[19] What Yorotomo finds in the rural area surrounded by nature where O Mimi San lives is a timeless world where only love exists. The literary works that Bakhtin examines are basically European ones, and the notion of the idyll he discusses comes from them. If the relationship of Yorotomo and O Mimi San fits the "love idyll," it is clearly within the European imagination regarding temporal and spatial articulation.

In the case of *O Mimi San*, this ahistorical and atemporal notion of the picturesque is especially emphasized by the film's intertextual reference to *The Mikado*. The plot summaries of *O Mimi San* in film trade journals identify the father of Yorotomo as the emperor of Japan (the Mikado) instead of the shogun.[20] These indicate Ince's commercial framework, which articulated *O Mimi San* in relation to *The Mikado*. In fact, *O Mimi San* refers to *The Mikado* in its narrative structure and visual reliance, even though the former ends on a tragic note and the latter is a comedy with a happy ending.

In *The Mikado*, Nanki-Poo, who has been ordered by his father, the Mikado, to marry Katisha, "an elderly lady" of the Mikado's court, flees to the town of Titipu. There, disguised as a wandering minstrel, he falls in love with Yum-Yum, who is about to marry Ko-Ko, the Lord High Executioner of Titipu. Ko-Ko needs to execute someone within a month in order not to lose his post, because the Mikado thinks the post is unnecessary given that there is no one to execute in Titipu. Nanki-Poo tells Ko-Ko that Ko-Ko can execute him after one month if he permits his marriage to Yum-Yum. Ko-Ko agrees. On the day of marriage between Nanki-Poo and Yum-Yum, the Mikado arrives with Katisha, looking for Nanki-Poo. Not ready to carry out the execution, Ko-Ko believes that the Mikado has come to check that someone has been executed and lies to him, saying that he has executed Nanki-Poo. When Nanki-Poo appears with his newly wedded wife, Yum-Yum, the Mikado feels so happy that he forgives his son's non-fulfillment of his engagement and accepts his marriage.[21]

The motifs of disguise of the prince, betrothal, a love triangle, and a love affair across class boundaries are the obvious affinities between the two stories. Both in *O Mimi San* and in *The Mikado*, the sons of the Mikado (or the shogun), who are betrothed to high-class women, go to a secret hideout in disguise and fall in love with innocent and cheerful young girls. As in *The Mikado*, Japan and Japanese people are represented as ahistorical and archetypal entities in *O Mimi San*. Japanese people and objects, depicted in great detail, were ideal embodiments of premodern ruralness and idyllness. When Hayakawa started his film career, the major emphasis in films with Japanese subjects was upon the picturesque, the nostalgic pursuit of authenticity, no matter how stereotypical and Eurocentric was the imaginary Japan in those films. Playing the son of the shogun/mikado, Hayakawa started his film career in *O Mimi San* merely as a human element, or an object of an American audience's gaze, to enhance the "authentic" atmosphere of Japan.

CHRISTIANITY VERSUS BUDDHISM

The Melodramatic Imagination

in *The Wrath of the Gods*

O n 12 January 1914, a volcano erupted on the island of Sakura-Jima in Kagoshima prefecture, in the southern part of Japan. Because of the stream of lava, the island of Sakura-Jima became connected to Osumi Peninsula on Kyushu, one of the main islands in Japan. It was one of the largest disasters in the history of Japan.

Thomas H. Ince lost no time in grasping an opportunity to make a film based on this event. Only two weeks after the eruption, the *Toledo Blade* (24 January 1914) and the NYDM (28 January 1914) reported that Ince was rushing to make a feature film entitled *The Wrath of the Gods* (also known as *The Destruction of Sakurajima*, Barker, 22 June 1914) with Aoki and her company of twenty Japanese players who had been working under Ince's direction. According to the *Toledo Blade*, "News of the eruption was hardly a day old before Mr. Ince had built in the Santa Monica Canyon a whole Japanese village."[1] Ince constructed a large and detailed Japanese village in his studio, Inceville, and used many Japanese people, not white American actors with makeup, as extras. On 31 January 1914, the *New York Clipper* reported that in addition to the Japanese company of performers, "Mr. Ince is scouring the lower part of California for Japanese laborers who are to be worked in as peasants."[2] The MPW reported that "actually 1,000 extras were used recently in a big Broncho picture, 'The Wrath of the Gods,'" and "most of the employees were Japanese people."[3] The filming of *The Wrath of the Gods* began on 27 January 1914, only fifteen days after the eruption, and finished on 13 February.[4] The eruption of Sakura-Jima was not only a subject with hot news value but also a good opportunity for Ince to make a spectacular film with an authentic depiction of Japan and its people.

Following the popularity of foreign imports, by 1914 the American film industry had begun to produce feature films with spectacles. The MPN announced the screening of "the super-spectacle" Italian film *Cabiria* (Giovanni Pastrone, 1914) and noted, "A NEW meaning was given to the words, 'motion picture,' and a new definition to the possibilities of Cinematographic art when 'Cabiria' . . . was displayed in the grand ballroom of the Hotel Astor on Saturday, May 9."[5] Set in the Roman Empire of the third century B.C., *Cabiria* tells a story of kidnapping and human sacrifice. Spectacular scenes in the film show a palace destroyed by an erupting volcano and a huge temple within which children are thrown into a fiery figure of the pagan god Moloch. *Cabiria* portrays these scenes effectively by using slow tracking shots toward or away from static action, which give a three-dimensional depth and solidity to the enormous sets. That traveling camera style was called the "Cabiria Movement" in the United States.[6]

Ince wanted to make *The Wrath of the Gods* his *Cabiria*. *The Wrath of the Gods* was far more than a news film or a travelogue. Ince made this project into a spectacular melodrama and sensational event movie by exploiting the exotic landscape and people. Hayakawa was not a star of this film. He was not even a leading character of this project but merely an ingredient to compose the melodrama. Aoki played a leading role in the film but in a strategic manner. First of all, Ince fictionalized Aoki's birthplace and connected it to the eruption of Sakura-Jima in a tear-jerking way. A report in the MPW stated,

> It so happens that Miss Aoki is a native of the Island of Sakura, which was practically destroyed by the eruption of the volcano Sakura-Jima. Miss Aoki, having lost practically all her relatives in this eruption, was inconsolable and Mr. Ince thought that he was due to lose her, that she would have to go back home. But in consoling her, he induced her to work in conjunction with him on a thrilling and powerful heart interest story, entitled "The Wrath of the Gods," a four reel Domino feature, evolving around Japanese legend and depicting the scenes and actions of her countrymen during the eruption, so that she could show the world the sufferings of her people.[7]

This report emphasized that Aoki was both the personal "eyewitness" and the melodramatic heroine of the event.

In real life, Aoki was not from the Sakura-Jima area but from Obara Tsuru, in Fukuoka prefecture, the largest city in the Kyushu area, which is located about 180 miles north of Sakura-Jima.[8] Moreover, the hierarchal race and gender relationship between an American man and a Japanese woman was implicitly indicated. Ince functioned to protect Aoki and provided her with the opportunity to work. In order to construct Aoki as a heroine of a melodrama that would appeal to middle-class audiences, Aoki's biography was thus fictionalized in the promotion of *The Wrath of the Gods*.

Aoki's fictionalized biography in *Reel Life*, the promotional magazine for Mutual, the distributor of NYMPC films, emphasized her Americanized character in order to make it easy for American audiences to identify with her as a melodramatic heroine. In the biography, Aoki became "the daughter of an illustrious Japanese artist who has done much to make the subtle art of his country known to the Occidental peoples," and the "influences which had shaped her growing years were American."[9]

Several articles also emphasized Aoki's Americanized education. Aoki entered a convent in Pasadena, California (her symbolic conversion to Christianity), where she studied the piano and vocal music.[10] Then, Aoki studied ballet in Chicago. According to an article that reported the marriage of Aoki and Hayakawa in the *New York Clipper*, "Just prior to the time Nat Goodwin was injured at Santa Monica, Miss Tsuru Aoki was rehearsing with Mr. Goodwin in a vaudeville sketch, which he had booked on the Orpheum Circuit, but owing to the disastrous outcome, his propect [*sic*] had to be given up, and Miss Aoki turned to the pictures."[11] In real life, Aoki did not go to the convent but studied at the Egan Dramatic School in Los Angeles before she joined Fred Mace's company and Ince's company.[12] The publicity that fictionalized Aoki's biography for American audiences indicated that *The Wrath of the Gods* mixed actual news with melodramatic fiction. For Ince, Japan and its people were merely raw materials for his project and their historical and biographical backgrounds were easily transformable.

Ince made the release of *The Wrath of the Gods* itself a sensational event specifically targeting middle-class audiences by way of a large-scale publicity campaign. As early as 14 February 1914, nearly four months before the film's release, the NYMPC put a fair-sized ad in the *New York Clipper* announcing "Wait for *The Wrath of the Gods*."[13] Right before and after the film opened, major trade journals carried one-page ads of the film every week with different pictures, still photos, and such sensational ad lines as: "THE MOST THRILLING AND GRIPPING PRODUCTION OF THE AGE,"[14] or "A STUPENDOUS AND GORGEOUS SPECTACLE: THE VOLCANO OF SAKURAJIMA IN ACTION—LAVA FLOWING—ASHES FALLING—HOUSES CRUMBLING—VILLAGES BURNING—THOUSANDS FLEEING FOR

THE MOVING PICTURE WORLD 929

5 *An ad for* The Wrath of the Gods. Moving Picture World *20.7 (16 May 1914): 929.*

THEIR LIVES—THE TYPHOON AT SEA—SHIPS DESTROYED BY FIRE
AND WATER—DAZZLING IN ITS MAGNIFICENCE."[15] These ads simultaneously exploited exotic Japanese people and objects with detailed "picturesque" illustrations, such as an angry-looking statue of the Buddha and a
Japanese woman in a kimono praying in front of it (see fig. 5).[16]

Even the marriage of the leading performers of *The Wrath of the Gods*, Aoki
and Hayakawa, became included in this publicity campaign as an attraction.[17]
This was the first time the portrait of Aoki appeared in the major film trade
journal MPN, and it was also the first time the name of Hayakawa appeared
in a news column in MPN. Hayakawa's private life was thus connected to his
public image for the first time in the ad campaign for *The Wrath of the Gods*.

The Wrath of the Gods opened on 7 June 1914, at a new "Million-Dollar"
New York theater, the Strand.[18] A review of *The Wrath of the Gods* in MPN

reported, "The lobby display not only rivaled the efforts of the best legitimate houses, but in many respects surpassed them. Fourteen magnificent framed oil paintings, colored drawings and photographs were on exhibition. The frames, six feet high by four feet wide, were decorated in the subdued shades of old gold. The most graphic scenes of the drama were shown in a blend of harmonious color; the clear perspective and the expression on the features of the characters indicated the work of an artist and showed that as much thought had been employed on this detail as on the pictorial details of the play."[19]

The NYMPC ad proudly announced on 20 June 1914, that *The Wrath of the Gods* "SCORED THE BIGGEST HIT EVER RECORDED AT THE STRAND THEATER, New York: BOX OFFICE RECORDS BROKEN UNPRECEDENTED APPLAUSE."[20] After its premiere at the Strand, *The Wrath of the Gods* opened in "all first class houses in New York and Brooklyn, including The Strand, Broadway, Proctor's Fifth Avenue, Regent, The New Law, Odeon, Pictorium, Burland and the Lenox."[21] On Monday evening, 22 June, the exhibitor Marcus Loew opened up Ebbets Field, the National League's baseball ground in Brooklyn, whose capacity was about 20,000 people, to show *The Wrath of the Gods*. The NYMPC ad reported that on that night "over 40,000 tried to get in. Consequence was a riot ensued, quite a few people hurt and the Police Reserves from three different precincts had to be called. Over 15,000 turned away."[22] Thus, Ince publicized the exhibition of *The Wrath of the Gods* as a sensational event, specifically targeting urban middle-class audiences.

Ince had another strategy to attract middle-class audiences to *The Wrath of the Gods*. Using religious images, Ince made this film a morality tale with a melodramatic dichotomy between the East and the West. First and foremost, *The Wrath of the Gods* is an archetypal fable between the civilized West and the primitive East, presented as a religious battle between Buddhism and Christianity. The review in MPN noted that the "big themes" of *The Wrath of the Gods* included the "irreconcilable attitude of Orient and Occident" and the "polar antithesis of two great religions."[23] The eruption of the volcano, the spectacular device, also symbolized the collision between the cultures and the religions.

In *The Wrath of the Gods*, Hayakawa plays old Baron Yamaki, the last male descendant of an old samurai family of Japan. In this first feature-length film for Hayakawa, he does not play a heroic handsome lead but an elderly supporting character with heavy makeup. This indicates Hayakawa's nonstar, subordinate role at the NYMPC. Aoki plays his daughter, Toya-San. According to an old local legend of Sakura-Jima, Yamaki's family has been cursed by the Buddha. If Toya-San marries, it would displease the Buddha and the long inactive volcano, Sakura-Jima, would erupt. When an American vessel is shipwrecked off the coast, Yamaki rescues a sailor named Tom Wilson (Frank Borzage). Tom and Toya-San fall in love. Tom tells Toya-San about the Christian God, who is more powerful than the Buddha. The villagers try to prevent Toya-San from getting married to Tom. When a furious crowd is about to lynch Yamaki, the volcano erupts. Lava, fire, and an earthquake kill most of the villagers, but Tom and Toya-San escape to an American ship anchored in the harbor.

Using the characters' appearances, written words, and a cross-cutting technique, the film clearly represents the Japanese village as a superstitious community bound by a primitive religion. The opening scene emphasizes that Toya-San is a melodramatic victim of the primitive community. When young villagers speak to Toya-San, an old prophet named Takeo intervenes. Takeo warns the villagers that "She came from [a] family that [is] accursed." Takeo embodies a primitive religion with his broken English, dirty long hair, beard, a torn white kimono, and a large wooden cane. Toya-San bursts into tears and runs back home, which is a wrecked house that is segregated from the village. When she tells the prophet's words to her father, Yamaki, he brings out an old scroll. Japanese letters on the scroll that dissolve into English read "Buddha appeared and said thy daughter to be wife/curse on your race. . . ." It is significant that the term "race" is used, instead of "family" or "village." Japanese "race" is thus presupposed as primitive and superstitious in this letter.

Toya-San and Yamaki go out of the house to an altar next to the house, in which sits a statue of the Buddha. The stone-carved statue looks unsophisticated, as if to emphasize the primitiveness of the religion. Yamaki prays to the Buddha to lift the curse but then angrily cries out, "I renounce my faith." Then, the sky darkens and a strong wind blows. Yamaki says, "The heaven has heard me! God will [be] angry." He is irritated with the religion that victimizes him and his daughter, but still he is tied up with his superstitious belief in the Buddha, whose curse seems very strong to him.

The following sequence introduces the opposite religious belief. In bright daylight, Tom asks Toya-San to marry him. In front of the statue of the Buddha, Toya-San wipes her tears with a sleeve and tells Tom that the volcano is the "symbol of God" and will erupt if she gets married. A shot of Takeo is inserted as a flashback, enhancing Toya-San's superstitious fear of the threatening religion. Tom gives Toya-San a cross-shaped necklace and says that this represents the "god of justice." The cross is shown in the first close-up of the film, which emphasizes its importance in the narrative. Tom helps Toya-San put on the necklace. Toya-San throws herself into Tom's arms, like a heroine of a Western melodrama. Then the close-up of the cross is inserted once again. Symbolically, Toya-San converts to Christianity here. Using a melodramatic dichotomy between the good religion and the bad one, this scene emphasizes the American sailor's position as an enlightening force that paternalistically helps a Japanese girl to change her religious belief and to free her from the primitive culture.

The actual collision of cultures occurs in the following scene. The collision is displayed as a religious battle. Cross-cutting among three locations heightens a tension between the superstitious villagers and the Yamaki family, which converts to Christianity. Toya-San and Tom go to the American mission in town to get married. A sinister-looking rickshaw driver spies on the couple with a clergyman in the mission and tells the villagers about it. The villagers rush to Takeo. Takeo tells the crowd, "Look, birds and animals are leaving Sakura-Jima," and he suggests that they should regard it as a "bad omen from Buddha." The camera cuts back to Yamaki alone at his place. He makes a cross with two branches and walks up to the statue of the Buddha. Yamaki throws away the statue of the Buddha, replaces it with the cross, and pushes his arms to the sky. Here, Yamaki portrays his conversion to Christianity in a violent manner. The camera goes back to the mission, where the clergyman in a clean black sacred costume faces Takeo in a dirty torn costume. At Yamaki's place, Yamaki raises the cross, shaking his right fist, and addresses the angry crowd: "I deserted god as god deserted me. I will not forgive anyone who prevents my daughter's happiness." The crowd flinches from the cross for a moment but then starts to assault Yamaki. Dying, Yamaki hopes that Tom and the Christian God in America will protect his innocent daughter. Yamaki, the major Japanese male character played by Hayakawa, is a more feminized character than Tom, the American sailor.[24] Yamaki is clearly passive and susceptible to the American man's idea about religion. He is incapable of making Toya-San, a woman with whom he lives, satisfied and happy. Moreover, Yamaki is incapable of fighting back against the superstitious group of men. He is easily and passively swallowed up in the violent lynching mob. All he can do is to accept his victimized position in the community and to leave his daughter to the American man. This view of feminized Asian men self-sacrificing for the creation of an American family continued to be one of the bases of Hayakawa's sympathetic star image later.

At this moment, when the religious battle between the superstitious crowd and the newly converted Christian becomes violent, the volcano erupts. The result of the collision of cultures is displayed as a sensational cinematic spectacle. The village is covered with smoke, lava comes down, rocks fall from the sky. Takeo dies in the smoke. Many villagers suffer in the streets. In contrast, Toya-San and Tom safely reach an American vessel. The shots of the disaster-stricken streets of Kagoshima are cross-cut several times with those of the American vessel safely off the coast.

Thus, the final spectacular sequence emphasizes the fact that a Christian American man saves a Japanese girl from a primitive land inhabited by a superstitious lynch mob. Tom says, "Your God is powerful, but ours proved to be omnipotent." Tom's remark transforms the status of the volcano in the narrative. The volcano used to be the symbol of Toya-San's superstition, but eventually it turns into the embodiment of the omnipotent power of the Christian God, who destroys the superstitious and punishes primitive people. This narrative may also refer to the tale of Sodom and Gomorrah in the Old Testament, civilizations entirely destroyed by God because of the evil of their citizens. The curse of Buddhism was chosen arbitrarily to represent a primitive religion's superstitions, even though the idea of curses has no part in Buddhism.[25] The moral of this tale is that the power of the Christian God overcomes the obsolete religion and the value of humanism is emphasized as a result of this Christian power.

In this melodramatic moralistic dichotomy, Japan is not regarded as a modern nation. It is not an independent existence, but a place somewhere in a totalized primitive region. It is not so much a historical community as an atemporal space where superstitious savages live. In *The Wrath of the Gods*, the binary axis is not drawn between a historical region and a modern nation-state, but in a more archetypal way between the civilized and the savage. With this de-historicization, the film, which originally has a news or travelogue quality, turns into a melodramatic fable that regards the civilized America and Christianity as good and the primitive space and its religion as evil.

The theatrical nature of *The Wrath of the Gods* reinforces its melodramatic quality. The film opens with a shot that imitates stage curtains, on which the name "Ince Company" is written in Japanese. When the curtains are opened, as an introduction of the film, each actor as himself or herself appears behind the curtains and dissolves into a shot of the same actor in costume. Hayakawa turns from a bowing young man in a black kimono to an old man with a thick beard.[26] An actor who plays a rickshaw driver takes a particular pose drawn directly from one of the most typical kabuki styles, called *mie*. *Mie*, "exaggerated freezes in tableaux," in kabuki means to stop one's movement in the middle of the act and to stare forward with eyes wide open. *Mie* creates a moment of static time that functions to express the enhanced emotion of the actor in a "bombastic gesticulation" and "brings all action onstage to a halt with it."[27] The technique of *mie* is closely related to a kabuki genre called *aragoto*, which literally means a "rough" or violent style of acting, perfected by the famous Edo kabuki actor Ichikawa Danjuro I (1660–1704). Many audiences may not have recognized the origin of this pose in kabuki. However, they should have noticed the sense of theatrical stylization in the pose. In *The Wrath of the Gods*, the rough and violent connotation of the pose is connected to the primitive and savage quality of the rickshaw driver and enhances these characteristics.

After the introduction of the major characters, the black curtains open again onto a location shot on the beach. At the end of the film, the curtains close on the shot of a ship that Tom and Toya-San have boarded. A reviewer from *Variety* unfavorably pointed out the theatricality of the curtain device: the curtain "helps to heighten the picture facts, that everything is set or staged, that the camera is there, so forth and so on. It's not the best way to start off a picture. If the actors are to be featured in this way, it would be better for them to appear after the finale, bowing their thanks for the applause, if any."[28] In any case, the curtains theatrically declare the beginning and ending of a fable.

Thus, the ideological narrative of *The Wrath of the Gods* is constructed around melodramatic binary oppositions, good/evil, civilized/primitive, masculine/feminine, and West/East. The role Hayakawa played in *The Wrath of the Gods*, as a supporting character with heavy makeup, was the embodiment of the latter. It morally justifies a white American male character's religious view. Ince made *The Wrath of the Gods* not only as a sensational event movie, but also as a morality tale targeting middle-class audiences, in which the white American patriarchal system plays an overarching role.

DOUBLENESS

American Images of Japanese

Spies in *The Typhoon*

M otion pictures have been using spies and espionage as one of their favorite topics since the very beginning. *The American Film Institute Catalog* lists 18 films under the subjects "spies" and "espionage" from 1898 until 1910, and 156 from 1911 until 1920.[1] Most of the early spy films deal with the motifs of international political conspiracy and the tragic results. The first spy film listed in the *AFI Catalog* was *Execution of the Spanish Spy* (distributed by Sigmund Lubin, 1898).[2] Thereafter, many spies who end up with tragic fates in early American silent films were represented as holding nationalities other than American, as if their tragic fates were only caused by their non-American citizenship.

Japan was a popular subject of spy films from the early period. Japanese men appeared as spies in many early American films, especially after Japan defeated Russia in the Russo-Japanese War in 1905. Ten out of fifty-four films listed under the subject heading "Japan and the Japanese" from 1910 until 1920 in the *AFI Catalog* were spy films.[3] The first was *Capture and Execution of Spies by Russians*, which was distributed by the Edison Company and the Kleine Optical Company in July 1904, only five months after the beginning of the Russo-Japanese War on 8 February.[4] In this film, two Japanese spies, disguised as coolies, fail to dynamite railway tracks in Russia. After a chase, they are captured and sentenced to death. The spies give three cheers for their emperor and are shot dead.[5]

As this early example shows, Japanese spies on screen tended to have images of double identities. They were often in disguise as devoted servants in American households, or sometimes as refined gentlemen in the high societies in Europe or in the United States. Their peculiarly or exotically dignified deaths, often occurring at the end of the film, symbolically emphasized their inassimilability to American standards. The 1910 film *The Japanese Spy* (Kalem) tells a story of a Japanese spy who secures secret information about the latest maneuvers of the U.S. Army. He leaves his wife and children in Japan and, disguised as a peddler, pursues his mission in the United States. He is finally captured and "dies like a Samurai, committing hari-kari."[6]

The doubleness in the representation of Japanese people in spy films refers not only to a two-sided (disguised, double) character—that is, high-class gentleman or faithful servant and betraying enemy—but also to the two-sided (ambivalent, contradictory) image that American audiences had of Japan—that is, refined, attractive, and threatening; Westernized and inassimilable; Japanese Taste and the yellow peril; premodern and modern; primitive and civilized. The motif of spies' double identities in early American cinema corresponded to, and enhanced, the ambivalent popular image of Japan in international politics at that historical moment.

After the Russo-Japanese War, the supposed omnipresence of an international spy system run by the Japanese government drew the attention of the Americans and the Europeans, in accordance with their awareness of Japan as a modernizing nation. From 1900 onward Japan increasingly directed its intelligence services to take a keener interest in the United States, regarding the United States as a rival imperialist nation in the Pacific. From time to time Japanese warships and fishing vessels carried out extensive surveying, charting, and photography off the American Pacific coast. In one such incident in 1908, a number of Japanese officers took the opportunity to wade ashore and explore the whole area.[7] The U.S. Army and U.S. Navy started paying attention to these probes.

Similarly, in Britain, in 1907, Ian Hamilton, who was attached to the Japanese First Army as a British military observer, wrote, "The Japanese realized the weakness of Russia much better than any American or European observers. The British believed that Russia was in Manchuria to stay. Japan weighed the evidence—superior intelligence—and came to a precisely contrary conclusion. . . . The Japanese accept what their experts tell them."[8] In a report to the German General Staff in 1908, another British officer also attributed the swiftness of the Japanese victory over Russia to "superior intelligence—especially on the naval side."[9]

This concern about the Japanese spy system began to appear in popular media in the United States. In 1907, *Harper's Weekly*, a magazine for middle-class readers, noted, "During the war between Russia and Japan, Manchuria was inhabited by spies and soldiers. . . . We shall not know how the Japs did in their conduct of the elaborate spy system, save as the Russians tell of it in their present discussion. . . . The Japanese . . . were able to use the Russian spies for Japanese purposes, and in the end to outwit the Russians at every turn."[10]

The European and American conception of the Japanese spy system is an example of racist imagination that trapped Japan in the middle of a eugenicist evolutionary ladder, or a racial and cultural hierarchy. On the one hand, the Japanese spy system was praised for its order and effectiveness. Japan's technical advances in espionage were noted in order to picture the Japanese as more advanced than other "primitive" cultures and thus closer to Europeans and Americans. In this perspective, Japan was allowed to be a member of a modernized European league. On the other hand, Japan was considered threatening for the same reason. The fact that the "scientific" advances of Japan were placed in the service of a fanatical, ultra-nationalistic patriotism to its emperor, which Europeans and Americans deemed primitive, clearly implied that Japan was still different from the modernized nations, especially in the discourse of yellow journalism.

Ince was well aware of the popularity of spy films in the early period of cinema and of the suitability of Japanese characters in this genre. He cast his Japanese actors in several spy films, including his second feature with Japanese subjects, *The Typhoon* (Reginald Barker, 8 October 1914). Hayakawa had already played several spy roles and he achieved popular recognition as an individual actor for the first time when he played a Japanese spy in *The Typhoon*.[11] A review of *The Typhoon* in the *Milwaukee News* even called Hayakawa "a movie star" for the first time.[12] The role of a young Japanese man who displays his ambivalent characteristics, torn between Westernized gentleness and inassimilable Japaneseness, would be repeated in *The Cheat* and become one of the basic star images that would be developed a few years later.

Hayakawa himself regarded *The Typhoon* as the film that formed the basis for his later stardom. In most of his interviews or his memoirs, Hayakawa ignored all the other films in which he appeared at the NYMPC and identified *The Typhoon* as his first film. In 1914, Hayakawa said that his character in *The Typhoon* was "his favorite role."[13] He also said, "I am anxious to see the play as I consider it my very best work. . . . It is seldom that an Oriental is given such an exceptional opportunity to portray his dramatic skill in America, and I know I did my best in 'The Typhoon.'"[14] Hayakawa even said, "'Typhoon' opened at the Strand Theater in New York, and made a great sensation," but he, intentionally or not, confused the film with *The Wrath of the Gods*, in which he did not play a leading role.[15]

In *The Typhoon*, Dr. Nitobe Tokoramo (Hayakawa), a Japanese diplomat who lives in French high society in Paris, is actually on a secret mission for his country. He is creating a secret report on France. With his refined lifestyle, Tokoramo attracts a French sweetheart, Helene (Gladys Brockwell). She is more interested in Tokoramo than in her American fiancé, Renard Bernisky (Frank Borzage). However, for Tokoramo, "Nothing but death will make me forget my duty to Nippon." Once Helene insults his duty to his country, he becomes furious and strangles her to death. In order to let the spy complete his mission, Japanese officials choose a young student Hironari (Henry Kotani) to be executed instead of Tokoramo. Tokoramo suffers from his conscience and his love and commits suicide in the end.

The Typhoon depicts a more contemporary Japan with a more topical subject matter than do *O Mimi San* and *The Wrath of the Gods*. However, *The Typhoon* is still a fable rather than an actual depiction of Japanese culture and its people at that time. The film melodramatically displays Japanese spies' barbarous and primitive patriotism in opposition to Western people's civilized manners. Hayakawa's Japanese character is represented as the one who is caught between the melodramatic dichotomy and falls into a tragic fate in the end, as in *The Cheat* later.

The Japanese spies in *The Typhoon* are, in fact, depicted with twofold characteristics. On the one hand, they are disguised as men of respectable position, who appreciate the life of French high society. Their refined lifestyles and their embodiment of Japanese Taste are attractive to French people, women especially. On the other hand, they are the representatives of an inassimilable culture. They become threatening when it comes to the interest of their own country. They represent the yellow peril discourse.

The introductory shots of Hayakawa foreshadow the double identity of the Japanese spy whom he plays. The film opens with the device of drawing up the stage curtains as in *The Wrath of the Gods*.[16] Beneath the curtains, each actor is introduced as himself or herself, then the shot dissolves and each actor appears in costume for the film. As himself or herself, each actor smiles and bows toward the camera, and in costume, he or she makes some gesture or expression that is suitable for his or her role. The boundaries between the actors and the characters that they play are clear.

However, in the case of Hayakawa and the character that he plays, it is difficult to draw a distinctive line between fiction and reality. After an intertitle saying "Mr. Sessue Hayakawa as 'Tokoramo,'" in a medium-long shot, Hayakawa, in a Japanese kimono with a Japanese fan in his hands, looks right and left with a vacant expression. He turns to the front, grins while raising his right eyebrow, and then smiles and bows. The shot dissolves into a shot of Hayakawa, with a frowning expression, in a long black coat reading a book. He looks up with an embarrassed face and goes back to the book. Even when Hayakawa is supposed to be an actor himself, he shows exaggerated gestures and expressions. Therefore, it seems that the Japanese man in a kimono is a character that Hayakawa plays. At the same time, the man who is reading a book, which is supposed to be the character that Hayakawa plays, can be Hayakawa as an actor. Using Hayakawa's costume and expression, these introductory shots of *The Typhoon* strategically locate Hayakawa as an actor and his character in an ambiguous position between Japaneseness and Westernization, which would become the major thematic and visual motif in Hayakawa's later star vehicles.

The excessively theatrical quality of the opening scene, which is situated in Japan, makes a clear contrast to the other less theatrical scenes in Paris. It visually declares that this film is about the collision of two cultures and peoples. Medium-long shots of the first scene emphasize the function of the frame as a theatrical stage frame. The composition of the first scene in a Japanese room simulates a stage set. A dense collection of furniture, such as tatami mats, shoji screens, sitting mats, a vase, a pot, a Japanese-style writing desk, a hanging scroll, and a Japanese plant, creates a claustrophobic and stage-like space. Three people enter the crowded room from the right side of the frame as if they had appeared on a stage. The theatrical set of the opening scene in the Japanese room emphasizes the exotic and premodern quality of Japanese culture.

At the same time, the opening scene portrays Japan as a modernizing nation. Japanese people in the scene read a letter, the content of which emphasizes Japanese nationalism. It is a letter of reference introducing Hironari, a young Japanese student who is entering a French university, to Baron Yoshikawa (Joshikawa, in the letter in English) in Paris. On the screen, the letter written in Japanese dissolves into English for American audiences.

The English translation emphasizes the young student's strong patriotism and Japan's ultra-nationalism, not mentioned in the Japanese original. The Japanese letter reads, "Hajime Hironari comes to Paris to study at a university. I would be grateful if you could take good care of him and introduce him to other Japanese people in Paris."[17] The English version reads, "This will introduce Hironari, who leaves to enter a French University. The Young man is ambitious to serve his country. Advise him in what capacity he can serve Nippon." The choice of the term "Nippon" rather than "Japan" may serve to emphasize a nationalistic tone to the letter. Thus, the opening scene of *The Typhoon* uses theatrical spaces filled with objects of Japanese Taste and strategically juxtaposes the nostalgic image of a premodern region with the topical image of a nationalist modernizing nation.

The following scene in Paris introduces the Japanese protagonist, Tokoramo, as a twofold character, portraying him as a metaphorical embodiment of the collision of two cultures. The shots of Tokoramo's room display his refined European lifestyle surrounded by luxurious European furniture. The house in which Tokoramo lives is a large European-style mansion. In the first shot, Tokoramo is wearing a suit and reading a book that is not written in Japanese. The only Japanese decor in this shot is a small Japanese inkstone on a desk. In a frame hung on the wall is a calligraphy that is possibly Japanese but looks more like hieroglyphics. When his French servant brings him tea in a Japanese teapot, Tokoramo frowns and makes a gesture that he does not want it. He looks as if he is refusing a Japanese lifestyle. The limited number of Japanese objects does not function as a symbol of Tokoramo's Japaneseness but as his refinement in appreciating Japanese Taste.

By 1905, Colonel Akashi Motojiro, the supreme Japanese intelligence officer in Europe, who worked as a Japanese attaché, had, according to his own claim, seven spies and five assistants working for him on a regular basis, within a network that extended to Paris, Zurich, Geneva, Copenhagen, Rome, Lisbon, and even to Warsaw. Colonel Akashi, who was both a poet and a painter, was described as "most conscientious, hard-working, considerate . . . a trifle over-careful, ponderous and precise from the military attaché point of view, but obviously upright and reliable in every sense" and became a favorite in the European salons.[18] Such figures as Akashi possibly served as models for Tokoramo's Westernized surface in the original play *Taifun*, on which the film version was based.

In opposition to Tokoramo's Westernized appearance, his hidden Japaneseness is also visually displayed in the mise-en-scène of the scene. When Helene disturbs Tokoramo's work for his country, he stares at her with a severe expression. In this brief shot, chrysanthemums and the hieroglyphic calligraphy suddenly occupy the background. This framing implies Tokoramo's Japanese traits hidden behind the Westernized surface. At this point, Tokoramo's Japaneseness is only briefly indicated. He takes her hand and gently says, "My work is of the utmost importance. It will soon be finished, when I can give more time to you." Helene reaches her arms to his shoulder and kisses him. When they kiss, the shot regains a Western-style painting in the background. The Japanese traits inserted into the previous shot completely vanish.

It was rare to show a kiss between a nonwhite man and a white woman in this period because it would cause the anxiety of miscegenation. In the case of Hayakawa's career, as far as the available film prints are concerned, this scene in *The Typhoon* is the only case that shows an "ordinary" kiss between Hayakawa and a white actress. The kiss in this scene basically functions to emphasize Tokoramo's Westernized character, which hides his Japanese traits at the core. Yet, it is still possible to argue that this kiss is not "ordinary" but indicates an unequal racial status between the two. Since Helene sits on the arm of the chair, she kisses Tokoramo from above, as if she is trying to conquer him. This may suggest a European subject's imperialistic possession over an Asian object.

The twofold characterizations of Japanese people in *The Typhoon*, hiding their inassimilable Japaneseness behind their Westernized disguise, are most typically displayed in a later party scene, in which Japanese diplomats/spies in Paris celebrate "Nobori no Sekku," a national holiday in Japan. In the scene, Tokoramo's refined European room turns into an extremely exotic Japanesque space. Japanese spies set up a white portable folding screen on which Mount Fuji is painted, Japanese-style sitting mats, Japanese-style paper lanterns, and Japanese teapots. They open the doors, on which the hieroglyphs are written, in the background. A little statue of the Buddha appears from behind the doors. The spies put on Japanese kimonos over their Western suits and start drinking sake and dancing Japanese style dances. Japanese ornaments cover all the European furniture and become dominant in the room. This is the only scene in Paris in which the mise-en-scène emphasizes the theatrical quality as does the opening scene in Japan.

When Helene comes into the ornamented room, she looks extremely out of place in the Japanese surroundings. Helene's entrance indicates the mutual incompatibility of the two cultures. Her intrusion causes the party to end prematurely. All the Japanese people apparently welcome Helene very politely, but behind her back, Yoshikawa gets furious at Tokoramo. While Tokoramo sees his colleagues off, Helene drinks and smokes in front of the statue of the Buddha and laughs at it. With a severe face, Tokoramo forces her to stop touching the statue. Helene says, "Can't you appreciate my great love for you?" Her question implies that it is her love that rescues Tokoramo from the world of premodern Japan, symbolized by the the statue of the Buddha, and helps him to achieve a Westernized self.

In the scenes that follow, the lovers' quarrel is cleverly transformed into an archetypal collision of the two different cultures. The French woman's words question the discrepancy between the Westernized surface of Tokoramo and his hidden inassimilable Japaneseness. Bernisky appears and confesses that Helene is his fiancée. After he leaves, Tokoramo shouts at Helene. "You told me there was no other man in your life. You have deceived me. Go, and never return." This behavior of Tokoramo is simply that of a jealous man. Tokoramo is not depicted here as a stereotypically ultra-nationalistic Japanese man, but as a man expressing a rather universal human emotion. In turn, Helene chides Tokoramo for his sense of obligation to his country and makes him a parting threat in racist terms: "All right I will go, but my face will ever come between you and your work for you love me in spite of all. I am going back to Bernisky and laugh with him at you—you whining yellow rat—and at your Japan, a dirty yellow blot upon the face of the earth."

As a result, within the narrative of *The Typhoon*, Tokoramo's jealousy is replaced by his anger, caused by Helene's debasing of his nationalist duty. What is presupposed behind Tokoramo's character is a stereotypical image of the Japanese people, who are viewed as being dominated by their ultra-nationalist duty. Helene's words function to reveal the inassimilable core of Japanese people in spite of their superficial assimilation. Her lines encapsulate Hayakawa's Japanese character in a stereotypical image of Japan and emphasize the archetypal binary opposition between the East and the West. The significant narrative motif that *The Typhoon* employs concerns a Japanese man who shows a possibility of Westernization/modernization, psychological as well as apparent. Yet, he is eventually positioned within a cultural stereotype of primitive and premodern Japan, which is visually emphasized from the beginning in a melodramatic dichotomy between the East and the West.

Helene's clear insulting attitude toward Japan turns Tokoramo into a stereotypical embodiment of the yellow peril. Tokoramo attacks Helene and strangles her to death. The novelization of the original stage version, *Taifun*, published in 1912, clearly locates Tokoramo's assault within the yellow peril discourse. "Gone was the carefully taught self-control of generations! Gone was the thin varnish of culture that hid the fighting, yellow savage of the Pacific! The long-schooled features were twisted into a horrible grimace of anguish and rage. The dark eyes flamed with a maniacal fire. He crouched forward like a beast about to spring. His strong fingers were crooked like the talons of a carrion bird and his breath escaped through the clenched teeth with a hissing, rattling sound."[19]

The Japanese portable folding screen appears in the background behind Tokoramo and visually emphasizes the abrupt gush of Tokoramo's threatening Japaneseness. As soon as Tokoramo hears Helene's racist line, he widens his locked lips and opens his eyes wide to gaze at Helene. Then, he stops his movement for a while with this expression before he assaults her. His way of posing, which creates a moment of static time and brings all action onscreen to a halt, imitates the *mie* posture, the style taken right before an act of violence in kabuki. The positioning of his legs (placing one leg forward) is similar to the *ashi o waru* in the *mie* pose. The positioning of his arms (raising one arm high and the other fist in front of the chest) follows the stance of Ichikawa Danjuro I, the famous Edo kabuki actor of the *aragoto* genre. Hayakawa claimed in a later interview that Danjuro inspired his performance.[20] Hayakawa explained his experience of watching Danjuro's gaze and his ability to create a dramatic moment of static time: "In Japan we had a great actor, his name was Danjuro. I remember one time seeing him come into the middle of the stage and fix the audience with his gaze. He didn't speak a word. His face was absolutely immovable. Every trace of expression was gone from it. It was set like stone. He just stood there and looked, and as he looked you could feel the audience catch its breath. He kept on looking. The audience became so tense that it seemed as tho [*sic*] you must scream if he did not move. I remember that I myself was almost hysterical when Danjuro finally relaxed and released his hold."[21]

This imitation of the stylized pose of kabuki and the resulting static moment reinforce the image of violent collision of cultures between the East and the West. The stylized kabuki pose emphasizes that Tokoramo's hidden cultural trait has superceded his Westernized appearance, even if only a few U.S. viewers would have recognized Hayakawa's performance as a reference to kabuki.

The shots of Baron Yoshikawa and his men dressed in European suits enjoying themselves in their European-style office are cross-cut several times in this sequence of Tokoramo's assault on Helene. A shot of Yoshikawa and his men laughing is inserted right after the shot of Tokoramo strangling Helene. They look as if they were laughing at Helene being strangled by Tokoramo. This cross-cutting enhances Tokoramo's unquestionable bond with Japan and the image of the Japanese people as cruel.[22] This cinematic technique functions to identify Japanese people's savagery as the reason for the breach between Tokoramo and Helene, rather than Helene's deception. The cross-cutting embodies a line that appears later in the film as an intertitle, "East is East and West is West and the twain shall never meet."

In spite of the melodramatic binary structure of the narrative, the character of Tokoramo still shows possible room for his psychological development beyond the cultural stereotype. He does not look triumphant after murdering the person who insulted Japan. His hair is disheveled and his lips are distorted. He falls down on the chair and bends over the desk. He turns to his left absentmindedly and desperately combs his hair with his hand. However, the possibility of Tokoramo's psychologically detaching himself from this Japanese cultural stereotype is soon denied by the intrusion of other Japanese people.

Tokoramo's attempt to express his humane emotions is hampered by Japanese ultra-nationalism, stereotypically represented by Yoshikawa, Hironari, and the other Japanese men. Yoshikawa insists, "Your country is first in importance. You must finish your report. Hironari will confess [to] the crime." Hironari looks extremely happy to sacrifice himself for his country. Tokoramo's choices to faithfully follow the decision of his countrymen and then commit suicide for his own honor evoke a stereotypical image of Japan, a country of *bushido*, the code of the samurai and their honor. As a result, the representation of Tokoramo in the finale of *The Typhoon* comes close to that of Hironari, who sacrifices himself for the sake of ultra-nationalist duty.

Baron Yamaki in *The Wrath of the Gods* also has a distorted self, a hybrid between a superstitious Japanese samurai descendant and a "human being" who converts to Christianity. Just as Yamaki is swallowed up by the barbarism of the stereotypically primitive and superstitious Japanese crowd, Tokoramo's depth of psychological development is denied in the narrative of *The Typhoon*. In the beginning, the imaginary Japan embodied by Tokoramo is an ambivalent mixture of a modernizing nation and a premodern space. However, eventually, Hayakawa's character falls into a cultural stereotype of ultra-nationalism, which is completely in accordance with the popular yellow peril discourse. The Jesse L. Lasky Feature Play Company and Hayakawa himself, when they shaped Hayakawa's star image, had to deal with the existence of such a strong cultural stereotype of Japan that prevented the Japanese protagonist from expressing sympathetic human emotions and from displaying any psychological development on the screen.

5

THE NOBLE SAVAGE AND
THE VANISHING RACE

Japanese Actors in "Indian Films"

Hayakawa's role in *The Typhoon* indicated a possibility of further psychological development beyond a mere cultural stereotype. Yet, Ince never decided to promote Hayakawa as his star. No star vehicle for Hayakawa was made at the NYMPC. In spite of the fact that many stars, including William S. Hart and Sessue Hayakawa, started their careers under Ince, Ince's films, mainly "authentic" spectacles that fully utilized cultural stereotypes, did not need movie stars. By 1915, when the NYMPC aligned with the newly formed Triangle Film Corporation and Ince joined D. W. Griffith and Mack Sennett in filmmaking, Ince came to admit the necessity of stars for product differentiation. He disclosed that his idea was "to get stars, teach them the tricks of the camera and then keep them at salaries high enough to restrain them so that they cannot work first for one company and then for another."[1] Still, it seems that at least before 1915, stars were "workers" who were "interchangeable part[s] in the script" for Ince, who pursued the specific division of labor in his studio.

Under Ince before 1915, Hayakawa appeared as a Native American in four "Indian films," a genre that constituted a separate popular genre from Westerns in the early 1910s. Ince specialized in the genre. The film historian Eileen Bowser claims, "Authenticity was an important advertising point for Indian films and was used with even more emphasis here than for the Westerns of the period."[2] According to the film historian Steven Higgins, Ince used Japanese and Native American performers in order to achieve the "authentic" feeling.[3]

In fact, the status of both Native Americans and Japanese were similar in the popular American imagination of the time. While Native Americans were often highly regarded as "noble savages," Japanese were regarded as sophisticated in the middle-class discourse of Japanese Taste. Both Japanese and Native Americans had been considered as descendants of the Mongoloid race, lower levels on the human ladder envisaged by the thought of social Darwinism or eugenics, but yet higher than the Negroid in the racial hierarchy. In Ince's supposedly "authentic" films, there were no big differences in the thematic motifs and narrative structures between the films with Japanese subjects and those with Native American subjects. Both of them circled around the cultural conflict between the civilized and the primitive.

Moreover, in a broad trade journal discourse of the time, both Japanese and Native American actors' acting abilities were praised, or publicized, for their dignity and restraint. Ince used Japanese and Native American actors interchangeably. While Hayakawa played some Native American roles in Ince's films, some Sioux Indians played Japanese villagers in such films as *The Wrath of the Gods*. Ince cast Hayakawa as a dignified son of a Native American chief in *Death Mask* (Jay Hunt, 25 September 1914) and as a wayward son of a dignified Native American chief, played by William Eagle Shirt, a member of the Sioux Nation, in *The Last of the Line* (probably directed by Jay Hunt or C. Gardner Sullivan, 24 December 1914). Steven Higgins argues, "Ince might have recognized dignified and refined features in the Japanese performers including Hayakawa that were necessary for his authentic Indian characters."[4] In 1977, four years after Hayakawa's death, the film critic Harvey Elliot stated, "Hayakawa's countenance was that of the noble savage."[5] Elliot emphasized the dignified and restrained acting styles of Hayakawa, compared to other actors of the period, and consciously or unconsciously explained the Japanese actor's acting skill using the term that signified Native Americans.

The major theme of the two extant Indian films in which Hayakawa appeared as Native Americans, *Death Mask* and *The Last of the Line*, is a racial and cultural middle-groundness of a certain group of Native Americans. Some Native Americans in these films accept the American middle-class discourse of home and family and distinguish themselves from the more primitive others. As a result, these films provide narratives that naturalize the construction of white supremacy, as do *The Wrath of the Gods* and *The Typhoon*.

In *Death Mask* and *The Last of the Line*, the binary axis between the civilized culture and the primitive one is indicated in melodramatic structures and with the motif of death. This connection of melodrama and the motif of death would later be one of the most important elements in Hayakawa's star vehicles. The connection in the Indian films also refers to the social discourse on Native Americans in early twentieth-century America.

Peter Brooks argues that the world of melodrama is imbued with moral Manichaeism and that characters in melodrama are either morally good or evil with no one in the middle. Moral conflicts between heroes and villains are unambiguously presented and often violently played out. The character system necessarily reflects this clear-cut division within the melodramatic worldview: characters in melodrama are either morally good or evil.[6] The film scholar Gregory S. Jay argues that the "ability of the melodrama to represent so expertly stark confrontations of good and evil proved to fit Indian subjects nicely, and not because the Indians were evil and the whites were good. On the contrary, many of the films create sympathy for the Indians, who are often the victims of the whole catalogue of historically documented white oppressions." According to Jay, the melodramatic mode in Indian films functioned to translate the political conflict between Native Americans and the United States into a "domestic tragedy" that was "seemingly unconnected to contemporary political decisions." The viewer "can feel sympathy for the individual victims without questioning the larger dominant narratives of white manifest destiny and racial superiority that these films presume."[7]

The melodramatic structure in Indian films coincided with Frederick Jackson Turner's famous thesis of the "closing of the frontier" in 1893, which implied the belief that Native Americans were inevitably vanishing before the power of America's "Manifest Destiny." As Jay points out, in Indian films, the "Indian served both as a nostalgic reminder of what was purportedly passing away," whose nobility lies in a "primitive defense against the complexity of modernity," and a "focus for perceiving the superior qualities of the dominant culture."[8] The melodramatic imagination thus functioned to turn Native Americans into the imaginary "noble savages" and the "vanishing race."

Death Mask, the third film in which Hayakawa played a Native American character, is a melodramatic adventure film. Its narrative emphasizes a certain hierarchy within Native American cultures and justifies white supremacy in a twisted manner. Hayakawa's character obtains the status of a "noble savage" only because he belongs to a tribe that is more civilized and moralistic than other primitive tribes. Hayakawa's character believes in romantic love, monogamy, and chivalry. He saves an innocent girl who has been trapped within a community of superstitious beliefs and despotism, as the American sailor in *The Wrath of the Gods* saves a Japanese girl from a primitive community.

In *Death Mask*, Hayakawa plays Running Wolf, the son of the high chief of a Southland tribe. In the opening scene, Running Wolf gently repulses the advances of Little Fawa, a maiden of his own tribe. In the council lodge, asked by his father, "Can my son find no maiden of all the tribe that pleases him?" Running Wolf answers, "There is a maiden in my heart but I have seen her only in my dreams—some day I shall find her." The next day of the council, an exhausted wanderer from the far north staggers into the village and tells the villagers of "a tribe of warriors fierce and cruel, ruled over by three brothers." The wanderer also describes a beautiful girl in the tribe (Tsuru Aoki). "With them dwells their sister, of whose beauty men sing from the lakes to the sea. Many young men have come to woo her; none have returned." Imagining the girl as the one of his dreams, Running Wolf starts for the far country that night. After many perils, Running Wolf sights the lodges of the three brothers, but a storm forces him to seek shelter in a cabin near the village. That night, he saves a Native American girl who is soaking wet from the storm. Running Wolf realizes that she is his dream girl. At dawn, Running Wolf wakes up and finds that the girl has gone. When the sun is highest, Running Wolf enters the village. When Running Wolf easily defeats the first two brothers, the tribe calls for the third brother, who wears a Death Mask, whom they regard with superstitious awe. When Running Wolf makes a dash for the third brother, the third brother throws away his spear and runs away. Infuriated by the astonishing cowardice of the third brother, the fanatic tribe clamors for his death. The chase leads into the forest, where Running Wolf unmasks the third brother and reveals the face of the Native American girl he had sheltered the previous night. She says, "There is no third brother; my brothers forced me to play the part." They run off.

From the opening scene, *Death Mask* emphasizes the civilized characteristic of Running Wolf's tribe. The tribe's patriarchal system maintains the order of heterosexual monogamy. The son of the chief (Hayakawa) is depicted as gentle and well mannered. He does not take advantage of a woman's approach to him. His vision of his dream girl emphasizes his romantic nature.

The existence of a more primitive tribe enhances the civilized image of Running Wolf's tribe in comparison. The wanderer compares the rulers of the warrior tribe to animals. Together with the tribe's superstitious awe of the Death Mask, this comparison emphasizes the image of the tribe as more primitive than Running Wolf's. The wanderer says, "The first brother is like the panther." A shot is inserted showing a Native American man jumping around. "The second's strength is that of a great white bear." A shot of a masculine Native American man, chopping woods with an axe, is inserted this time. "The third brother no man may meet and live. His face is ever hidden in the 'Death Mask.'" Several shots are inserted: that of a man with the Death Mask, sitting with snakes and skulls; that of a Native American child attempting to peep into the house of the third brother and stopped by others; scared Native American men watching the third brother coming out of his house. Thus, the structure of the narrative of *Death Mask* is clearly based on a melodramatic binary opposition: between the civilized, "noble" tribe and the primitive, superstitious one. As in *The Wrath of the Gods* and in *The Typhoon*, the collision of cultures occurs when a couple is being created between two different cultural origins. Running Wolf's quest for his dream girl turns into a chivalric romance to save an innocent victim from an uncivilized group of people.

The scene of the night storm emphasizes Running Wolf's civilized characteristic once again. Running Wolf does not take advantage of a suffering woman. His respect for an unmarried virgin is extreme. He goes out of the cabin into the storm with only a blanket and sleeps outside of the door.

In contrast, the primitiveness of the warrior tribe is emphasized when the actual face under the Death Mask is revealed. An innocent woman with a Death Mask, an object of superstitious awe, has been made into a taboo. Because of Running Wolf's intrusion into the tribe, the tribe's superstitious belief is overthrown, as the American sailor in *The Wrath of the Gods* helps to destroy the superstition toward the Buddha.

Running Wolf's refined characteristic is also indicated by his actions in the climactic fight scene. Running Wolf stops his movement, holding the knife with his right hand, raising it, and putting his left leg forward. He stares at the people of the tribe with his eyes wide open. As with Tokoramo's pose in *The Typhoon* before he strangles Helene, this pose of Running Wolf creates a static moment in which the action onscreen comes to a halt. It looks exactly like the *mie* posture in kabuki, with his legs in the *ashi o waru* pose and his arms positioned to mimic Ichikawa Danjuro I, the famous kabuki actor. *The Wrath of the Gods* also utilized the rough and violent connotation of this pose to imply the primitive quality of a Japanese man. Here, the pose may suggest the primitive characteristic of Native American culture.

However, simultaneously, this pose distinguishes Running Wolf from the opposite tribe. His *mie* pose also signifies his grandiose heroism right before the act of violence. Kabuki was considered a refined art form from Japan in early-twentieth-century America. To some audiences who were familiar with kabuki, Running Wolf's kabuki-style pose functioned to enhance his embodiment of higher cultural status, despite the fact that the issue of authenticity in this artificial connection of Japanese Taste and the Native American culture is never questioned.[9]

Thus, the motif of cultural hierarchy among Native American tribes is clear in the narrative of *Death Mask*. The melodramatic binary distinction between the civilized and the primitive constructs this chivalric romance narrative. Japanese Taste serves to enhance Running Wolf's image of embodying a refined culture. The hero from the more civilized and refined culture encounters a primitive culture. As a result of the collision of cultures, the hero destroys the superstition and saves an innocent girl as does the hero in *The Wrath of the Gods*. The nonwhite hero functions to defend the Victorian morality of heterosexual monogamy in the end.

While *Death Mask* is a romantic story of a cultural collision, *The Last of the Line* is a story of a tragic encounter between Native American culture and white American culture. In *The Last of the Line*, Hayakawa again plays a son of the chief of a Native American tribe. Gray Otter, the last of a long line of powerful Sioux chiefs, prepares for the return of his son Tiah (Hayakawa) from a white American school. At the frontier station, the tribe's men are embarrassed when Tiah, who is supposed to be the most educated and civilized future chief, arrives completely drunk. Even though Gray Otter scolds Tiah, he keeps drinking and tries to take advantage of women. He also endangers the tribe's livestock and children. Following a new peace pact with the U.S. commander at the frontier garrison, Gray Otter pledges his word that no white man shall be molested by Native Americans while Tiah plots with a band of renegades to rob the Army paymaster. Enraged at the attack, Gray Otter shoots down his own son. Wishing that his son should be honored in death, Gray Otter seeks to make it appear that his son gave his life defending the paymaster. When the belated rescuers arrive, he tells them, "Word came to our village that those not our tribe had attacked the paymaster. My son went to help him. I now seek him." The commander says, "Gray Otter, your son died a hero." The army men bury him with military honors. The coffin is covered with the star-spangled banner, and at the conclusion of the ritual a priest reads lines from the Bible. Alone after the funeral, Gray Otter holds a cross over the grave with his hands, looks up at the sky, and then looks down absentmindedly.

In *The Last of the Line*, the heroism of the Native American people is demonstrated through their moralistic attitude toward alcohol and women and eventual sacrificial commitment to the U.S. nation. Parallel editing is extensively used in *The Last of the Line* and clearly displays two possible types of behaviors of Native Americans. When Gray Otter gives the commander his pledge and shakes hands with him, the scene is cross-cut to that of Tiah drinking at a bar with his follower Native American and Mexican renegades. When the band lead by Tiah ambushes the coach of the army paymaster, the parallel editing shows Gray Otter prancing on his beautiful white horse. He uses a saddle in a civilized manner while Tiah does not. Since Tiah has been continuously shown mounting the horse awkwardly and riding on it wearily, Gray Otter's dignified riding style stands out. The MPW points out, "The old Indian is fine. He has all the dignity and grandeur that one could want."[10]

The collision of cultures is represented in a form of family melodrama, when the battle occurs between the band of the renegades and the army paymaster. The cross-cutting that has been used throughout the film ends here and, thus, visually emphasizes the collision of two types of Native Americans in the tragic form of a dual between the father and the son. When Gray Otter witnesses his son shooting at the army wagon, even though Tiah is not aiming at Gray Otter, the use of shot/reverse shot editing between Gray Otter and Tiah makes Gray Otter and Tiah appear to be facing each other.

Thus, the collision depicted in *The Last of the Line* is not between white Americans and Native Americans but between two Native Americans. The actual cause of Tiah's fall is hidden from the surface on the screen, and only the tragic result is shown. What is hidden in this narrative is the fact that Tiah has learned to drink and has been spoiled in white American culture. Historically, many Native Americans educated at the schools created for them by white Americans eventually found themselves rejected by both Native American and white societies. The ordeal of separating children from their families and cultures through the Indian boarding-school policy—and the trauma of their return home as outsiders—is fully recognized in silent Westerns and "Indian dramas" from 1908 to 1916, which were produced during a time when federal Indian policy encouraged both assimilation and removal from the land. During the silent film era from the turn of the century through the 1920s, the primary federal policy structuring Indian-white relations was the drive for assimilation through the General Allotment Act (1887) and the removal of Native American children to government boarding schools. Many of the Westerns produced during this period reflected, if not a sense of national guilt, then certainly a public and cultural awareness that despite the rhetoric of assimilation as progress, children and land were being siphoned away from Native American peoples and placed under white control with devastating consequences.[11]

The historian Joanna Hearne suggests that the Western genre's special reliance on costume to signify social roles and ethnic differences leads to a fluidity when clothes, props, and identities are exchanged during the course of the action. In *The Last of the Line*, Tiah's appearance—short hair, a jacket, a tie, pants, a cowboy hat, and heavy makeup that makes Hayakawa's skin look darker—stands out among the Sioux Indians and emphasizes his alienation from his tribe. With his dark skin he looks like a failed white "wannabe."

The Last of the Line tapped into this widespread popular ambivalence about the negative aspects of the federal Indian policy. However, in *The Last of the Line*, the existence of white American culture is not directly questioned within this narrative of a family melodrama. Since Gray Otter serves for the white American army in a civilized and obedient manner, the white American culture maintains its symbolic status as a moral and civilized center. From the very beginning, Gray Otter is depicted as a person who acknowledges the value of modernization and the importance of learning white American civilization: the typical image of the "noble savage." In the opening scene, Gray Otter, in his tent with his large authoritative pipe, which signifies his authority in the tribe, remembers the past. The flashback shows the time when Tiah was born. The medium shot of Gray Otter smoking dissolves into a medium shot of him holding a baby accompanied by his wife on his right. A close-up of the baby is inserted here. Gray Otter says, "He shall grow up to be a great chief and the white man's wisdom shall be as an open book to him." The parents nod happily to each other. Gray Otter, with his baby in his arms, goes outside the tent where his men are waiting to salute their future chief. This shot dissolves back to Gray Otter smoking and smiling. What he remembers is not the past when he was deprived of his lands and people by white Americans, but the one when his baby was born and promised the bright future of his tribe with his understanding of white American culture. *The Last of the Line* legitimates the dominance of white American culture in the form of a family melodrama.

Gray Otter looks wretched in the end of the film because of the loss of his own son. However, his blame is not aimed at white America. Tiah is buried as a national hero. Positioned in opposition to the more primitive and barbarous Native American and Mexican renegades, the civilized chief Gray Otter thus comes to embody the stereotypical image of the "vanishing race."

After the success of two feature films, *The Wrath of the Gods* and *The Typhoon*, Hayakawa was "well regarded at Ince," but he kept being cast in "odd stories" with archetypal narrative structures and stereotypical characters.[12] Casting Japanese actors in Indian films was an example of such oddities. Ince simply did not want to leave "this prestigious group of Japanese actors," especially Hayakawa and Aoki, jobless. Even after the successful features *The Wrath of the Gods* and *The Typhoon*, the Japanese actors were cast for a series of two-reelers until their year-long contract expired in late November 1914. It was a business and aesthetic decision for Ince as a producer having an eye on the bottom line.[13]

There was no consistency in roles in which Hayakawa was cast. In both *Death Mask* and *The Last of the Line*, Hayakawa played sons of Native American chiefs, but their characters were completely opposite: a relatively civilized romantic hero and a drunk prodigal son. The latter was not even a leading role. Ince also cast Hayakawa in non-Japanese, non–Native American roles. In *The Chinatown Mystery* (Barker, 10 February 1915), for instance, Hayakawa played a Chinese murderer, Yo Hung, who is captured by a hero, an American reporter, in the end.[14] Hayakawa, as a supporting character, was treated only as a component of the chaotic landscape of Chinatown. *Nipped* (George Osborne, 19 November 1914) is another example of such "odd stories." It is a spy film with an interracial love story set in Mexico. Hayakawa played a Japanese protagonist in this film, but his character was a stereotypically ultra-nationalistic spy. Because of the spy's conspiracy, a Japanese girl, who reveals the conspiracy to her American boyfriend, dies in the end.

In 1915, Hayakawa decided to quit the NYMPC and moved to the Jesse L. Lasky Feature Play Company. It was unusual behavior for an actor to walk away from Ince, who was a big name in the industry at that time.[15] By 1915 Hayakawa must have felt strongly that his career under Ince was headed toward a dead end.

TWO

Villain, Friend, or Lover

Sessue Hayakawa's Stardom at Lasky-Paramount (1916–18)

6

THE MAKING OF
AN AMERICANIZED JAPANESE
GENTLEMAN

The Honorable Friend and *Hashimura Togo*

Sessue Hayakawa's role as Tori in *The Cheat* was so sensationally received that the creation of Hayakawa's star persona inevitably started with that image. One natural strategy that the Jesse L. Lasky Feature Play Company could undertake was to make Hayakawa a refined-looking villainous star with his embodiment of the yellow peril and ultimate inassimilability into American society. Yet, Lasky did not simply undertake this strategy. Hayakawa played villainous roles in his star vehicles at Lasky, but these roles were carefully constructed in order not to offend middle-class morality.

Around the time when *The Cheat* was released, the Hollywood film industry was in the middle of an attempt to acquire cultural legitimacy for middle-class audiences. Movie stars were meant to assert that the cinema was morally a "healthy phenomenon," compared with the scandalous theater world.[1] Since Hayakawa's role was a supporting one in *The Cheat*, it was not necessary to make his villainous character sympathetic. In the film, there were heroic white characters with whom audiences were able to sympathize. It was possible to make star vehicles with stars as villains, as in the gangster films in the 1930s. However, even these villains were usually given some sympathetic characteristics in order to lead in feature-length films that would not subvert the morality of middle-class audiences.

Another option of Lasky's company was to turn Hayakawa into a heroic star. Many early stars played on-screen roles as virtuous heroes and heroines whose moral course withstood whatever challenges were put in their way. Charles K. Field wrote in 1916, "Had he [Hayakawa] kept on playing villains, he might have veiled his good looks in the whiskers of the hairy Ainu and never won the feminine admiration which now unquestionably greets his picture."[2] However, right after *The Cheat*, it seemed too adventurous for Lasky to create a brand new heroic star image for Hayakawa that would be substantially different from his sensational image in the film.

The film scholar Paul McDonald claims, "Star discourse picked out certain film actors as worthy of identification and desire."[3] For "identification," the threat and villainy that Hayakawa showed in *The Cheat* needed to be tamed, but at the same time, for "desire," the consumerist and sensual attraction that Hayakawa represented in *The Cheat* needed to be maintained. Hayakawa later said, "Sessue Hayakawa double character . . . very, very complicated."[4] Lasky had to employ a "complicated" strategy of creating Hayakawa's star image that would strike a balance between following *The Cheat* and deviating from it. The whole complication of Lasky's twofold strategy came from the fact that the studio had to enable white American middle-class audiences to sympathize, or identify, with Hayakawa's characters and his star image, as well as to let them safely desire those characters and image, despite Hayakawa's nonwhite cultural origin.

In short, Lasky's strategy was to locate Hayakawa in the movable middle-ground position in the racial and cultural hierarchy between white American and nonwhite other. On the one hand, Hayakawa's (and his characters') status had to be raised and distinguished racially or culturally from other nonwhite actors (and their characters) in order for the American middle-class audiences to sympathize with, identify with, or even desire Hayakawa more easily. On the other hand, Hayakawa's status had to be clearly differentiated from white Americans in terms of race. Any sexual relationship between Hayakawa's characters, no matter how heroic they were, and white women must be avoided in order not to cause any anxiety around miscegenation. The control of a Japanese man's racial, cultural, and sexual transgression within the discourse of white American middle-class family and domesticity, which was the thematic motif of *The Cheat*, came to play a dominant role in the formation of Hayakawa's star image at Lasky.

"Americanization" was a feasible strategy for Lasky to take to make this Japanese actor heroic and sympathetic enough for middle-class audiences. According to the final result of the "Motion Picture Hall of Fame" popularity contest in the *Motion Picture* magazine in December 1918, five of the male stars listed in the top ten, Douglas Fairbanks Sr., Harold Lockwood, William S. Hart, Wallace Reid, and Francis X. Bushman, were from the "clean-living group of all-Americans."[5] When the most popular stars of the time embodied this "all-American" image, it was a proficient strategy for Lasky to provide its new, promising, but non-American, star with this image.

In fact, the popularity of the stars with "all-American" images corresponded to a nationwide "Americanization" movement by middle-class Americans in the early twentieth century. According to Philip Gleason, the words "Americanize," "Americanizing," and "Americanization" came into common usage during the antebellum nativist controversies of the mid-nineteenth century, when many Irish Catholic immigrants arrived in the United States, and clearly referred to the immigrants' assimilation into American life. The idea of "Americanization" was that immigrants must change.[6] Even if the wide-spread expression "the melting pot" may imply America's cosmopolitan nationality based on diversity or pluralism (at least among Europeans) and Israel Zangwill's 1909 play *The Melting Pot* appeared to express Americans' confidence in the nation's absorptive powers of differences, the fact was that immigrants were expected to merge into the national community by being willing to identify themselves with American principles and customs.

From the eighteenth century on, white Anglo-Saxon Protestants (WASPS) had been viewed as the dominant ethnic majority and touted as a people distinguished by their desirable qualities without being basically changed themselves. Therefore, basically, Americanization was Anglo-conformity, based on this Anglo-Saxonism.[7]

Then, beginning in the 1890s, Americanization and Americanism became attached to a more specific movement. As a result of rapid industrialization, urbanization, and the increase of immigrants by the early twentieth century, reorganization of the social order was debated, especially among middle-class Americans. More Americans began to feel that the United States as a nation would require a higher level of cohesion, homogeneity, and solidarity, a closer conformity to the cultural majority (WASP) in language, religion, and manners, and a more active policy of purposeful Americanization, or more forceful assimilation.[8] The historian Lynn Dumenil claims that there was a strong undercurrent during this period of using numerous federal laws "to control and assimilate immigrants to American Protestant morality and standards."[9] Immigrants were required to learn the middle-class sense of values, that is, to learn English, the American concepts of law and order, and the work ethic.

In 1907 the North American Citizens League started using the term

"Americanization" for its activities that helped new immigrants understand American ideas in their daily lives. The ethnic reverberation set off in the United States by the outbreak of World War I in 1914 marked the opening of a far more intense phase of the Americanization movement.[10] In 1915, the National Americanization Committee was organized. On 4 July 1915, "Americanization Day" was celebrated by the Chambers of Commerce and Industry, churches, organizations of mutual aid in immigrant communities, and so on, in more than one hundred cities all over the United States. In 1916 Royal Dixon, an activist of the Americanization Movement, published a book entitled *Americanization* and insisted on refocusing of the nation on Americanization.[11]

The Americanization movement had two orientations. One insisted that Americanization was needed to protect the national character, which was based on the dominant white Anglo-Saxon Protestant principles, from the dangers posed by the immense immigration of the time. The other desired to assist the immigrants in adjusting to the different conditions of life they encountered in the United States. Eventually, the former emphasis dominated and, by the 1920s, the Americanization movement became more nativist and came to mean the exclusion of people on an ethnic or racial basis. Therefore, Americanization meant at the same time forceful assimilation and nativist exclusion of the inassimilable.

The early Hollywood film industry, which pursued legitimatization and institutionalization of cinema, needed to respond to this middle-class movement, which stressed Americanization. Motion pictures, thus, tended to become a medium that institutionally supported the Americanization movement that forced assimilation of immigrants to white Anglo-Saxon Protestant thoughts and customs. They also began to exclude inassimilable immigrants on and off the screen. On the screen, "bad" immigrants are punished in opposition to "good" immigrants. Off the screen, for instance, Chinese immigrants, who had been prohibited from entry to the United States since 1882, rarely obtained jobs in film studios until the early 1920s, when anti-Japanese movements became severe and many Japanese actors decided to go back to Japan.

Hayakawa's star vehicles displayed an acceptance of immigrants who were willing to identify themselves with American principles and, especially, to adopt white Anglo-Saxon Protestant customs. The negotiation between assimilation to white Anglo-Saxon Protestant customs and inassimilable Japaneseness became the first major motif for forming Hayakawa's star persona, both on and off the screen. Hayakawa came to embody an image of a successfully Americanized immigrant from Asia, beginning with his first star vehicle, *Alien Souls* (Frank Reicher, 3 May 1916), and continuing throughout his Lasky years. In complex manners, these films portrayed the implicit tensions in becoming Americanized: the choices one must make between the older culture and group and the new, and between the way one views oneself as either American or ethnic.[12]

Even though no film print or film script of *Alien Souls* exists any longer, Lasky's strategy of Americanizing Hayakawa's image in the film is indicated in reviews. Thomas C. Kennedy of *Motography* regarded the character that Hayakawa plays as the paradigmatic Japanese merchant who "would become American in customs and ideals."[13] The *Philadelphia Telegraph* also noted, "An Americanized Japanese gentleman (Sessue Hayakawa) . . . must educate and support the Japanese daughter (Tsuru Aoki) of a patriarch in old Japan."[14] A still photo published in trade journals with Kennedy's review emphasizes Hayakawa's Americanized image in the film.[15] In the photo, Hayakawa is wearing a suit, sitting at a desk with an open book, and talking with a white American man. The photo also shows such Japanese-style objects as a vase and a screen in the background, indicating Hayakawa's exotic foreignness. However, these objects are carefully arranged in an American room. They certainly indicate Japanese Taste in the room but they do not dominate the space as if emphasizing the exotic and foreign nature of the Japanese character. In general, publicity photos tend to emphasize the more spectacular elements of a star persona and reduce the star's meaning to certain foundational essences that lodge quickly and easily in public consciousness.[16] The photo from *Alien Souls* reprinted in the journal indicates that Americanization was one of the "spectacular" and "foundational essences" of Hayakawa.

A reviewer wrote, "The bad memory left by Mr. Hayakawa's villainies has almost been erased by his splendid heroic work as Sakata in *Alien Souls*."[17] Another reviewer claimed that Hayakawa's character "seizes and holds the [spectators'] sympathy with ease."[18] Hayakawa himself wrote, "It was in *Alien Souls* that I was seen in one of my sympathetic roles, and one which helped redeem me with those who damned me for my portrayal in *The Cheat*."[19] Thus, Lasky's strategy to emphasize Americanization and make Hayakawa's star image sympathetic and heroic was successfully launched.

Lasky took the same strategy in *The Honorable Friend* (Edward J. LeSaint, 24 August 1916), the second Hayakawa star vehicle, whose print is lost but whose script is extant. Contrasting two types of Japanese immigrants, the film makes Hayakawa's character stand out because of his faith in and obedience to the American legal system and his successful assimilation to the American way of life.

In *The Honorable Friend*, Hayakawa's character is portrayed as an ideal Japanese immigrant, who Americanizes himself by learning American laws and the American way of life. Hayakawa plays Makino, a young, honest, and industrious Japanese-American man. Makino works for Kayosho, an old, ugly, unscrupulous, and greedy Japanese-American art dealer. Kayosho has an affair with Hana, his servant Goto's daughter. When Kayosho sees a photo of Hana's pretty cousin Toki-ye (Tsuru Aoki), he conspires to make her his mistress also. Kayosho promises Makino, who is anxious to get married soon, that he will bring a pretty girl from Japan as Makino's fiancée. When Toki-ye arrives in the United States, Kayosho tries to make her his mistress. One night, Kayosho is found dead. To protect Toki-ye from a police investigation, Makino tells the police that he murdered Kayosho. Later, Goto confesses to having murdered Kayosho out of revenge for his daughter, whom Kayosho had betrayed. Makino is freed and reunites with Toki-ye.

There was a general dramatic approach in films of this era to the portrayal of immigrants of all ethnicities by dividing them into "good" and "bad" characters. For instance, it is very frequent in D. W. Griffith's films that deal with Italians and Chinese. Hayakawa's role in *The Honorable Friend* is fit into this larger pattern. According to *Variety*, the story of *The Honorable Friend* "is of a melodramatic turn."[20] Using the melodramatic binary structure of conflict between good and evil, *The Honorable Friend* emphasizes the differences between the two Japanese immigrant types and characterizes Makino as the moralistic hero of the film in opposition to the sensual and deceitful villain.

As Japanese immigrants, Kayosho and Makino are the mirror images of each other. The MPN claims that *The Honorable Friend* "deals with Japanese aliens who bring to this country their oriental customs and manners and who have difficulty in conforming to the occidental idea of law and honor."[21] Only the levels of assimilation to Anglo-American society define the differences between Makino and Kayosho. One group of "Japanese aliens," represented by Makino, tries to "conform to" the American "idea of law and honor" and to form an ideal American family, fighting against obstruction from the other group. The other group of immigrants, represented by Kayosho, sticks to "oriental customs and manners" and consciously violates both American laws and the U.S.-Japan diplomatic agreement.

The one-page ad for *The Honorable Friend* in MPN uses photos to visually

6   *An ad for* The Honorable Friend. Motion Picture News *14.10 (9 September 1916): 1449.*

contrast the favorable and unfavorable images of Japanese immigrants (see fig. 6). The ad effectively uses racial stereotypes emphasized by makeup, costumes, and gestures of the actors for this purpose.[22] Kayosho, who was played by a white American actor, Raymond Hatton, wears a luxurious black Western-style suit, a tie, and a hat. Because of a special makeup his eyes look extremely slanted. He is grinning, looking up slightly, showing his buckteeth, and putting his hands on his fat belly, like an ugly and vulgar nouveau riche. His catfish-like mustache is one of the significant visual marks of Fu Manchu, the notorious Asian character in American pulp novels.[23] The exaggerated ethnic stereotype created by special makeup for a white actor emphasizes the threat of collapsing nationalities intrinsic to the Fu Manchu narratives.

In contrast, Makino wears a poor-looking white work shirt. He does not have any exaggerated makeup that emphasizes his Japanese traits. He is young and smiling. Makino also places his hands in front of his body, but his hands touch each other, as if he were shy and did not know exactly where to put them.

Similarly, the script of *The Honorable Friend* clearly differentiates Makino from Kayosho.[24] Following the intertitle, "Kayosho, Japanese-American of 'honorable' wealth, dishonorably gained," Kayosho is introduced in a shot in which he puts a high price tag on a piece of broken china that he has dropped. This shot is in accordance with the anti-Japanese discourse in the Pacific states, which insisted that Japanese immigrants were "dishonorably" committing to commerce and agriculture in the United States and stealing jobs and profits from American workers.

Moreover, Kayosho embodies a stereotypical image of the sexually threatening, lustful Oriental male. When he looks at a photo of Toki-ye, he "gloatingly, covertly, moisturizes his thin lips, as he looks greedily at the fresh beauty of the girl in the picture." The script stresses that his "Desire Breeds Cunning." When Toki-ye arrives in the United States, Kayosho tries to fulfill his desire in a barbarous manner. The script reads, "Kayosho towers over the terrified Toki-ye as though about to draw her into his embrace."

The historian David Grimsted claims that the melodramatic villain's "vileness was proved by his deceit toward women."[25] Kayosho deceives two women for the fulfillment of his sexual desire. This proves his melodramatic "vileness." He double-crosses Toki-ye because he sends Makino's portrait to her and invites her to America as Makino's wife, but he has intended to make Toki-ye his mistress from the very beginning. At the same time, Kayosho has pledged to wed his servant Goto's daughter but breaks his vow.

Betraying women, Kayosho simultaneously dishonors the U.S.-Japan diplomatic agreement, the 1907–8 Gentlemen's Agreement, which prohibited unmarried Japanese women from entering the United States. What he practices is the infamous "picture marriage." The original purpose of this agreement was to decrease the number of Japanese laborers, who were blamed by working-class Americans in the Pacific states for unfairly stealing jobs from other American laborers.[26] The agreement was meant to force single male laborers to go back to Japan to get married. However, the agreement had a flaw. It allowed Japanese women to immigrate to the United States as family members. Picture marriage, which rapidly became popular among Japanese immigrants in the 1910s, played a role in exploiting this flaw. One characteristic that facilitated picture marriage was that arranged marriage itself had been customary in Japan. Parents often consulted go-betweens to help them select partners for their sons and daughters. An exchange of photographs often took place in the screening process. The picture bride practice conformed to this marriage custom. The prospective groom in America and the bride in Japan exchanged their photos before the initial meeting, and eventually they got married in Japan only on paper. Then, the brides crossed the Pacific Ocean. From 1912 to 1919, there were at least 6,321 "picture brides" who comprised over half of all the married women arriving in the United States through Seattle and San Francisco.[27]

No matter how customary arranged marriage was in Japan, some agitators of the anti-Japanese immigrant movement in the United States criticized the picture bride practice. The large number of anti-Japanese articles in West Coast newspapers, such as the *San Francisco Chronicle* and the *San Francisco Examiner*, contended that the picture bride practice was a strategy to outwit the agreement. Also, some women's groups regarded the picture bride custom as savage human traffic and criticized it as violating "women's rights."[28] Such negative views on the practice of picture bride marriage tended to enforce the notion that Japanese people were uncivilized savages who were able to marry strangers.

Another major issue in the accusation of the picture bride practice was the supposed high birthrate of Japanese immigrants, "the purported enormous fertility of Japanese women, when mated to persons of their own race."[29] The increase of the childbirth rate of Japanese immigrants was considered threatening, especially by white landowners and farmers in the Pacific states. Even though the 1906 naturalization law did not clearly define the Japanese as "aliens ineligible for citizenship," an administrative measure in the Pacific states regarded that definition as a fact and prohibited Japanese immigrants from owning land based on the 1913 alien land laws. Yet, this administrative measure was not applied to those newly born Japanese children, because then, as now, every American-born child was an American citizen by birth.

The actual size of the Japanese population and the amount of land owned by Japanese immigrants were relatively limited compared with the white population and land owned by whites.[30] However, exclusionist agitators in the Pacific states tried to connect the threat caused by the increase of American-born Japanese children and their eventual land ownership to the discourse of yellow peril. They insisted that those children would not be assimilated into American society and would become the forerunners of a Japanese invasion of the United States.

In *The Honorable Friend*, Kayosho is portrayed as the most typical and vulgar embodiment of the picture bride practice. Kayosho's old and ugly appearance relates to numerous incidents in which picture brides arrived in the United States and discovered that their husbands did not resemble the photographs they had sent.[31] A large portrait of Kayosho on the wall is described in the script as "even more hideous than Kayosho." When the heroine Toki-ye looks at Kayosho's portrait, she says, "Kayosho is like ape, is he not?"

The narrative of *The Honorable Friend* emphasizes how Makino, in opposition to Kayosho, departs from the old Japanese custom and accepts the American way of life. In the beginning of the film, Makino is characterized as a man with stereotypical Japanese traits, similar to Kayosho. Makino shows feudalistic loyalty to his Japanese boss and displays his expertise in Japanese martial arts. He saves Kayosho from two gangs at the dock using jiu-jitsu. When Kayosho orders him to treat Toki-ye as a guest, he "respectfully holds out sword," and says, "Honorable guest is safe here—none shall intrude." Makino here sounds like a samurai with his sword, who is loyal to his master.

However, as the narrative progresses, Makino learns American ways. While Kayosho only uses servants with "Samurai blood" and tries to be like a feudalistic Japanese lord, Makino has an Irish-American man as his "guardian angel," who teaches Makino about American lifestyles. He teaches Makino how to drive a nursery wagon for flowers and instructs him in American laws on immigration. The Irish-American man, as another new immigrant in the United States in the late nineteenth century to early twentieth who has already assimilated into American society, functions as a mentor who has experienced the Americanization process and helps Americanize Makino, as Lasky attempted to Americanize Hayakawa's image.

Another example of Makino's Americanization process is his American-style wedding. Makino and Toki-ye marry at the dock in San Francisco in order to bring her into the United States as his legal wife. Kayosho insists that this marriage between Makino and Toki-ye is invalid because it was not done in a Japanese way but in an American manner. Kayosho misrepresents American law, saying, "The ceremony at the dock is only a part of the Immigration routine. You are not yet legally married." Despite Kayosho's efforts at obstruction, Makino and Toki-ye choose to follow the American way for their marriage instead of obeying the Japanese method. In a still photo published in *Motography*, Kayosho wears a luxurious kimono, while Makino is in a suit and Toki-ye is in a Western dress. Here, the contrast between Kayosho and the newlyweds is visually transferred into the difference between Japanese-ness and Americanization.[32]

Makino also facilitates the heroine's process of Americanization. Makino shows the heroine around his room while the two are alone, as Tori does to Edith in *The Cheat*. Toki-ye is very curious about American domestic objects, such as a gas stove, an American bed, and so forth. Toki-ye's Americaniza-tion process is slow and comical. She uses a dustpan, instead of a cooking pan, to make a pancake. Makino enjoys explaining how to use the American products to Toki-ye, much as Tori shows Japanese objets d'art to Edith. How-ever, unlike Tori, Makino never tries to take advantage of her appreciation of these things. As a helping hand for Americanizing the female Japanese immi-grant and rescuing her from the "exploitative" Kayosho, Makino functions as a teacher of the American lifestyle to a newly arrived Japanese immigrant.

In the end, a baby is born to Makino and Toki-ye. The birth of a Japanese baby in America was what the yellow peril rhetoric feared most. However, in *The Honorable Friend*, this racial issue is cleverly replaced by an image of the creation of an Americanized family. The MPW published a still photo of the final scene of the film in its review of *The Honorable Friend* (see fig. 7).[33] The photo shows a smiling Hayakawa embracing Aoki. Aoki holds a baby with her left arm and a dog in her right hand. Hayakawa is wearing a black three-piece suit and tie, and Aoki is in a middy blouse and skirt. Hayakawa is handing a candy-like toy to the baby. Even though their faces are Asian, their costume, the bulldog, and their pose, a husband gently embracing his wife, child, and dog, make them look more like an ideal middle-class American family. This obvious manner of suggesting an ideal image of a middle-class American family does not follow the more "restrained" ways in which Japanese hus-bands of the time should have behaved despite how much they loved their wives and children. Usually, a husband did not physically embrace his wife in public in Japan, no matter how deeply he loved her. Most Japanese husbands at that time did not consider it proper behavior to embrace their wives in public.

The couple's Americanized lifestyle was reproduced in fan magazine articles as the actual life of Mr. and Mrs. Hayakawa in their American-style bungalow. Lasky's strategy was to make Hayakawa's screen persona and his real-life actor identity go hand in hand in order to form his Americanized star image. This strategic blurring of the line between the private personality and the on-screen personality constituted the basis and powerful appeal of movie

7   *A still from* The Honorable Friend. Moving Picture World *29.11 (9 September 1916): 1685.*

stardom of the period. Hayakawa's case initiated this consciously confusing nature of the publicity in film trade journals and fan magazines.

Sociohistorically, in the 1910s before the end of World War I, the nation-wide discourse on Japan and Japanese immigrants observed in articles in middle-class magazines was generally positive and sympathetic to Japan and Japanese immigrants. According to the *Nation*, the "Japanese problem" in the United States "almost limits itself to California, where the climate is thoroughly congenial to Japanese habits."[34] David Starr Jordan claimed, "Japan is a nation of hard working people, very peaceful, very poor, very heavily taxed, with a huge war debt," and insisted that the "rulers of Japan are sagacious and cautious men, largely educated in American universities" and well-Americanized.[35] In August 1913, in an article titled "Can We Assimilate the Japanese?" the *Literary Digest* quoted "Mr. Takekoshi, a leading publicist and a well-known author in Japan" and indicated how the assimilation of Japanese immigrants into American life would become possible. "Mr. Takekoshi" said, "If assimilation means preference on the part of Japanese for American civilization and institutions, political and social, as well as a desire to adapt themselves to the new surroundings, then the Japanese are assimilable and are being assimilated."[36]

William Elliot Griffis insisted in 1914 that the Japanese "are so wickedly zealous in reclaiming our waste land, so offensively industrious, and so shamefully eager to learn our language, read newspapers, patronize libraries and life-insurance companies, become builders and supporters of Christian churches." Overall, Griffis favorably described the Japanese people as eager to Americanize themselves, despite the fact that his choice of terms such as "wickedly" and "shamefully" ironically implied his innate unfavorable view of Japanese people. Griffis claimed that the "recent hostile anti-Japanese legislation in California—race hatred in its most immoral form—violates in spirit and letter the treaty with Japan, to which we promised the same treatment as to 'the most favored nation.'"[37] While Kayosho embodies such "wicked" and "shameful" images of Japanese immigrants, Makino plays a role of reconciling the images of Japanese immigrants with Griffis's more favorable and optimistic view. In 1917 Tully C. Knoles wrote that the United States was a nation composed of people who would love America, respect its government, and desire to become Americans.[38] By emphasizing the process of Americanization of Makino, who desires to become an American and respect the American legal system and customs, *The Honorable Friend* tells an ideal assimilation narrative of Japanese immigrants into American society. Playing Makino, Hayakawa's star image turned from inassimilable Japaneseness to successful Americanization.

The Honorable Friend was a film written for Hayakawa. Yet, star vehicles are often based on popular fictions or novels with famous characters. Sometimes, such popular characters are changed into ones that fit stars' existing personas and vice versa. Lasky's strategy of Americanizing Hayakawa's star image is observable in one such film, *Hashimura Togo* (William C. DeMille, 19 August 1917). *Hashimura Togo* is a film adapted from Wallace Irwin's popular short stories, "Letters of a Japanese Schoolboy," first published in *Collier's* on 2 November 1907, and in such publications as the *American Magazine, Good Housekeeping, Sunset, Life*, and the *New York Times* after that.

"Letters of a Japanese Schoolboy" comically tells stories of Hashimura Togo, "a 35-year-old Japanese schoolboy" in the form of unsolicited letters from Togo to an editor of a New York newspaper. "Letters" has a form of a first-person narrative written by a Japanese man, a fictional character created by an American author. In this form, American views on Japanese people are presented as if they are innate Japanese points of view, no matter how imaginary and stereotypical they are. The first-person narrative enhances the fictional authenticity of the stereotypical views and normalizes the alien image of Japanese people.

In "Letters," Hashimura Togo is clearly a caricature of inassimilable immigrants. Togo keeps being fired from his jobs because of his ignorance of American customs. For instance, Togo misunderstands what Thanksgiving Day means. He believes that the Pilgrim Fathers were thankful because they did not have an appetite when they had no food. Therefore, Togo cannot understand why his employer serves a huge dinner on Thanksgiving Day. When the employer's dog steals a cooked turkey that Togo has left to cool at a window, everybody gets angry because the Thanksgiving dinner is spoiled. Togo says, "You should all be very thanksgiving. . . . He [the dog] should be gave medal of Pilgrim Fathers for eating a bird you would not dare to bite."[39]

Even though Togo is conscious about his alienness as a "heathen" Japanese, he does not intend to change his Japanese way of thinking. In a letter talking about Christmas in America, Togo writes,

Japanese can not be Christmas persons, thank you. Why so is it? Because Japanese is all heathens, which is not eligible to Christmas present. If Japanese would obtain valuable presents on this date they must become Christians. This is too much trouble to do. . . . In getting civilized all over herself must Japan do this Hon. Christmas also? I do not require this, because many Christmas customs is not best good for all human races. Therefore Japan can get along more quicker without Hon. Christmas. . . . I am going to eat like heathen, think like heathen, act like heathen, so that everything about me shall remain in good-healthy condition for 4th of July, when it is unnecessary to be a Christian, thank you.[40]

Even though Togo supports the value of family as do middle-class Americans, what he is highly proud of is the feudalistic family system in Japan. Togo gives advice to a henpecked American husband to be like "a Japanese father." Togo says, "Japanese father are steam-roller Czar. Wife are sipposed [sic] to approach him with frightened elbows, daughter must be sipposed [sic] to ask for favors and not get it. All parties, presents, etc. are given by him. All servants must attend his selfishness while neglecting females around house."

As a result, Togo is fired, being told by the American husband, "I am very respectful to your Oriental uncivilization and know what you snuggest [sic] can be accomplished 10,000 miles distant from New Jersey. . . . And since you are so crazed about Japan, maybe you should return there and teach Domestic Science where it shall be understood."[41] Thus, "Letters" emphasizes Togo's Japanese characteristics that are inassimilable to American customs and family living. Togo even states that one of the reasons why he has come to America is "To go back to Japan."[42]

The film *Hashimura Togo* follows such stereotypical views of the original stories. Lasky's massive ad campaign for the film emphasized the stereotypical aspect of Japanese culture. Lasky surely regarded the images of Japan as marketable product distinction. To publicize the film, letters from Hashimura Togo in his "twisted" English to exhibitors appeared in major trade journals: "'Dearest Sir' Next August P. M. Boss he tell me he release great picture. Him funny like nothing so much. 'Togo' he report 'this is great statistics which I make on last Paramount Picture with Mr. Susie [sic] Hayakawa.' So now, sh-sh-sh!! a state sneckrut [sic]—get ahead from all picture house in your city. Hoping you are the same, yours truly 'Hashimura Togo' P. S.—I make love like anything."[43]

These ads utilized Japanesque designs, such as bamboo-shaped letters, illustrations of a Japanese shrine gate, a statue of the Buddha, and so forth, together with still photos of Hayakawa in a white kimono committing hara-kiri.[44] When the film was released, the NYDM put Hayakawa in a Japanese kimono on its cover for the first time on 8 September 1917.

According to the script, the film opens with a scene of a tea ceremony in Japan. A middle-class American mother and her daughter, who are visiting Japan as tourists, perform the tea ceremony. This opening scene emphasizes the exotic foreign atmosphere of Japan, viewed from the American perspective. At the same time, this scene depicts Japanese culture within the middle-class imaginary framework of refined Japanese Taste.

However, contrary to the ad campaign, which emphasized exotic Japanese culture in the film, the narrative of *Hashimura Togo*, a prequel to "Letters," which shows how Hashimura Togo came to the United States and started writing his famous letters to newspapers and magazines, does not emphasize Hashimura Togo's Japanese traits. In the film, the Japanese schoolboy's inassimilable point of view in the original stories is carefully eliminated. As a review in MPN correctly suggests, "It is only in the substitutes and the main title that the picture discloses a relationship to the popular magazine and newspaper stories. Togo performs none of the extravagant pieces of foolishness on the celluloid that he did on paper."[45]

Instead, the emphasis in the film is on Hashimura Togo's successful process of Americanization. In fact, the film *Hashimura Togo* upgrades the negative discourse of Japanese immigrants in American yellow journalism to a more favorable one. Purposefully or not, this film, as a result of Lasky's star-making strategy, offers a more progressive view on racial integration than the original stories. Even a racist attitude toward the Japanese immigrant is treated as villainous in *Hashimura Togo*. A racist chauffeur calls Togo "you Yeller Peril," but in the end he comes to respect Togo's Americanized attitude.

In *Hashimura Togo*, Young Baron Katsu (Hayakawa) lives in Japan and industriously studies American language and history. His brother loses his father's important document when he is drunk. A wily old proprietor finds the document and blackmails Katsu's father. Katsu is disowned by his father in place of his brother and decides to go to America. Katsu changes his name to Hashimura Togo. On his way to America, Togo falls in love with an American girl, Corinne (Florence Vidor), at first sight. He is so devoted to Corinne on the ship that she hires him as a servant in her home. Even though Corinne is in love with a young doctor, Garland, she is forced into an engagement with Anthony, who secretly forges a document to withdraw all the property from Corinne and her mother. Togo finds out about the conspiracy and writes to an American newspaper, explaining the entire situation and demanding that George Washington stop this marriage. Learning that Washington has been dead for a long time, he sees a district attorney next. The district attorney and a newspaper reporter help Togo. In the end, Togo's father, who has found out the truth of the stolen document, comes to the United States and forgives Togo.

According to the script, Katsu is first introduced in a room, surrounded by Japanese objects. He is "in very dignified native costume, sitting on floor before 'alcove'—a recess in the shoji containing [a] figure of large and impressive god. Hanging 'sacred lamps' on either side of recess." Katsu sits in front of an altar in a room with a tatami floor and shoji screens and looks at a statue of the Buddha.[46] Katsu's brother, who is not in the room, though, is absorbed in two Japanese ways of indulgence: sake and geisha.

Even though he is surrounded by these Japanese objects and customs,

Katzu aspires to Americanize himself. In the introductory scene, the script describes how Katzu is studying English "laboriously." In front of Katzu, on a low Japanese writing table, there is "an open Japanese-English Primer on [sic] First Reader." In the following scene, Katzu "delightedly" buys a book, *Life Story of Hon. George Washington: Most Truthful Father in Native Country* by I. Ta-Naka.

When Katzu decides to go to America, he changes his name to Hashimura Togo. This change of name is a sign of his disconnection from his past in Japan. At this point, Togo's Americanization is not yet sufficient. He still shows his attachment to Japanese culture. He does not change his name to a Western one like George or Abraham. The suit he chooses is too small and is inappropriate by American standards. Togo packs the English textbook and the Washington biography, but simultaneously he brings a Japanese white burial robe and a hara-kiri sword to America.

However, from then on, the film shows how Togo becomes Americanized, even though in a comical way. Like *The Honorable Friend*, *Hashimura Togo* is a story of a Japanese immigrant who is eager to Americanize himself. As soon as Togo realizes his suit is improper, he changes it to a cabin boy's white uniform, the only American-style clothing that is available on a ship to America. After that, he never puts on Japanese dress, except when he attempts to commit hara-kiri for the sake of a white American girl whom he loves.

When Togo is told by an American man, "To get job in America you must have boastful manuscript telling all things you can do—written by former boss," he follows his advice right away. Since he does not have any former boss, he has to write a letter of recommendation by himself. The content of the letter implies that Japanese people of the day could not function well in the United States: "To lady, Dir [sic] Sir: Hire Togo and you will wonder why! He can cook without pain. O see. See how well he boils pies and other American vegetables. Can ron [sic] furnaces, babies and ottomobiles [sic]. Behaves like sweetheart to strangers. He will be a nice trial for you. I have know [sic] Togo since baby. Yours truly, Togo." Yet, later in the narrative, Togo makes every effort to learn how to do these things properly.

Togo is hired as a servant by Corinne, a middle-class white woman. Togo falls in love with Corinne, but contrary to *The Cheat*, his desire for the white woman never becomes threatening in this film. As soon as Togo learns that she loves a young white American doctor, he gives her up. Togo's attitude looks moralistic and heroic in contrast to the melodramatic villain of this film, who deceives Corinne to obtain her. As in *The Honorable Friend*, the vileness of the villain is proven by his deception of women, and the Japanese hero is clearly contrasted to the villain.

Togo's heroism mainly comes out of his self-sacrifice for a white American woman, which is one of the major motifs of Hayakawa's star vehicles and will be discussed in the next chapter in detail. The MPW regarded *Hashimura Togo* as "a story of attempted sacrifice on the part of Togo to save his family honor, while he becomes the unwitting instrument of saving an American heroine from a sacrifice at the altar to save her family honor."[47] In some advertising photos of the film, Hayakawa protects a woman in a kimono.[48] Since the woman in a kimono is obviously played by a white actress, these photos appear to show Hayakawa protecting a white woman. This motif of self-sacrifice for a white woman was not observed in the original stories by Irwin and was newly added to the film version.

Togo's heroism is also generated from his Americanized behaviors. He respects the Founding Fathers of America and is obedient to American laws. When Togo finds out about the villain's conspiracy against Corinne, he does not resort to any Japanese method, using jiu-jitsu or his sword, to solve the situation, but asks for help from the American legal system and from American journalists. First, he tries to find George Washington for help. Then, he writes a letter of protest to an American newspaper, not with a Japanese brush and ink but with a typewriter. In the course of this search, Togo sees a district attorney. Since Washington has been dead for a long time, Togo's act would look silly and inappropriate to American viewers. Hayakawa said about his characterization of Togo in an interview: "It is not a true Japanese nobleman to rush into the courts and into the newspapers with his family troubles."[49] Yet Togo's behavior indicates his efforts to Americanize himself.

Like Makino in *The Honorable Friend*, Togo has mentors for his Americanizing process. The district attorney and the reporter stop Togo from committing hara-kiri, a Japanese method of suicide. They help Togo deviate from Japanese customs. In the end, Togo's "well-fitting American clothes" signify his successful Americanization and Anglo-conformity.

In the American suit and a pair of black-framed glasses, Hayakawa as Hashimura Togo looks like Harold Lloyd, a popular comedian with the star image of a middle-class white-collar worker, or the "city boy next door." It is significant that Lloyd suddenly started wearing the pair of horn-rimmed glasses in a baseball comedy, *Over the Fence*, and changed his comic persona from the more clownish "Lonesome Luke" to the normally dressed and everyday-appearing youth in June 1917, only two months before *Hashimura Togo* was released. Lloyd began to merge the physical comedy of slapstick tradition, which targeted working-class audiences, with the situation comedy, which had more realistic characters and events, which middle-class audiences were accustomed to.[50] Even though it may not be possible to find any records of a direct influence of Lloyd's characters on Hayakawa's Hashimura Togo, the comic elements of the film, which relate Hayakawa's character to Lloyd, a popular comedian of the time, provide Hayakawa with a more escapist image, deviating from the actual sociopolitical issue of Japanese immigration. Albert F. McLean Jr., argues in his book on vaudeville in America that humor based on ethnic stereotypes functioned primarily "to encourage a sense of community among the diverse groups constituting the American city." McLean states, "When this humor began to single out its scapegoats, and when its appeal became limited to narrow and particular areas of discontent, it was losing its essential character as mass humor."[51] Without "singling out" a Japanese immigrant as a scapegoat, *Hashimura Togo* utilizes ethnic stereotypes to create "mass humor" for middle-class audiences, especially those in urban areas experiencing ethnic diversity.

Thus, *Hashimura Togo* is another ideal assimilation narrative of a Japanese immigrant. In both *The Honorable Friend* and *Hashimura Togo*, Lasky made Hayakawa's characters heroic and sympathetic by showing their processes of Americanization in their lifestyles and in their obedience to American law and order. Hayakawa's characters obtain higher positions in the racial hierarchy than other nonwhite characters because they make every effort to Americanize themselves. Lasky's star-making strategy on Hayakawa began in this manner, focusing on Americanization.

7

MORE AMERICANIZED
THAN THE MEXICAN

The Melodrama of Self-Sacrifice and the

Genteel Tradition in *Forbidden Paths*

According to the film scholar Linda Williams, melodrama has been "a central *mode* of American popular culture" since the mid-nineteenth century, "a major force of moral reasoning in American mass culture," and "the basic vernacular of American moving pictures."[1] In fact, Lasky used the melodramatic structure in many of Hayakawa's star vehicles. It was a common device to provide the status of melodramatic heroes to stars all through the silent period. This strategy of Lasky was again meant to make Hayakawa's star image heroic and sympathetic.

Williams also points out melodrama's "incalculable influence on American attitudes toward race." In American melodramas with black and white characters, "the emotionally charged 'moral legibility' . . . [that is] so crucial to the mode of melodrama is intrinsically linked to a 'racial legibility' that habitually sees a Manichaean good or evil in the visual 'fact' of race itself." According to Williams, the dynamics of American melodramas with black and white characters make the viewers "feel for the raced and gendered sufferings of some and to hate the raced and gendered villainy of others."[2]

In Hayakawa's star vehicles, racial issues are almost always connected to moral issues. Through self-sacrifice and self-victimization, the virtues of the nonwhite characters played by Hayakawa are recognized. As a result, they earn the sympathy of other characters and the viewers. Even when Hayakawa played villains, Lasky characterized them as racially beset virtuous victims, in order to make them sympathetic and heroic.

One of the major thematic motifs in melodrama is a hero's self-sacrifice, especially for a white woman. At the same time, the film historian Robert Sklar claims that noble sacrifice of oneself for womanhood or honor was a major character trait of the romantic hero of the genteel tradition, which was "so ubiquitous a part of American culture as it was like air" for about half a century until World War I.[3] According to Sklar, the aim of genteel culture was "to teach how to behave, and to do so in the guise of disinterested benevolence — or of noble self-sacrifice. The ultimate weapon of control was the censorious power of social opinion, but the everyday forms of persuasion and manipulation were the schools, literature, the press, the pulpit. The basic trick, the most subtle and challenging, was getting people to adopt the desired manners and morals as if they had been spontaneously generated and freely accepted from within."[4] The genteel tradition was a conservative attempt at social control by middle-class Americans, who faced such social issues as the arrival of new immigrants, the rise of the New Woman, urbanization, and industrialization.[5]

Motion pictures became one of such "everyday forms of persuasion" in the genteel tradition. In the movement toward refinement for middle-class audiences, the film industry took part in the genteel tradition. Hayakawa's star image followed the romantic heroes of the genteel tradition to a certain degree, with the melodramatic motif of self-sacrifice.

In fact, the motif of self-sacrifice was very useful for the creation of Hayakawa's star image. It could place Hayakawa's nonwhite characters at the moral center of the narrative while keeping them out of full assimilation into American society and prohibiting them from interracial marriages. If Hayakawa's romantic heroes of the genteel tradition sacrifice themselves and die for the good of white American women, such anxiety as that caused by miscegenation will never occur. Sklar argues, "Danger and sexual allure are not alien to the genteel romantic hero in his performer's role."[6] Even when Hayakawa's characters show any sexual threat to white American heroines, the motif of self-sacrifice compensates for the "danger and sexual allure" in the end. With this motif, Hayakawa's characters became safely desirable for the middle-class white women on the screen and for the middle-class audiences. Hayakawa's nonwhite heroes gain the hearts of white women, and their places in America, with their self-sacrificial deaths. Consequently, the status quo of white American society is maintained because the inassimilable nonwhite characters willingly destroy themselves. While Tori in *The Cheat* is capable of social assimilation but remains morally inassimilable, the motif of self-sacrifice can make Hayakawa's characters morally assimilable but racially inassimilable in American society. There is no room for fearing that nonwhite men might ascend the steps of the racial and class hierarchy.

The boundaries posed by race and by conventional morality of the genteel tradition are entirely insurmountable. Thus, the motif of self-sacrifice, which serves to maintain the genteel American racial and social order, could safely provide Hayakawa with a high degree of moral stature.

Another use for the motif of self-sacrifice is to maintain the unique Japanese traits in Hayakawa's star image for the purpose of product differentiation. The motif of self-sacrifice connected Hayakawa to the traditional Japanese idea of *bushido*, the code of samurai, one of the stereotypical images of the Japanese people. In the thought of *bushido*, a samurai warrior should serve his master for life and be willing to sacrifice himself for the honor of his family name.[7] Lasky and Paramount, the distributor, had publicized the notion of self-sacrifice as one of the prominent traits of Japanese men. In its own promotional magazine, Paramount reported that a "magazine writer, while presenting 'Japan's Commercial Crisis' recently, had this to say: 'Woman has no place in the much-talked-of and boasted 'bushido,' or self-sacrifice of the man.'"[8] Here, the notion of self-sacrifice was treated as a synonym of *bushido*, which was already "much-talked-of" as a trait of Japanese men.

The motif of self-sacrifice was also a typical device in romances of chivalry used to turn a masculine protagonist, who is at the beginning of the story misogynistic, brutal, and terrorizing, into a hero genteelly devoted to concern for a heroine's pleasure. T. J. Jackson Lears argues that *bushido* and European chivalry were integrated into American anti-modernist thought in the late nineteenth and early twentieth centuries, in terms of the notion of self-sacrifice.[9] This coincidence of values, despite their different cultural origins, was conceived as another convenient proof given for the popular discourse that regarded the Japanese people as closer to whites than other nonwhites. Along with this mechanism, which enhanced Japan's position in the racial hierarchy, the motif of self-sacrifice even placed Hayakawa's nonwhite characters within the tradition of European chivalry.

In *Forbidden Paths* (Robert T. Thornby, 5 July 1917), Hayakawa's character becomes sympathetic, moralistic, and heroic mainly because of his self-sacrificial act for a white woman and for a white American family. This act favorably distinguishes Hayakawa's character from other nonwhite characters in this film. Yet, eventually, this motif of self-sacrifice prevents Hayakawa's character from completely assimilating into American society.

In *Forbidden Paths*, Hayakawa plays Sato, a young Japanese man who is a devoted assistant of James Thornton, a wealthy white American importer of Japanese art in San Francisco. Sato secretly loves Thornton's daughter Mildred, but Mildred loves Harry Maxwell, a young white American diplomat. In Mexico, Harry is seduced by Benita Ramirez, "the most notorious woman in the capital" of Mexico, and marries her.[10] When Harry realizes Benita is unfaithful, he leaves Mexico. In San Francisco, when Thornton dies, he asks Sato to take care of his business. Harry sees Mildred again, but Benita comes from Mexico to bring back her husband. Sato gets angry at Harry because he betrayed Mildred, but he decides to sacrifice himself to Mildred's love for Harry. Sato seduces Benita onto a boat and sinks the boat in the middle of the ocean.

One of the most obvious narrative devices in *Forbidden Paths* that serves to make Hayakawa's character sympathetic is the melodramatic binary structure between good and evil. The binary line is drawn between the two nonwhite characters, in terms of their relationships to a white American family. While Sato devotes himself to the happiness of a white American family, Benita seduces a young American man and endangers the formation of a white American family. The continuous use of the parallel editing technique throughout this film emphasizes the distinct contrast between Sato and Benita. In this melodramatic structure, Japanese people, represented by Sato, occupy a more favorable position than Mexican people, represented by Benita. Not only are national, racial, and cultural stereotyping used here, but so too are gender politics: the nonwhite male is more highly regarded than the nonwhite female. However, Sato is never fully accepted into American society. A racial hierarchy is formed among Japanese, Mexican, and white American people.

The cross-cutting that opens the film emphasizes the distinction between the two nonwhite characters. In Mexico City, the extravagantly but indecently gowned Benita drinks liquor in a squalid bar and mingles with Luis Valdez, "Her Latest Conquest," according to the intertitle. In San Francisco, James Thornton admires a Japanese-style pot in front of a small statue of a Japanese god, and Mildred in a Japanese-style kimono enjoys a branch of a cherry tree in blossom in a Japanese-style vase. While Mexican culture is introduced as dirty and sexually indulgent, Japanese culture is so refined that white American people can appreciate it without lowering themselves. Nevertheless, Japanese culture here stays in an inferior position. It is commodified and consumed by white Americans as a refined but exotic art form and safely incorporated into the middle-class American family space. The script emphasizes that Mildred, like her father, "loves the Art of Old Japan." The way

Thornton and Mildred appreciate Japanese artifacts literally represents Japanese Taste, which was so influential among white middle-class American families.

Together with Japanese objets d'art, Sato, the Japanese assistant, is safely accepted both in a white American family space, the realm of women according to the discourse on the cult of domesticity, and in an American business space, the realm of men. First, Sato in a kimono teaches Mildred how to draw a picture on a plate, using a Japanese brush, in his Japanese-style room in Thornton's house. Sato's room is furnished with a shoji screen, a pot, and a Japanese-style desk. A Japanese stone lantern and a plum tree in Thornton's garden behind the shoji screen are also observable. Despite this intimate atmosphere, like Tori and Edith in a Japanese room in *The Cheat*, there is no sexual tension between Sato and Mildred.[11] Mildred never regards Sato as her love or sexual interest. For Mildred, as the script states, Sato is just "Good Old Sato."

At the same time, Sato is depicted as a repressed, or even castrated, person. Sato feels sexual attraction toward Mildred, but it is always curtailed. With this desexualized characterization, Hayakawa's star image is safely immune from the fear of miscegenation. Moreover, Hayakawa's character obtains a genteel image of chivalry. The hero is masculine enough to remove a threat to the heroine but is rather feminine when it comes to romance. In the case of Hayakawa, there is no actual romance between the hero and the heroine in the film. The Japanese hero literally sacrifices himself for the heroine. The hero's repression is a major characteristic of Hayakawa's star vehicles.

In regard to Sato's repression, in one scene, when Sato hears Mildred come into his room, he cannot even turn to her at first. He keeps looking down shyly. He can only say, "Today, in Japan, begins the Fete [Festival] of the Cherry Blossoms." He finally turns to her, but he looks down to a pot that he has at hand and draws something on it with a brush. Shots of the sensual-looking Benita and her boyfriend with a dark beard who says brutally, "Your smiles belong to me—I pay for them," are inserted several times into this sequence and create a clear contrast between the sensual Mexicans and desexualized Sato.

Sato is also accepted into an American business space without any sign of difficulty. The narrative of *Forbidden Paths* carefully avoids anxiety about any possible economic yellow peril, in addition to the sexual one—fear of miscegenation—in the domestic sphere. Sato is faithful to Thornton. He never shows any ambition to take over Thornton's business. When Thornton tells

Sato, "Sato, you're a better business man than I am—I have decided to make you an equal partner," Sato is simply astonished. The script states, "His face loses its Oriental inscrutability overcome with the honor."

Moreover, Sato is depicted as Americanized enough to succeed in Thornton's business. Symbolically, Sato never wears a Japanese kimono when he works in Thornton's shop. When Sato accepts Thornton's offer by shaking hands, he shows his feelings outwardly, not like a stereotypically restrained Japanese man. He looks like an American businessman in a black tuxedo suit. The script even uses a Christian religious term to describe how Sato takes Thornton's hands when he accepts the offer. It is "as if he were fulfilling a sacrament."

A parallel editing in the following scene, between the two couples, Sato and Mildred in San Francisco, and Benita and Harry in Mexico, reinforces the contrast between the desexualized Japanese man and the sensual Mexican woman. In Thornton's garden, Mildred prepares Japanese tea while wearing a kimono. She turns around and shows the obi of her kimono to Sato. Sato first shows his embarrassment but then happily looks at Mildred in kimono in his point-of-view shot. He says, "You are very beautiful, little Cherry Blossom." Here, for the first time, the subject-object relationship between Mildred and Sato is reversed. Mildred becomes objectified in Sato's gaze. Yet, this reversal of their positions becomes possible only because she has put on Japanese commodities and has "Japanized" herself. She takes on the stereotypical role of an obedient Oriental woman. Sato symbolically takes off his kimono-style gown before he comes out to join Mildred in this scene. Sato is in Western clothes, while Mildred is in a Japanese kimono. Sato's Americanized appearance allows him to be in a superior subjective position over Japanized Mildred.

In this complicated racial masquerade, a sexual tension, or the anxiety of miscegenation, between the white woman and the nonwhite man comes to the surface for the first and only time in *Forbidden Paths*. Mildred's Japanese kimono hides her normally superior white position to Sato, who is wearing a Western suit, and thus almost reverses the power relationship between the two. Sato leans toward Mildred. His hand touches Mildred's on the table for the first time. Their hands are shown in an irised close-up. According to the script, a "wild hope flares in his breast. She does not realize this. Sato almost loses control of himself." Sato comes close to crossing the prohibited line of miscegenation because of Mildred's masquerade, imitating in her imagery an obedient Japanese woman.

However, Sato abruptly stops his act himself. According to the script, when Sato looks at their hands in his point of view, their hands' "difference brings to his mind the difference of race." A stern expression comes back to his face. He moves his hand away from Mildred's. Mildred restarts preparing tea as if nothing has happened. This complex masquerade scene depicts Sato not only as a desexualized man who attempts to reject his sexual impulse toward Mildred but also as a man of restraint who consciously maintains the unconquerable barrier of different races in American society. In other words, a racialized object, Sato's hand, controls his emotion here. Sato is depicted not only as a person who can perfectly control his feelings but also as a man who perfectly understands the ideology of race and the unsurpassable power relations between white and nonwhite, subject and object. Sato remains safe and faithful to the white American family. Sato's desexualized status in the narrative does not allow him to approach Mildred, and simultaneously his well-tempered self as an Americanized gentleman forbids him to take advantage of the Japanized Mildred.

In contrast, Benita seduces Harry in her room, "furnished garishly and untidy. Bottle, cigarettes, ashes, etc.," contrary to the gay and beautiful Japanese flower garden in San Francisco. Benita cunningly appeals to Harry's imperialist point of view. From the beginning, Harry is portrayed as a young and naïve American imperialist with a "slight shade of race prejudice." He dreams of Mexican people obeying him. In this sense, no matter how innocent and naïve, Harry, in contrast to Sato, is ignorant and exploitative about the racial hierarchy. At Benita's place, Harry tries to save Benita from Valdez, a sexually abusive Mexican man. Listening to Benita's honeyed words filled with racism, "Ah Señor—men of your race are so quick to protect the weak and innocent," Harry becomes overjoyed. As Mildred imitates a Japanese girl, Benita pretends to be a coy and bashful Mexican girl. She keeps tempting Harry by saying, "I couldn't go out alone, señor." Sato can control himself not to make advances to a woman, even when he appears to be in a superior position to her because of their racial masquerade. In contrast, Benita skillfully makes advances to a naïve man and Harry easily yields to Benita's temptation, which appeals to his superior position vis-à-vis his gender and race. She purposefully emphasizes her victimized position as a doubly inferior existence: nonwhite and female. Benita lures Harry and forces him to protect her. Harry is trapped by Benita's seduction. He kisses Benita and proposes to her. "Marry me. Let *me* protect you." When Harry leaves, Benita becomes triumphant and says, "I've got him." Contrary to Sato, Benita thus represents the sexually threatening aspect of nonwhite people. Harry and Benita's wedding in Mexico is cross-cut with the scene in San Francisco in which Thornton is dying. The trouble at home enhances the vicious atmosphere in Mexico City.

Moreover, Benita threatens the monogamy of the American family system. She seduces a young and naïve white American man, even when she has a Mexican husband. At Harry's and Benita's wedding, the American ambassador angrily says to Benita, "Tell him you are married to Luis Valdez!" Benita does not give up and says to Harry, "It's true what he says, but I love you!" Seeing Harry still disappointed, she threatens Harry by saying, "You lied to me. I'm your wife. You can't undo that."

In addition to the cross-cutting technique, the narrational focalization differentiates Hayakawa's character from Benita's.[12] The main focalization in the narrative of *Forbidden Paths* goes to Sato and constructs Sato as a main character with a full psychological development beyond just a stereotypical representation as with Benita.

First, the longest screen time is given to Sato, clearly indicating that he is the protagonist of the film, even though the opening credit states, "Vivian Martin supported by Sessue Hayakawa." Since Hayakawa is the star of the film, this credit also implies the motif of a nonwhite man's self-sacrificial "support" of a white woman.

Second, all of the point-of-view shots in the film are from Sato. Point-of-view shots lead particular characters to be narrative agencies of the films. Sometimes, point-of-view shots even create a way for the audience to psychologically identify with or sympathize with the characters, because they usually place the viewers in the identical position with the characters in terms of their visual perspectives. In comparison, there is no point-of-view shot provided for other major characters, Mildred, Harry, or Benita. In this sense, they are objectified characters from the focalized perspective of Sato: the one to sacrifice himself for (Mildred), the one to save from evil (Harry), and the one to eliminate from American society (Benita).

Third, most of the close-ups in *Forbidden Paths* are of Sato's face. Not only is Sato's visual point of view often provided, but also his facial expressions are clearly displayed many times and eloquently indicate his psychological state or his emotions.

The focalization on Sato is particularly enhanced in a scene in which he observes a quarrel between Benita and Mildred from behind a curtain. The repeated close-ups of Sato and his point-of-view shots depict his gradual psychological development until he comes to realize that "Love is Sacrifice." In this scene, Sato is visually and stylistically connected to the thematic motif of the film: self-sacrifice for a white woman.

The first close-up of Sato shows his stern expression, raising his left eyebrow slightly. In the next close-up, after Benita tells Mildred, "Love him—till your heart breaks—you'll never get him," Sato squints, grabs a curtain with his right hand, and makes a cold-hearted expression. In Sato's point-of-view shots, Benita is seen as a melodramatically evil character enjoying the fright of her victim. Even after knowing Mildred's devotion to Harry, Benita does not become remorseful and cease her revenge. Then, after Benita says, "Love is sacrifice—if you want him, you'll have to be—what I was [a mistress]," Sato opens his eyes wide, clenches his teeth, frowns, closes his mouth tightly, and squints. This close-up of Sato indicates his fury against Benita, but, at the same time, it implies his astonishment at the words "Love is sacrifice," which have come from Benita's mouth, because that is the rule that he is to obey.

Sato then hears Mildred make up her mind and say, "Love *is* sacrifice—I will go with him." Sato frowns several times and, finally, achieves a concretely decisive expression. The thematic line "Love is sacrifice" is delivered by Benita and Mildred, but it is Sato who shows his sacrificial act for his love. He leaves the room with dignity to go to a climactic showdown with Benita, the melodramatic encounter between the Americanized hero versus the inassimilable villain. Sato puts on a black bow tie and formal dress, as if attempting to show his complete Americanization.

Yet, the Japanese character's Americanization is achieved in a twisted manner. The finale of *Forbidden Paths* even uses such stereotypical images of Japan as the embodiment of threatening sensuality to make the motif of self-sacrifice more dramatic. Sato approaches Benita, using his sensual appeal. They sit on a sofa. Sato lights a cigarette for Benita in a very polished way and says to her, "Our interests lie together. I have come to help you. Your husband is in the position of my worst enemy." The strong lighting from above and below creates stripes of shadows on his face, which may remind the viewers of Tori in *The Cheat*. Sato comes near to her, looks ardently at her, and says, "If your husband does not appreciate your beauty there is one who does." In the script, Sato's approach to Benita is written in more direct mode. Sato says, "Your beauty is maddening." Benita answers, "Not so fast." At this point, the viewers do not know whether Sato's act is for the purpose of protecting Mildred and Harry from the evil nonwhite woman. Since Sato never clearly declares his self-sacrificing aim in words at this point, Sato's true intention remains ambiguous. There is a possibility that Sato will betray Mildred to take advantage of her.

Eventually, both Sato's Americanized aspect, which has been established early in the narrative and signified by his American costume, and his stereotypical Japanese traits, indicated by his conspiring sensual behavior, are intertwined in his self-sacrificial act for a white woman. Sato, in the clothes of a Western leisure-class gentleman, with a hunting cap and leather gloves, visits Benita, with a gentle smile on his face. He cheerfully says to her, "It is too beautiful a day to remain indoors, Señora. You like yachting—a motor boat?" Once she turns her back to him, his disguise as an Americanized gentleman is gone. Sato grins and his expression indicates that he has a secret scheme. When Benita is pleased and goes out of the room, Sato starts writing a letter and asks a servant to deliver it to Mildred. The intertitle reads "The Greater Love."

The parallel editing shows the anguish of the young white American couple in opposition to the apparent joy of the nonwhite couple. This parallel editing emphasizes the greater price that Sato is ready to pay for "The Greater Love." While Mildred and Harry hold each other in tears, Sato throws away the steering wheel and pulls off the stopper at the bottom of the boat, avoiding Benita, who resists and cries out, "Why do you do this?" Black water comes into the boat. Sato shakes off her hands and says impassively, "I love her." When Benita prays with her knees already under water, the letter from Sato reaches Mildred: "Little Cherry Blossom: When you receive this—you will not have loved in vain. Sato." The shot of a life buoy, an oar, and Sato's hunting cap is inserted. Mildred shows a mournful expression for a while, but Harry turns to her with a cheerful smile.

With his own death, Sato accomplishes his mission, "love-is-sacrifice," for Mildred and his duty to Thornton, who has helped him to live in American society. Not only does Sato eliminate the unwelcome nonwhite alien to protect the white American family, but also he makes up for the mistake that the naïve white American imperialist (Harry) has made. Thanks to the suicidal act carried out by Sato, Harry's error, caused by his imperialistic naïveté and by the devious act of a nonwhite evil woman, is compensated. Sato provides an opportunity for Harry, the imperialist and racist, to change into an ideal husband in a white American family. According to the script, even Benita, an unwelcome immigrant to the United States, "is fascinated by his calm." She becomes "overcome with wonder and into her mind creeps a realization of how great is this man's love and how petty her own. . . . She looks into his face, admiration growing on her own." Sato eliminates the seductive Mexican woman from America. At the same time, he even educates her to understand the American way of thinking about love and family.

Forbidden Paths is a tragedy of interracial romance. Yet, at the same time, it is a morality tale, in which a nonwhite man devotes himself to protecting a young white American couple from a devious outsider and helps them form an ideal American family. It is indicative that the credit of *Forbidden Paths* declares, "Vivian Martin supported by Sessue Hayakawa," despite the fact that this film is a Hayakawa star vehicle, according to the listings in trade journals. William Elliot Griffis wrote in his pro-Japanese essay in *North American Review* in 1914, "We need the Orientals among us for our refinement and best development."[13] Hayakawa's character in *Forbidden Paths* works for a white man's "refinement and best development" as the moral center of such a narrative.

There is a definite racial hierarchy among the Thorntons (James, Mildred, and her future husband Harry), Sato, and Benita. Sato occupies a more morally civilized and socially Americanized position than the other nonwhite people. Sato's act is chivalrous in a European sense. Simultaneously, it can be derived from the feudalistic notion of *bushido*, which requires subjects to devote their lives to their lords. Sato faithfully obeys his master's will to look after his daughter. Sato's self-sacrificial decision functions to maintain the status quo of the white American family system, but, simultaneously, it can be regarded as a primitive act. Thus, the motif of self-sacrifice in *Forbidden Paths* is a valuable device to naturalize the racial hierarchy that prohibits interracial romance, avoids miscegenation, and keeps nonwhite people out of white American society.

The reviews of *Forbidden Paths* in trade journals indicate that the motif of self-sacrifice was considered to be effective in making Hayakawa's star persona heroic and sympathetic. The NYDM stated, "It [*Forbidden Paths*] presents Sessue Hayakawa in one of his most sympathetic and touching roles. . . . [The situations of the plot] end in a tragic solution with the Oriental idea of poetic justice."[14] The MPN also claims it is "a powerfully dramatic story that has as its climax the well-known Japanese personal loyalty equal even to the sacrifice of life itself—in this case for his love of an American girl whom he cannot honorably seek in marriage because of his race."[15] Thus, the motif of self-sacrifice was explicitly and overtly used to enhance Hayakawa's heroic and sympathetic star image based on the racial hierarchy.

SYMPATHETIC VILLAINS
AND VICTIM-HEROES

The Soul of Kura San and The Call of the East

After *The Cheat*, some spectators wanted Hayakawa to play villainous roles and Lasky dared not completely ignore their demand. The popular reception of Hayakawa's first two vehicles, *Alien Souls* and *The Honorable Friend*, in which Hayakawa played Americanized heroes, had been merely "not bad." Beginning 14 September 1916, a trade journal, *Wid's Films and Film Folk Independent Criticisms of Features*, published weekly exhibitors' reports on the number of "pleased patrons" and "box office" by percentage. "Exceptional" was 100 percent, "Excellent" 80 percent, and "Poor" 20 percent.[1] *Wid's* reports may not have been factually accurate, but they surely convey certain tendencies of industrial practices consistent with the discourses of exhibitors. According to *Wid's*, *The Cheat* received sixteen reports by 1 February 1917, and the average "pleased patrons" figure was 94 percent, more than "Excellent."[2] In contrast, the average "pleased patrons" figures of *Alien Souls*, based on twelve reports, and of *The Honorable Friend*, based on twenty-one reports, were 69 percent and 65 percent respectively.[3] *The Soul of Kura San* (Edward J. LeSaint, 30 October 1916), in which Hayakawa played a villainous role for the first time in his star vehicles after *The Cheat*, received a better figure, 90 percent, from four reports.[4] The *New York Times* noted that Hayakawa's role in *The Cheat* was "better adapted to his talents" than that in *Alien Souls*.[5] Consequently, Lasky began to provide Hayakawa with more villainous roles.

However, in the context of legitimization of cinema, film studios ascribed their stars with images consistent with middle-class morality, even when they played villainous roles. Hayakawa, especially given his non-American nationality, should not have been exceptional. A trade journal reported that *The*

Soul of Kura San "is a picture that ought to have a wide appeal, especially to people of refinement."[6] As this report suggests, Lasky took a specific strategy to make Hayakawa's nonwhite characters moralistic and sympathetic, in spite of their vileness. Lasky again utilized the melodramatic structure and its major motif of self-sacrifice for this purpose. Lasky provided Hayakawa with roles of racially beset victims with virtues the audiences could relate to, thus making the characters sympathetic and heroic for genteel middle-class viewers.

In most cases, Hayakawa's villainous nonwhite characters are not ultimately evil from the beginnings of the films to the ends. They usually transform themselves twice in the narratives. In most cases, they become villainous to enact revenge on the racist and imperialist white American male characters, but, in the end, they turn remorseful for their vengeful thoughts after being moved by the pure love of white heroines. They accept their victimized position in white American society and often decide to sacrifice themselves to help white middle-class families. These transformations in the narratives differentiate Hayakawa's characters in his star vehicles from his villainous role in *The Cheat*, where the Japanese character expresses no remorse and is punished by white American men.

In these narratives, the racism and imperialism of white American male characters, which make Hayakawa's characters villainous and vengeful, are not seriously questioned. The main issue of these stories is whether, and how, the villainous characters accept their victimized positions. Conversion narratives then substitute for revenge stories. The motif of self-sacrifice for white women makes this conversion possible. Hayakawa's characters give up their vengeful desires because of white women's devotion or petition for their loved ones. Through victimization and self-sacrifice, the victim-heroes played by Hayakawa achieve recognition of their inner virtue, earn moral sympathy, and find their appropriate positions in America. In this manner, the status quo of white male dominance in American society is safely maintained.

The Soul of Kura San and *The Call of the East* (George H. Melford, 15 October 1917) are typical films in which Hayakawa played villainous victim-hero roles.[7] In *The Soul of Kura San*, Hayakawa plays Toyo, a young Japanese man, who is in love with Kura San (Aoki). Kura San's greedy father prohibits their love affair only because Toyo is poor. When Toyo and Kura San attempt double suicide out of despair, Toyo receives news that he will inherit his uncle's business in America. Toyo asks Kura San to wait for him until he becomes rich in America. However, Kura San's father hides all of Toyo's letters from America and forges a letter saying that Toyo is getting married there. Kura San is heartbroken and becomes a geisha. When she poses for an American artist, Graham, as a model, Graham takes advantage of her, even though he has a fiancée in America. When Toyo returns from America, Kura San commits suicide out of shame. After Kura San's death, Toyo goes back to America to take revenge on Graham. Using his wealth, Toyo seduces Anne, Graham's fiancée. As he is on the verge of murdering Anne and Graham, Toyo's conscience comes back, only because of Anne's devotion for Graham. He forgives Graham and kills himself at the foot of the portrait of Kura San.

In *The Call of the East*, Hayakawa plays Takada, a young Japanese aristocrat, who falls in love with Sheila, an American woman who is visiting Japan. At a street festival in Tokyo, Takada mistakes Sheila as Japanese because she is in a Japanese kimono. Sheila falls in love with Takada, too. In the meantime, Alan, Sheila's brother, makes love to Omitsu (Aoki), Takada's sister, just for fun. Takada plots revenge on Alan and his sister, not knowing that his sister is Sheila. After running Alan into debt by cards, Takada takes Alan to his home on a distant island, Hakoshima, and tortures him. Hearing from Omitsu, who loves Alan in spite of what he has done to her, Sheila sails to the island. When Takada learns that Sheila is Alan's sister, he forgives Alan because of Sheila's devotion to her brother. Takada also decides to give up his love for Sheila because of their racial differences. However, Alan tells them that Sheila is half-Japanese.

Both *The Soul of Kura San* and *The Call of the East* follow *The Cheat* in the characterizations of the Japanese protagonists: the simultaneous embodiment of a refined American lifestyle on the surface and of ultimate inassimilable and threatening Japaneseness at the core.[8] The villainy of these protagonists stems from their double identities. In *The Soul of Kura San*, Toyo looks Americanized in a "natty American business suit" in his office in America. Furniture, files, phone, and so forth, are "up-to-date and prosperous looking." The script clearly notes that the "only Japanese flavor [in his office] is from objects of art, scattering about . . . evidently not part of the permanent furniture." In contrast, Toyo's private room, which signifies his hidden self, is described as a "Japanese room, richly furnished according to Japanese ideas which preclude crowding or over-ornamentation."

When he becomes vengeful, Toyo turns into a typical yellow peril villain like Tori in *The Cheat*. Toyo's vileness is described in the script in sexually threatening terms. "Toyo grimly eyes painting (CU [close-up]). A vision of Anne disheveled, clothes torn as if in struggle, face tear-stained and convulsed with horror and shame. Toyo bestial expression, crouches to spring upon her (FI, FO [fade-in, fade-out])." Toyo seduces a white American woman with his masquerade as a refined Americanized gentleman, as Tori does. The heroine Anne is characterized as a New Woman, like Edith in *The Cheat*. She is introduced in the film as a connoisseur of Japanese art. She joyfully purchases an "antique Japanese bronze" at a shop filled with such Japanese art objects as a "big, forbidding figure of warrior or athlete." Graham, Anne's fiancé, like Richard in *The Cheat*, becomes jealous of Toyo, the rich and refined art dealer, who offers luxury to Anne.

The villainous aspect of Toyo's character bursts out on the eve of the wedding between Anne and Graham. Disguising his vengeful thoughts with "respectful, friendly intimacy," Toyo invites Anne to his place to show her the portrait of Kura San painted by Graham. When they are alone in Toyo's private room, Toyo "gazes passionately into her face" and "laughs savagely." Even though Anne becomes terrified by Toyo's fiercely implacable look and pleads for mercy, he attacks her, tears the clothes from her neck and shoulders, and kisses them fiercely until she faints. Toyo appears to rape Anne, as Tori does to Edith in *The Cheat*. A still photo used in a one-page ad of *The Soul of Kura San* emphasizes the twofold image of Hayakawa's character, refined on the surface and threatening to a white woman underneath the surface (see fig. 8). In the photo, Toyo in a tuxedo spreads his arms over an unconscious Anne and approaches her from above.[9] The scene depicted in the photo looks similar to the one in *The Cheat* in which Tori steals a kiss from the unconscious Edith. Toyo even looks like a vampire coming close to a white woman's naked shoulder, as Tori does in *The Cheat*. Two Japanese paintings, hung in the background, which have been signs of refinement in different settings, create an eerie atmosphere in the very low-key lighting.

Similarly, in *The Call of the East*, Takada is a villainous character with two different faces. A scene of an "American club" in Tokyo emphasizes how Americanized Takada is. In this scene, Takada is "in European evening dress, seated with a small table at his elbow, taking his after dinner coffee." In Tokyo, "by sharpest possible contrast with Hakoshima," where his house is located, Takada is seen as "the modern Japanese, graduate of Yale, man of the world, a veritable product of New Japan."

However, in Hakoshima numerous Japanese objects surround Takada. In a "room of a high caste Japanese of wealth, who keeps up the old customs," Takada, "about 30, in Japanese dress" is "seated on floor, with a cup of sake on low table before him." This is "Takada's main room: House com-

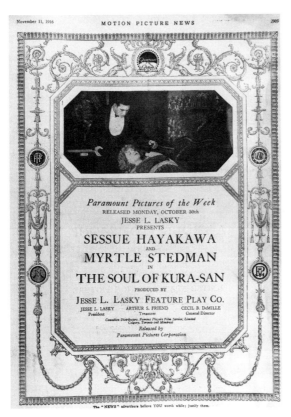

November 11, 1916   MOTION PICTURE NEWS   2909

Paramount Pictures of the Week
RELEASED MONDAY, OCTOBER 30th
JESSE L. LASKY
PRESENTS

SESSUE HAYAKAWA
AND
MYRTLE STEDMAN
IN
THE SOUL OF KURA-SAN

PRODUCED BY
JESSE L. LASKY FEATURE PLAY CO.
JESSE L. LASKY   ARTHUR S. FRIEND   CECIL B. DeMILLE
President   Treasurer   General Director
Canadian Distributors, Famous Players Film Service, Limited
Calgary, Toronto and Montreal
Released by
Paramount Pictures Corporation

The "NEWS" advertisers believe YOU worth while; justify them.

8   *An ad for* The Soul of Kura San. Motion Picture News *14.19 (11 November 1916): 2909.*

pletely Japanese in character and furnishings," such as "shoji to veranda," and "bronze gong." Later in the narrative, when Alan visits Takada, "white clothes of Alan—[are] startlingly exotic in the completely Japanese environment." A still photo published in a trade journal shows the out-of-placeness of Alan's white shirt and pants in a dark Japanese-style room, with Takada in a black Japanese kimono glaring fiercely at Alan. There is one Japanese-style lantern in the room. The shot is in a very low-key and Alan's white clothes stand out in the dark.[10] In Hakoshima, Takada is completely different from a white American man and fits into "Oriental" surroundings.

In reality, there is no place called Hakoshima in Japan. It is an imaginary space.[11] The script emphasizes Hakoshima's "wilderness and desolateness of the place." The melodramatic binary opposition is clear between a wild/primitive Japanese space and a civilized/Americanized urban space. Takada moves back and forth between these spaces. While Tokyo is a background for the "boy-meets-girl" style romance between Takada and Sheila, Hakoshima becomes a place where Takada's primitive and savage character is revealed.

From the beginning, Sheila, the heroine of *The Call of the East*, is attracted to and anxious about Takada's twofold nature: his refined and Americanized appearance and his racial difference. When Sheila looks into a mirror, Takada's eager and enkindled face appears in double exposure as her point-of-view shot. The script describes Sheila's ambivalent reaction to the image of Takada, from which she "gets delight" first. "Sheila lets herself dream happily forgetting that she is 'American.'" "Sheila is yielding to his spell, trying to remember that she is Caucasian and must not fall in love with this alien." Then, she feels "terror." Sheila takes off the kimono that she wears and orders her maid, "Put it away—out of sight! I'm American—and I mustn't forget it!" The kimono here signifies the materialized attraction and threat of Japanese Taste, which Takada embodies, for the middle-class American woman. Sheila's anxiety is clearly represented as the fear of miscegenation. An ad for *The Call of the East* in a trade journal exploits this issue of miscegenation between the Japanese man and the white woman in order to emphasize Takada's twofold characteristic. The ad places a still photo of a serious-looking Hayakawa in a Japanese kimono facing and holding a white-looking woman in a trench coat with a loving and dreamy expression on her face (see fig. 9).[12]

Takada's threatening demeanor is revealed when he hears that Alan is playing around with Takada's sister, Omitsu, and is not promising anything for their future. He becomes vengeful and decides to attack Alan and his sister. The MPW emphasizes Takada's Japanese nature here in its review of the film: "[This is] a Japanese bent on revenge—a revenge fiendish in its cruelty. . . . It is the revenge of the Oriental, not of the Caucasian. . . . We see the Japanese of high position, of education molded by contact with men of other races suddenly revert to the primitive."[13] Takada takes Alan to Hakoshima and drops him into quicksand. Takada says, "Tonight—your sister—she shall pay the price." No matter how Americanized and refined on the surface, Takada is depicted as a villain of a different race who threatens a white woman.

However, unlike Tori in *The Cheat*, Hayakawa's characters in *The Soul of Kura San* and *The Call of the East* are not ultimately evil. Eventually, both of them give up their villainous plots for white American families. Neither character's vengeful thoughts come from their innate sexual desires, in contrast to Tori, but only from the fact that white American men deceive Japanese women. Tori attacks a white woman because she betrays her contract with

MOTION PICTURE NEWS   Vol. 16. No. 18.

Jesse L. Lasky presents
SESSUE HAYAKAWA
"The Call
of the East"

By Beulah Marie Dix.
Directed by George   Melford

Facts and
Conclusions

The facts are that Sessue Hayakawa has never had a weak picture. "The Cheat," "The Jaguar's Claws," "The Bottle Imp"
and "Hashimura Togo" were
all successes of no uncertain
order.

The conclusion is that exhibitors are well within the bounds
of conservative business when
they put all the power of their
advertising and local prestige
behind "The Call of the East."

Paramount Pictures Corporation
FOUR EIGHTY-FIVE FIFTH AVENUE AT FORTY-FIRST ST.
NEW YORK

A Paramount Picture

Be sure to mention "MOTION PICTURE NEWS" when writing to advertisers

9   *An ad for* The Call of the East. Motion Picture News *16.18 (3 November 1917): 2992.*

him, but Tori's sexual desire for the white woman is indicated clearly from
the beginning. In the cases of Toyo and Takada, their vengeful acts are only
generated from white American men's racist and imperialist behaviors.

White American men victimize Japanese women in these films. In *The
Soul of Kura San*, Graham betrays Kura San because he has his fiancée waiting for him in America. Similarly, in *The Call of the East*, Alan treats Takada's
sister, Omitsu, not as a "legal wife" but merely as his mistress. Both Toyo's
and Takada's acts of revenge are against the white men. Even though their
methods of revenge are savage and cruel, the reasons for their acts are moralistic in terms of a discourse on family. They try not to allow Graham and Alan
to victimize Japanese women. They also attempt to defend monogamy.

Nevertheless, in the end, the Japanese characters in *The Soul of Kura San*
and *The Call of the East* give up their vengeful plots and accept their victim-

ized positions in favor of the white American characters. In *The Soul of Kura San*, Toyo eventually decides to give up his revenge plot in favor of preserving a white American couple, no matter how racist and imperialistic Graham's behavior was. Similarly, in *The Call of the East*, Takada forgives Alan for the sake of a white American family (a brother and a sister).

As a result, the white male characters are not blamed for their immoral and contemptible conduct within these narratives. The main issue of the narratives moves away from accusing them of racist and imperialist behaviors and turns to questioning whether the nonwhite protagonists can give up their vengeful thoughts and accept their victimized positions. By focusing on the process in which the Japanese characters accept their victimized positions for the good of white American families, these narratives allow the Japanese men to be more sympathetic and, simultaneously, let the racism of the white male characters escape from being problematized. As a result, white male supremacy, the status quo of American society and international relations, is safely maintained within these narratives.

Takada is characterized as the one who strictly tries to maintain the racial boundary in America. From the beginning, Takada has no intention of attracting a white woman, no matter how the promotion (and presupposition) of this film exploited the anxiety of miscegenation. Takada falls in love with Sheila and approaches her only because, and only as long as, he thinks she is Japanese. Takada thinks of Sheila as Japanese because Sheila wears a kimono when they first meet at the Boy's Festival in Japan. Unlike Tori in *The Cheat*, Takada is excused from any intention of miscegenation within the narrative of *The Call of the East*. He does not know that he is attracted to a white woman. When Takada learns that Sheila is Alan's sister and supposedly a white American, Takada instantly gives up his desire for Sheila, acknowledging that she is untouchable to him because their union would cause miscegenation. In spite of Sheila's affection for him, Takada declares, "You forget. East is East—and West is West!" Takada's self-consciousness and self-restraint about miscegenation and his self-sacrifice for the maintenance of a racial boundary make him moralistic and sympathetic.

The Call of the East, however, presents a twisted device to provide a happy ending. As the moral center of the film who defends the white American family and the status quo of the racial boundary between the white and the nonwhite, Takada is rewarded a status that goes beyond a mere victim-hero. *The Call of the East* is the first Hayakawa star vehicle in which Hayakawa's character happily unites with a white-looking heroine in the end.

In order to unite Hayakawa's nonwhite character with a white woman without breaking the taboo of miscegenation, the white-looking woman in *The Call of the East* is explicitly explained to the viewers as half-white and half-Japanese. From the beginning, an intertitle clearly notes, "In reality her [Sheila's] mother was a Japanese." Therefore, the viewers know that within the narrative Sheila is half-Japanese no matter how white she looks (she is played by Margaret Loomis, a white actress). Thus, *The Call of the East* is a meta-fantasy whose audience can safely enjoy the interracial romance.

Hayakawa once claimed, "I have never done a part where the 'bad guy' is stupid, crude or vicious. . . . I try to give him reasons, to make him understandable. The men I play are intelligent and, in their way, honorable—but on the wrong side of life."[14] Even when Hayakawa plays villainous nonwhite roles, his star vehicles characterize him as sympathetic with the motif of self-sacrifice. Accepting their victimized positions, Hayakawa's nonwhite villains become virtuous and heroic because they consequently serve to maintain the ethical and structural status quo of white American patriarchy, no matter how racist and imperialistic it is.

By the time *The Honor of His House* (William C. DeMille, 1 April 1918), in which Hayakawa played another Americanized but ultimately inassimilable Japanese character who sacrifices himself for the maintenance of white supremacy, was released, Hayakawa's star vehicles had become standardized in their content and publicity.[15] By the late 1910s, the Hollywood film industry was operating on a mass-production basis. Eager to maximize profits, filmmakers had seized upon the concept of standardization as the key to industrial efficiency.[16] After *The Honor of His House*, in all three Lasky films in which Hayakawa appeared, *The White Man's Law* (James Young, 6 May 1918), *The Bravest Way* (George H. Melford, 16 June 1918), and *The City of Dim Faces* (Melford, 15 July 1918), he played nonwhite (not always Japanese) victim-heroes in melodramatic binary structures with the motif of self-sacrifice.[17] Standardization of star vehicles was a regular strategy adopted by Hollywood film producers in this period.[18]

The standardization of Hayakawa's star vehicles is clearly indicated in reviews in trade journals. The motif of self-sacrifice was unanimously pointed out in the reviews of *The Bravest Way*. The MPN claimed,

> The Lasky company has been generally wise in its selection of stories for Sessue
> Hayakawa, the Japanese star, and "The Bravest Way" might have ranked with

the best of these had it not been developed so artificially. Tamura, Hayakawa's latest characterization, is as usual the soul of honor. He makes a sacrifice to protect the wife of his dead friend that paints him very black in the eyes of the girl he loves. Every one appreciates noble self-sacrifice, it is true, but when a few words would clear the whole situation and prevent the sorrow without injuring a single character, the situation becomes plainly artificial while the bid for sympathy quite collapses. . . . And it seems to the writer that the self-sacrifice of Tamura could have been made a real self-sacrifice by the use of a little imagination.[19]

Variety also noted on the same film, "Like all the Hayakawa features, the story is built on heroic self-sacrifice, along which lines it seems to be necessary to lead all the stories for the Jap."[20] The MPW clearly called *The Bravest Way* "a Drama of Sacrifice . . . Hayakawa, in the role of sacrifice," and ETR pointed out that "Hayakawa in typical role . . . Hayakawa plays the lead and succeeds in making the self-sacrificing but somewhat impractical Tamura a very appealing youth."[21] These reviews demonstrate that by 1918 Lasky and Paramount had standardized Hayakawa's star image.

Hayakawa himself promoted this image. He said in one interview, "In my coming picture, 'The Honor of His House,' I take the part of a Japanese nobleman who marries an American girl who brings disgrace upon him. . . . My latest part calls for the supreme sacrifice and I decide to kill myself."[22] Hayakawa's recognition of his standardized image at Lasky-Paramount and its popularity among American audiences became his dilemma, especially when he established his own production company in 1918 and tried to appeal to Japanese spectators in addition to American ones.

SELF-SACRIFICE IN THE FIRST WORLD WAR

The Secret Game

I n April 1917, the U.S. government decided to participate in World War I and Japan became an allied country. In the U.S. diplomatic discourse on Japan during World War I, the U.S. trusted, or at least desired to trust, Japan's policy in Asia and the Pacific. The *Nation* insisted that the United States should confide in "Japan's sincerity rather than pursuing Machiavellian conspiracy."[1] *Outlook* also declared its "faith that Japanese leadership in the East is not the origin of danger to America as well as to the world."[2] The U.S. government accepted Japan's expansion in China with the Ishii-Lansing Agreement in November 1917.[3]

As a part of its war efforts, the Hollywood film industry began to resort to the U.S.-Japanese alliance in the promotion of Hayakawa's star vehicles. Even regarding films in which Hayakawa did not play Japanese roles, such as *The White Man's Law*—Hayakawa played a Sudanese man—trade journals suggested they be advertised with reference to the U.S.-Japanese alliance: "Advertising Suggestions: With Japan an ally in the war there is opportunity to strengthen the bonds. Show the Japanese flag, decorate the lobby with lanterns and paper flowers to lend an Oriental atmosphere."[4]

The threatening image of Japan that had existed in the past was rewritten in favor of the Japanese people. When *The Cheat* was re-released on 24 November 1918, Tori was no longer a Japanese art dealer, but a Burmese ivory king, in order not to offend the audiences of the allied country.[5] In Japan, it was reported that even the title of *The Cheat* would be changed to "I Owe You," and the Japanese character would be changed to an "East Indian."[6]

The U.S.-Japanese allied conditions came to work as a safety valve for Hayakawa's star image. An article on Hayakawa in a fan magazine noted, "The

Allies need not fear for Japan's part. Honor is a sacred thing in Japan, and we are bound in honor by our treaty with England. Japan is prepared to send millions of Japanese troops to Europe and to turn over her whole merchant marine. Japan is willing to take charge of transporting the American troops to Europe on either ocean and to furnish the warships to convoy the transports as well."[7] Thanks to these historical conditions, no matter how immovably Hayakawa's persona might contain unique Japanese traits, it was not supposed to generate anxiety about the inassimilability of the Japanese people in American society or to cause fear of a Japanese political and economic invasion.

The Japanese actor was also provided a star image as a "mediator" in the war. In May 1917, right after the United States began to participate in the war, the *Los Angeles Times* published a photo of Hayakawa serving as a "mediator, in a threatened war at the Lasky studio" between a dog and a cat. The caption of the photo notes, "Wouldn't Mr. Boston Bull just like to drop a bomb on the other fellow, who seems to have adopted the policy of defensive preparedness."[8]

Hayakawa's tenth star vehicle, *The Secret Game* (William C. DeMille, 3 December 1917), took advantage of such historical conditions. *The Secret Game* was in accordance with the diplomatic discourse that desired Japan to be trustworthy in Asia and the Pacific and to be helpful in American society. *Variety* claimed, "The interest that attaches to anything in the nature of a picture or story dealing with the present war situation naturally accentuates the value of 'The Secret Game.'"[9] Similarly, ETR noted, "At a time when the war is almost the sole topic of conversation, when eyes are turned on Japan, and when the secret service is kept busy with the plots and counterplots of the traitors to our country, this story is one of most timely interest."[10] The MPW also noted, "Finely exemplifying the change in international relations as regards Japan and the United States. . . . In this story the representatives of the two countries are not at odds, they are working hand in hand against a common enemy—Germany. . . . Mr. Hayakawa as Nara-Nara has a role that wins the sympathy."[11]

In *The Secret Game*, Hayakawa plays Nara-Nara (again an improper Japanese name), a Japanese secret service agent in the United States. Nara-Nara is sent to Los Angeles to see that no information about the sailing of Japanese transports, which carry American soldiers across the Pacific to surprise the Russian front, leaks out of the U.S. quartermaster's office. Major Northfield is in charge of the office and Kitty Little (Florence Vidor) is a stenographer there. Kitty is actually a member of the German secret service, who takes orders from Dr. Ebell Smith. Nara-Nara, disguising himself as an art dealer, takes the office next to the quartermaster's. He learns of Kitty's mission to get the sailing information into the hands of the Germans. Northfield, who is in love with Kitty, also discovers her taking orders from Dr. Smith. He gives her a blank paper instead of the sailing orders. Nara-Nara pursues Kitty, who brings the paper to Dr. Smith. Nara-Nara kills Dr. Smith and attacks Kitty. Kitty's plea awakens his honor and loyalty to his country. He helps Northfield and Kitty and is stabbed by one of Dr. Smith's aides. Northfield forgives Kitty in the end.

In disguise in the United States, Nara-Nara works for his duty to Japan, like many Japanese characters in early spy films, including Tokoramo in *The Typhoon*. While Tokoramo embodied the discourse of the yellow peril, Nara-Nara is depicted as if his existence in American society would cause no threat. Nara-Nara's ultra-nationalistic behaviors of espionage follow Tokoramo's in *The Typhoon*. Yet, they are not depicted as being as threatening as those in *The Typhoon*. This is simply because Nara-Nara does not kill and die only for Japan, but also for the United States. Even though Nara-Nara's behavior symbolizes his ultimate bond with Japan, he helps a white German American woman assimilate herself into American society. In the end, Nara-Nara sacrifices himself for the good of the German American woman and for a white American family. Under the U.S.-Japanese allied conditions, Hayakawa's Japanese character could be heroic, not necessarily because of his Americanization but because of his loyalty to Japan and the alliance.

The introductory shots of Nara-Nara clearly indicate his innate Japaneseness and his loyalty to the United States, "A patriot of Japan and sincere friend to America," as the intertitle declares. Wearing a tuxedo, Nara-Nara enters a shop to purchase a cigar. He looks at a small object on the counter and smiles. The following close-up shows a small stand on the counter, on which a lot of little silk flags of the United States, Japan, and France are pinned. Smiling, Nara-Nara first takes a pin of the Japanese flag and then that of the United States and puts both of them on the lapel of his tuxedo. These introductory shots are not necessarily located in the linear temporality of the narrative. They function to visually signify the presupposed characterization of Nara-Nara. His formal costume and cigar signify his status as an Americanized gentleman, and his gesture of putting on two flag pins indicates his loyalty to the U.S.-Japanese alliance.

The melodramatic binary structure is used again in *The Secret Game* to distinguish Japanese spies from German ones. The boundary line is drawn according to the level of their loyalty to the United States. While the Japanese spies are depicted as good because they devote themselves to supporting the U.S.-Japanese alliance and to maintaining peace in American society, the German spies are evil because they conspire to subvert American society.

A parallel editing sequence that opens *The Secret Game*, after the introductory shots of Nara-Nara, establishes the contrast between the Japanese and the German spies in the United States. In the Japanese embassy in Washington, D.C., Nara-Nara and the Japanese ambassador, in correct morning dress—Nara-Nara has transferred the little flags that he bought in the introductory scene to this coat—talk about America sending troops to the Russian front to surprise the German army. The ambassador says, "I have sent for you because *Japan* has offered to convoy the American transports," but "New German raiders are known to be in the Pacific. This means there has been a 'leak'. . . . Find the traitor behind that 'leak' before he divulges the transports' sailing date and route. *Japan's honor* is staked upon their safety."[12] Nara-Nara bows to the ambassador in a dignified manner. The words of the ambassador and the final bow of Nara-Nara emphasize Japanese nationalism and loyalty. There still are possibly threatening Japanese images here, such as the high value placed on honor, the highly developed espionage system, and the superficial Westernized appearance. However, the characters' eloquent statement that Japan works to serve America and the success of American military strategy prevents the viewers from easily associating these possibly threatening images with the Japanese characters in this film. Instead, the calm conversation style of the characters and the furniture of the room, which has no particular emphasis on Japanese objects, are displayed as appropriate to a modernized nation and reinforce the safely loyal image of Japan to the alliance.

Contrary to these Japanese spies, two German spies in Los Angeles are visually emphasized as evil. One is the middle-aged Dr. Ebell (implying Evil?) Smith. His attempt to hide his German origins using an American name is emphasized by an intertitle: "Schmidt, in Germany." Smith, with dark circles under his eyes, watches American children with "a slow sneer, the look of traitor, slowly into his eyes contemptuous and sinister," according to the script. The other spy is the young and white Kitty Little. According to the intertitle, she is "Katrinka Littlehaus in Germany," "with a deeply concealed hyphen in her name, and, in her heart a romantic love for the 'Fatherland.'" Smith and Kitty are in Smith's laboratory, where a lot of test tubes, skeletons, and an anatomical chart create a horrifying atmosphere that reminds viewers of a room of a mad scientist. The lighting of this laboratory is much darker and more ominous than that of the Japanese embassy. Kitty's facial expression and behavior in front of Smith are not willful. She keeps looking away from Smith with a reluctant expression. The scene looks as if a despotic man is forcing an innocent white woman to do a dirty job. Later in the narrative, Smith kidnaps Northfield's secretary, Miss Loring, and threatens her with a needle and syringe to obtain information. Thus, Smith clearly embodies a threat to white women in America.

The compositions of settings of these two rooms are exactly the same, in spite of the completely opposite use of lighting techniques and props. Both pairs—Nara-Nara and the Ambassador, and Kitty and Smith—sit at desks in consecutive medium shots. The mise-en-scène of the opening scenes enhances a clear contrast between these spies from two different nations.

While both Nara-Nara and Kitty are bound up with their national duties as secret agents in disguise, this opening parallel editing clearly contrasts them. Nara-Nara, a nonwhite who is not considered to be eligible for American citizenship, is depicted as working for maintaining peace and order in American society. Kitty, who is a white immigrant from Germany who is eligible for citizenship, is on the verge of betraying the American people, no matter how reluctantly. The contrast between these two "aliens" in American society, in terms of their loyalty to the United States, is the driving narrative force of *The Secret Game*. Eventually, the Japanese spy helps the German woman to transform herself into a patriotic American and to create a white American family. The continuous use of parallel editing throughout the narrative emphasizes the similarities and differences between the two.

The Secret Game is an antithesis to *The Cheat*, which also depicts the similarities and differences between a Japanese man in the United States and a New Woman. (At one point, Kitty even says, "I feel like a cheat.") Exactly like Tori, Nara-Nara, with his Americanized appearance in costumes and manners, seduces a white woman with luxurious Japanesque consumer products. He invites Kitty into his office, which is filled with objets d'art of Japanese Taste. Kitty exclaims over the brocade, silk, a small box, a Japanese sword, and so forth, just as Edith does in *The Cheat*.

However, contrary to *The Cheat*, this scene, in which Kitty is attracted to Japanese objects, is not meant to emphasize Nara-Nara's threat to the white woman in *The Secret Game*. Nara-Nara is depicted as an inassimilable Japanese man who lives a double life and uses deceptive methods as a spy, but not as a dangerously sexualized one, as opposed to Tori. In the script, Nara-Nara studies the vivacious Kitty and says to her temptingly in improper English, "American girl have beeg round eye instead of the beautiful slant—but some of her have beauty." In the film, Nara-Nara's obsession with a white woman is minimized. He does not say these words to Kitty but to his servant with an innocent smile and a playful big gesture. The threateningly sensual implication of the line is therefore reduced.

Also in the film, Nara-Nara touches Kitty's hand when he shows her a small pot. He even shows her a Japanese sword, which can be read both as a phallic symbol and as an embodiment of a Japanese samurai warrior's ultra-nationalistic oath of honor. However, at this point, Nara-Nara does not say any words that could be seductive to a white woman or subversive to the order of American society, but only ones patriotic to America: "You're a loyal little American—eh? Will you help me to protect the soldiers of your country—and the honor of mine?" Nara-Nara points his right finger at Kitty, and his pose exactly follows the famous pose of Uncle Sam. In this sense, Nara-Nara is not a Japanese man full of sexual desire toward white women; rather, he functions as an educator of immigrants for loyal Americans.

Moreover, in the script, there is another scene in *The Secret Game* that exactly follows one in *The Cheat*. When Nara-Nara secretly searches Kitty's room, the Lasky lighting creates a high contrast between the light and shadow of the scene and emphasizes Nara-Nara's double identity as it did Tori's. Then, on his way back, he sees Kitty in the corridor. Remembering Smith's threatening order to steal important documents from Northfield, Kitty faints in front of Nara-Nara, as Edith does in front of Tori when she knows that she has lost money from the Red Cross Fund. Kitty falls helplessly against Nara-Nara, as Edith does against Tori in *The Cheat*. In *The Cheat*, this scene enhances the eminent fear of miscegenation. According to the script of *The Secret Game*, Nara-Nara looks ardently at the fainted Kitty in a close-up. However, this close-up, which could emphasize Nara-Nara's threateningly sensual characteristic, is entirely omitted in the film.

At the climax of the film, when Nara-Nara climbs up the wall outside of Smith's house and kills him, he looks much like an American action film star, such as Douglas Fairbanks Sr. Right after that, when Nara-Nara finds out that Kitty has deceived Northfield and has stolen secret documents, he tries to take advantage of Kitty's crime, as Tori does. This is the only scene in *The Secret Game* in which Nara-Nara's sexual desire for a white woman is indicated. Nara-Nara grabs Kitty and swings a knife in his right hand up toward Kitty's naked shoulder. Then, Nara-Nara embraces her and insists, "You are too beautiful to die! I will take you to Japan with me." Kitty frantically tries to free herself from Nara-Nara. Nara-Nara threatens her, "You need not fear Northfield. I will never tell him you are a traitor if you come with me. If you won't come with me you'll never see Northfield again." *Wid's Independent Reviews of Feature Films* noted, "Hayakawa's Nara-Nara, the Japanese spy who works in behalf of the United States, is an admired figure until he turns around [and] attacks the girl. This action instead of thrilling, mystifies unpleasantly."[13]

However, the Japanese man's sexual desire for the white woman in this scene is not visually emphasized as much as in *The Cheat*. Nara-Nara's pose when he threatens Kitty with a knife exactly follows that of Tori when he brands Edith. But in *The Secret Game*, this shot is not a close-up. A long shot reduces the brutality of the image. In the script, Kitty's expression is "full of horror and loathing," and she cries out, "No! I loathe you!" In the film, she does not show such an expression or say such words.

Eventually, Nara-Nara stops assaulting Kitty when Kitty reminds him of his duty to Japan. He suddenly stops his threatening action toward Kitty. Then he chooses to sacrifice himself to "protect" Kitty and Northfield. He points Northfield in a safe direction, provides him with all the useful spy-related intelligence that he has obtained from deliberate privacy infringement, and waits alone in Smith's room to be assassinated by Smith's man (Raymond Hatton, who played the villainous Japanese Kayosho in *The Honorable Friend*). In this sense, even though Hayakawa is credited as the star of *The Secret Game*, he plays more of a "supporting" role for the good of a white American couple.

Nara-Nara's self-sacrifice is absolutely unnecessary in a narratological sense. He does not have to be killed by Smith's man, who is not even attacking Kitty and Northfield and is about to be arrested by the police. Nara-Nara does not have any reason to commit suicide, either. He has killed Smith, but that is justifiable because he has to protect a secret document of the U.S. government. The only possible "cheat" that Nara-Nara has attempted is to cover Kitty's crime and threaten her. He has told Kitty that he will not report her crime to the police if she stays with him. Yet, this is exactly what Northfield does to protect and obtain Kitty in the end. Northfield shuts his mouth to cover up Kitty's crime only for his personal reason: his desire for Kitty. For conducting the same "cheat," Northfield does not die, but Nara-Nara has to. The only difference between them is that Northfield's possession of Kitty will not cause any racial fear of miscegenation, but Nara-Nara's would.

Mixed feelings in a contemporary review revealed this contradiction in the characterization of Nara-Nara and Northfield at the climax. A reviewer in *Wid's Independent Reviews of Feature Films* pointed out,

> Since the Jap had been the central figure all the way, I can't in any way see the advisability of having this character practically commit suicide in order that the hero and shero [heroine] might get together—because it would certainly have been just as reasonable to have allowed the clutch with the Jap devoting his life to the Secret Service work and still retaining a certain element of sympathy. This unhappy ending is going to disappoint a great many people in this film. It is absolutely illogical to figure that a successful Secret Service man, a Jap, should permit himself to be shot just because a white girl wanted to marry an American officer. That was certainly a bad break.[14]

Nara-Nara's death in *The Secret Game* is ultimately necessary, only because it emphasizes the thematic motif of self-sacrifice of a nonwhite man for a white American woman. It ends the triangular relationship among Nara-Nara, Kitty, and Northfield, and opens a way for the white woman's appropriate assimilation into American society. As a result, it helps to create a patriotic white American couple and family. In the final scene, Northfield completes Nara-Nara's work: to Americanize the white German woman. He salutes the U.S. flag, takes Kitty's hand, lets her salute the flag, and then he kisses her hand. In this manner white male supremacy and patriarchy is maintained.

Simultaneously, Nara-Nara's unnecessary death emphasizes his embodiment of a mysterious Japanese code of honor. Flashbacks are used effectively in *The Secret Game* to connect Nara-Nara's self-sacrificial act and his ultimate bond to Japan. In a scene at his office with Kitty, Nara-Nara explains about his Japanese swords. After Nara-Nara's spoken title, "When I left Japan, my father, like a Samurai of old, sent me forth sworn to the service of my Emperor," the following shot shows a room of a Japanese house. Many paper lanterns and a shoji screen emphasize the Japanese atmosphere. In front of the room, Nara-Nara, in a Western suit, bids his father farewell. The old father, in a Japanese kimono, takes a sword from the servant. Nara-Nara takes the sword and bows with profound filial respect. Nara-Nara's spoken title concludes the flashback, "And he bade me return, at the end of my service, and lay my sword—unstained—at his feet." At the end of the film, another flash-back reunites Nara-Nara to his past in Japan. Nara-Nara's spirit, in a double-exposure, goes back home to return the sword to his father.

In this sense, contrary to Hayakawa's characters in his many other star vehicles, Nara-Nara does not necessarily show his process of Americanizing himself, despite his demands for Kitty to be loyal to the United States.[15] His unnecessary self-sacrificial death functions only as a consequence to help an-other immigrant to become a loyal American. Nara-Nara's ultimate bond to Japan is emphasized in the finale, which stereotypically depicts Nara-Nara's self-sacrificial death for honor. Only because Japan was in alliance with the United States is Nara-Nara's ultimate inassimilable Japaneseness construed as favorable. Under the allied situation, Lasky was allowed to freely empha-size the image of Japanese traits in Hayakawa's star persona, mainly for prod-uct differentiation. Despite Hayakawa's character's ultimate inassimilability to the United States, audiences favorably received The Secret Game. The MPN reported a response from an exhibitor: "[The Secret Game is] Great—one of the Jap's best yet."[16]

THE COSMOPOLITAN
WAY OF LIFE

The Americanization of
Sessue Hayakawa in Magazines

Since the emergence of the star system, publicizing actors' private lives in the film trade press (*MPW*, *MPN*, *NYDM*, and so forth), film fan magazines (*Photoplay, Motion Picture Classic, Picture-Play,* and so on), periodicals on art, politics, and religion (*Harper's, Atlantic Monthly, Outlook, Nation,* and so on), mass-circulated magazines (*Saturday Evening Post,* and so forth), and newspapers has been the Hollywood film industry's typical strategy to construct its stars' images.[1] Hayakawa's emergence in extra-filmic sites was as important as his star vehicles in constructing his star image. The major purpose of the publicity of stars' private lives in early Hollywood was to distinguish the moral healthiness of work in the cinema as opposed to life in the theater. The moral healthiness of cinema was considered proven effectively through reference to the stars' family lives.[2]

Under the industrial conditions of the time, Hayakawa's star image was no exception. Lasky and Paramount employed the strategy of Americanization and gentrification of Hayakawa's star image and established his screen persona as a heroic and moralistic defender of white American families. At the same time, they started publicizing Hayakawa's private life in many magazines, particularly in fan magazines, most of which began to be published in the early 1910s. Since the extra-filmic identity tended to reproduce the representations of personality already produced in the films of the 1910s, Hayakawa's home and lifestyle were displayed in the magazine articles as overly Americanized in accordance with his star vehicles.

The most prominent image of Hayakawa in magazine articles was his Americanized family life with his wife. Even when the unique Japanese traits of Hayakawa were emphasized for product differentiation, such articles incorporated them into the popular discourse of Japanese Taste, a signification of cultural refinement among middle-class American families. The emphasis was not on Japaneseness per se, but on how Hayakawa was using Japanese Taste in his Americanized domestic sphere. Both filmic and extra-filmic images of Hayakawa valued the down-to-earth pleasures of American family life.

The fairly thorough articulation of Hayakawa's private life in magazines began after the release of *Alien Souls*. One of the first articles that referred to Hayakawa's private life appeared in *Photoplay*, arguably the most popular fan magazine of the time, in March 1916.[3] Grace Kingsley's article, suggestively titled "That Splash of Saffron: Sessue Hayakawa, a Cosmopolitan Actor, Who for Reasons of Nativity, Happens to Peer from Our White Screens with Tilted Eyes," effectively incorporates Hayakawa's "native" background with his "cosmopolitan" star image. A still photo accompanying the article, in which a grinning Hayakawa, dressed in a three-piece suit, is seated on a cushion while wiping a Japanese sword, supports her argument: the Americanization of Hayakawa's innate Japaneseness.

Even though Kingsley exoticizes Hayakawa's Japanese national and cultural origin by referring to Japanese religion, she puts more emphasis on Hayakawa's Americanized lifestyle. Kingsley writes, "No, Sessue Hayakawa, the world's most noted Japanese photoplay actor, does not dwell in a papier-mâché house amid tea-cup scenery. He is working in pictures in Los Angeles, and he lives in a 'regular' bungalow, furnished in mission oak, and dresses very modishly according to American standards. Even his gods are forsaken, for he owns an English bull-pup, named Shoki, which means 'destruction,' and is the name of a Japanese god."[4]

In the paragraphs that follow, Kingsley fictionalizes Hayakawa's biography and emphasizes his Americanized career. She writes, "He has played American and English roles in Japan, having the distinction, indeed, of having introduced American and English drama in his native land. He played 'The Typhoon' there; also Ibsen and Shakespeare, making an especial hit as 'Othello.'" According to Kingsley, Hayakawa came to the United States on an international tour with Otto Kawakami, "his uncle," and Madame Yacco, "the aunt of Sessue's wife," because he had been in the company of Kawakami since he had been a child. Hayakawa "studied English drama and literature at the Chicago University for a year, and translated a number of the English classics into Japanese." Kingsley's source on Hayakawa's stage career was the actor's profile, which was published in many trade journals and newspapers and undoubtedly followed studio publicity department releases.[5] A trade journal claimed, "Sessue Hayakawa is a *good* type of the educated Japanese. He studied drama at the University of Chicago and then returned to his native country with Japanese translations of the English classics. He was the first Japanese to appear in Shakespearean productions in that country."[6] The studios, which had control over actors' biographies, emphasized that Hayakawa's acting skill was "good," because it came from a Westernized acting career and lifestyle, in spite of his different cultural origin.[7]

Even Hayakawa's own words are quoted in Kingsley's article and reinforce the authenticity of the article's content, even though we do not know to what extent Kingsley edited, or even fabricated, Hayakawa's comments. Hayakawa is quoted as saying, "When playing an American or English character, even in Japan, I find it necessary to use the English language. I find it impossible to get the proper facial expression or the right action when I translate the words of an American or English character into Japanese. Most of the Japanese understand English nowadays, and they did not really like your drama until I gave it to them in English."[8] In this comment, Hayakawa insists upon the importance of differentiating between the English and Japanese languages. This bilingual attitude with more emphasis on the superiority of English in dramatic use makes Hayakawa's Americanized position stand out.

In real life, there is no official record that Hayakawa had an acting career in Japan before he arrived in the United States, except that he appeared in several stage dramas for Japanese American audiences at Little Tokyo in Los Angeles just before he signed a contract with Ince. He never went back to Japan to play in adaptations of Ibsen and Shakespeare after graduating from the University of Chicago. Also, Hayakawa did not enter the University of Chicago to study drama but rather political economy in order to help his family business later. Furthermore, Kawakami was not Hayakawa's uncle but rather that of his wife, Tsuru Aoki. Thus, Hayakawa's career was fabricated by the publicity departments of the NYMPC and Lasky and functioned to emphasize his legitimate acting capability by Western standards and his Americanized image.

Similarly, an article by Pearl Gaddis in *Motion Picture Classic* fictionalizes Hayakawa's Americanization process in the manner of an old romance and articulates Hayakawa's star image within the genteel tradition. Gaddis begins her article as if it were an old fairytale: "Once upon a time, in faraway Nipponland, where the moon hangs heavy o'nights; where the lazy breeze brings odors of indefinable sweetness; where the cherry-blossoms sway gently, casting fantastic, witching shadows, the God-of-Things-as They-Ought-to-Be planned a romance." Gaddis continues: One day, during a tour of Otto Kawakami and Madame Yacco, Hayakawa was shown a photograph of Aoki by Madame Yacco and instantly fell in love with her. Two years later, when Hayakawa played the leading role in *The Typhoon*, he finally met his dream girl. They fell in love right away. During the filming of a love scene in *The Typhoon*, Aoki got jealous and cried stormily, saying, "You say you love me—yet all the time you kiss her." To ease her feelings, Hayakawa made love to her that night; and the next day, they got married. It was "an American wedding, in an American church, with bridesmaids, orange-blossoms, Mendelssohn's Wedding March, and all the lovely, useless finery so dear guests [sic] who thronged the church and crowded the house for the reception were all American."[9]

This love affair between Hayakawa and Aoki that Gaddis reports is meant to enhance the American readers' psychological identification with the Japanese star couple. The more banal the story sounds, the more Americanized the couple looks. The structure of Western style romance turns the actual life of Hayakawa into that of a genteel romantic hero.

Gaddis also mixes Hayakawa's screen persona and his biography and fictionalizes Hayakawa's actual life story in accordance with his "Americanized Japanese" image in his star vehicles. According to Gaddis, Hayakawa's father recommended that Hayakawa should be Americanized in order to enlighten other Japanese people. He said to Hayakawa, "Go to America, to an American college. Learn the American ways—the American plays—all that is best in American drama. Then bring it back to your countrymen." This was almost exactly the same plot that was used in such Hayakawa star vehicles as *Hashimura Togo* and *The Secret Game* to emphasize Hayakawa's characters' Americanization.

An article by Warren Reed in *Picture-Play*, with its suggestive title, "The Tradition Wreckers: Two People Who Became Famous, Though Few People without Almond Eyes Can Pronounce Their Names," presupposes the Eurocentric notion of racial hierarchy. Reed emphasizes that Hayakawa and Aoki became successful in American films because they came out of their closed shells of Japaneseness and learned to become Americanized. Reed argues,

> We consider the Mongolian as uncannily intelligent and shrewd, and as a rice-eating athlete of endurance and prowess. Beyond that we scarcely consider him at all. But the Hayakawas contradict the common belief about the Easterner.

Their success is all the more splendid in contrast to their fellow countrymen who have from time to time played in America without gaining much popularity. . . . Hayakawa and his wife have pluckily overcome many obstacles. . . . By long and untiring effort they mastered the English language, . . . step by step [Hayakawa] has advanced in the art of dramatic interpretation, . . . his ability to register emotion by facial expression and gesture—something that could hardly be expected of a Jap.[10]

Reed thus claims that the Hayakawas ascended the steps of the racial hierarchy in the process of their Americanization.

The photos attached to the article emphasize the Hayakawas' Americanized lifestyle using Japanese Taste (see figs. 10, 11, and 12). In these photos, Hayakawa and Aoki wear Western clothes and dance a Western-style dance in front of Japanese-style furniture; Hayakawa reads English literature surrounded by Japanese objets d'art; Hayakawa and Aoki have tea while seated at a dining table; and the Hayakawas appear in Western clothes in front of the American-style bungalow with their dog. In these photos, the Hayakawas' Japanese traits symbolize their refined taste, a product of their own choice rather than a meaningful state of being in its specific cultural and historical context. It is a visual display of consumer culture that allows the middle-class readers to imitate them through the purchase of furniture of Japanese Taste.

Moreover, the third photo, because Hayakawa is wearing a Western suit and lighting a cigarette while being served tea by Aoki, who is wearing a kimono, also functions as a reminder of the race and gender relations of *Madame Butterfly*, in which a Japanese woman faithfully serves her American lover.[11] In a somewhat twisted manner, this photograph emphasizes the image of a patriarchal Victorian family.

The Cheat and Lasky's star-making strategy for Hayakawa changed not only the status of Hayakawa in the Hollywood film industry and among motion picture fans, but also that of Aoki. Aoki had started working in films earlier than Hayakawa did.[12] Aoki was the one who had introduced Hayakawa to Ince. The leading characters of Thomas Ince's "Japanese film" series, which started with *O Mimi San*, were originally played by Aoki.[13] The title role of *O Mimi San* was played by Aoki and the heroine of *The Wrath of the Gods* was Aoki.[14] Hayakawa merely played a supporting role in the latter as the heroine's elderly father. The *Reel Life*, the promotional magazine for films distributed by the Mutual Film Corporation, placed a still photo of Aoki, not Hayakawa, in *O Mimi San* on its cover on 7 February and on 20 June 1914.[15]

10 *The cover page of an article about Sessue Hayakawa and his wife.* Picture-Play Magazine 4.1 *(March 1917): 61.*

11 & 12 *Interior photos of the Hayakawas from the same article.* Picture-Play Magazine 4.1 *(March 1917): 63 and 64.*

The *Reel Life* had placed Aoki in *The Oath of O'Tsuru San* on its cover as early as 1 November 1913.[16] A NYMPC ad for *O Mimi San* in MPW and in MPN also used Aoki's photo, not Hayakawa's.[17] At the release of *O Mimi San*, MPW reported, "Lovers of motion pictures may soon see a most interesting actress in the Mutual 'movies,' Miss Tsura Aoki, a Japanese star of recognized ability in her own country, is competing for film honors."[18] Despite misspelling Aoki's first name, the MPW report featured Aoki, not Hayakawa. The MPN reported Aoki and Hayakawa's marriage in May 1914, but the report only included Aoki's portrait, not Hayakawa's.[19] At least during their careers at the NYMPC, Aoki had a more prestigious position than Hayakawa. As proof, the *Reel Life* published a one-page special article on Aoki in May 1914, but it never had an article specifically on Hayakawa until he left the company.[20]

However, the sensational success of *The Cheat* led Lasky to create a star image around Hayakawa that consequently drastically changed Aoki's public image. Aoki, who had married Hayakawa in 1914 after the shooting of *The Wrath of the Gods*, came to embody the image of ideal American middle-class domesticity. Aoki's image of a faithful wife in the domestic sphere enhanced that of Hayakawa's as a patriarchal husband in the United States, which functioned as a safety valve to reduce the threatening image of an alien of a different race. After *The Beckoning Flame* (Charles Swickard, 16 January 1916) at the NYMPC, Aoki eventually stopped playing leading roles. After 1916, in addition to fan magazine articles featuring Hayakawa, she only occasionally appeared as supporting characters in Hayakawa's star vehicles, such as *Alien Souls* and *The Honorable Friend*. In these films, her characters often served as ideal female immigrant bodies that are open to Americanization with the support of Hayakawa's characters. As a helping hand for Americanizing the newly arrived female Japanese immigrants, Hayakawa's characters functioned as an American regulatory agency. As a result, Aoki's characters functioned to enhance the heroic and successfully Americanized status of Hayakawa's characters.

Aoki thus played an important subordinate role in the formation of Hayakawa's stardom. Politics of gender were clearly observable in this formation, which placed certain constraints upon Aoki in defining her role in domestic settings. In fan magazine articles, Aoki mainly served as an ideal wife who would stay at home and create a refined domestic space with consumer products. Possibly, the image of *Madame Butterfly*, a devoted self-sacrificial Asian woman, was so strongly inscribed upon the Asian actress's on-screen image that it was difficult to distinguish Aoki's individual image as a star in early-twentieth-century America. Even a Chinese American actress, Anna May Wong, played a *Madame Butterfly* type of role in her early career in *The Toll of the Sea* in 1922. Compared to this persistent Asian female image based on an extremely popular narrative that was in accordance with the U.S. imperialist policy, an Asian male such as Hayakawa had relatively more flexibility to form his own star image.

An article in *Photoplay* titled "How to Hold a Husband: Mr. and Mrs. Hayakawa, in an Oriental Lesson in Four Chapters" more boldly places the Hayakawas as the model of an ideal Victorian family. This article first declares, "One may turn to Tsuru and Sessue with a considerable belief that they can really show a way to keep papa in nights. The divorce courts will now be watched for dwindling business, and more lessons will be published if necessary in this great cause." Even though part of the title of this article is "An Oriental Lesson," the captions for four photos of the couple are consistent with suggestions and "don'ts" from patriarchal Victorian family life, especially targeting wives, such as "Silence when he reads the paper at breakfast" or "Be artistic everywhere. Few men would chase a roof garden if they had a garden like this in the backyard."[21]

In Reed's article in *Picture-Play*, the Hayakawas are described as "cosmopolitan in their tastes."[22] Reed claims that there is "still another nationality represented—by the English bulldog." In Gaddis's article, the bulldog was publicized as American.[23] In 1916 the social philosopher Randolph Bourne proposed the notion of "cosmopolitanism" in American society, declaring "the failure of the 'melting-pot'" by the "discovery of diverse nationalistic feelings among our great alien population" at the advent of World War I. For the first time it was seen that the specific ethnic components did not necessarily disappear and assimilate. Bourne wrote,

> Whatever American nationalism turns out to be, it is certain to become something utterly different from the nationalism of twentieth-century Europe. . . . What we have achieved has been rather a cosmopolitan federation of national colonies, of foreign cultures, from whom the sting of devastating competition has been removed. America is already the world-federation in miniature, the continent where for the first time in history has been achieved that miracle of hope, the peaceful living side by side, with character substantially preserved, of the most heterogeneous peoples under the sun. . . . It is for the American of the younger generation to accept this cosmopolitanism, and carry it along with self-conscious and fruitful purpose.[24]

Bourne insisted, "Immigrants do not simply assimilate themselves to WASP culture, nor the reversal of that, but their dynamic mutual interference creates a brand new image of Americans." It was true that the majority of Americans still believed in the Anglo-conformity of immigrants and Bourne's cosmopolitanism was limited in its scope to a European multiculturalism. Yet, such cultural pluralists as Bourne formed a middle-class sociopolitical discourse toward cosmopolitanism at that time.

Lasky's strategy in forming Hayakawa's star image in magazine articles and Hayakawa's willingness to Americanize himself despite his Japanese cultural origins were mainly in accordance with Anglo-conformity. The *Los Angeles Times*, for instance, noted in December 1917, "Hayakawa still considers the land of the cherry blossoms as his home, but has lived and learned so much in the United States that he looks upon it as the land of his adoption."[25]

However, to a certain degree, Lasky and Paramount promoted the Japanese aspect of Hayakawa's star image along with the cosmopolitanism discourse, an image of transnational America, in addition to his Americanized image. Specifically, they emphasized Hayakawa's unique acting skill within the discourse of Japanese Taste and its cultural refinement and legitimacy. As Richard deCordova points out, the discourse on acting was "an important part of a larger strategy which asserted the respectability of the cinema and worked to guarantee the expansion of the audience."[26] The NYDM insisted that Hayakawa's way of performance would make motion pictures more legitimate. The report noted,

Once again he [Hayakawa] has proved the enormous effect that can be gained by repression. He seems to have applied the Japanese system of jiu jitsu to his acting, for nearly all of his effects are gained by yielding rather than by strenuous forcefulness. The expression of his face changes very little, yet that slight change is more than what he means but what he is thinking as well. He has the art of transmitting thought by means of facial expression down to an exact science, with the result that his acting never appears forced, and is for that reason all the more forceful and effective. We believe that he will advance very far on the motion picture stage if he is given the right opportunity.[27]

Lasky's and Paramount's strategy to attribute Japanese Taste to Hayakawa's star image was extensively exploited in articles in general magazines for middle-class readers. Charles K. Field's article in *Sunset* was one of these.[28]

Following Kingsley, Field first describes Hayakawa's Americanized family life: With a "bundle French bull" whose name is "Puppy" and "as Western as any Los Angeles bungalow-building," Hayakawa's lifestyle was, according to Field, "as far from Japan as possible," and apparently "nothing Japanese is left."

Field then moves on to locate Hayakawa's acting style in the line of Japanese theatrical arts, instead of Shakespeare and Ibsen, and to connect it to a renowned Japanese kabuki actor, Danjuro, in particular. Kabuki had been performed in the United States since 1904 and was considered a refined theatrical art form in the trend of Japanese Taste. Field concludes his article by emphasizing Hayakawa's Japaneseness, which was hidden behind his Westernized persona. He writes, "Watch Hayakawa on the screen some day; note how that subjective tension gets over to you, across the stage, across the ocean, indeed; observe how the corners of his handsome mouth, drawn suddenly down under emotional stress, or some swift posture of his body, albeit Western-clothed, will recall whatever you may have known of the tragic note in Japanese art. . . . Or, it may be Danjuro, come back in the ultra modern vehicle of the movies."[29]

Similarly, an article in the *Literary Digest* in November 1917, which was based on a report in the *Los Angeles Times*, articulates Hayakawa's star persona, based on his Japanese cultural background.[30] It describes how Hayakawa explains jiu-jitsu, his Japanese styles of acting, the meaning of death in Japan, the drama of Japan, and life in Japan. According to Hayakawa's explanation, "An old Samurai who had really studied ju-jutsu [*sic*]" can make someone who points his revolver at him put it down just by his "mysterious force." Hayakawa claims that the Japanese people "are all trained from childhood never to betray emotion with" their faces. This article regards Hayakawa as if he were a Japanese philosopher and a specialist of Japanese culture and assumes his unique performance was completely based on his Japanese philosophy. Hayakawa says, "To a Japanese death is nothing and is welcomed joyously," and "the favorite native Japanese plays are still full of sorrow and tears." According to Hayakawa, even though "the conditions of life are not soft in Japan," life is "more pleasant there," because "the amenities of life are more harmonious."[31]

The conversation between the interviewer and Hayakawa in this article is as if it were between a master of Japanese arts, culture, and religion, and a disciple. Despite his position of mastery, Hayakawa shows modesty to the American interviewer by wondering whether his opinion would hurt his feelings. Emphasizing Hayakawa's modesty and his sincere attempts to explain his cultural origin to middle-class readers and to adapt his cultural background to American filmmaking, this article provides Hayakawa with an image of an Americanized star, in spite of his mysterious different national background.

An article in *Current Opinion* properly locates the Japanese traits in Hayakawa's acting style and star persona in the middle-class discourse on Japanese Taste, cultural refinement, and morality.[32] Significantly, this article emphasizes that Hayakawa and Japanese filmmaking embody moral codes that are appropriate to middle-class American audiences. According to Hayakawa in this article, Japanese filmmakers have a "code of movie ethics" and avoid such motifs as "the sex triangle," "divorce, domestic infelicity, and belligerency between husband and wife," "murder, burglary, arson, crime of nearly every sort, treason or disloyalty to country," and ridiculing "persons in authority."

In fact, *jun'eigageki undo*, or the Pure Film Movement, sought to modernize and nationalize the film culture in Japan, especially in the Taisho period (1912–26). The movement, as I will discuss in more detail in a later chapter, corresponded to the "high-minded cultural aspiration of Taisho intellectuals" to "defend *bunka* [culture] before the onslaught of debasement which the masses promised to bring in their wake."[33] In the first two decades of the twentieth century, Japan was forming a culturally and politically active urban working class. The historian Carol Gluck argues that on a nationwide scale, with the rise of the urban lower class and worker agitation, "the greatest threat to the nation appeared . . . to come from within."[34] The *Tokyo Nichinichi Shinbun* stated, "As a result of motion picture theaters' showing sensational films competitively, they endanger public safety, throw social behavior into disorder, provide too much sensation to human minds, damage young people's character, make them sensual, and spoil their whole lives."[35] One of the major goals of the movement was to raise the status of motion pictures, which had been considered to be entertainment for the working class, up to high culture that would properly express middle-class culture as the national culture.

Simultaneously, the movement emphasized the social mission of cinema to enlighten the working class and stressed cinema's educational applications. As early as 1910, the film magazine *Katsudo Shashin Kai* insisted that motion pictures had to work to improve the taste of Japanese people, and the development of the motion picture would have an influence upon the Japanese national character.[36] The sociologist Gonda Yasunosuke claimed that Japanese-made films had "educational merit" in terms of "national morals."[37] The Ministry of Education started recommending particular films to Japanese audiences in 1916.[38] It is symbolic that *Katsudo no Sekai*, an educational magazine that originally started with the intention of advising Japanese young people on how to obtain success in their lives, turned in its third issue into a magazine devoted to cinema. The first essay of the inaugural issue, "Sokan ni nozomite" [For the first issue], announced that the magazine's goal was to "activate Japanese people's energy and spirit, to accompany their vigorous activities, and to move toward progress together with them," because "the development of a nation depends on its people's spirit, and its people's energy comes from their activities," and because "a nation will die out if its people do not act vigorously."[39] In the same magazine, Kamata Eikichi, the president of Keio University, proposed an application of the motion picture for education and "for the national interests."[40]

With these middle-class-oriented, education-oriented, and nationalist viewpoints on cinema's role in Japanese society, the movement even admitted governmental intervention into film culture. A film-journal editor wrote, "I would like to force the improvement of cinema in this regard by borrowing the power of the authorities."[41] In response, Numata Yuzuru, the chief of motion picture censorship at the Tokyo Metropolitan Police Department, insisted, "[motion pictures] have become a national and social enterprise. . . . It is necessary by any means to improve it. . . . No art form will progress without a true protector, and [the protector for motion pictures is] a nation, . . . and the Police Department is the direct force of the nation."[42] Then, the Tokyo Metropolitan Police established and enforced *Katsudo shashin kogyo torishimari kisoku* (Regulations on the motion picture exhibition) in 1917. The Tokyo Metropolitan Police started regulating films in the name of "public safety" and "public education."[43] In fact, the examples that Hayakawa gave of taboo subjects for Japanese filmmakers followed the Tokyo Metropolitan Police's list of prohibited subjects in "films," which was established along with the regulations and included such topics as "treason to the imperial or royal family," "opposition of the rebel against authority, or the defeat of authority," "criticism of and disloyal thoughts on the state and the government," "destructive thoughts on the current social system," "subversive thoughts on international relations," "slander of heroic historical figures and sacred figures," "display of criminal acts in such a way as to inspire imitation," "cruel torture or brutal penalty for good men, otherwise even for bad men," "obscenity," "adultery," "arousing low passions," "comic sarcasm or violation of domestic privacy," "any possibility that induces children to do various ways and sorts of mischief," and "any possibility that prevents education of children."[44]

It is significant that Hayakawa's examples of taboo subjects, most of which were in fact observed in the Tokyo Metropolitan Police's regulations, were very similar to those regulated by the National Board of Censorship (Reviews) of Motion Pictures in the United States. Generally, in 1917, the National Board would condemn or not permit,

[1] suggestive comedy;[45] [2] the details of uses of habit-forming drugs; [3] sex-suggestiveness;[46] [4] tampering with the mails and the equipment of railroads; [5] pernicious reflections on the army and navy; [6] emphasized brutality; [7] situations [that] tend to cause race hatred; [8] adulation of criminals in such a way as to inspire imitation;[47] [9] the details of suicides and murders; [10] the brutal treatment of women, children, and animals; [11] misrepresentations of ecclesiastics and criticism of the churches which might be considered slanderous; [and 12] detailed exposition of criminal incidents of such character as to be considered instructive in crime.[48]

In fact, the National Board already knew of the existence of the regulations in Japan in September 1916, even before the regulations were enforced. In a press release dated 1 September 1916, the National Board introduced Japan's "official pre-publicity censorship of motion pictures" with translations of some of the regulations.[49] From January 1918 until at least 1923, T. Tachibana, an officer of the Censor Section of the Tokyo Metropolitan Police, and the secretaries of the National Board corresponded with numerous letters and exchanged their opinions and information about motion picture censorship.[50]

The National Board of Censorship, which was established in 1909 by the People's Institute of New York as a voluntary extra-legal organization, started as an advisory committee for the New York exhibitors of motion pictures to evaluate and preview films prior to their public release. The National Board, with its continual correspondence with city officials and numerous social organizations (mayors, license bureaus, police departments, and boards of public welfare), attempted to improve the quality of popular motion pictures and to quell the wave of protests and attacks by social and religious groups against motion pictures. The National Board advised "regarding morally objectionable elements" in motion pictures and tried to codify films into workable middle-class standards, "morally, educationally and artistically," to guide the production and exhibition of motion pictures.[51] The major film producers later came to agree to submit their films to the committee and comply with any recommended changes.[52] Even though the National Board had no legal powers, there was very little indication that the producers deliberately ignored their suggestions. Moreover, for "the improvement of the public's taste in motion pictures," another prime aim of the board, the National Board held special programs, such as "family nights" or "children's matinees." Even though the National Board had a "compromise status" between the film industry and local or state censorship and its ability to effect any real changes in production and exhibition was questionable, according to the film historian Garth Jowett, it was "a prominent organization in the motion picture world before 1922," and its standards and policies were reported in many periodical and newspaper articles.[53]

Hayakawa certainly knew about the regulations in Tokyo, because some of his films, including *Alien Souls* and *The Wrath of the Gods*, were banned from exhibition by the regulations, even though his citation of the regulations was not necessarily exact. Hayakawa must have been familiar with the standards and policies of the National Board of Censorship, too, because his star vehicle *The Bottle Imp* (Marshall Neilan, 26 March 1917), a fantasy drama set in Hawaii based on Robert Louis Stevenson's novel, was exhibited at the Strand Theatre in New York in April 1917 and chosen as the first demonstration of the Better Films Movement initiated by the National Board, in cooperation with the New York Teachers' Association.[54] The National Board of Review thus had an influential role in regarding Hayakawa's star vehicles at Lasky as "better" films. The board codified Hayakawa as a master of refined culture using his image of the embodiment of Japanese Taste.

By referring to Hayakawa's version of the Japanese reform movement toward cinema and by implicitly locating his choice of words within the context of the National Board's "moral reform," articles in U.S. general magazines tried to fit Hayakawa's star image safely into the American middle-class sense of value.

THREE

Triple Consciousness

Sessue Hayakawa's Stardom at Haworth Pictures Corporation

(1918–22)

BALANCING JAPANESENESS
AND AMERICANIZATION

Authenticity and Patriotism in

His Birthright and *Banzai*

After two years of stardom at the Jesse L. Lasky Feature Play Company, Sessue Hayakawa established his own film production company, Haworth Pictures Corporation, in March 1918.[1] Already in 1916, before the release of *Alien Souls*, Hayakawa told a fan magazine that he was not satisfied with his roles in the films in which he had already appeared. He said, "Such roles [in *The Wrath of the Gods*, *The Typhoon*, and *The Cheat*] are not true to our Japanese nature. . . . They are false and give people a wrong idea of us. I wish to make a characterization which shall reveal us as we really are."[2] During the shooting of *The Cheat*, Hayakawa was said to have requested that Cecil B. DeMille correct the details of costume and behavior of Tori, but DeMille did not do it and simply calmed Hayakawa down by praising his performance in *The Typhoon* and *The Wrath of the Gods*.[3] Also in 1916, a newspaper reported Hayakawa's desire to portray a Japanese person "as he really is and not the way fiction paints him."[4]

Hayakawa's dissatisfaction with his roles in films by the NYMPC and Lasky was partly caused by the Japanese American communities' unfavorable reactions to them. Right after the release of *The Cheat*, the *Rafu Shimpo* severely criticized Hayakawa's character in the film and Hayakawa had to publish an apology immediately.[5] When *The Honorable Friend* was similarly criticized, Hayakawa quickly made an excuse that the film was not an anti-Japanese film.[6]

After these incidents, Hayakawa became anxious about his reputation among Japanese people in the United States and tried to get along with Japanese American communities, particularly in California. Hayakawa appeared in stage plays for Japanese audiences in Los Angeles to keep in touch with the Japanese community.[7] One article reported, "Hayakawa is continuing his daily work at the Lasky studios, aided by a big company of Japanese players, and at night these same actor folk appear in stock dramas at the newly opened Japanese theater. One wonders when Sessue is going to find time to sleep, but perhaps he, like Edison, is tireless and works on and on, with no need for sleep."[8] Hayakawa was also planning to open "a Japanese style theater," after the filming of *The Soul of Kura San*.[9]

Hayakawa became an associate member of Rafu Nihonjin-kai (Japanese association of Los Angeles) in April 1917.[10] When Nihonjin Katsudo Shashin Haiyu Kumiai (Union of Japanese motion picture actors) was established on 4 September 1917 for mutual communication and benefit and for prevention of anti-Japanese films, Hayakawa became the director.[11] On 4 July 1918, many ethnic communities, including the Japanese community in Los Angeles, paraded in their cultural costumes and dances to celebrate the Independence Day of America. Hayakawa coordinated with Rafu Nihonjin-kai to present a Japanese float at the patriotic fair. Ince asked Hayakawa to ask the Japanese people to participate in his twenty-four-foot float with eight horses, which cost about eight hundred dollars and was intended as a representation of Japanese warriors, past and present. It was meant to publicize Japan's co-operation with its ally.[12] Thus, Hayakawa actively worked as a connection between the U.S. and Japanese American communities.[13]

Under these conditions, what Hayakawa could have done at his company was to replace his star image created at Lasky with a more authentic image of a Japanese man that would not offend Japanese spectators. It could have been a nationalistic attempt to satisfy Japanese communities in the United States, which had been frustrated by the stereotypical images of Japan constructed in mainstream media. A declaration of independence from Lasky could have led Hayakawa to pursue this nationalistic goal, because Hayakawa had obtained enough power to control his films at Haworth. Hayakawa told trade journals that the first several films at Haworth were selected by himself.[14] According to Hayakawa, "300 people were working for me at the [Haworth] studio. . . . [The films made at the Haworth studio were] Mine. Just mine. . . . Nights I had to work, on cutting and writing scenarios. I had a scenario writer, but I had to go over it with him. All those things."[15]

In fact, at the launching of Haworth, Hayakawa declared that he would introduce authentic Japanese characters in realistic surroundings in his films. He announced that he would "produce eight films each year, and all of them would have plots dealing with Japanese subject matters."[16] The MPW reported,

> In these first productions and others which are to follow, he [Hayakawa] said a few days ago while discussing his work, 'I am happy to say I will have splendid opportunity for the kind of acting which most appeals to me and, I am sure, makes the most profound impression upon the audience—the repressive, natural kind, devoid of gesticulation and heroics. Danjuro, idol of the Japanese stage, was this sort of an actor. My aim is to be like him, and if I succeed I shall feel that I have not labored in vain before the camera.' . . . Hayakawa sent several of his company to Japan . . . to film scenes for the initial production. They have just returned, bringing with them about four thousand feet of film taken in Tokio and Yokohama and in the wonderfully beautiful Mt. Fujiyama region.[17]

Here, Hayakawa explained his aim to show more realistic Japanese characteristics, using Danjuro as an authentic model of the Japanese people. He also mentioned the departure of his production group to shoot actual images of Japan. According to Tsuru Aoki, Hayakawa was even planning to go back to Japan to make a film about Japan.[18]

Nevertheless, it is doubtful that Hayakawa seriously wanted to make films that would portray more authentic Japanese people and their characteristics. The method that Hayakawa took was hardly original. Many early travelogue filmmakers had been sent to Japan to obtain images that would look authentic to foreign audiences, such as Mount Fuji or geisha dances. Moreover, reference to Danjuro was the strategy that Lasky repeatedly took in fan magazines to construct Hayakawa's refined star image.

While admitting the fact that "the bias of those days against Orientals was a great help to me [and] we underscored it in our story-lines,"[19] Hayakawa confessed later, "[At Haworth] I was not about to change away from the type of picture which had earned me my fame and following." Hayakawa wrote,

> In these pictures and others [at Lasky] I was able to dispel the deep-stained conception of the Orient[al] as a man of mystery and a traditionally sinister figure. . . . Public acceptance of me in romantic roles was a blow of sorts against racial intolerance, even though I lost the girl in the last reel. . . . In my picture I often played a Japanese or a Chinese; but, thankfully for artistic reasons, not all of the time. In *The Jaguar's Claws*, for instance, I performed the role of a Mexican—a

man with a character like Juarez, subtle in his general conduct, rational, but stern, and when pressed, vicious. I liked the part very much.[20]

Hayakawa pragmatically realized that too faithful an adherence to Japanese realities might not be pleasingly exotic to American audiences. In order to make profits at his company, it was by all means necessary for Hayakawa to maintain, or enhance, his star image, which had been made for middle-class American audiences. Hayakawa's strategy at Haworth was a simultaneous campaign of winning the hearts of American audiences by clinging to his already established star image and convincing Japanese American communities of his more authentic depiction of Japanese characters.

A report in MPN implies that Hayakawa regarded it as more important to maintain his popularity among American audiences. "Hayakawa . . . has refused an offer to appear personally in the theaters of Japan. This would require at least three months, it is said, and the star does not wish to discontinue his motion picture work for that length of time."[21] While Hayakawa proudly announced that *Alien Souls* had a Japanese role "who shall do justice to the real Japanese characteristics," in reality, the film was banned from exhibition in Japan because the Japanese censors believed that "the film would insult Japanese people and enhance anti-American thought."[22] After *Alien Souls*, Hayakawa kept playing stereotypical characters for more than two years at Lasky. Therefore, Hayakawa's claim in 1916 to make films that would do justice to the Japanese national character sounded like a temporary excuse to Japanese American spectators who severely criticized *The Cheat*.

Before anything else, the name of Hayakawa's company, Haworth, symbolizes the careful mediation between his Americanized star image and his Japanese national identity to reestablish his popularity, which cut across racial lines. No record is left concerning the details of naming his company, but Haworth seems to be the combination of "Ha" from Hayakawa and "worth" from William Worthington, who was Hayakawa's right-hand man and directed twelve out of the first thirteen Hayakawa vehicles at Haworth. Hayakawa wrote in his autobiography, "Bill Worthington, and Jim Young [the director of the one other film out of the first thirteen Hayakawa films] directed all scenes except the ones in which I appeared. I preferred to direct those myself."[23] If Hayakawa had total control and intended to produce films targeting Japanese American audiences as he said, the name could have been "Hayakawa Pictures Corporation," because Worthington was just a director of the company. By adopting the Anglo-Saxon name Haworth Hayakawa paid particular attention to the Americanized aspect of his star image.

As for his own name, Hayakawa's real name was Hayakawa Kintaro. Sessue Hayakawa was a stage name. Moreover, Hayakawa Sesshu is the correct way to write and pronounce his stage name, according to the Chinese characters. Yet, it was written and pronounced Sessue Hayakawa and Hayakawa never changed it. Hayakawa's name itself is thus doubly fictionalized, targeting American audiences.

Even at his company, Hayakawa reconfirmed his biographical legend, especially the details about his career prior to making motion pictures, details that were created at the publicity departments of the NYMPC and the Jesse L. Lasky Feature Play Company.[24] In 1919, Hayakawa said, "I had been acting for several years in Japan before taking up motion picture work in this country."[25] Later, in his autobiography, Hayakawa finally confessed that he did not have any experience of acting before entering the film business.[26]

Thus, at his company, Hayakawa strategically chose to represent stereotypical Japanese traits for American spectators while at least verbally stressing authenticity in them to appeal to Japanese American audiences. There was a war of images that Hayakawa had to deal with in his stardom, at least among three elements, after the establishment of Haworth: the cultural stereotypes of Japanese people versus Hayakawa's star image made at Paramount-Lasky versus the identity politics that Hayakawa took on as Japanese at his company. Hayakawa's star image at Haworth can be called a product of Hayakawa's "triple-consciousness." W. E. B. Du Bois theorizes "double consciousness" as a "sense of always looking at one's self through the eyes of others."[27] Hayakawa, as a star and the center of the creative force, always looked at himself through the eyes of two different others: American audiences and Japanese spectators both in Japan and in the United States. As an American star, he had to think about adjusting his made-in-the-U.S.A. star image to Japanese spectators. As a Japanese actor, he needed to be conscious about his image of "otherness" for American audiences. And as himself, Hayakawa Kintaro, he was conscious of his alter ego's stardom. For Hayakawa both American and Japanese fit into Du Bois's sense of "others." In other words, Hayakawa stood in a "trans-position," distancing himself from American audiences and Japanese spectators in order to satisfy them both.[28]

He had to display Japaneseness that looked authentic to several different audience groups. He had to negotiate between his star image, created at Lasky to appeal to American audiences, and a more realistic image of Japanese people, an alternative to the stereotypical image in the dominant medium, which would please the Japanese spectators. Between 1910 and 1922, many audiences in the United States believed that, through their own initiative and action, they could directly influence the content and presentation of motion pictures. Moviegoers and exhibitors interacted on a regular basis until at least the end of 1922, when Paramount Studios came to acquire nearly six hundred theaters around the country in a process of vertical integration. As other studios followed Paramount, the relationship between the exhibitors and spectators became increasingly impersonal.[29] Yet, in 1918, the direct influence of the audiences' demands should have had significant influence on the newly established studio, Haworth.

Therefore, there was a performative nature in Hayakawa's re-creation of his star image. As Andrew Parker and Eve Kosofsky Sedgwick claim, "performativity" is an act of constructing "identities . . . through [a] complex citational process."[30] Judith Butler insists, "Gender is an 'act,' as it were, that is open to splittings, self-parody, self-criticism."[31] In the case of Hayakawa's star image, his racial, cultural, or national identity somewhat appeared as an "act" "through [a] complex citational process." No matter how stereotypical, or authentic, the Japaneseness Hayakawa represented in his films made at Haworth was chosen strategically by Hayakawa himself. It was role-playing of an imagined self for others and left a certain degree of authority to Hayakawa over his star image and his portrayal of his nationality. In other words, when he had an opportunity to obtain authority over his star image for the first time, Hayakawa needed to "mimic" the stereotypical Japanese image in American popular discourse.[32] The self-reconstruction of Hayakawa's star image thus appeared at the dialogic focal point of three different groups: himself, Japanese communities (and eventually Japan, across the Pacific),[33] and American spectators.

Advertisements of Haworth that appeared in trade journals indicate Hayakawa's well-balanced strategy to reconstruct his star image. The emphasis of an ad of Haworth that appeared in *MPW* on 9 March 1918 was on Hayakawa's Americanized image; the ad featured a large portrait photo of Hayakawa in a tuxedo (see fig. 13).[34] In contrast, an ad that appeared in the next issue of *MPW* emphasized Hayakawa's Japanese characteristics. A small photo of Hayakawa in a kimono was displayed together with his signature in Japanese and a caption that said, "Watch for Hayakawa Productions made by most unique of all screen stars: son of Japan now heading his own company." These images were surrounded by drawings of stereotypical Japanese objects, such as a torii, a shrine gate, and a stone lantern (see fig. 14).[35] Then, a third ad, which appeared in *MPW* two months later, provided an eclectic image of Hayakawa that emphasized both his Japanese traits and his Americanized image by using a photo of him in a suit surrounded by drawings of stereotypical Japanese images: a torii and Mount Fuji (see fig. 15).[36]

Hayakawa's attempt to balance his Americanized star image and a more realistic representation of Japanese characteristics is also indicated in an article in a fan magazine. Truman B. Handy, in his article titled "Kipling Was Wrong!: West Isn't West, nor Is East East, as Far as the Hayakawas Are Concerned," emphasizes Hayakawa's conscious struggle to reconcile or compromise between East and West. Even though "Hayakawa's great ambition is to epitomize the history of his country in films," according to Handy, Hayakawa admitted "how extremely difficult it is for him to get vehicles that are Oriental, and yet have an Occidental appeal. Japanese legends aren't at all satisfactory. They're not dramatic enough, and they're . . . too strictly local, without enough universal appeal."[37]

Hayakawa's strategy for reconstructing his star image at Haworth is typically observed in *His Birthright* (William Worthington, 1 or 8 September 1918), the first film released by Haworth. Hayakawa was one of the authors of the original story and therefore had full control over the plot material.[38]

In *His Birthright*, Hayakawa plays Yukio, a young Japanese man born of a Japanese mother and an American father, Lieutenant John Milton of the U.S. Navy. Yukio has been raised in a Japanese fishing village by a servant of his mother. When he turns twenty-one, he learns that his mother, who had been brokenhearted at the desertion of her husband, had stabbed herself to death while he was still a baby. He goes to America as a cabin boy to take revenge on his father. He confides his intention to Edna, a German spy. She persuades Yukio to steal important documents from his father, in return for which she promises her love. When he learns that her professed love is false, Yukio's sense of honor leads him to fight the German spies. Realizing that his father has always loved his mother, Yukio abandons his ideas of revenge and determines to enlist in the service of America.

The only surviving print of *His Birthright* opens with a shot on the deck of a boat.[39] Yukio, in the white uniform of a cabin boy, walks toward the camera, with a tray of cocktails in his left hand. Since there is no explanation about the character and the situation, the original opening sequences, supposedly set in Japan, are clearly missing in this print. The *MPW* noted, "A Japanese

13 *An ad for Sessue Hayakawa and Haworth Pictures Corporation.* Moving Picture World 35.9 (9 March 1918): 1332.

14 *An ad for Hayakawa Productions sponsored by Haworth Pictures Corporation.* Moving Picture World 35.10 (16 March 1918): 1467.

15 *An ad for Hayakawa Productions sponsored by Haworth Pictures Corporation.* Moving Picture World 36.8 (18 May 1918): 960.

atmosphere has been cleverly contrived as a background for the opening of the story."[40] According to a Japanese film trade journal, *Kinema Junpo*, the first shot of *His Birthright* is Mount Fuji and the story starts at Port Uraga, where Commodore Matthew Perry arrived in the 1850s. The journal notes, "It is clear from its opening shot of Mt. Fuji and its opening scene at Uraga port that this film was made to make foreigners understand our country's culture and custom."[41] According to the review in ETR, "The scenes in Japan are exquisite with the Japanese gardens, wisteria bowers, tea houses, geisha girls and cunning Japanese children."[42] The MPW and EH also stated in reviews of Hayakawa's next film, *The Temple of Dusk* (James Young, 13 or 20 October 1918): "As in 'His Birthright,' the first production, many of the scenes are laid in Japan. The settings and locations show with wonderful fidelity the exquisite beauty of the Kingdom of Flowers and the quaint and picturesque life of the Nipponese."[43]

In this extant print there are only three shots that are supposedly set in Japan, all of which appear in flashbacks. Probably, these three remaining shots were not shot in Japan but in Los Angeles, because Tsuru Aoki appears in these shots and there is no record that Aoki went back to Japan for the filming of *His Birthright*. It is a pity that we cannot thoroughly examine how authentically *His Birthright* presented Japanese landscapes and characters in its opening scenes, which were supposedly shot in Japan. Yet, it is noteworthy that the re-created Japanese landscape in the remaining three shots does not particularly emphasize exoticism or theatrical Japaneseness as did some of Hayakawa's films at the NYMPC and at Lasky.

The first of these three shots is Milton's flashback. Milton, in his naval uniform, flirts with a Japanese woman in a kimono. The location is a Japanese garden. There is a temple-like building and a balustrade of a Japanese bridge in the background. Other than these objects and the two people, we only see trees in this long shot. The garden is not filled with strange Japanesque objects. It does not look as theatrical as the Japanese sequences in *O Mimi San* and *The Typhoon*.

The second shot, which is also Milton's flashback, is a long shot of the Japanese woman who flirted with Milton in the first shot holding a baby. The third shot, Yukio's flashback, is a frontal medium shot of the Japanese woman in a white kimono. She looks up and raises both of her arms. She has a small Japanese sword in her left hand. Even though the third shot looks more theatrical because of her ritualistic action, there is almost no strange exoticization with her kimono and Japanese-style hair in any of the shots. The sleeves of her kimono in the second and third shots are short and are appropriate for a married woman, while those in the first shot are long and are only for un-married women. Her hair in the second and third shots looks like *marumage*, a hairstyle for a married woman, while in the first flashback her hair looks like *shimada*, a more garish hairstyle usually for a young woman. Also, there is no forced emphasis on Japanese traits in these shots, except for a stone lantern. If we presume from these shots with their more precise details in the sets, costumes, and makeup, Japanese landscape and characters in *His Birthright* look much more authentic than those in Hayakawa's films made at the NYMPC and at Lasky.

The name of Hayakawa's Japanese character, Yukio, is authentically Japanese. While Hayakawa had earlier played stereotypical Japanese characters with strange Japanesque names, such as Nitobe Tokoramo (*The Typhoon*) or Hishuru Tori (*The Cheat*), at Haworth Hayakawa played six Japanese characters with correct Japanese names in a row before he returned to playing other Asian roles in *The Man Beneath* (Worthington, 6 July 1919): Yukio, Akira, Sasamoto, Sakurai, Toyama, and Goro Moriyama. As Hayakawa declared, the first film made at Haworth looked more authentic on its surface than his previous films.[44]

However, beneath its surface, *His Birthright* exploits the same motifs as Hayakawa's star vehicles at Lasky. The plot of *His Birthright* utilizes the archetypal narrative of *Madame Butterfly*, which Lasky often referred to in Hayakawa's star vehicles. *Variety* points out that the film "followed the lines of John Luther Long's story."[45] In fact, *His Birthright* was originally entitled "Butterfly's Son," something "like a sequel of *Madame Butterfly*."[46] As the flashbacks set in Japan suggest, a U.S. naval officer falls in love with a Japanese woman but leaves her in Japan. After giving birth to her son, she takes her own life with a dagger, like Cio-Cio-San.

Moreover, the plot of *His Birthright* follows that of *The Soul of Kura San*, in which a Japanese man travels to America to avenge a Japanese woman's death. Frances Guihan, the writer of *The Soul of Kura San*, wrote the scenario of *His Birthright*. *His Birthright* is also a spy film like *The Secret Game*, as MPW summarizes the plot, "How a Vengeful Heart Was Turned to Loyalty by Voice of Conscience. . . . Thrilling Story of Vengeance and Retribution in Spy Plot. The Strange Case of a Japanese Villain Who Reformed."[47]

More than anything else, *His Birthright* uses one of the most prominent devices that Lasky took to form Hayakawa's star image: the motif of Americanization that positions Japanese people in the middle ground of a racial and cultural hierarchy between white and nonwhite. In Hayakawa's star vehicles at Lasky, Hayakawa's characters become sympathetic first and foremost because they aspire to Americanize their lifestyles. Similarly, *His Birthright* depicts how Yukio Americanizes himself.

In the beginning, Yukio is characterized as a culturally unrefined person. In one scene, Yukio works as a valet at a party and watches an African American orchestra. He moves his hands exactly in rhythm with the orchestra. Then, he turns to the guests dancing gracefully. In his point-of-view shot, the guests do not look in harmony with the rhythm. Yukio frowns and tilts his head. Here, the Japanese man and the African American people are juxtaposed in terms of their way of appreciating music. They are clearly contrasted to white people.

Yukio's barbarous nature is most strikingly portrayed in a scene in which he brutally attacks a white woman. When Yukio finds out that the female German spy has cheated him, he jumps at her, grabs her by the neck, and pushes her down on a sofa. He tries to strangle her. The medium shot of Yukio grabbing her naked shoulder exactly follows that of Tori, branding a white woman in *The Cheat*. When her bodyguards enter the room, Yukio throws them away one by one, using jiu-jitsu, a Japanese martial art, which could function as a visual signifier of premodern culture.

However, in this scene it is very clear that Yukio shows this "primitiveness" only for the good of the American people. The white woman who angers Hayakawa is a villainous character who attempts to subvert the order of American society. In a sense, this visual reference to Tokoramo and Tori, who try to avenge their tragic interracial romances, paradoxically functions to express the Americanized characteristic of Yukio, who tries to defend the peace of American society by attacking the villainous woman, as Hayakawa's character did in *Forbidden Paths*. In other words, by referring to those stereotypically villainous characters that he played, Hayakawa tried to overcome or reverse the threatening image of an inassimilable Japanese man in those films and transform it to that of an Americanized one.

In other scenes, Yukio is regarded as an illiterate child. Yukio shows his unreadable handwritten memo to his mistress and is scolded by her. When his female friend helps him remember what he wrote, he puts his hands together in front of his chest and jumps for joy like a child. Then, when Yukio wears a tuxedo and a top hat, a maid laughs at him and says, "What an enfant terrible!"

According to the film historian Gaylyn Studlar, youth culture reformers of the early twentieth century "agreed that the instincts of boys from nine to fourteen were 'savage.'"[48] For instance, George Walter Fisk stated that, "the whole process of child development like race development is a climb upward from savagery through barbarism to civilization."[49] Douglas Fairbanks Sr., Hayakawa's friend and another big star at the early period of the Hollywood star system, represented an ideal model of primitive boys becoming civilized American men. In the 1910s and into the 1920s, Fairbanks Sr. embodied this "development" of "boys" with "instinctive behaviors of animal origin to be modulated by morality and other qualities (such as sexual purity)." The star image of Fairbanks Sr. was "a perfectly balanced, vigorous manhood that combined the primitive and the genteel."[50]

Similarly, *His Birthright* is a story of Yukio's growing up from a boy to a man, juxtaposed as his development from savagery to civilization. Yet, contrary to Fairbanks Sr., in the case of Hayakawa in *His Birthright*, a racial discourse was clearly woven into the child discourse. Both childlikeness and racial difference were to be Americanized.

By the end of the narrative, Yukio becomes a loyal son of America. He is actually half white American in the narrative. As ETR notes, "The birth of patriotism in the heart of the young Japanese boy is graphically pictured" in *His Birthright*.[51] When Yukio attacks the female German spy at the climax, he looks directly toward the camera in a medium close-up and points at the camera with his right forefinger. Frowning a little, Yukio exactly copies the famous pose of Uncle Sam in patriotic posters, saying "I Want You for U.S. Army." In this shot, the makeup, the lighting, and the performance style function to emphasize Yukio's Americanization. Yukio's face looks white in the strong key lighting and with the white makeup.

In the final scene, Yukio hears something, stands up from his working desk, and walks to a window. He moves his hands in rhythm with the music that he hears. This time, it is not a dance number played by an African American orchestra, but a march played by a U.S. Navy band. In the beginning, Yukio identifies himself with an African American orchestra, but in this final sequence, he comes to identify himself with a U.S. Navy band. As Yukio climbs up the racial hierarchy, his music preference changes. Thus, in *His Birthright*, music signifies a racial identification.

In the final spoken title, in which a picture of an American soldier and a Japanese soldier saluting each other in front of their national flags is drawn, Yukio states, "I am willing to give my life for the Stars and Stripes—your country—OUR country." Yukio's white American father embraces his son at this point as if he were blessing him as a completely Americanized man.

In the publicity for *His Birthright*, Hayakawa again followed Lasky's strategy, which mainly targeted American middle-class audiences: mixing actuality and fiction. The fusion was achieved on two levels: between Hayakawa's biography and the story of *His Birthright*, and between an authentic Japanese object and a stereotypical image of the object. Hayakawa was quoted in a report in *ETR*:

> "His Birthright," in which the famous sword of the Samurai is involved, uses a sword in the production which has been in the Hayakawa family for 400 years. Hayakawa belongs to one of the oldest families in Japan, one whose traditions involve the succession of the oldest son to the family troubles and guardianship of the family honor. He is also custodian of the family sword—most precious of family possessions.
>
> "Time was—not so long ago either"—remarked the actor a few days ago, "when a man's honor consisted in his preservation of certain traditions that in some instances were not worthy of preservation. Among these was a too ready use of the sword to avenge insults, sometimes imaginary ones."
>
> "Now we take our troubles to the courts, just like Americans. The sword of the Samurai is a noble tradition, but we don't use it with old time indiscriminacy. It hangs on the wall in the place of honor among the portraits of our ancestors who were good old fighters of a different regime."[52]

Here, Hayakawa fictionalized his biography and the origin of the sword in accordance with the plot of *His Birthright* and the stereotypical images of Japanese culture.

Hayakawa's strategy to appeal to American audiences in *His Birthright* was successful, according to the reviews in trade journals. A reviewer at *ETR* claimed, "one of the best things he [Hayakawa] has done, and promises well for future Hayakawa pictures under this management."[53] According to the two-page ad for *The Temple of Dusk*, Hayakawa's next film, *His Birthright* "proved one of the big box office winners of the season."[54]

After *His Birthright*, Hayakawa made a short film, *Banzai*, a promotional film for the Liberty Loan Campaign. When the U.S. government announced the third Liberty Loan Drive for April and May 1918, which aimed to raise three billion dollars to support the war effort, Hayakawa joined a large group of speakers, including such movie stars as Charlie Chaplin, Douglas Fairbanks Sr., and Mary Pickford. The MPW reported, "Sessue Hayakawa, the Japanese star of the Haworth Pictures Corporation, was the first screen player to appear at the tank, and in less than an hour disposed of bonds valued at $6,500."[55] The *Rafu Shimpo* proudly reported that Hayakawa sold $25,000 in bonds, which "surpasses that of Griffith and Fairbanks," and "Sessue's act to sell bonds the other night contributed to promote Japan's reputation."[56] The purchase of the bonds was a visibly Americanized, or patriotic, activity. Thus, while publicizing his loyalty to the United States to American fans, Hayakawa acted as an ideal representative of Japanese American communities in California who would enhance the favorable national image of Japan among Americans.

Not only his patriotic public performance but the film *Banzai* clearly indicates Hayakawa's intention to enhance his popularity among American audiences, while being conscious about his reputation among Japanese American communities. In *Banzai*, Hayakawa adopted two devices to emphasize his and Japan's loyalty to the United States. First, *Banzai* confirms a favorable image of Japan in opposition to that of Germany. *Banzai* forces the image of the yellow peril upon German soldiers. German soldiers are demonized with the images of an ape, death, alcoholism, and a threat to white women. The film opens with a theatrical set of German headquarters. The intertitle, with pictures of an ape-like man with big ears and fangs wearing a helmet, reads, "Swine! Filthy Yanks! Who produce money-mad weaklings to fight [the] U.S. Their talk of billions is 'Bluff.' All 'Bluff.'" A soldier with a bottle of champagne in his hand and two white women under his arms enters the room and asks the general, "How about that champagne party in Paris, General?" The general grabs a woman's arm, forcefully embraces her, and says, "Next month. Then in the Fall, a celebration in New York, and all American women will belong to German Soldiers." The intertitle has a picture of white people captured by the hands of a huge black monkey.

Second, a racial masquerade positively blurs the difference between an Americanized Japanese man and an American man in *Banzai*. The NYDM notes, "Sessue Hayakawa as a Japanese soldier in the United States Army in his Liberty Loan film 'Banzai,'" while the synopsis that the Library of Congress provides writes that he plays an American soldier who saves white women from the Germans.[57] Thus, Hayakawa's character's nationality was conceived ambiguously in the film's reviews.

In the film, an American soldier with a blonde mustache comes into the German headquarters right after the German general attacks the white woman. He shoots the German general and opens the door for other American soldiers. He tears down the German flag on the wall and replaces it with an American flag. Then, he says, "The bluff called, Four Liberty loans oversubscribed. Your dollars, turned into bullets, won the war. The Victory is ours. The war is over." The following extreme long shot reveals that the sequence has been played on a stage. The shot/reverse shot structure shows American audiences in the theater clapping at actors, who play American soldiers in front of the American flag on the stage.

The American soldier takes off his helmet and peels off his fake mustache. Hayakawa's dark hair and his Japanese face are revealed. Hayakawa frowns slightly, posing like Uncle Sam with his finger pointing at the camera, and says, "Applause didn't win the war. The boys backed by your Liberty bonds, did. Applause will not bring them home or pay the war bills. Your dollars in the victory Liberty Loan will. I am not talking to the man near you— but to you—the real American." In the following medium shot Hayakawa raises his right fist and cries out, "Banzai!," then raises both arms and repeats "BANZAI!" Even though the Japanese word "Banzai" indicates Hayakawa's Japanese nationality, what Hayakawa represents is a completely Americanized Japanese man. Hayakawa masquerades as a white American man and makes the audience conscious of his racial difference as Japanese. However, at the same time, by playing a patriotic white American role, he emphasizes his appropriately Americanized self. Studlar suggests, "Americans had regarded the Great War as a moral crusade that, in the words of the *Washington Post*, could turn any 'slacking, dissipated, impudent lout' into a[n American] man."[58] Hayakawa does not intend to pass as white, but tries to display his pseudo-white American status (again, a racial middle ground) in *Banzai*.

Thus, the first two Hayakawa films made at Haworth were, in fact, pro-American war propaganda films. While "more realistic" Japanese landscapes or characters certainly exist in both films, as proofs of Hayakawa's concerns about his reputation among Japanese American communities, the more significant motifs in these films are the protagonists' Americanization and their loyalty to the United States. Hayakawa strategically followed these motifs, which had been continuously exploited in his star vehicles at Lasky. Therefore, Hayakawa's first two films at Haworth can clearly be called the products of "triple consciousness": a result of Hayakawa's negotiation among himself as the head and the star of his own company, American audiences, and Japanese American spectators.

RETURN OF THE AMERICANIZED ORIENTALS

Robertson-Cole's Expansion and Standardization
of Sessue Hayakawa's Star Vehicles

Т he structure of the film distribution system, which connects film
production and exhibition, was fully developed in the American film
industry in the 1910s. It was inevitable that the distributor, which
would directly know exhibitors' demands, would eventually obtain a certain
degree of influence upon the independent studio's policy and the contents
of its films. Since Haworth was an independent production company, it required a dependable distributor that would secure exhibitors to show its films.
Haworth contracted with the Robertson-Cole Distributing Corporation, a
new face in the film distributing business. Since Haworth did not enter the
distribution business, Hayakawa did not acquire complete autonomy regarding his work. Sooner or later, this split between production and distribution
would come to have a serious influence upon Hayakawa's star image.

The English-born Harry F. Robertson and the American Rufus Sidman
Cole formed Robertson-Cole as an import-export firm in 1918. For them,
the film business was originally a sideline to that of automobiles and tea.[1]
In the beginning, with its ample funds, Robertson-Cole functioned as the
connecting link between independent film production companies, including
Haworth, and the distributor, the Exhibitors' Mutual Corporation, an out-
growth of the Mutual Film Corporation, which had distributed films for many
years. Robertson-Cole purchased films from independent manufacturers and
sold them to Exhibitor's Mutual, which then sold the films to exhibitors.

The *MPW* reported in December 1918, "The Robertson-Cole Company
buys the subjects purely on their merit, not permitting the influence of . . .
distributor to play any part in the transactions. This allows the manufacturer
to devote his entire time to the manufacture of good subjects."[2] Yet, the

"manufacture of good subjects" did not mean that Robertson-Cole allowed filmmakers to have complete freedom. Robertson-Cole requested films that would appeal to the popular audience. Percival M. Reynolds, a traveling special representative of the Robertson-Cole Company in New York, suggested that it is important "to learn the needs of the exhibitor and just the kind of film subjects which [Robertson-Cole's] patrons like best, and also the kind they don't like. . . . In this way the Robertson-Cole Company is aiming to produce films which will make the widest possible appeal."[3]

In October 1919, Robertson-Cole restructured its distributing system and expanded its influence in the film distributing business.[4] The MPW reported, "There is no more pronounced evidence of the rapid growth of the Robertson-Cole Company than the extremely large number of first run houses which are booking its pictures. . . . Less than five months after its initial feature had been distributed in the domestic field, Robertson-Cole is now placing its output in many of the highest type of motion picture theatres in the United States and Canada."[5] Robertson-Cole continued to distribute Haworth films through 1920, when Haworth was integrated into Robertson-Cole, which by then had also begun producing films. As Robertson-Cole rapidly expanded its position in the film distribution and production businesses, it became necessary for Hayakawa to negotiate more seriously with it regarding the production of his star vehicles.

No official record is left that describes how the relationship between Hayakawa and Robertson-Cole changed after Robertson-Cole expanded its film business. However, the reports and advertisements in trade journals and the contents of Hayakawa's films indicate that, throughout the year 1919, Robertson-Cole began to take the initiative in its business relations and to have a stronger influence on Haworth's films, with a corresponding decrease in Hayakawa's control over his own company.

With *Bonds of Honor* (William Worthington, 19 January 1919), the third feature film of Hayakawa at Haworth, the name of Robertson-Cole began to appear in ads in trade journals. With *A Heart in Pawn* (Worthington, 10 March 1919), the following film, trade journals came to regard Robertson-Cole, instead of Exhibitors Mutual, as the distributor of Hayakawa's star vehicles. As Mori Iwao, a Japanese film critic and screenwriter, reported, the films made at Haworth were distributed by Mutual in the beginning, but as Mutual became stagnant, Robertson-Cole took over.[6] With *His Debt* (Worthington, 25 May 1919), trade journals started calling Haworth one of "the Robertson-Cole Company's various units."[7] In June 1919, Robertson-Cole, instead of Haworth, started publicizing Hayakawa's films in trade journals. With *The Man Beneath* (Worthington, 6 July 1919), reviews in trade journals stopped calling Hayakawa's vehicles "Mutual-Haworth Productions" and identified them as a "Robertson-Cole feature" or as the films "released by Robertson-Cole."[8]

In August 1919, Robertson-Cole made a new contract with Haworth. After that, in the ads for Hayakawa's films, the words "Robertson-Cole Productions" were printed at the top of the page and the size of the letters were larger than "Produced by Haworth" at the bottom of the page (see fig. 16).[9]

In September, Robertson-Cole announced that it would start a new series called "Hayakawa Superior Pictures."[10] Robertson-Cole made an arrangement to distribute this series on an expanded scale. It announced, "The series of eight Hayakawa productions will start in over 4,000 houses. . . . When the first Hayakawa picture was released just a few years ago it was shown in a few first run houses."[11] The *EH* noted, "Almost five thousand theaters will show the new Hayakawa pictures and this number will without doubt be greatly increased before the first is released."[12] Robertson-Cole even started issuing extensive press books of the Hayakawa Superior Pictures brand. According to *MPW*, they were "the most elaborate" press books, which included advance notices, reviews, stills, lobby display photos, catchlines for ads, projectionists' cues, musical settings, and so forth, and they were extended to exhibitors as "a complete guide and advertising aid."[13]

Right before Robertson-Cole and Hayakawa signed their new contract, Robertson-Cole placed a two-page ad for Hayakawa in *EH* and a four-page one in *MPN*. Both ads clearly stated that Hayakawa was "a Robertson-Cole star." These ads did not emphasize Hayakawa's Japanese traits, as Haworth had done. Instead, Robertson-Cole's ads underscored that Hayakawa had an "Oriental" characteristic, stating, for instance, "He [Hayakawa] adds the distinction of being alone in his chosen sphere, the interpretation of those parts which only an Oriental can successfully portray for an audience of the Western World. Sensational or unpleasant subjects are always avoided and Hayakawa carries with him the full support of those who love the mystery and beauty of the Oriental World as well as the superb finish of a great actor."[14] Apart from Haworth's limited but purposeful emphasis on the "authentic" Japaneseness in Hayakawa's films, Robertson-Cole's promotional campaign for Hayakawa more intensely targeted the reception by American audiences. Robertson-Cole deviated from a specific representation of Japan and the Japanese people in its films and ads and decided to revitalize Hayakawa's

ROBERTSON-COLE PRODUCTIONS

S E S S U E

HAYAKAWA

in

The Gray Horizon

A PRODUCTION of the most gorgeous beauty, pronounced by great artists a master-piece of photography. The splendor of the set-tings is equalled only by the powerful dramatic intensity of the theme.

Produced by
HAWORTH

Distributed by
Exhibitors Mutual

16   *An ad for* The Gray Horizon. Moving Picture World *41.9 (30 August 1919): 1234.*

popularity by emphasizing his more inclusive and stereotypical "Oriental" images.

In December 1919, Robertson-Cole published a one-page ad in trade journals that thanked Thomas Ince for discovering Hayakawa. The ad noted, "Thank you Mr. Ince. We noticed with extreme pleasure in the trade papers of November 15th that you took pride in announcing Sessue Hayakawa . . . as [a star] of your discovery."[15] This ad indicated Robertson-Cole's intention to follow Ince's stereotypical portrayal of Japan and the Japanese people in its films with Hayakawa.

In the beginning, Hayakawa did not seriously oppose Robertson-Cole's intervention because Hayakawa himself had been desirous of enhancing his popularity among American audiences when he established Haworth. There were even some mixed reviews of Hayakawa's first several films at

Haworth in trade journals, in spite of their overall critical successes. In April 1919, MPW reported, "Beyond question, he [Hayakawa] is one of the most popular players on the screen today, and a glance at the Exhibitors Mutual booking records is sufficient to prove this assertion."[16] Yet, in September 1918, a reviewer at Wid's Daily had criticized His Birthright by noting that the film was "carefully produced as to characterizations and atmosphere but is held down by much unnecessary detail and painfully slow tempo."[17] The "unnecessary detail and painfully slow tempo" were possibly caused by the film's too serious attempt to "do justice to real Japanese character." Too much emphasis on detailed Japanese traits might not have an appeal to the mainstream American audiences. This was why trade journals suggested to exhibitors regarding Hayakawa's films at Haworth: "Fix your ad copy up with Japanese trimmings, always, however, making sure to mention the fact that an American drama is presented."[18] In a fan magazine, it was even reported in 1919 that "The Great Sessue Hayakawa Has Not Been So Successful Since He Left Lasky."[19]

By 1919, some trade journals began to problematize Hayakawa's stardom in terms of his nationality. On Bonds of Honor, Wid's Daily commented, "Sessue Hayakawa is a difficult star to fit with screen material. So many things are of necessity eliminated, for social or political reasons, that he is fortunate when a story of good quality and free from anything likely to give offense comes his way."[20] Some fans in early 1919 worried about Hayakawa's possible decline in popularity because of his nationality. A magazine editor responded to a fan's question about Hayakawa:

Sanatorium Intern: I have not seen Sessue Hayakawa featured very much lately, and as he is a great favorite of mine, would you kindly give me a few facts concerning him, if space will permit? Is his popularity decreasing or is it because of his nationality that he is held back?

A: While Sessue Hayakawa is not shown as much as heretofore it does not reflect upon his talent or ability, and being a Japanese does not handicap him in his film work, for he has shown that he is equally as capable in the histrionic art as some of the more widely exploited artists. Personally, he is a man of many and varied accomplishments, and being an expert linguist, he is thoroughly conversant with American and Oriental customs.[21]

These views that questioned the popularity of Hayakawa's films and his star image made Hayakawa more anxious about his appeal to American audiences. Under such conditions, Hayakawa was willing to fully utilize the motifs and characterizations that popularized him at Lasky.

The film historian Richard Koszarski writes, "More conservative business practices adopted during the twenties acted to freeze many stars into repeated variations of familiar routines. Performers who a decade earlier had constantly developed and expanded their roles were now content to exploit their audience-tested images."[22] This was what Hayakawa did after 1919. Especially after *The Courageous Coward* (Worthington, 14 April 1919), using standardized plots, motifs, and characterizations, Hayakawa's films and his star image began to "repeat" his "audience-tested images," which had been successfully made at Lasky. Symbolically, for the first time at Haworth, in *The Courageous Coward*, Hayakawa accepted a character's name, Suki, which is not appropriately Japanese.

Then, the most prominent thematic motif of Hayakawa's star vehicles at Lasky returned in full. Hayakawa had already used the motif of self-sacrifice in the second film at Haworth, *The Temple of Dusk*, which MPW called a "Story of Great Love and Final Sacrifice in Living True to Ideal Devotion. . . . Photoplay of Deep Interest Typifying Oriental Ideals and Devotion."[23] Hayakawa hired Frances Marion, who wrote *The City of Dim Faces*, a self-sacrificial melodrama made at Lasky, as a writer of the scenario of *The Temple of Dusk*. Hayakawa declared confidently, "*The Temple of Dusk* will be received well among Americans."[24] In *The Temple of Dusk*, Hayakawa plays Akira, a young Japanese poet "of the Samurai clan." Akira falls in love with a young American woman who is under his father's care in Tokyo after her father has died. To be faithful to her father's will, she marries an American millionaire. After the woman dies three or four years later, her child is left in the care of Akira. The American man marries a new wife, but he shoots her former lover out of jealousy. Akira takes the blame for the crime for the child's sake. When the child writes to him that she is lonesome, he escapes from prison to see the child. He is shot to death. At the Temple of Dusk, his loved one welcomes Akira and he and the white woman unite in heaven.

Reviewers welcomed Hayakawa's self-sacrificial Japanese role in the film. The EH noted, "We see Sessue Hayakawa in a role that best becomes this favorite of the silver screen. The love and devotion of a Japanese youth for a child . . . and his final sacrifice to save the baby's name from disgrace, forms the basis of the story."[25]

Yet, it was after *The Courageous Coward* that the motif of self-sacrifice for a white woman was used more obviously and continuously.[26] The MPW called *His Debt*, the film that followed *The Courageous Coward*, a story "of Self-sacrifice by a Japanese for the Sake of the Woman He Loves."[27] The MPW regarded the following film, *The Gray Horizon* (Worthington, 18 August 1919), as an "Absorbing Story of a Japanese Who Sacrificed His Own Happiness for the Sake of the Woman he Loved," and "Powerful Tragedy of Thrilling Vengeance and Self-Sacrificing Love with Sessue Hayakawa in Leading Role."[28] As a result of the constant play of this theme of self-sacrifice, one Japanese fan pointed out, in a bored tone, the "worn out thematic motif of self-sacrifice" in *His Debt*.[29]

Robertson-Cole's promotional materials exploited the motif of miscegenation in Hayakawa's films. A one-page ad of *Bonds of Honor* in trade journals uses a drawing of Hayakawa and a white woman that implies an indulgent interracial love scene. Hayakawa lies on a sofa with a glass of wine in his right hand. A wine bottle is lying on a table and Hayakawa looks drunk. He draws the white woman close to him with his left arm. The white woman has put her right hand on his head, left hand on his left arm, and bends over Hayakawa, as if she is about to kiss him. Clearly, this ad campaign was meant to appeal to American spectators' curiosity concerning the racial taboo, but not exceedingly.[30]

Finally, Hayakawa decided to play non-Japanese roles again. At Lasky, Hayakawa played seven non-Japanese leading roles: two Indians, two Hawaiians, a Mexican, an Arab, and a Chinese. At Haworth, he did not play any non-Japanese role until *The Man Beneath*, the eighth Hayakawa film at Haworth. A one-page ad for *The Man Beneath* in trade journals emphasized the strange Oriental atmosphere of the film, which is a mixture of Japan and India. In the ad a close-up drawing shows Hayakawa, playing a young Indian doctor, wearing an Indian-looking turban in front of a drawing of Mount Fuji, the moon, the sea, and a plum tree (see fig. 17).[31] Even so, *Wid's Daily* praised this role of Hayakawa as "the best in his recent film" and "the sort of stuff the women like to see the Japanese star do."[32] The MPN also stated, "Hayakawa is far too versatile to confine his work to the portrayal of Japanese roles only."[33] George T. Pardy of ETR even insisted, "The versatile Hayakawa is never seen to better advantage than as a film adventurer of the Orient."[34]

After *The Tong Man* (Worthington, 14 December 1919), the third of the "Hayakawa Superior Pictures" initiated by Robertson-Cole, Hayakawa played eleven more non-Japanese roles until he left Hollywood in 1922, while playing only one Japanese role.[35] In this manner, Hayakawa followed Robertson-Cole's strategy of standardizing his star vehicles based on a stereotypically

17   *An ad for* The Man Beneath. Moving Picture World *41.4 (26 July 1919): 463.*

Orientalist imagination of Japan and Asia, but not on a more realistic depiction of Japanese people.

Hayakawa may have chosen not to play Japanese roles in order to avoid playing stereotypical Japanese roles, thinking about his reputation in Japanese communities especially in the postwar revival of the anti-Japanese movement in California. *Photoplay* noted, "So long as it must be a 'heavy' part, Sessue Hayakawa prefers that his villainy be consummated in the guise of a Chinese. As is generally known, the relations between the Celestials and those of the Flowery Kingdom are not unlike those existing between the Teutons and the Sons of Albion."[36] This claim juxtaposed Britain versus Germany and Japan versus China to indicate Hayakawa's intention of differentiating Japan from the rest of Asia. By masquerading as other Asians, Hayakawa tried not to enhance stereotypical views of Japan among American audiences.

No matter what Hayakawa's intention was, ironically, Hayakawa's choice resulted in the blurring of national boundaries and cultural differences among Asian countries. It helped to form a collective and imaginary space called "the Orient" or "Asia" and strengthened the Orientalist mode of representing Asian people in the 1920s. In fact, after this point, reviewers often confused the nationalities of Hayakawa's characters. For example, Akbar Khan, a Hindu novelist in *The Devil's Claim* (Charles Swickard, 2 May 1920), was mistakenly identified as "a Persian author" by Matthew A. Taylor of MPN.[37]

Robertson-Cole's strategy to revitalize Hayakawa's popularity was successful. The EH reported that *His Debt*, *The Man Beneath*, *The Gray Horizon*, and *The Dragon Painter* (Worthington, 28 September or 4 October 1919) "were all accorded splendid receptions by the press and public."[38] The MPW noted that in the course of the year 1919 Hayakawa "steadily advanced in popularity."[39] In the beginning of 1920, MPW reported, "So overwhelmingly [sic] has been his success that Hayakawa's name is used in lights at almost every first-run house in the United States. On account of this enviable record, many of the best known exhibitors have contracted for every picture turned out by Hayakawa for Robertson-Cole."[40] It was reported that Haworth earned more than two million dollars by early 1920 and Hayakawa was able to pay back the one million that he had borrowed for the initial establishment of Haworth.[41]

The Dragon Painter was the first of Robertson-Cole's new series of "Hayakawa Superior Pictures." Despite Robertson-Cole's overall strategy, which treated Hayakawa not as specifically Japanese but as ambiguously Oriental, *The Dragon Painter* was publicized as if it showed authentic Japanese landscapes and characters. In a one-page ad in MPW, all eight still photos show Hayakawa in a Japanese kimono amid Japanese scenery. One photo was even framed in the shape of a Japanese lantern (see fig. 18).[42] A two-page ad in EH displays a drawing of dragons and Hayakawa's name written vertically on one page and Hayakawa and Aoki in kimonos holding each other in a Japanese-looking garden on the other.[43]

Trade journals reported that *The Dragon Painter* successfully reproduced "authentic" Japanese atmosphere. Margaret I. MacDonald of MPW wrote, "One of the especially fine features of the production is the laboratory work, mountain locations of extreme beauty, chosen for the purpose of imitating Japanese scenery, and supplying Japanese atmosphere, are enhanced by the splendid results accomplished, in the work of developing and toning."[44] The MPW also reported, "In this setting the village of Hakone, Japan, was duplicated even to its famous Shintu [sic] gates. Each setting is so naturally beau-

18   *An ad for* The Dragon Painter. Moving Picture World *41.13 (27 September 1919): 1943.*

tiful that it is hard to realize the perfection of the interior detail. The pictur-
esqueness of 'The Land of the Rising Sun' has been fully retained in 'The
Dragon Painter.'"[45]

However, contrary to these reports, the Japanese landscapes and characters that *The Dragon Painter* represented were the careful result of Robertson-
Cole's high standardization, which stressed an Orientalist recreation of Hayakawa's star image. In fact, *Kinema Junpo*, a Japanese film magazine, pointed
out, "[*The Dragon Painter*] did not show either contemporary or actual Japan."[46]
The Dragon Painter displayed the imaginary, exotic, and picturesque Japan
that many American audiences had been accustomed to seeing in films and
travelogues about Japan since the late nineteenth century. Robertson-Cole
and Hayakawa fully exploited this expectation of American audiences.

The Dragon Painter was based on a story written by Mary McNeil Fenollosa.[47] Her husband, Ernest, was a famous Japanologist, whose collection

became the basis of the Japanese art collection of the Boston Museum of Fine Arts. Ernest Fenollosa had an influential role in forming Japanese Taste among middle-class Americans. His wife's novel was written in this trend. Robertson-Cole relocated the Japanese aspect of Hayakawa's star image not in its cultural authenticity but in the context of Japanese Taste.

In *The Dragon Painter*, Hayakawa plays Tatsu, a young Japanese painter who madly seeks a dragon princess, who, he believes, is hiding under the surface of a mountain lake. Undobuchida, a friend of Kano Indara, the aging master of Japanese painting, is impressed by Tatsu's paintings and his talent and invites him to Tokyo. Undobuchida convinces Tatsu to learn the art of Kano. In Tokyo, Umeko (Aoki), the daughter of the artist, poses as the dragon princess for Tatsu. Tatsu is impressed by Umeko's refined beauty. Umeko is fascinated by Tatsu's talent. Yet, after Tatsu marries Umeko, he becomes unable to paint. She decides to sacrifice herself and so leaves Tatsu in order to save his talent. Tatsu leaps into the pool in which he believes his wife has drowned herself. He is rescued, and afterward, he succeeds with his art. After his successful exhibition, Umeko, who has actually been hiding at a temple, comes back to him.

The imaginary Orientalist aspect of *The Dragon Painter* is indicated, first, by its choice of strange Japanesque names: Undobuchida; Kano Indara, which may be a mixture based on a Japanese painter named Kano and a fourteenth-century Chinese painter named Indara;[48] and Hanake for the place where the hero lives. In the only surviving print, restored at the George Eastman House, the hero's name is not Tatsu, which is more suitable for a Japanese name, but Ten-Tsuou. *Katsudo Kurabu*, a Japanese film magazine, pointed out, "Even though Mr. Sessue Hayakawa took subject matter from Japan, Japanese names and styles in *The Dragon Painter* are very inappropriate. . . . A film about Japan that does not properly depict Japanese customs is very hard to watch for us Japanese."[49]

Second, *The Dragon Painter* utilizes the archetypal dichotomy between wilderness and civilization, the concurrent notion extensively used in Hayakawa's films at the NYMPC and at Lasky. The Eurocentric notion of a racial and cultural hierarchy in the representation of Japan and its people functions within this dichotomy. The opening shot, an extreme long shot of Hanake, artificially combines the actual location of Yosemite Valley and Japanesque objects, such as a torii and a straw-thatched hut, and establishes Japan as a wild, premodern, and picturesque place. The mountains, waterfalls, and rocks of Yosemite are displayed in the background, signifying nature and wilderness. Clouds move fast, as if they were shown in fast motion, and thus enhance the fantastic atmosphere. A Japanese critic described the landscape of Hanake as "the mysterious region of the age of the Gods."[50]

Throughout the film, Tatsu, a painter madly obsessed with completing a masterpiece of a legendary dragon princess, moves back and forth between savagery/wilderness and refinement/civilization and embodies the movable middle-ground position of Japan in the racial and cultural hierarchy, in accordance with the popular American discourse of the time.[51] Tatsu is introduced literally as a savage in his appearance, with his untidy hair and worn-out kimono. The second shot of the film shows Tatsu painting. He tears the piece that he has just painted and tries to summon a dragon from the mountains. Then, a high angle shot shows Tatsu lying on the ground and emphasizes that Tatsu is in the middle of nature and wilderness. Even when Tatsu arrives in Tokyo, he cannot stay in a house at night and sleeps by the stream in the garden. The original novel begins in Tokyo, and there is no opening scene that describes Tatsu in the wilderness. In the film, instead, a scene at Kano's refined house in Tokyo is inserted into the opening scene at Hanake. This cross-cutting between Hanake and Tokyo emphasizes the image of Japan positioned in the middle ground between wilderness and civilization.

Despite his uncivilized behavior, Tatsu is characterized as a creator of sophisticated art, Japanese paintings. Especially after his wedding to Umeko, Tatsu shows his gentle, civilized, and refined aspect. He wears an authentic black Japanese kimono with family crests on the chest. His hair is neatly set as he speaks of love with a flute in his hand, kneeling down before Umeko under a pine tree. He paints at a table sitting neatly on a tatami floor.

Umeko embodies Japanese Taste more clearly. Umeko's room is filled with typical signifiers of Japanese Taste: a Japanese garden with a gate, a stream, a small bridge, stone lanterns, and a peacock in front of a small shrine; a room with tatami mats, *fusuma,* Japanese sliding doors, and shoji; paintings of Mount Fuji and a dragon; paper lanterns. She wears a luxurious kimono and the beautiful hairstyle of an unmarried woman, *shimada.* After applying her makeup in front of a Japanese-style mirror table, she dances a Japanese dance with a silver fan in front of flowers arranged in a Japanese style, while her housemaid plays the samisen, a Japanese banjo-like musical instrument, and Japanese drums. She sits beside a shoji window under the beautiful moon. Even after the wedding, possibly to exaggerate her showy display of Japanese Taste, Umeko keeps wearing her long-sleeved kimono, which married women traditionally do not wear, and her *shimada* hairstyle, which should have changed to the less showy *marumage* of married women. Umeko even shows her extremely obedient and self-sacrificial nature as a stereotypical Japanese woman by committing suicide as Cio-Cio-San does in *Madame Butterfly.*

However, too much gentrification makes Tatsu lose his talent. To regain his artistic inspiration, Tatsu has to go back to the wilderness and savagery once again. The final shot of the film is symbolic. Tatsu, even though neatly dressed and accompanied by Umeko in a kimono, sits and paints in the wilderness. Tatsu and his embodiment of Japaneseness are kept on the edge of savagery/primitiveness and refinement/civilization.

Thus, *The Dragon Painter* rearticulated the Japanese aspect of Hayakawa's star image in the context of Japanese Taste, the archetypal dichotomy between primitive and civilized, and the motif of self-sacrifice in the style of *Madame Butterfly*. The result was very favorable. A reviewer in EH even claimed, "Optically this is one of Sessue Hayakawa's best offerings. In pictorial appeal it is the strongest thing the Haworth Company has ever done."[52] The EH also noted, "Hayakawa's recent pictures, produced by Haworth, have been triumphs in the art of production and it is generally agreed that 'The Dragon Painter,' the latest picture, will take its place among the few best pictures produced this season. The critics who reviewed it were enthusiastic and some of them said it was the best picture play shown in years."[53] Helen Rockwell of ETR wrote, "By far the best thing he [Hayakawa] has done since his well remembered performance in 'The Cheat.'"[54] The *New York Times* even selected this film as one of "The Year's Best."[55]

In the same year of 1919, Thomas C. Kennedy of ETR praised *The Tong Man*, another "Hayakawa Superior Picture," because it was "produced with such realism."[56] The MPW also pointed out the film's "authentic" depiction of the Chinese people and stated, "It is so typically Chinese that it carries with it all the mystery of the Orient."[57] However, when *The Tong Man* was released, it caused an uproar in Chinese communities in the United States.[58] Chinese residents in Rochester, N.Y., and in San Francisco tried to ban the film, insisting that the film misrepresented the lives and customs of the Chinese people.[59] However, according to the film historian Stephen Gong, the presiding judge in the case had the film screened in court and denied the protestors' request for an injunction. The judge said, "This is a picture that shows action of real life. There is nothing misleading about it. It is entertaining, gripping and instructive."[60] This controversy over *The Tong Man* reveals the film's Orientalist traits that looked "realistic" only to American audiences.

In fact, EH reviewed the film, using the term "Orient" over and over again: "The transplanted Orient which is San Francisco's Chinatown is the perfect setting against which Sessue Hayakawa portrays the sort of role that Sessue Hayakawa should portray in this his latest and most fitting production. . . . Oriental drama, along with the host of other things from the dimly apprehended East, has a peculiar charm for American audiences."[61]

In *The Tong Man*, Hayakawa plays Luk Chan, a Chinese hatchet man in San Francisco's Chinatown. Luk Chan falls in love with Sen Chee, the daughter of Louie Toy, a wealthy merchant of the opium trade. Ming Tai, who rules the powerful secret society Bo Sing Tong, desires Sen Chee and Louie Toy's fortune. When Louie Toy refuses to pay protection money, Ming Tai orders Luk Chan to kill Louie Toy. When Luk Chan refuses, Ming Tai kills Louie Toy, kidnaps Sen Chee, and informs the police that Luk Chan is responsible. Eventually, Luk Chan and his friend Lucero rescue Sen Chee from Ming Tai and the three get on a ship to China.

Not realistic but sensationally and stereotypically negative images of Chinatown are clearly established in the opening scenes of *The Tong Man*. The opening shot, which follows the intertitle with its photos of an altar and paper lanterns saying, "In the heart of Chinatown," shows a dark street in Chinatown at night. A man is suddenly shot and a policeman runs up to him. An intertitle, "The Bo Sing Tong[,] the most powerful and dreaded of Chinatown's secret societies; dealing in blackmail and assassination" is followed by a shot that shows the meeting of the Bo Sing Tong. In the dark room where an altar and a poster with Chinese characters that spell "sacred" dominate the space, most of the men hold long pipes and smoke opium. The Bo Sing Tong worships the "great Joss," the big statue of a dragon, whose eyes glow when it shows "a divine token," which appears in later shots. These images of Chinatown, dominated by the members of a superstitious and violent cult group, follow those of anti-Chinese discriminatory cartoons in popular American magazines in the late nineteenth century. One illustrated image of a Chinese gambling place in New York in *Leslie's Illustrated Newspaper* published in 1887, for example, shows a dark room filled with smoke and many Chinese people in Chinese caps and black Chinese dress playing a board game.[62]

Hayakawa's character, Luk Chan, "the Bo Sing Tong's most feared hatchet man," is certainly characterized as one of these stereotypical Chinese people. When he first appears on the screen, smoking a cigarette, he throws a hatchet to surprise a sleeping old Chinese man and laughs at him savagely. However, at the same time, Luk Chan is clearly distinguished from other Chinese char-

"So intense, so thrilling it's almost terrifying."

Sessue Hayakawa in *The* **TONGMAN**

Produced by
HAWORTH
Directed by
William
Worthington

Available at all Robertson-Cole Exchanges

19   *An ad for* The Tong Man. Moving Picture World *42.8 (20 December 1919): 929.*

acters. Luk Chan wears a European dress hat while other Chinese characters wear Chinese caps (see fig. 19). After Luk Chan pulls out his hatchet from the pillar, a Chinese man with a Chinese cap lights Luk Chan's cigarette extremely respectfully. Luk Chan's white made-up facial skin makes him stand out in the scene because other Chinese characters, mostly played by white actors, wear dark makeup and catfish-like whiskers. Moreover, even though Luk Chan is a hatchet man for a barbarous Chinese tong, he rarely actually kills people on the screen. In most cases Lucero, "a Lascar" (Indian) sailor, who has been saved by the heroine from policemen, kills villainous men for Luk Chan. Lucero, who is called "this poor creature" by the heroine, looks more like a Chinese teenager than an Indian, especially when he wears a Chinese cap.

The Tong Man characterizes Luk Chan as a genteel hero, referring to the narrative of *Romeo and Juliet,* which portrays an innocent and melodramatic love affair between the hero and the heroine. The motif of self-sacrificial devotion of a genteel hero for a white woman functions in the process. Herbert J. Hoose of MPW claimed that *The Tong Man* was a "Very attractive . . . 'Romeo and Juliet' episode in Chinatown."[63] Sen Chee, "A Juliet of Chinatown," according to an intertitle, falls in love at first sight with Luk Chan, a hatchet man of the enemy group. Luk Chan promises Sen Chee to quit the Bo Sing Tong and to become "a merchant prince." He betrays the tong and tries to protect Sen Chee and her father. When the villains assault Sen Chee, Luk Chan desperately runs to her. Parallel editing enhances the melodramatic tension until "the last minute rescue."

Even though a white actress, Helen Jerome Eddy, plays the Chinese woman and always wears a Chinese dress, she does not look Chinese at all with her blonde hair and makeup. She simply looks like a Caucasian girl in Chinese dress, as Vivian Martin in *Forbidden Paths* does not look Japanese when she puts on a Japanese kimono. Thus, both the hero and the heroine of this film are visually distinguished from other Chinese characters, with their costumes, makeup, and their innocent and romantic love affair. They are, in this sense, treated as an Americanized genteel couple. Tom Hamlin of MPN correctly pointed out, "[*The Tong Man*] does not portray the usual finale of so many of his [Hayakawa's] pictures that showed that 'East is East and West is West and the twain shall never meet.' . . . This picture does not have the sad ending most Hayakawa pictures have with romance blasted at the end because of race."[64]

The nonwhite hero played by Hayakawa and the nonwhite villain played by a white actor, Marc Robbins, are the two melodramatically opposite types of Chinese immigrants in the United States, like the two Japanese immigrant characters in *The Honorable Friend*. In both films, stereotypical Asianness is exaggerated by racial masquerade, with characters played by white actors with their makeup, costumes, facial expressions, and gestures. The goodness of Hayakawa's nonwhite characters is emphasized in comparison to their opponents.

Regarding this issue of racial masquerade in their characters' representations of Chinese traits, *The Tong Man* stands in marked contrast to *Broken Blossoms*, D. W. Griffith's interracial melodrama set in a Chinatown, which was released several months earlier in May 1919. In *The Tong Man*, Ming Tai, who always wears a Chinese cap, is frowning all the time and imitates Chinese posture with a slight stoop, placing his hands in front of his chest. This posture is exactly what the white actor Richard Barthelmess displays in *Broken Blossoms*. Barthelmess always wears a Chinese cap, is always half-closing his eyes or frowning because of his makeup, has a slight stoop, and walks slowly with his hands in front of his chest.

Yet, the Chinese character in *Broken Blossoms*, played by Barthelmess, is divided into two Chinese characters in *The Tong Man*. First, the implicitly threatening sexuality of Barthelmess's Chinese man becomes more obvious in the character of Ming Tai, who kidnaps a white heroine. In *Broken Blossoms*, Griffith transformed the Chinese protagonist from a vengeful schemer of the original short story, Thomas Burke's "The Chink and the Girl" (1916), to "a disillusioned romantic, brutalized by a callous urban environment" with his passive and protective gesture.[65] Barthelmess's Chinese character does not kidnap the white heroine, played by Lillian Gish, but cares for her after she wanders into his store and collapses, dazed from a beating given by her father. Yet, the Chinese character in *Broken Blossoms* is still threatening to white womanhood in terms of the anxiety of miscegenation. The white heroine's father interprets the Chinese man's act as an illicit love affair. Moreover, there is an extreme close-up of Barthelmess's face with half-closed eyes approaching the heroine in bed. This shot appears as a point-of-view shot of the horrified heroine. Barthelmess ends up kissing the sleeve of the heroine's Chinese dress, but the heroine's horrified facial expression clearly indicates the implicit fear of miscegenation with the Chinese man. "The Chink and the Girl" existed within the late-nineteenth-century genealogy of a popular Victorian imagination of Chinese kidnapping white women to make them "white slaves." Within this popular discourse, no matter how sympathetically the Barthelmess character is depicted in the film version, he signifies a sexual threat to white womanhood to a certain degree.[66] He treats the white heroine as an object of worship: in other words, he fetishizes her.

Ming Tai is much more aggressive and obviously threatening to the white heroine than Barthelmess's character. From the beginning, Ming Tai spies on the heroine from behind a curtain, playing with her bird on a balcony, grinning and wiping his mouth with his hand. The deep space composition emphasizes Ming Tai's voyeuristic act, which treats the heroine as an object of his gaze. In contrast, the first meeting of Sen Chee and Luk Chan is shown in shots/reverse shots that indicate their relatively equal relationship as a man and a woman. After Ming Tai murders Sen Chee's father, he approaches Sen Chee with an obviously lustful expression, emphasized in a close-up. Even though both Ming Tai and Sen Chee are Chinese characters and played by white actors, the different tactical uses of their makeup, costumes, and gestures function to cause anxiety of miscegenation in this scene.

In contrast, the good aspect shown in Barthelmess's character—rescuing the white heroine from a brutal villain—is displayed in a more gentle and heroic manner in the character of Luk Chan. Luk Chan, in spite of being played by Hayakawa, an Asian actor, always stands straight, walks actively, and never places his hands in front of his chest. He deviates from the "Oriental" postures and facial expressions represented by Barthelmess and Robbins. Luk Chan's black silk dress shines and even looks white in the lighting effects in night scenes, while Robbins and Barthelmess wear dull black clothes.

Most strikingly, any sexual implication is excluded from the love affair between Luk Chan and Sen Chee. The most significant device to eliminate the anxiety of miscegenation between the characters played by the Japanese actor and the white actress is the persistent avoidance of a kiss between them. Even after exchanging affectionate words, they just press their cheeks together. Many films of this period often fade out or cut to other scenes when couples in the films start kissing and so hide their actual kisses. However, in *The Tong Man*, a kiss between Hayakawa's character and the white actress's character is not even suggested or hidden. They do not start kissing at all. They repeatedly press their cheeks, even in Luk Chan's flashback, his supposedly subjective memory. Even in the finale, on the deck of a boat to China, they merely embrace each other in silhouette.

This no-kiss policy was adopted in other Hayakawa films at Haworth in order not to cause a fear of miscegenation between Hayakawa's nonwhite characters and the heroines played by white actresses. In fact, the *Rafu Shimpo* reported about *A Heart in Pawn* (Worthington, 10 March 1919): "This can be called a 'kiss-less picture,' and there is no kiss scene between a man and a woman. It is a rare case in contemporary cinema."[67] The French impressionist filmmaker Jean Epstein, in his article that praised the silent language of cinema, described Hayakawa's kissless performance in a more poetic but Orientalist manner, "The glance of Hayakawa, clean, grave as an oath, crushes those who do not know the honor of the Orient, nor love without kissing, fire without ash, engagements that last 15 years."[68]

In *The Swamp* (Colin Campbell, 30 October 1921), which was written and edited by Hayakawa himself for the first time since he produced *His Birthright*, *Banzai*, and *The Temple of Dusk*, this no-kiss policy for Hayakawa was observable in an extremely twisted manner.[69] *The Swamp* is a story about Wang (Hayakawa), a Chinese vegetable peddler in the slums, who loves a white woman, Mary. Wang devotes himself to encouraging Mary to divorce her unfaithful husband. After helping her to form a new relationship with her old friend, Wang leaves her. Even though *The Swamp* is basically a tragic story of interracial love that concludes with Wang's self-sacrifice, in many scenes the film imitates Charlie Chaplin's film of the same year, *The Kid* (1921), a sentimental comedy set in the slums. One shot, in which Mary's child and Wang, both wearing berets, sneak behind a building away from a masculine boxer who has just hit Wang in the face, directly refers to a shot in *The Kid*, in which Chaplin and the kid hide behind a building from a policeman. In other scenes, Wang's behaviors follow those of the silent clown Chaplin: giving too many cabbages to the kid; being hit by the boxer and falling hard on the street; hopping and dancing with his Chinese guitar; playing around with his horse; or pretending to be a Chinese-style fortuneteller wearing a Chinese gown, a Chinese hat, and glasses in the style of Harold Lloyd's, and banging a tiny Chinese drum with a serious expression.

For Wang, this comical but affectionate relationship with Mary's son is in fact a substitute for his devoted love for Mary. Wang's fascination with Mary is clearly displayed in a very expressive and excessive manner in one scene when Wang looks at Mary lying sick in bed. Shots/reverse shots between close-ups of Wang's face with his seriously affectionate expression and Mary's face with her vulnerable expression are repeated five times, with very subtle or almost no change of their facial expressions. When Wang witnesses Mary kissing her old friend and decides to leave her, a medium close-up of Wang shows him touching the sleeping child's head, kissing his forehead, pressing his cheek against the child's, and kissing him probably on the lips. In the print of the film extant at Gosfilmofond in Moscow, the actual kissing on the child's lips is done barely off the screen and does not completely appear on the screen. After the off-screen kiss, a medium close-up of the kid's face shows Wang's right hand touching his head affectionately for a couple of seconds as if it did not want to leave him. Then, in the next medium shot Wong faces Mary with a calm expression, free from lust and sorrow. After all, Wang never touches Mary throughout the entire film: only in one scene does Mary touch his cheek when she treats his injury on his eye. Thus, Wang's desire to touch Mary and kiss her is completely replaced by his extremely affectionate behavior toward her son, but even his kiss to him is not represented on the screen.

It is ironic that in a lecture that Hayakawa gave at the Nippon Club in New York in 1921 he discussed actual kissing in motion pictures. Hayakawa said, "When I act in a film, I speak the lines in the film all the time and try my best to become a character in the film. In an emotional love scene, in which a couple embraces and kisses each other, each actor has to really think that the opposite one is his or her sweetheart. Otherwise, we cannot make a film that impresses viewers. Therefore, when I have an actress who plays my lover in a film, I go to eat with her, talk with her, and try to develop really romantic feelings between us, at least on the day of shooting. So, there is a danger, too."[70] In the last line, Hayakawa jokingly makes excuses for flirting with the actresses, but simultaneously, the line underscores his awareness of the anxiety of miscegenation between his nonwhite characters and the white female characters.

Thus, *The Tong Man* used very complicated strategies of representing race and sexuality to make Hayakawa's character a romantic genteel hero. Hayakawa as a nonwhite Japanese actor portrayed a nonwhite non-Japanese character, in opposition to nonwhite characters played by white actors. As a nonwhite star, Hayakawa was considered to be more appropriate, or "authentic," to play the Chinese hero than white actors. However, to become the hero of the film, Hayakawa's Chinese character had to be Americanized and detached from the stereotypical images of savage Chinese people. The narrational strategy in *The Tong Man* repeated that used by Lasky to form Hayakawa's star image. To establish Hayakawa's stardom among middle-class American audiences, Lasky provided Hayakawa with the motif of Americanization and helped him move up to the middle ground in the racial and cultural hierarchy between the civilized (that is, Americanized) and the uncivilized. However, in order to avoid offending the taboo of miscegenation, Lasky did not create ordinary couples between Hayakawa's characters and white actresses, even when these actresses played nonwhite roles. The no-kiss policy in *The Tong Man* corresponded to the Lasky policy of careful avoidance of the fear of miscegenation.

In 1920, Hayakawa played an Arab for the second time in his career in *An Arabian Knight*, another Hayakawa vehicle at Haworth. In the film, Hayakawa plays Ahmed, a young donkey boy in Egypt, who is hired as a guide for George Darwin, an American Egyptologist. Darwin's elderly sister believes that she is a reincarnation of an Egyptian princess and Ahmed is the prince she loved two thousand years ago. When Aboul Pasha tries to abduct George's fiancée, Ahmed becomes the defender of the white American couple.

The story of *An Arabian Knight* is set in Egypt. It is filled with American Orientalist images, while the film was again publicized as "a production of astonishing realism."[71] In the film, Egypt is depicted as a primitive and mystical, but simultaneously culturally refined space, as Japan is in *The*

Dragon Painter. As the site of a complex culture that built the pyramids and established an advanced ancient civilization, Egypt was viewed and accepted as part of Western civilization while its current inhabitants were viewed as primitive. The film historian Antonia Lant suggests that Egypt's status in the Victorian period was ambiguous as "a point of interchange between Europe and Africa, the Middle East, and beyond."[72] Richard White, whom Lant cites, also notes that while Egypt was "indisputably part of the Orient, the Orient being less a place in the East than part of a discourse in the West," it was not easily placed within Africa or Asia, or within the East or the West.[73] Egypt and Japan thus shared the image of a racial and cultural middle ground between the white and the nonwhite.

The opening of the film emphasizes the mixture of religious primitiveness and cultural refinement of Egypt. At the same time, the film connects imaginary Egypt (drawings and studio sets) and the actual landscape of Egypt with no interference. Following the initial title card with drawings of silhouettes of a palm tree, a pyramid, and the River Nile, the first shot of the film shows a palm tree, a pyramid, and the River Nile in reality. Nature and the old civilization coexist in Egypt. A drawing of silhouettes of a mosque and buildings in the following intertitle indicates the refined culture there, but, simultaneously, the words in the intertitle emphasize that Egypt is a land of a primitive religion: "The plaintive call of the Meuzzin [sic] arouses the children of Allah. There is but one God and Mohammed is his prophet." All the people in the following extreme long shots kneel down barefoot on the ground and pray toward the sunlight. Other intertitles similarly juxtapose the primitive characteristics and refined traits of Egypt with such drawings as mummies, ruins, harps, and half-naked Egyptian women.

If, in the Victorian vision, Egypt was considered as a place that was located in the cultural and racial middle ground between the East and the West, and between the primitive and the civilized, it was a suitable space to narrate a Hayakawa star vehicle. In *An Arabian Knight*, Hayakawa's character is clearly positioned in the middle ground in the racial hierarchy. Ahmed's father tells him, "Remember, the blood of Emperor runs through thy veins. When Napoleon of the French conquered our land he smiled upon thy great-grandmother." The father's words suggest that Ahmed is a descendant of Napoleon's encounter with an Egyptian woman.

Hayakawa again portrays a nonwhite hero, in opposition to a nonwhite villain played by a white actor. He is a sexually unthreatening genteel hero in

20   *An ad for* An Arabian Knight. Moving Picture World *45.8 (21 August 1920): 968.*

the film. At the same time, Hayakawa's nonwhite character stays in an ultimately inassimilable position to white culture, even though he plays a role of
the savior of a white woman. In a one-page ad for *An Arabian Knight* in trade
journals, the motif of self-sacrifice for a white woman is observable again.
The ad has a photo in which Hayakawa wears an oriental outfit and protects
a white girl, who is hiding behind him (see fig. 20).[74]

When Ahmed first appears in the film, his costume, a black T-shirt, white
scarf, and white short pants, does not emphasize his Egyptianness. Instead,
Hayakawa's makeup emphasizes Ahmed's white skin color and distinguishes
him from other sub-characters, who are allocated positions inferior to
Ahmed's. Wassef, another Arabian servant of Darwin, has darker makeup
and wears a tarboosh. Ahmed contemptuously bribes a black guard who is
depicted as lazy, falling into sleep right after Ahmed leaves. Ahmed forces an

Egyptian dancer, embodying the sensual image of the orient with her half-naked costume and erotic dance of poses from ancient Egyptian paintings, to light his cigarette and treats her like a child.

Moreover, Ahmed is clearly distinguished from the Arab villain, Pasha, who is played by a white actor, Fred Jones. Jones's racial masquerade exaggerates the stereotypically oriental characteristics of Pasha. He wears luxurious oriental clothes, including a tarboosh, and has a dark beard. His room is filled with oriental objects, such as Arabian tapestries. From a dark and dirty hasheesh den, full of addicted Arabs and black guards who brutally harass them, Pasha recruits drug addicts to assault white people. Pasha is, more than anything else, a sexual threat to white women and an embodiment of the anxiety of miscegenation. Pasha kidnaps Eleanor, Darwin's fiancée, and attacks her.

In contrast, Ahmed differentiates himself from Pasha in his relationship to matrimony. Ahmed's loyalty to his fiancée, Zinah, signifies his monogamist morality, even when he is allowed four wives "by the Prophet" in Egypt. In this sense, Ahmed is depicted as a Westernized (Americanized) and civilized man who pursues the "normative" model of heterosexual romance.

Moreover, Ahmed's physical strength, which is emphasized in this film, links Hayakawa to such contemporary white American action heroes as Douglas Fairbanks Sr. In fact, *An Arabian Knight* is a chivalry action film similar to such Fairbanks Sr. star vehicles as *His Majesty, the American* (1919) and *The Mark of Zorro* (1920).[75] When pursuing an enemy, Ahmed jumps out of a second-story window. He catches up with the enemy and shakes him violently to make him confess where he has hidden Eleanor. In another scene, Ahmed reaches up to the second-story window from the back of his donkey. In the climactic battle, he fights alone against many enemies on a staircase. After murdering Pasha, Ahmed jumps out of the window, climbs up a wall, jumps on a horse, and rides away. With his physical strength, Ahmed self-sacrificially fights against his ethnic fellow Egyptians for the sake of a white family.

Finally, Ahmed is depicted as a receptive person when it comes to his relationship with women, which emphasizes his sexually unthreatening nature. George's sister Cordelia believes that Ahmed is a reincarnation of her prince of two thousand years ago and makes him look like it. Ahmed functions as an oriental object to be consumed by a white middle-class woman.[76] Cordelia symbolizes New Women who actively engage in consumer culture. In her introductory shot, she wears an oriental cape and ornaments and stands in front of a tapestry with an Egyptian design. As if referring to the Oriental-ization of Hayakawa's star image by Robertson-Cole, Ahmed is Orientalized in a luxurious Egyptian costume when Cordelia hires him as a "new butler." Ahmed, with an embarrassed facial expression and moving his eyes to the lower right and left several times, has to turn around in front of Cordelia and show his costume to her and to the middle-class audiences who adore Hayakawa and his costume. Before Cordelia appears in this scene, there is a shot in which Hayakawa, looking into a mirror and checking his costume, suddenly turns to the camera, comes closer to a medium shot, smiles at the camera, and moves his eyes left and right in a serious facial expression. This shot looks as if he were modeling for the viewers of the film.

Right after Cordelia tells an Egyptian butler, "Hereafter you will take orders from Ahmed," Ahmed folds his arms in front of his chest and repeats what she has said in a dignified manner as if he were pretending to be a king. Thus, Ahmed masquerades and acts like a king to satisfy Cordelia's desire. In *An Arabian Knight*, Cordelia satisfies her—and the female film spectators'—fantasies and desires, as consumers, by turning Ahmed into an Orientalized object and commodity, like a mannequin in department store displays or a model in fashion shows.

This emphasis on Hayakawa's oriental costume and poses for the spec-tator, including Cordelia, implicitly acknowledges the gazes from the spec-tators, white female fans, in particular, as part of the scenario. A one-page ad for *The Brand of Lopez* (Joseph De Grasse, April 1920), another Hayakawa star vehicle, placed a framed photo of Hayakawa in a Western suit with a bullfighter cap. The ad adds a drawing of a white woman. She seems to be suffering from the brand on her shoulder, but still admiringly looks up at the photo. The ad regarded Hayakawa as the object of a female gaze (see fig. 21).[77]

The film historian Miriam Hansen claims that women's increased signifi-cance as consumers for the film industry was contradictory to the systematic imposition, on the level of film style, representation, and address, of mascu-line forms of subjectivity, of a patriarchal choreography of vision. The Valen-tino cult is a typical example in which Hansen indicates this ambivalence. Hansen argues that Valentino's films "offer women an institutional oppor-tunity to violate the taboo on female scopophilia" in order to cater to female audiences.[78]

According to Gaylyn Studlar, by the 1920s, when *An Arabian Knight* was released, public discourse posited women as the primary participants in

21   *An ad for* The Brand of Lopez. Moving Picture World *43.13 (27 March 1920): 2058.*

America's new consumer culture, in which "the consumption of cultural forms of masculinity" also emerged.[79] Studlar claims that the fan magazines of the postwar years began to cater more to women's express demand to see male stars. This visual objectification of the male in film and its surrounding discourses, especially when Rudolph Valentino became a star with his image of a "woman-made man" or a "creation of, for, and by women," gained enormous public attention as the act of women looking at men became symbolic of the tumultuous changes believed to be taking place in the system governing American sexual relations.[80] In *An Arabian Knight*, under such historical circumstances, Hayakawa was represented as a fascinating consumable ethnic other for the white female spectators.

On its surface, *An Arabian Knight* has the structure of a male-centered adventure comedy: kidnappings, escapes, chases on horseback, fights on stairs, and slapstick action. Ahmed becomes a hero because of his actions to save a white American couple. However, at its core, referring to romantic and mythical legends of Egyptian kings, the film displays a commodified male star "in ways associated with women's interest in objectifying men."[81] Stephen Kern claims, "Victorian artists allowed female desire to burn hottest when far away or long ago."[82] Post-Victorian theater and Hollywood films of the 1920s, Studlar argues, "could more overtly appeal to female spectators' libidinal passions when the male object of idolatry was allied to an exotic or historically distant rendering of erotic thrills."[83] Ahmed in *An Arabian Knight* is a passive oriental, a historically displaced consumer object and a "woman-made" matinee idol, made by Cordelia and female fans' interests in a man of a far away land and long ago. In this sense, Hayakawa in *An Arabian Knight* is a precursor of Valentino—a "Latin lover" who is not Caucasian but is obviously not Asian—and other white male stars in the 1920s adventure films set in oriental lands. Preceding Valentino, Hayakawa in this film combines masculine control of the gaze, as an adventurous hero, with the "feminine quality of 'to-be-looked-at-ness,'" as an Orientalized object.[84]

It is significant, however, that there is a distinct barrier between Ahmed and the women. He is carefully prevented from having an erotic sexual relationship with any white women in the film. This is one of the largest differences between Hayakawa's star vehicles and Valentino's *The Sheik*, which was released in 1921, one year after *An Arabian Knight*. There were similar tensions and anxieties raised by the images of Hayakawa and Valentino in the era of xenophobia and consumerism. Similar motifs, such as costuming, feminization, Orientalism, and consumerism, appeared in both stars' careers, but they did so in different cultural and racial contexts, which inform their meanings. In order not to enhance the fear of sexual arousal and the anxiety of miscegenation, Ahmed, and Hayakawa as a nonwhite star, is strictly kept at a certain distance only to be looked at, especially as a self-sacrificial genteel victim hero, and to be read about in fan magazines, as an Americanized model minority who embodies refined Japanese Taste but who cannot be touched and can never be kissed. Valentino, in contrast, in the finale of *The Sheik* unites with the white heroine when it is revealed that he is a son of European aristocrats.

Ahmed, "a playboy of the East," according to the intertitle, is clearly characterized as an object for white female gazes. When he appears in the film for the first time, he rides on a donkey. Many women with veils, played by white actresses, sit behind lattice windows, hailing him and throwing kisses one after another. He answers and waves to everyone with a smile. However, as is the case in *The Tong Man*, the actual kiss between the couple does not appear on the screen in *An Arabian Knight*. As soon as Ahmed and Zinah, his girlfriend, embrace each other, the shot turns to the next. Or, in a long shot, the kiss is hidden behind the woman's face. In another one, it is behind Hayakawa's head. Later, when he thinks about Zinah, a flashback shows the two embracing each other. When they are about to kiss, the shot dissolves back to Hayakawa and all viewers can see is Hayakawa kissing a branch of a tree and holding tightly to his hat. In the romantic final scene in the desert at night, before Ahmed approaches Zinah, the film ends.

13

THE MASK

Sessue Hayakawa's Redefinition
of Silent Film Acting

I n the introductory shot of *The Honorable Friend*, Hayakawa appears on
the screen as an actor himself. The shot of Hayakawa as an actor dissolves
into that of his role, Makino, according to the script of the film. In this
shot, "Sessue Hayakawa at desk, looking over script. He ponders—stoops
to make correction—the line. 'As Makin [*sic*]' fades in overhead—dissolve to
Makino in hot-house, working over plants. He mops brow—turns and looks.
. . . He smiles—calls dog—picks him up in his arms—(FADE OUT)." This
mode of presentation showing an actor first and his or her screen role next
was often taken in early feature films, but the actors in such introductory
shots were not usually reading scripts.

The shot that opens the second Hayakawa star vehicle indicates Lasky's attempt to emphasize legitimate acting as the essential element of Hayakawa's
star image, becoming another unique element in Hayakawa's stardom. The
Hollywood star system was very much associated with personification, with
the notion that the stars did not act but were themselves and that the pleasur-
ably recognizable repertoire of gestures, expressions, and movements were
the property of the star, not of any individual character.[1] As Miriam Hansen
argues, stars and stardom in Hollywood cannot be reduced to the narrative
function of character.[2] Actors' on-screen personae and their real lives were
connected with the emergence of the star system. The *New York Times* in
1920 noted:

A "star" in the film firmament is a man or woman, who by reason of looks,
personality or eccentricity—and, always, advertising—is considered a good

business asset by some promoter. Sometimes they can act and sometimes they cannot, but even when they have genuine pantomimic ability they are usually required by their stellar position to confine themselves to one role—that of being themselves, as they have become known to the public. The art of acting is the art of impersonation, and an actor really plays a part only when his own individuality is absorbed by that of the character he impersonates, but screen players who lose themselves in their roles are invariably catalogued as "character" actors and rated as of secondary importance by those to whom the screen is a matter of salaries, film rentals, box office receipts, electric lights, three-sheet posters, &c. Stars, with some notable, and enjoyable exceptions, are always themselves, each bringing the same appearance, mannerisms and expressions to every part, so that the presumably undiscerning public may recognize the well-advertised individual in every moment of his or her appearance and find all of the old familiar attributes on which the star's popularity is based.[3]

In contrast, Hayakawa was publicized and praised for his acting: his naturalism of "impersonation"—the gap between star and character—as the introductory shot of The Honorable Friend indicated. That is, Hayakawa was regarded as a character actor, as well as a star.

An article in Current Opinion in 1918 quotes Cecil B. DeMille's comment on Hayakawa's performance in The Cheat and enhances the novelty of Hayakawa's acting styles. DeMille stated, "I don't understand it [Hayakawa's acting style]; it is new and strange, but it is the greatest thing I ever saw."[4] Was Hayakawa's stardom based on his supreme quality as a character actor? Was he a pioneer in an acting style of restraint, as trade journals and fan magazines described? Was the reputation of his acting style simply an Orientalist promotional device for product differentiation in the emerging star system? Was his acting more restrained than his co-stars' acting? What was the actual quality of Hayakawa's acting?

The film scholars Ben Brewster, Lea Jacobs, Charlie Keil, Roberta Pearson, and Janet Staiger, among others, argue that at every American film studio in the period of 1908–13 there was a transition in acting styles from the one heavily influenced by theatrical melodrama to the one allied to realist movements in literature and theater.[5] Most popular acting styles at the turn of the century corresponded to the emphasis on the "pictorial" display of spectacles in theatrical melodrama.[6] Actors were charged with managing how they looked within the stage picture and were not necessarily required to create psychologically complex characters. Particularly, emotions and internal states should be externalized in gestures.[7] Actors were subject to a number of conventions that de-emphasized any need for inner realism or depth of character but displayed them in stereotyped postures. Pearson named this type of acting "histrionic" style, in which "the actors selected their gestures from a repertoire of standard, conventional gestures kept alive . . . through descriptions and illustrations in acting manuals and handbooks."[8] In the beginning, silent film acting followed this trend.

By 1913, following the emergence of internally coherent narratives centered on individuated characters and the emergence of feature film with its greater character development and more effective use of close-ups, "modification" of film performance occurred.[9] Citing Louis Reeves Harrison's 1911 comments in MPW, "the eyes and the lips are most effective in facial expression of any kind, whether the emotion be open or subdued," Staiger describes the change of the style of film acting as "from broad pantomimic gestures, to the face in general and, eventually, to the eyes as 'the focus on one's personality.'"[10] Pearson argues that in D. W. Griffith's 1913 films, compared to his 1908 films, the "gestural isolation and the elimination of little gestures of the histrionic code gives way to a continuous flow of movement linked by little gestures."[11] Griffith stated in NYDM in 1913, "Restraint in expression" would raise "motion picture acting to the higher plane which has won for it recognition as a genuine art."[12] Facial expressions were the replacement for the highly stylized and physicalized pantomimic gestures. They were regarded as more suitable for close-ups in cinema. Pearson calls this "modified" acting style "verisimilarly" coded performance that "came to dominate the classical Hollywood cinema and, by extension, world cinema."[13] She suggests, "Verisimilarly coded acting does not rely upon a standardized gestural repertory, which leaves room for greater individual interpretation of a part. . . . In the verisimilar style, the arms remain closer to the center of the body while the hands and face relay a good deal of information."[14] The transition from the "histrionic" to the "verisimilar" was not abrupt. According to Brewster and Jacobs, actors' assumption of stereotyped poses and attitudes continued in European and American filmmaking long after 1912. Coexistence of the histrionic and verisimilar codes within individual films or within individual performers was not unusual well into the 1910s.[15]

Hayakawa recalled in 1963, "I tried to distinguish myself as a Japanese actor from foreigners. . . . My facial expression was highly valued [in the United States] as expressionless expression."[16] Hayakawa's acting was promoted in trade journals, fan magazines, and general magazines as an ideal deviation from the pictorial style to the restrained one. Charles K. Field's article in *Sunset* was one of those.[17] Field locates Hayakawa's acting style in the line of Japanese theatrical arts and connects it to a renowned Japanese kabuki actor, Danjuro, in particular. In the 1910s, Danjuro was considered even in Japan to be the typical representative of the Japanese acting style that lacked facial expressions.[18] Field writes, "As he [Hayakawa] stands before the camera his thought goes back to that mighty personality, to the intense, subjective method of Danjuro's portrayal of emotion. He remembers how Danjuro could hold his audience for long tense periods without moving a muscle, with merely the power of his eloquent eyes, the potent set of his mouth."[19]

Hayakawa did not have an acting career and did not have a particular interest in kabuki when he was in Japan. Field's argument was, therefore, based on his imaginary comparison between Hayakawa and the Japanese kabuki actor, or on Lasky's promotional materials. Moreover, strategically or not, Field's article combines two different Danjuros as if they were one person. Hayakawa's static posing in *The Typhoon* and his facial expression with special makeup in the branding scene of *The Cheat* look similar to the *mie* pose in the *aragoto* genre, the violent act, in kabuki that Ichikawa Danjuro I established in the late seventeenth-century Edo period.[20] Danjuro I stylized *mie*, or *nirami*, glaring, as a physical movement of an actor that should display outwardly his inner emotions in a somewhat exaggerated manner.

However, the "Danjuro" whom Hayakawa was compared to in this article must have been Danjuro IX, who was popular in the Meiji period in the late nineteenth century. Danjuro IX "starred" in the oldest remaining Japanese film, *Momijigari* [Maple viewing] (1899), the film that captured his performance on the stage. Danjuro IX was famous for his rebellion against the performance style from the Edo period that physicalized characters' emotions on the surface. Danjuro IX articulated his famous style, *haragei*, saying, "Once on stage, I cannot show the real thing unless I forget myself and the stage and turn into the character, the person. In order to do this, *hara* [literally speaking the term translates as "stomach," but it seems closer to "soul" or "mind"] is important as well as the surface, because the real feeling must be transmitted from heart to heart. Therefore, I know it is important to imitate some shapes or styles on a certain occasion, but rather I try to show the heart. To show the heart, the most important thing lies in *hara*."[21] Danjuro IX did not wear any makeup in many cases, and other actors complained because he did not move much on stage.

Hayakawa's acting styles, particularly those in climactic scenes in *The Ty-*

phoon, in *Death Mask*, and in *The Cheat*, were much closer to the stylized performance of Danjuro I than that of Danjuro IX. Yet, Field explains Hayakawa's performance in terms of Danjuro IX's method. Even though Hayakawa's acting style was praised as "repressed" or "restrained," the kabuki-style performance that Hayakawa showed on the screen was not necessarily based on the "restrained" performance but on the highly "stylized" one.

Similarly, an article in the *Literary Digest* in November 1917, which was based on a report in the *Los Angeles Times*, praised Hayakawa's restrained acting style.[22] The article emphasizes that Hayakawa's performance is not based on exaggerated pantomime ("expression") but on nonverbal gesture ("repression") and explains it in terms of his Japanese cultural origin. The article begins with the quotation of Hayakawa's theory for gestures: "If I want to show on the screen that I hate a man I do not shake my fist at him. I think down deep in my heart how I hate him, and try not to move a muscle of my face—just as I would in life."[23] The article then notes, quoting the *Los Angeles Times*, "It would seem that Sessue Hayakawa injects something of the mysticism of the East into the development of his work in motion picture. . . . His fine patrician face gives a hint of a thousand years of aristocratic ancestry in the proud old Samurai of Japan. In his own country he was a naval officer, in America he is the most subtle motion picture actor the screen has produced. Everything else about him is shrouded in mystery." In reality, Hayakawa was not a naval officer in Japan. He had wanted to become one but failed. This article once again fictionalizes Hayakawa's biography to enhance the mystically refined image of his acting styles.

The praise of Hayakawa's restrained style of performance, referring to Danjuro IX, appeared to go along with the trend toward the verisimilar style. The film scholar Mary Ann Doane, in her essay on the close-up and the concept of "photogenie" in cinema, also notes that Hayakawa had "relative restraint as an actor of the silent cinema, rejecting the histrionics usually associated with the era. Given the stony immobility of his face, a slight twitch of an eyebrow could convey extraordinary significance."[24]

However, Hayakawa's acting styles should not be located simply within the historical transition from an emphasis on broad athletic and pantomimic gestures (the "histrionic") to an emphasis that values facial expression and more restrained and individualized gestures (the "verisimilar"). Despite the fact that trade journals, fan magazines, and general magazines praised Hayakawa for his restrained acting styles and connected them to Japanese cultural and theatrical traditions, it seems difficult to articulate Hayakawa's actual acting as simply contrasting exaggeration and restraint. Hayakawa's face is not simply expressionless, in spite of his own comment. Instead, it is like a mask. The implication of the mask is twofold: first, it is static and therefore hard to read since it does not change (but it cannot be called "expressionless"); second, it seems to conceal something else. Both implications are applicable to Hayakawa's face. The second implication, in particular, is crucial to his ethnic identity and stardom: stereotypically, the mask-like expression is easily connected to the Oriental inscrutability, but also Hayakawa, as a Japanese actor, needed to wear a mask in "triple consciousness."

By the use of mask-like facial expressions (tightened mouth and unmoving eyes) and his controlled pauses (stilled gestures), Hayakawa was able to freeze an action in intense ambiguity and/or ambivalence. Therefore, in Hayakawa's acting, the moments of restraint—that is, repression of emotions or motivations—were also those of being exaggerated and vice versa. The uniqueness of Hayakawa's acting styles lay in the specific fact that, consciously or not, he uniquely employed the existing vocabulary in film acting, such as restrained facial expressions suited for close-ups and pantomimic gestures, and redefined them with inscrutable facial expressions and economy of gesture.

Further, in place of familiar pantomimic gestures Hayakawa inserted such body language as *mie*-like stances, moments of stillness before a sudden burst of violence, which were based on Japanese theater but which he used in a completely different context. He could be said to still use the pictorial style, but without its traditional meanings. In this sense, he also redefined Japanese theatrical acting styles in early Hollywood cinema. His mask-like facial expressions and stilled body language, which emphasized ambiguity of the emotional, psychological, and physical states of the characters, impressed, or offended, viewers with a sense of potential but not explicit cruelty and an odd eroticism.

A reviewer of *Photoplay* points out Hayakawa's momentary frozen posture in *The Cheat*: "His [Hayakawa's] very lack of gesture emphasized the ferocity of his sudden attack on the white woman."[25] French intellectuals of the period also valued highly the impassive mask of Hayakawa. Jean Epstein, a film critic who had worked for the Lumière brothers and would become a film director in 1922, compared Hayakawa's expression as "a revolver" and described how the viewers were flabbergasted by the intense moments created by Hayakawa's acting style and his economical use of gesture: "Hayakawa aims his incandescent mask like a revolver. Wrapped in darkness, ranged in the cell-like seats, directed toward the source of emotion by their softer side, the sensibilities of the entire auditorium converge, as if in a funnel, toward the film. Everything else is barred, excluded, no longer valid."[26] Hayakawa's acting is extraordinary precisely for his mask-like face and his stilled pause: his intense ambiguity or ambiguous intensity.

At the beginning of his film career, at the NYMPC under Ince, Hayakawa mostly appeared in films whose emphasis was on the theatrically melodramatic and pictorial display of Japanese people and landscapes, and he often used pantomimic gestures in the surroundings. However, in some cases, Hayakawa displayed his mask-like facial expressions and *mie*-like stilled postures to create intense but ambiguous moments in the films.

In his debut film, *O Mimi San*, Hayakawa resorts to pantomimic gestures to clearly represent his emotional states in pictorial Japanese surroundings. When Yorotomo (Hayakawa) receives a letter from the prime minister saying that his father is dead and he has to go back to the court, he expresses his grief with his body language. He drops the letter, covers his face with both hands, faints, and is supported by an errand boy. Full of tears in his eyes, he turns to his left and spreads both his arms, as if he longed for O Mimi San. With his powerlessly extended arm Yorotomo asks the errand boy to leave and wanders out of the frame. The following scene emphasizes the pictorial quality of Japan and its people. Yorotomo and O Mimi San walk to a Japanese-style wooden bridge under a willow tree in a Japanese garden and slowly and affectionately embrace each other.

However, in the final scene, Hayakawa's acting displays a more intensely ambiguous quality. After the royal wedding between Yorotomo and Sadan San, Yorotomo looks at the wisteria outside a shoji window in a medium shot. Within the window frame, the shot of Yorotomo and O Mimi San embracing each other at the Japanese-style wooden bridge under the willow tree appears in double exposure. Framed in the window frame, the pictorial quality of the scene in the Japanese garden is emphasized. When the double exposure ends after a few seconds, Yorotomo turns toward the camera, opens his eyes wide, keeps his mouth tightly shut, and pauses before slowly looking down. While Hayakawa's acting in *O Mimi San* is captured in a theatrical space that emphasizes the pictorial display of an imaginary Japan and quite often uses pantomimic gestures, this final image of the film is full of intensity and looks rather horrific, despite the fact that Yorotomo's emotional state is left ambiguous.

In *The Wrath of the Gods*, as a supporting actor with the heavy makeup of the elderly father Yamaki, Hayakawa uses pantomimic gestures throughout the film. However, Hayakawa's movements of his body, such as the respectful bows, were not necessarily typical pantomimic gestures in Western theatrical melodrama. They surely function to display pictorial and stereotypical images of Japan, but at the same time they provide unnamable tension in the scenes. In the opening of the film, when Toya-San runs back home in tears after the old prophet's severe warning based on his superstitious belief, Yamaki's reaction is intense but his emotional state stays ambiguous. With his eyes wide open and his mouth tightly closed, he pauses, slowly looks up, ritualistically brings out an old scroll, and explains to Toya-San about the Buddha's curse. He does not clearly display his emotions in a typically pantomimic mode until the very end of the scene, when he makes two fists, raises both of them to the sky, looks straight up, and cries out in fury, "I renounce my faith."

It is significant that Hayakawa constantly uses more straightforward pantomimic gestures after the scene in which Yamaki decides to convert to Christianity. In the melodramatic narrative of *The Wrath of the Gods*, pantomimic gestures and clearly expressed emotional states are connected to Christianity (Tom and Toya-San openly express their affection by embracing each other, and so forth), while ambiguity in gestures and emotions is related to the primitive and the superstitious. After the conversion, Yamaki makes a cross with two pieces of wood and raises it high with his arms. He walks up to the statue of the Buddha, violently throws it away, replaces it with the cross, and pushes both arms to the sky in fury to renounce the Buddha, his arms fully extended upward at about a forty-five degree angle. When the angry crowd comes close to lynching Yamaki in front of the altar, he excitedly but proudly raises the cross high in front of the crowd. Thus, in *The Wrath of the Gods*, Hayakawa employs both nontraditional manners of body language and typical pantomimic gestures to represent the different positionings of his character in the archetypal dichotomy between the primitive and the civilized religions and regions.

The introductory shots in *The Typhoon* are indicative of Hayakawa's unique acting styles. After an intertitle saying "Mr. Sessue Hayakawa as 'Tokoramo,'" a medium long shot shows Hayakawa as an actor appearing in a Japanese kimono with a Japanese fan in his hands. When he turns right and left his facial expression is so vacant and mask-like that it is impossible to read any feelings or emotions. After he turns to the front, he grins a little toward the camera. Then, he stops grinning and raises his right eyebrow. At this point, his eyes are slightly wider open than before, which makes his facial expression more intense. Yet, still, it is difficult to interpret any specific meanings in it. Finally, after a moment, he smiles and bows. The shot dissolves into a shot of Hayakawa as Tokoramo, the character in the film, in a long black coat reading a book with a clearly frowning expression. He looks up with a noticeable movement and with an obviously embarrassed facial expression and goes back to the book. Playing the character in the film, which has a narrative about a melodramatic dichotomy between the primitive East and the civilized West, Hayakawa resorts to the acting style with more explicitly pantomimic gestures and obvious facial expressions.

However, his pantomimic acting in *The Typhoon* has moments of intense ambiguity, which render nonspecific psychological or emotional meanings. Right after Tokoramo hears Helene's line, "I am going back to Bernisky and laugh with him at you—you whining yellow rat—and at your Japan, a dirty yellow blot upon the face of the earth," he widens his locked lips and opens his eyes wide. Quickly turning to her with his arms slightly widened, he stops his movement for a while and simply gazes at Helene. His lips are tightly closed and bent. Is he mad? Is he sad? Or, is he about to betray Japan for his love? This is a moment of intense ambiguity. His pose and facial expression, which create a moment of static time and bring all action onscreen to a halt, look exactly like the *mie* style right before the abrupt violent acts in kabuki. After this tense but emotionally ambiguous moment, Tori finally attacks Helene.

The contract with Lasky brought more complicated issues into Hayakawa's acting. The ambiguous intensity in his acting became publicized and promoted as his "restrained" style of acting. In trade journals and magazine articles it was connected to Japan's traditional theatrical acting with reference to the renowned kabuki actor Danjuro IX and thus was culturally authenticated. The ambiguity was given a clear name: the traditional Japanese method of acting. This was Lasky's strategy of Orientalizing Hayakawa for product differentiation. At the same time, Hayakawa began to use more mainstream acting styles that were used by other contemporaneous actors: using both pantomimic gestures and the "verisimilar" style in close-ups with less emotional and psychological ambiguity. This might have been the result of Lasky's strategy of Americanizing Hayakawa and giving him the image of a model minority, who adopts the American way of life, behavior, and acting, in order to make Hayakawa a star for middle-class Americans. Thus, as a result of the star system at Lasky, Hayakawa was placed in another movable middle-ground position with regard to his acting styles: ambiguity versus clarity, that is, Orientalized versus Americanized.

In *The Cheat*, on the one hand, in the scenes in which Tori (Hayakawa) acts like an Americanized gentleman, there is no big difference in acting styles between Hayakawa and Jack Dean, for instance. Hayakawa smiles, salutes, shakes hands, wonders, smokes cigarettes, and offers cigarettes, as other white American characters and actors do.

On the other hand, Hayakawa's acting displays intense ambiguity, which can be interpreted as gentle, cruel, feminine, and masculine all at once. Even though Tori turns into an obvious melodramatic villain toward the end of the narrative, Hayakawa's acting does not correspondingly transform into something more pantomimic and expressive to clearly indicate his villainy. Instead, on most occasions, Hayakawa's stilled postures and mask-like facial expressions leave room for ambiguity.

In Tori's shoji room, when Tori demonstrates to Edith how to brand, Edith looks obviously frightened because of Fannie Ward's pantomimic gestures. Tori remains at the table with a poker in his hands and does not change his countenance, although he pauses as if he had something on his mind, even though the viewers are not sure what it is. According to the script, after the spoken title, Tori "points toward himself—comes very close to Edith—passion and determination in his face indicates—almost whispering 'As I want you to be'—Tori takes her hand in one of his—He reaches with the other hand as if to caress her hair which is just under a spray of cherry blossoms—He crushes the petals of the cherry blossoms in his hand, letting them shower over her— His hand sliding from her hair down to her shoulder—Edith watches him half-fascinated with strange atmosphere and determination of the man." On the screen, however, Hayakawa does not resort to such pantomimic gestures and the obvious facial expressions that express Tori's desire. The change of Tori's facial expressions is so subtle, if there is any, that it is difficult for the viewers to decide his emotional state.

In the following scene, when Edith is scared by her thought of a newspaper headline, Tori grins and shows an "expression of sinister satisfaction," according to the script. After Edith has left, in the script Tori even shows a face "full of relentless determination" when he picks up the chiffon scarf that she has left behind and inhales a whiff of her perfume from it with "a *slow* oriental smile."[27] However, on the screen, Hayakawa's facial expression does not change much. It is possible to say that Tori shows slightly surprised and slightly conspiring expressions when he hears that Edith has lost the Red

Cross Fund, but overall he does not make provocative gestures and facial expressions. Yet, simultaneously, Hayakawa's mask-like face underscores the heightening threat that pushes a white woman into a situation of white slavery.

In the branding scene, when Tori is shot by Edith in the shoji room, Hayakawa does not display pantomimic gestures of pain and suffering but effectively utilizes repressed movements and pauses to extend the moments of violence. After being shot, he holds his chest with his left hand, pauses, raises his right arm, pauses, looks up at the sky with wide open eyes, pauses, staggers up front, pauses, and then slowly falls down on his back against the shoji screen. He gradually moves toward his right when he displays these physical actions. The camera slowly pans in accordance with his movement until he falls down. Based on Lasky's promotional device that connects Hayakawa and Danjuro, this dotted lingering movement could be related to kabuki's stylized act of dying, but it is used in a completely different context: silent cinema that was based on both pantomimic and verisimilar acting.

At the climactic trial, Tori's facial expressions are displayed in quite a few close-ups. Staiger argues that these close-ups "convey interior thoughts and feelings" of Tori.[28] However, contrary to her claim, Hayakawa's mask-like facial expressions and his stilled body language create ambiguity about the character's inner emotions and extremely heighten the tension of the scenes. The changes of his facial expressions are very slight compared to those of Edith, whose emotional states are clearly displayed in her reactions to the testimonies and the verdict. Edith's emotions are conveyed through exaggerated facial expressions, such as biting her lips and restlessly moving her eyes, and gestures, such as making fists, moving her hands to her mouth, and shaking her body. In the script, Tori was supposed to have more obvious facial expressions that deliver his emotional states, such as smiling "with satisfaction" when Richard testifies that he shot Tori and reacting with "surprise and dissatisfaction" when Edith starts to talk. On the screen, he smiles slightly or worries, but he does not show exaggerated facial expressions or pantomimic gestures, in opposition to Edith, who tells the courtroom audience what happened to her with overly extreme actions (jumping up, taking off her hat, waving her arms, showing her naked shoulder, crying hard onto a desk, and opening up her arms while begging for mercy) and emphasized facial expressions of fury, sadness, and even insanity.

Consequently, Tori's emotional state stays ambiguous in the scene (and throughout the film), despite the fact that his role in the narrative of *The*

Cheat is clearly the melodramatic villain as an inassimilable alien who threatens the lives of the white American middle-class couple. Even though the film historian James Card insightfully calls Hayakawa's ambivalent acting technique in *The Cheat* "eloquent restraint," the close-ups in the courtroom scene, for instance, are not "eloquent" at all but, instead, ambiguous and repressive in terms of the expression of his emotional states.[29]

The film's melodramatic inclination in the narrative eventually confines Tori within the image of a stereotypical villain. However, the focalization on the heroine and the deprivation of eloquent voices and facial and bodily language from Tori in the courtroom scene caused an unprecedented result. The close-ups of Hayakawa's muteness (vocal, facial, and physical) become paradoxical in meaning, coming closer to what Walter Benjamin calls cinema's "optical unconscious," which opens up hitherto unperceived modes of sensory perception and experience and suggests a different organization of the daily world.[30] According to Benjamin, photography inaugurated a mechanically reproducible means to arrest and congeal life in a split second. Siegfried Kracauer argued that the cinema was able to assemble these "still" images and put them into motion, or back into the "flow of life."[31] Hayakawa's acting, particularly his mask-like facial expressions captured in the close-ups here, comes to embody the tension between this stillness of photography and the flowingness of cinema, or to problematize the innate contradiction of cinema: stillness and motion; timeliness and timelessness.

Hayakawa's body in this scene is a field of betrayal of meanings more than a ground of communication.[32] Despite the continuous close-ups that are narratologically meant to express Tori's villainous characteristics, the evil of Tori becomes shaded gray because of his noneloquent facial expressions and repressed gestures. Even Hayakawa himself as an actor might not have realized the uniqueness of his acting style. Probably, he did not have any intention to redefine the vocabularies of acting in silent cinema. He was not trained as an actor at all before he entered the film business. He did not study European styles of stage acting. He might have seen Danjuro IX in Japan before he came to the United States, but it is doubtful that he completely understood the very stylized methods of acting in kabuki. He might have remembered some impressive movements, such as an act of dying or the famous *mie* pose, but he did not know how to use them structurally. Instead, it can be assumed that Hayakawa was not really sure what he was doing in front of a movie camera, at least when he was not routinely appearing in films. He might have stopped moving his body and making obvious facial expressions at certain points when he was playing characters in films. Yet, it was the camera that examined the expression of ambiguity and enhanced the moments of intensity in Hayakawa's acting.

In any case, Hayakawa's acting in *The Cheat*, which left room for intense ambiguity, made Hayakawa a more appealing screen presence than his white co-stars, according to the reviews in film trade journals, even though these reviews were struggling to find appropriate terms to describe Hayakawa's acting styles. *Wid's Films and Film Folk Independent Criticisms of Features* correctly noticed Hayakawa's effective use of pauses and subtle facial expressions and claimed that Hayakawa "surely does some wonderful work. His careful timing of his slow movements and the wonderful control he has over his facial muscles, makes his work grip you in a truly effective manner."[33] The NYDM praised Hayakawa's "thoroughly enjoyable piece of acting": "he has displayed a new method of portraying villainly [sic], a method that many of our Western actors would do well to emulate. It was comprehensive, convincing and effective, and throughout his whole characterization, there was not an unnecessary gesture or expression."[34]

In Hayakawa's star vehicles that followed *The Cheat*, in order to construct Hayakawa's star image for the mainstream middle-class audience, Lasky strategically created a balance between the ambiguously intense acting style, which was publicized as "restrained" with reference to Japanese traditional culture, and the more expressive acting style that signified the image of an Americanized star and a model minority.

In *Forbidden Paths*, Hayakawa's intensely ambiguous acting style functions to place his character in an awkward position in relation to the heroine. On the one hand, he looks shy, but on the other hand, he also looks to be restraining himself from his deep desire to obtain the heroine by violating the taboo of miscegenation.

The intertitles of the film explicitly state that Sato (Hayakawa) is in love with the heroine, Mildred, but he rarely expresses his emotions in obvious manners, even in the close-ups of his face. He keeps his mask-like countenance. In the script, in one scene, when Sato realizes that Mildred has dropped a flower, he looks at it "with reverent affection." There is no such implication of Sato's fetishistic behavior in the film. This change from the script functions to desexualize Sato, while at the same time the omission functions to emphasize ambivalence in Sato's psychology. Even when Sato looks at Mildred and Harry, whom she loves, he does not change his facial expressions much. He simply pauses in a close-up when he sees Harry take

Mildred's hand. He looks a little stunned, but it is not clear from his facial expressions whether he is jealous, furious, sad, desperate, or conspiring. When Mildred's father dies, he looks at her with eyes wide open and tries to embrace her from behind her back—but he eventually pauses and decides not to do it. After a stilled moment, he retains his mask-like face.

At the climax of the film, Hayakawa drastically changes his acting style. In a scene in which Sato decides to sacrifice himself for the white American heroine, Hayakawa starts to use more pantomimic gestures and more obvious facial expressions. The close-ups in the climactic scenes in *Forbidden Paths* begin with intensely ambiguous appearances of Hayakawa's facial expressions, but, contrary to those in *The Cheat*, they function to eloquently express Hayakawa's character's psychological states and his emotions in the end. The repeated close-ups of Sato when he listens to the conversation between Mildred and Benita from behind the curtain display Sato's gradual psychological development until he comes to a point of being clearly convinced that "Love is Sacrifice." In the close-up after Benita's words to Mildred, "Love him—till your heart breaks—you'll never get him," Sato opens his eyes wide, clenches his teeth severely, and closes his mouth tightly. He grabs a curtain strongly with his right hand. Yet, at this point, his face is still mask-like. He pauses. This makes another stilled moment. Then, after Benita says, "Love is sacrifice—if you want him, you'll have to be—what I was [a mistress]," he strongly frowns, severely clenches his teeth, and furiously squints. This close-up of Sato clearly indicates his furious emotion against Benita, and then his astonishment at the words "Love is sacrifice." After Benita leaves, Sato comes close to Mildred. At this point, he shows her a facial expression that he has never shown to her: deep frowning. After Mildred leaves, he moves his eyes right and left many times to show his embarrassment, makes a desperate expression, frowns several times, and, finally, comes to his concrete decision. Then, finally, he regains a calm face and leaves the room with dignity to face Benita for a melodramatic showdown.

In a scene where Sato invites Benita out, Hayakawa uses more pantomimic acting. Narratologically, the viewers already know that Hayakawa's exaggerated style of acting emphasizes the fact that Sato is acting in this scene to deceive Benita. He opens his arms wide, and, with a big smile, says to her, "It is too beautiful a day to remain indoors, Señora. You like yachting—a motor boat?" Sato looks at Benita ardently. Once she turns her back to him, Sato shows a conspiring glance at her and grins. These expressions are exclusively for the viewers. On the boat, he crosses his arms on his chest and looks absentmindedly far away in an obvious manner. Consciously and strategically using the pantomimic gestures, Hayakawa (and Lasky) confirms the melodramatically heroic image of Sato, a model minority who devotes himself to the good of a white American couple.

The Secret Game takes a similar strategy. On one hand, when Nara-Nara (Hayakawa) speaks to Kitty of patriotism toward the United States, saying, "You're a loyal little American—eh?," he makes a pantomimic gesture that signifies Uncle Sam in patriotic posters, saying "I Want You for the U.S. Army": he points his index finger at her with his eyes wide open. Then, saying, "Will you help me to protect the soldiers of your country—and the honor of mine?," he raises his right fist high. Hayakawa repeats the same gesture in other films. In *Banzai*, Hayakawa, in a role of an American soldier with a blonde mustache, explicitly imitates the pose of Uncle Sam with his finger pointing at the camera. In *His Birthright*, when Yukio (Hayakawa) attacks the female German spy, he looks directly at the camera in a close-up and points at the camera with his right forefinger and frowns a little.

On the other hand, Hayakawa (and Lasky) strategically uses his intensely ambiguous acting, explicitly referring to *The Cheat*. In a scene in which Nara-Nara attacks Kitty with a knife, Hayakawa's facial expressions and gestures imitate those in *The Cheat*. In a medium close-up, with white makeup on his skin and dark makeup on his eyes and eyebrows that seem to imitate *kumadori*, a special makeup for kabuki theater, Hayakawa appears to be taking the *mie* pose, a stylized expression of kabuki: the frozen moment. Nara-Nara's death scene also refers to a scene in *The Cheat*. When the knife stabs Nara-Nara's back, he stops twice in the middle of his movement with his eyes wide open until he falls down on the floor over Smith's dead body.

Moreover, *The Secret Game* attempts to connect Hayakawa's acting to stereotypically Japanese cultural traits. When Nara-Nara explains to Kitty how honorable his Japanese sword is, his eyes become intensely wide open and his mouth becomes sealed tightly. He ritualistically raises the sword with his both hands and bows to it. The shot dissolves to a scene in front of Nara-Nara's house in Japan with shoji screens, shadows of bamboo, paper lanterns, and a willow tree—a flashback in which Nara-Nara receives a Japanese sword from his father, also in a Japanese kimono, and bows with profound filial respect. When the scene dissolves back to the shot at Nara-Nara's office, he says to Kitty, "And he [my father] bade me return, at the end of my service, and lay my sword—unstained—at his feet," and he respectfully places the sword on the shelf. In the final scene of the film, the spirit of Nara-Nara, who chooses a self-sacrificial death to save his honor, brings the sword back to his father.

At Haworth, despite the fact that Hayakawa theoretically obtained freedom to choose his own films, he came to play more straightforward romantic heroes. Hayakawa's acting styles became closer to those of white male actors in contemporaneous action and comic films.

In *His Birthright*, Hayakawa clearly uses his intensely ambiguous acting style. When Yukio (Hayakawa) thinks of his mother committing suicide in a flashback, in an extreme close-up Hayakawa compresses his lips and slowly looks up into a mirror. The close-up only displays Hayakawa's static mask-like facial expressions with widely opened eyes and tightly closed mouth, even though this is an emotionally loaded scene.

Yet, overall, in *His Birthright*, Hayakawa employs more pantomimic gestures and obviously emotional facial expressions, which emphasize Americanized characteristics of Yukio but often make him look comical. Yukio's Americanization is physicalized by Hayakawa's pantomimic performance. In the opening scene (of the extant print), when Yukio finds a cheat in a card game, he expresses his disappointment in obvious gestures and facial expressions. He looks at the card, moves his eyes to the upper left, bends his neck a little, then shakes his head, and sighs. On the same boat, when Yukio happens to pick up a name card, he tries hard to remember the name on the card, blinking many times. When he remembers it, in a medium close-up, he opens his mouth and expresses his astonishment in an unambiguously emotional manner.

In action scenes, Hayakawa clearly imitates such white American male stars as Douglas Fairbanks Sr., who was famous for his physical strength. When Yukio sneaks out of the boat, extreme long shots capture Hayakawa's bodily actions—jumping off the deck, clinging to the rope to the dock, and running away very fast on the shore.

In other scenes, Hayakawa often uses his hands to reflect his emotional states. When Yukio's female friend helps him decode his own handwriting, he first places his left hand on his head to express his perplexity, and when he finds out what is written on the paper, he puts his hands together in front of his chest, jumps up for joy, and holds up his fist in triumph.

In *The Tong Man*, Luk Chan (Hayakawa) appears with the mask-like expression on his face. Without changing his countenance at all, he throws a hatchet at a sleeping old Chinese man. Yet, when the old man is astonished, he suddenly starts laughing at him, wildly moving his body and arms. Thus, his ambiguous restrained-looking facial expression at the beginning is quickly replaced by his pantomimic gestures.

Similarly, in a scene when Luk Chan follows the tong's order and tries to murder the heroine's father, Hayakawa uses his ambiguously intense acting style. With his eyes wide open he raises his hatchet and pauses momentarily. Yet, despite the frozen movement and moment, Luk Chan's emotional state here is not ambiguous at all. A shot of his affair with the heroine is inserted here as a flashback. His suffering is clearly displayed by the form of flashback and leaves no ambiguity as to his psychological state.

Throughout the film Hayakawa uses pantomimic gestures, eloquent words, and obvious facial expressions to express his affection to the heroine. Like Romeo in *Romeo and Juliet* or like the characters played by Douglas Fairbanks Sr. in his star vehicles, Luk Chan easily climbs up the wall and jumps over the bamboo fence to see the heroine. He takes the heroine's hands, saying, "You are my love calling," and embraces her shoulder. In another scene, he even presses his cheek to hers.

It is significant that Hayakawa's pantomimic acting in *The Tong Man* avoids any stereotypically racialized characteristics. The white actor who plays Ming Tai, the Chinese villain, displays racialized performances, such as standing with a slight stoop and placing his hands in front of his chest. Resorting to more pantomimic gestures and emotionally explicit facial expressions, Hayakawa's acting in *The Tong Man* comes closer to those of other American heroes and stars.

In *An Arabian Knight*, Hayakawa's gestures and facial expressions are the most pantomimic of all his films made at Haworth. Hayakawa comes much closer to a mixture of such white American action heroes as Douglas Fairbanks Sr. and such white American comic stars as Harold Lloyd and Buster Keaton. The difference in performance in *An Arabian Knight* likely also reflects ethnic stereotypes about Arabs.

When Ahmed (Hayakawa) appears, he speaks to his donkey with comical gestures, with his arms stretched and his mouth wide open. When many women with veils, sitting behind lattice windows, hail him and throw kisses one after another, he waves his right hand widely to everyone and wears a big smile on his face. In the middle of his secret meeting with his girlfriend he is caught by her mother. Hayakawa shows an extremely surprised expression with his eyes and mouth, jumps out of the window, and runs away, insanely whipping his donkey. Looking at the mother, who is angrily raising her fist, he fully puffs out his cheeks contemptuously.

When Cordelia keeps treating Ahmed as her king, Hayakawa portrays Ahmed's embarrassment in comical gestures: bowing extremely respectfully to Cordelia, sneaking away from her with stealthy steps and hiding behind a tree, trying hard to avoid Cordelia's embrace, spreading his hands and praying for mercy to escape from Cordelia's fanatic thoughts. Moreover, when he goes back to his girlfriend's neighborhood in the Egyptian king's costume, he pretends to be a king, playfully using dignified gestures and facial expressions. In medium close-ups, Ahmed, this time not on a donkey but in a car, folds his arms in front of his chest and looks at the people in the neighborhood with exaggeratedly cold-looking eyes. He taps the driver on the head, makes him open the door for him, and gets out of the car in a dignified manner. In front of his girlfriend, who has been sleeping, he once again folds his arms. He stops her coming near him by raising his left hand and says with emotionless expression, "I have royal blood in my veins." She starts laughing and so does Ahmed. As soon as her mother appears and gets angry again, a surprised Ahmed runs away quickly to his car. As the car starts moving all of a sudden, he falls down completely into the car as a silent clown often does. In this manner, in *An Arabian Knight*, Hayakawa consciously imitates acting styles of silent comedians.

At the same time, this film emphasizes Hayakawa's physical strength as if he were an action star. Tied up by an enemy to a table, Ahmed acrobatically moves his body and frees himself. When pursuing an enemy, Ahmed runs extremely fast and climbs up to a second-story window from the back of his horse, as Fairbanks often does. During the climactic battles, after throwing a villainous woman into a chest and locking her up, Hayakawa uses both of his hands to make a pantomimic gesture of wiping sweat from his forehead. Having the heroine back, he playfully throws a kiss to the villain. Ahmed shows a triumphant smile, jumps out of the window, jumps on a horse, and rides away. Hayakawa's more pantomimic acting in *An Arabian Knight* thus simultaneously places him among the group of action and comic stars of the time.

Hayakawa's pantomimic gestures and psychologically explicit facial expressions in the films made at Haworth moved Hayakawa's stardom closer to that of contemporaneous white American actors. In comparison, *The Dragon Painter* placed Hayakawa in a supposedly Japanese landscape. However, even in this surrounding, Hayakawa resorted to more pantomimic gestures and emotionally filled facial expressions.

Hayakawa used explicit facial expressions to clearly deliver Tatsu's emotional states. When Tastu (Hayakawa) learns that the heroine Umeko self-sacrificially commits suicide, he shows his astonishment with his eyes and mouth and then cries out in distress. When Umeko reappears after the success of Tatsu's exhibition and touches Tatsu's hand, Tatsu, who has been embracing her kimono to remember her, shows his astonishment by using his extended arms and his wide-open mouth. Then, they affectionately embrace each other. Astonishment, grief, and affection—these emotional states of Tatsu are clearly represented by Hayakawa's gestures and facial expressions.

In *The Dragon Painter*, Hayakawa also displays the physical strength of an action star. Tatsu jumps off the rocks and runs in the wilderness. He raises his fists and tries to summon a dragon. Despite its setting in a supposedly Japanese space, *The Dragon Painter* exists along with a certain tendency of Hayakawa's star vehicles at Haworth: more pantomimic gestures and emotionally filled facial expressions to emphasize Hayakawa's Americanized star image. However, ironically, Hayakawa's attempt to imitate more mainstream acting and to become more like other contemporaneous actors ended up with him losing his uniqueness and even his fan base. By 1921, Hayakawa's performance was criticized for the first time in his career. *Variety* criticized Hayakawa's change of performance styles in *Five Days to Live* (Norman Dawn, 8 January 1922): "Dollars are going sadly to waste trying to make the Japanese star into a washed-out imitation of an American screen hero. The man has unlimited ability, particularly as a heavy. Why not let him loose on a lot of sweet Americans who foil him in the end? Make him a George Arliss of the screen. But perhaps Mr. Hayakawa objects."[35]

Thus, Hayakawa's acting had a fair degree of latitude, from the mask-like intense ambiguity in facial expressions to the mainstream pantomimic gestures, but in a strategically organized manner. The complex mixture of acting styles in Hayakawa's star vehicles indicates Hayakawa's and the studios' continuous efforts to strike a balance between Americanization and Japaneseness in his star image. At the same time, it could be their attempt to pursue the possibility of something new, whether it would be the uniquely Orientalized "ambiguous" style for the American domestic market or the "universal" style of acting that mixed pantomimic, "verisimilar," and Japanese "traditional" acting methods for foreign markets, within the context of Hollywood's globalization in the latter half of the 1910s.

14

THE STAR FALLS

Postwar Nativism and the Decline

of Sessue Hayakawa's Stardom

I n spite of Robertson-Cole's strategic standardization of Hayakawa's star vehicles and its extensive publicity for them, Hayakawa's popularity started to decline in the early 1920s. According to a popular poll of film stars conducted by the *Motion Picture Story Magazine*, Hayakawa was ranked number 44 in December 1918, but in December 1920 his rank had dropped to number 124.[1] Then in 1921, a reviewer of *Where Lights Are Low* (Colin Campbell, 4 September 1921), a Hayakawa vehicle, pointed out, "This Jap star is either popular with your fans or he is unpopular."[2] It was the first time that Hayakawa's unpopularity was reported in trade journals. In 1924, a Japanese film magazine noted, "Hayakawa knew his popularity in the United States was gradually declining" by the early 1920s.[3] Hayakawa's American stardom, which experienced "the best year" in 1919, thus came to a turning point by 1921.

Behind the decline of Hayakawa's popularity there was a change in the sociopolitical discourse in the early 1920s. The period between 1918, when Hayakawa established Haworth, and 1922, when he left Hollywood, witnessed the rise of strong American nationalism, or nativism, in the aftermath of World War I. The film historian Diane Negra observes, "All of the foregrounding social, economic, and political phenomena contributed to the formation of a climate in which the American film industry self-consciously structured itself to meet the requirements of American nationalism."[4] Indeed, Frederick H. Elliot, the executive secretary of the National Association of the Motion Picture Industry, stated on 19 December 1920, in a press release, "The motion picture industry of this country has been mobilized to make the fight for Americanism. The leading men of the industry have pledged to Franklin K. Lane, Secretary of the Interior, all the resources of their organizations, the services of the stars and directors, and the co-operation of the exhibitors in a country-wide screen campaign to combat Bolshevism, and in the words of Vice President Marshall, to fight for 'the winning of America for Americans."[5]

More specifically, according to the historian Walter Benn Michaels, the nativist discourse of the 1920s denied the possibility of Americanization for immigrants and emphasized the ultimate difference between "American" and "un-American." In "progressive racism," Michaels argues, "projects of 'Americanization'" of immigrants always existed behind the racist discourse. The "inferiority of 'alien' races" was emphasized in regard to new immigrants, but eventually they were considered to be able to assimilate into American society as Americans. However, in the nativist discourse of the 1920s, immigrants' ultimate "difference" was emphasized. "American" came to be regarded not as "a set of social and economic conditions" but as "an identity that exists prior to and independent of those conditions," and "the qualities that constituted the American could not be taught."[6] In fact, Frances Kellor, who used to be the central figure of the Americanization movement in the 1910s, stated in 1921 that American people began to think it was wrong to consider that all foreigners were future American citizens and that political, economic, and educational opportunities should be equally provided.[7]

The notion of racial hierarchy, which left room for Americanization of nonwhite races and was the keystone of the formation of Hayakawa's star image, was, thus, transformed into racial difference, which admitted the existence of races that were different from the Caucasian race and difficult to Americanize. The image of the racial and cultural middle-ground position in Hayakawa's star persona, which had been attained by way of careful negotiation between the image of Americanization and that of Japaneseness, suddenly lost its balance.

As the wider discourses on race and immigrants changed after World War I, the more specific social and cultural discourses on Japan and Japanese people, which formed the basis of Hayakawa's stardom, also changed. Roger Daniels writes, "In the years after the war, the real rather than the imagined acts of the Japanese government were of growing concern to many Americans."[8] More than ever, images of Japan became politically and economically concrete to the American people, mainly because of Japan's strengthened imperialist policy after World War I.

At the 1919 Paris Peace Conference, Japan made European countries and the United States accept the imperialistic Twenty-one Demands upon China. Japan also continued its subjugation of Korea and obtained economic bases in the Shantung Peninsula and the Pacific Islands formerly held by Germany. When the Allies sent forces to Siberia to oppose the Russian Revolution in 1918, Japanese troops stayed in Siberia two years longer than other countries' troops. It was even reported that Japanese troops came into direct conflict with American troops several times. Moreover, at the Paris Conference, Japan requested the "Racial Equality Clause," opposing "white supremacy" in the world order under the rules of the League of Nations, which directly went against the nativist racial discourse in the United States. All of these postwar Japanese actions were regarded as directly opposing American economic interests in Asia, such as the "open door" in China, maintenance of territory in the Pacific, and safety of Americans in the Philippines. Especially after 1918, both Japan and the United States turned from debtor to creditor nations. Both governments began to recognize each other as economic and military competitors in the Pacific and Asian regions.

These imperialist activities of Japan became more and more visible through increasing media coverage. Fox Films, for instance, announced the release of a news film series entitled "Face to Face with Japan," which would question "the so-called peril of Japanese expansion and territorial aggrandizement in respect to the effect of these upon American interests" and reveal "the secrets of Japan's Army and Navy."[9]

As Japan's imperialist policy became more visible to the American people, the anti-Japanese movement was resurrected in California. During the war, anti-Japanese sentiment was quiescent because Japan was an allied nation. Yet, right after the war, such groups as the California Oriental Exclusion League and the Los Angeles County Anti-Asiatic Society were organized by labor unions, farmers' unions, and politicians who aimed at votes from those unions in the election of 1920. In 1920 these groups were reorganized and named the Japanese Exclusion League of California.

The league tried to spread its anti-Japanese message nationwide by sending out lecturers to the East and the Midwest. One such lecturer, Valentine Stuart McClatchy, the head of the league and the former publisher of the *Sacramento Bee*, which had initiated the prewar anti-Japanese movement, insisted that Japanese immigrants would become a military threat because they would never lose their bonds with the Japanese government and never assimilate to America.[10] Wallace Irwin, who wrote the original stories of *Hashimura Togo*, published an anti-Japanese novel, *Seed of the Sun* (1921) and warned that Japanese immigrants could be spies for the Japanese government. Even though these lectures and novelists were highly propagandistic, they linked Japan's postwar imperialistic expansion into China and the Pacific to the American people's more concrete concern about Japanese immigrants in the United States. They effectively reformulated the decades-old ambiguous yellow peril rhetoric with more specific images of Japan's economic and military threat.

Because of the increasing media presentation of imperialistic images of Japan, and because of the persistent anti-Japanese propaganda from California, the anti-Japanese movement rooted in the Pacific states started to have an influence on nationwide public opinion for the first time. Even easterners and midwesterners, who had barely supported anti-Japanese movements in the Pacific states before the war, began to oppose Japanese immigration. A renowned writer on the East Coast, Lothrop Stoddard, warned against Japan's economic expansion in racist terms in 1920: "There is a very immediate danger that white stocks may be swamped by Asiatic blood."[11] A writer for the *Nation's* special issue on Japan on 2 February 1921, admitted, "It is not as easy to champion Japan before America as it was a few years ago," even though the writer "still believe[d] the attitude of California and her politicians to be all wrong."[12] Another writer for the issue clearly stated, "Japanese immigration should, in my judgement, be flatly prohibited," even though he tried to differentiate himself from politicians in California by admitting that those "Japanese already in the United States should, however, be given all the privileges which are accorded to other aliens in this country."[13] Thus, as the historians Eleanor Tupper and George E. McReynolds insist, "the American public as a whole" became "greatly excited and shocked" by Japan's postwar imperialistic acts and showed its "irritation" and "distrust" at Japan's intentions in the Far East.[14]

Under these conditions, federal judgment and policy came to embed anti-Japanese sentiment into laws. The 1922 Ozawa case at the U.S. Supreme Court and the Immigration Act of 1924 legally denied Japanese immigrants the opportunity to become U.S. citizens. Ozawa Takao originally filed an application for U.S. citizenship on 14 October 1914, after twenty years of studying in an American university and working in an American company. After his application was denied, Ozawa challenged the rejection in the Federal District Court for the Territory of Hawaii in 1914, but the court ruled that Ozawa was not eligible for naturalized citizenship.[15] In 1922 Ozawa Takao informed the Supreme Court that "at heart" he was "a true American." Ozawa insisted that he did not have any connection with the Japanese government or with any Japanese churches, schools, or organizations. His family belonged to an American church and his children attended an American school. He spoke English at home so that his children could not speak Japanese. He even chose for a wife a woman educated in American schools, instead of one educated in Japan. Ozawa thus Americanized himself as Hayakawa's characters in his star vehicles did. However, Ozawa lost his petition, because, according to the verdict, he was "clearly not Caucasian."[16] No matter how Americanized in his lifestyle, Ozawa was regarded as racially different and thus had no right to be completely assimilated into America. According to this ruling, Hayakawa's stardom, which was mainly based on the balance between the image of Americanization and the image of Japaneseness, was deprived of one of its wings.

Then, in 1924, the new immigration act, passed by the U.S. Congress, prohibited the entry of "aliens ineligible for citizenship." This act crystallized the quota system for immigration, which continued until 1965: there was no quota for Japanese people, who were categorized as aliens "ineligible for citizenship."[17] Roger Daniels argues that the "California position" regarding the anti-Japanese movement, which "did not win national favor in either 1906–1907 or 1913, was written into the statute book in 1924."[18]

As the social and legal discourses on Japan changed after World War I, the cultural discourses on Japan also altered. Japan's safely exotic and artistically sophisticated image, which had led middle-class American women to consume and domesticate Japanese Taste as an emblem of cultural refinement, gradually lost its appeal. The third volume (1910–14) of the *Readers' Guide to Periodical Literature* has forty-four entries of articles about "Art—Japan," the fourth volume (1915–18) has fifteen, and the fifth volume (1919–21) has only eleven.[19]

The number of fiction films with Japanese subjects also decreased. According to the subject index of the *AFI Catalog*, in 1921 there were only two films about "Japan," the "Japanese," and the "Japanese American," in 1922 only one, and from 1923 through the rest of the 1920s there were none. In contrast, the number was six in 1920, eight in 1919, nine in 1918, seven in 1917, and many more in the early 1910s and before.[20] As a result, in 1921, a Japanese film magazine reported that in the United States "there is no film about Japan this year, even though there were many last year."[21] Yamamoto Togo, a Japanese journalist and actor in Los Angeles, reported in the same year that films about Japanese subjects suddenly became "unwelcome" because they "would need expensive costumes, props, and so forth," and "because they may offend the anti-Japanese problems and they are not popular."[22] In 1922, the actor and journalist Aoyama Yukio wrote in the *Rafu Shimpo*, "Without relaxation of Japanese exclusion, there won't be any drama of Japan."[23] A Japanese film magazine reported in the same year, "in these couple of years when Japan and the U.S. had the most delicate problems in the world, there was no drama, educational film, or even films with Japanese landscape."[24]

At the same time, anti-Japanese films came into existence. Even Robertson-Cole made one such film, *Who's Your Servant?* (director uncredited, February 1920). In the film, villainous Japanese spies threaten American military secrets and white American women.[25] George T. Pardy of ETR clearly pointed out the obvious anti-Japanese content of the film: "Whenever you see a soft-footed Jap gliding unobtrusively around in the background of a picture whose plot turns upon the theft of U. S. Navy official documents, it is a fairly safe bet that the slant-eyed son of the Orient is the guilty party."[26] A reviewer of *Wid's Daily* compared the anti-Japanese content of the film to that in *The Cheat*: "[There are] sequences of gripping power in the development of the business between the girl and the Jap," which can "bring in a climax to rival the time-honored denouement in 'The Cheat.'"[27]

Under such anti-Japanese conditions in Hollywood, Japanese actors, one after another, went back to Japan.[28] Remaining Japanese actors stopped playing Japanese roles and decided to play mainly Chinese characters.[29] In fact, in spite of the unpopularity of Japanese subjects, Aoyama reported in the *Rafu Shimpo*, "[1922] saw the peak of the dramas set in the East. Most of those films were set in Turkey or China."[30] The *Rafu Shimpo* tried to explain this popularity of films about non-Japanese Asia, especially China: "In California, increase in fearing the Japanese, and decrease in abhorring the Chinese."[31] Before World War I, the popular image of Japan was the movable middle in the racial and cultural hierarchy. When Japanese people were deprived of this image, Chinese people replaced it. The Japanese actor Inoue Masao wrote, "I cannot deny that in American people's view Chinese people are closer to Americans than Japanese people are."[32]

Hayakawa's willingness to continue playing Oriental roles, Chinese roles in particular, corresponded to the decline in popularity of films set in Japan and the increase in favorable views toward Chinese. After 1921 Hayakawa played only one Japanese role and kept playing non-Japanese roles until he left Hollywood in June 1922. A Japanese film magazine reported that "Hayakawa had not made films about Japan in order to avoid anti-Japanese sentiments" until *Black Roses* (Colin Campbell, 22 May 1921).[33] It was Hayakawa's desperate attempt to maintain his stardom, clinging to the image of a racially middle-ground position. Yet, ultimately that attempt was in vain.

The decline in popularity of films about Japan seriously influenced Hayakawa's popularity. In fact, after 1921, the number of films in which Hayakawa appeared decreased. Exhibitors from all over the United States started reporting Hayakawa's loss of appeal among audiences. In December 1921, an exhibitor in Virginia reported that *The First Born* (Colin Campbell, 30 January 1921) was a "very good drama, but Hayakawa [is] not popular with my patrons." An exhibitor in New Jersey said that *Black Roses* "did not seem to please as other Jap pictures."[34] An exhibitor in Arkansas considered *Five Days to Live* to be "a poor offering from an entertaining standpoint."[35] Another exhibitor called Hayakawa a denigrating term: "Personally I thought this [*Five Days to Live*] a beautiful picture, but my patrons were only 50 percent pleased. Didn't pay for the rental. The 'Jap' is no card here. — Harold F. Wendt, Rivoli theater, Defiance, O. — General patronage."[36]

Gaylyn Studlar argues that in the 1920s "fan magazines increasingly encouraged a distanciation between screen persona and actor-identity."[37] If so, even if extra-filmic anti-Japanese sentiment had influenced the image of Hayakawa's identity as a Japanese actor, his screen persona would have been safely distanced from the outside world, especially when Hayakawa avoided playing Japanese roles. However, in the case of Hayakawa, his screen persona was not able to escape from the public knowledge of his actor-identity as a Japanese man. Hayakawa's actor-identity was too deeply rooted as a representative of Japanese art, culture, nation, and race, even when he stopped playing Japanese characters, no matter how deliberately Lasky and Robertson-Cole emphasized the Americanized aspect of his star image. Already in 1918, *MPW* noted, "The essential character of Mr. Hayakawa is that of gentle manliness, and, if it is representative of his race, it contributes to a more complete understanding of his people."[38]

The image of a representative of Japan was so strongly inscribed into Hayakawa's actor-identity that it subtended his fictional roles even when he played non-Japanese characters. In the reviews in trade journals, Hayakawa's filmic characters in the 1920s were always regarded as Japanese, even when he played other nationalities. The *ETR* confused Chinese and Japanese in *Li Ting Lang* (Swickard, July 1920), in which Hayakawa played a Chinese student: "Interesting photoplay woven around race prejudice with Hayakawa in the role of Japanese college youth who falls in love with an American girl."[39] Even though the story of *Where Lights Are Low* is set in China, a reviewer at *Variety* wrote, "The picture presents the Japanese star in almost entirely native atmosphere and this is the background in which he is at his best. . . . No one has yet been able to make him a romantic figure in American or any other Occidental surroundings."[40] Reviews of *The Swamp* in EH and *Variety* stated that Hayakawa plays a "Japanese vegetable vender," even though the story is set in the tenement district of New York where few Japanese people lived and the names of the characters, such as Wang, are clearly Chinese.[41] The EH called Hayakawa's Chinese roles Japanese again in *Five Days to Live* and *The Vermilion Pencil* (Dawn, 19 March 1922), both of which were set in China: "Like his former vehicle, 'Five Days to Live,' the scene of 'The Vermilion Pencil' is laid wholly in Japan."[42] These reviews indicate the reviewers' Orientalist confusion of national boundaries in Asia, and, at the same time, they demonstrate that Hayakawa's extra-filmic actor-identity as Japanese was strongly imprinted on the spectators' consciousness and expectations.

Hayakawa's status as a representative of Japan in American minds was also the result of Hayakawa's outstanding extra-filmic activities. By the early 1920s, Hayakawa came to regard himself as a representative of Japan. Yukio, Hayakawa's son, wrote later, "My father even made himself look more Japanese than necessary."[43] Hayakawa declared that his "West Coast lifestyle," including the extravagant parties that he threw at his luxurious house, which was called the Argyle Castle, and the gold-plated Pierce Arrow that he drove, was meant to demonstrate that Japanese people were able to live just as lavishly as American.[44] Important Japanese political figures, such as Nitobe Inazo, vice secretary of the League of Nations, visited Hayakawa's studio when they were in the United States.[45] Parties for a famous Japanese opera singer, Miura Tamaki, who played Cio-Cio-San in *Madama Butterfly* at the Metropolitan Opera House, were held at Hayakawa's residence.[46] Hayakawa also cooperated with Japanese communities that protested an anti-Japanese film, *Shadow of the West*.[47] The *Rafu Shimpo* favorably reported, "Even though Hayakawa is very busy shooting his new film, he is making every effort to prevent the film from exhibition."[48]

When Hayakawa visited Washington, D.C., on his way back to Los Angeles from his recuperative trip to the East Coast following an operation for appendicitis, President Warren G. Harding invited him to the White House on 27 June 1921.[49] Harding needed to publicize his friendly relations with Japan while he was taking a cautious diplomatic policy toward that country in international conferences, including one in Washington, D.C., in 1921. The *Nyu Yoku Shimpo*, a Japanese newspaper in New York, reported Hayakawa's East

Coast trip: "After *The Cheat* was severely criticized by the Japanese audience, he [Hayakawa] realized the impact of his art upon the U.S.-Japan relations. Hayakawa declared that he would contribute to the mutual understandings between the two countries. . . . Hayakawa is Americanized, but as a Japanese man, he insists that he would make every effort to the mutual understandings between the Japanese and American people using motion pictures."[50] The *Nyu Yoku Shimpo* thus expected Hayakawa to play an active role in the United States as a representative of the Japanese people. Its editorial note on 6 July 1921, read,

> The motion picture industry has recently become one of the top industries together with steel and automobile industries in the U.S. Motion pictures exist as essential elements in the lives of American people. Therefore, his [Hayakawa's] role is undoubtedly significant. His decision, his creativity and his responsibility have become extremely important. . . . Now that he is the only Japanese actor who has been actively engaged in the American film industry, we strongly hope he will do his best and will not degrade his international fame. . . . He should fully understand his responsibility as a Japanese and do his best mastering his art. He must do good for Japan.[51]

Hayakawa's personalization of the political as the representative of the Japanese people had an inevitable influence on his status at Robertson-Cole and eventually led to his declining popularity among American audiences under postwar nativist conditions.

During his silent film stardom, Hayakawa's persona maintained an effective tension between representing the popular images of Japanese culture and embodying the American assimilationist narrative. However, in the nationwide anti-Japanese nativist atmosphere and with the legalization of Japanese inassimilability, it became difficult for the Japanese actor to maintain his stardom, which had been based on a well-balanced cross-cultural star image. Symbolically, the year Hayakawa left Robertson-Cole and Hollywood was the year in which the U.S. Supreme Court officially denied naturalization to Japanese immigrants in the Ozawa case of 1922.

As a result, Robertson-Cole became inclined to use Hayakawa in films that contained fairly anti-Japanese sentiments. *The Vermilion Pencil*, the last film Hayakawa made with Robertson-Cole, was based on a story written by Homer Lea, the author of an infamous anti-Japanese novel, *The Valor of Ignorance* (1909). *The Vermilion Pencil* was a rehash of *The Wrath of the Gods*.[52]

Both films depicted Asia as an uncivilized and premodern region controlled by a religious cult, connected with a volcano eruption.[53] Hayakawa had to re-play a religiously primitive old man, a role very similar to the one that he had played in *The Wrath of the Gods* when he was not yet considered a star.

Hayakawa later recalled the production of *The Vermilion Pencil* and said:

> The last story was picked like the toss of a penny. I was given three stories to choose from. I do not like any of them. Still they insist I must choose one of these. . . . I was associated with certain men in motion picture enterprise. They owe me $90,000. I never ask for this money. I think there is plenty of time to pay. Perhaps it was that they think too much about this debt. They think it good to goad and humiliate me—to pick a quarrel. . . . He called me by a name. It is something should not come out of the mouth. Something that is unpardon-able insult to me and an affront to my nationality. No man can help where he is born—what is his blood. Only an ignorant coward throws up to a man that he does not like his race. I come of a proud people—a man of my quality could not endure such insult. . . . He say then: "People in this country have no use for *Chinks.*" I am not *Chink.* I am Japanese gentleman, and the word *Chink* is not fit to be spoke. . . . I take many little insult and humiliation—but no—nothing so big as this.[54]

Hayakawa did not clearly state who "they" were, but it is obvious that "they" were the executives of Robertson-Cole, who came to share the nativist and anti-Japanese sentiment in American society in general.

The case of *The Vermilion Pencil* suggests that Hayakawa was seriously losing control over his films and his star image. By 1921, Robertson-Cole had started producing films with a rationalized and standardized basis and be-came "foremost of the independent motion picture producers and distribu-tors," according to its own declaration in trade journals.[55] Haworth was virtu-ally integrated into Robertson-Cole when Hayakawa signed a new four-year contract with Robertson-Cole on 28 March 1920.[56]

As for this new contract, both an American journalist, Grace Kingsley, and a Japanese film critic, Mori Iwao, claimed that Hayakawa became indepen-dent from Haworth, established his own company, the Sessue Hayakawa Fea-ture Play Company, and made an exclusive contract with Robertson-Cole.[57] It is ironic to claim that Hayakawa had finished his contract with Haworth be-cause Haworth was originally Hayakawa's own company. This claim reveals Hayakawa's loss of control at Haworth by 1920. Probably, the truth was that

Hayakawa's new company was merely nominal and was set up by Robertson-Cole. In spite of its name, Hayakawa, his films, and his star image entered under the total control of Robertson-Cole. In fact, after *The First Born*, the first film under the new contract, the name "Hayakawa Feature Play Company" vanished from film ads in trade journals. Instead, there were only the words "Produced by R-C [Robertson-Cole] Pictures."[58]

In his autobiography, Hayakawa wrote, "The integration of the Haworth Pictures Corporation into Robertson-Cole, begun in 1920 when we changed studios, was almost complete" by the time *The Swamp* was made.[59] In an interview conducted in the 1950s, Hayakawa simply explained that the integration happened only because "the studio [of Haworth] was prohibited by the Fire Department" because the studio did not "have [an] iron building." Therefore, he "moved into that unit, a huge studio, new, everything terrific, proper conditions." However, in the same interview, Hayakawa said, "I wasn't quite happy after that."[60] His confession indicates that the integration was not what Hayakawa really wanted.

Under the new contract, Hayakawa's loss of control over his production was obvious. When Hayakawa's new contract was announced, the NYDM and the *Los Angeles Times* reported that Hayakawa's own play, *A Man's Name*, in which Hayakawa had appeared on the stage for Japanese audiences, would be the second production.[61] However, a film version of *A Man's Name* was never made. Moreover, even though *The First Born* was Hayakawa's "dream project"—he had wanted to make the film version ever since he had seen the stage play at the Alcazar Theater in San Francisco years earlier—he was not satisfied with the completed film.[62] The reception of the film was great. The National Board of Review included *The First Born* in one of the nineteen "exceptional pictures" of 1921.[63] However, Hayakawa did not like the film because, according to him, the producers did not let Hayakawa play the character as he wanted but made him "weep with glycerin tears."[64]

In May 1920, Robertson-Cole published a multi-page ad for its "Super-Special" series, including Hayakawa's star vehicles, in trade journals. The ad read, "Robertson-Cole makes the positive assertion that none of these productions shall be released unless they pass the test which classes them as 'Specials.' Robertson-Cole is in a position to make this declaration because its contracts with producers provide for the rejection of pictures until they are of the highest standard of excellence."[65] According to this ad, Robertson-Cole began to execute the ultimate authority to decide the content of films that it would distribute. During his courtesy visit to the Robertson-Cole executives in New York, Hayakawa had to promise them that he would be "selecting the best stories which the market affords," each of which would "be one of great appeal to Americans, and at the same time of international appeal."[66] *A Man's Name* did not "pass the test." *The First Born* had a "great appeal to Americans," but not to Hayakawa.

At the end of 1921, Hayakawa published his view on film in the *Rafu Shimpo*. What Hayakawa emphasized again was his intention to make films with truthful and authentic Japanese characters. He wrote,

> [After World War I] motion pictures started representing the world more truth-
> fully. . . . See films about the East, for example. Screenwriters have to study
> social problems more seriously. . . . It is noteworthy that racially discriminatory
> films have not been made any longer and works that publicize authentic racial
> characteristics have appeared. For instance, *Humoresque* was written and pro-
> duced by the Jewish people. Also, there are works that depict beautiful human
> nature observed in Chinatown. . . [Therefore,] I am willing to make films . . .
> that will publicize authentic racial characteristics [of Japanese people].[67]

Hayakawa, then, announced through the Ministry of Foreign Affairs that he was seeking scripts of Japanese drama that dealt with Japanese protagonists in Japan, with a prize of thirty thousand dollars.[68] In reality, Hayakawa appeared in one standardized Orientalist film after another. Hayakawa's announcements functioned merely as an excuse to target Japanese spectators.

By 1921, however, standardization and Orientalization were no longer able to support Hayakawa's stardom. The *New York Times* criticized the standardized quality of *Where Lights Are Low*: "It remains a movie melodrama, which is to be regretted, because Mr. Hayakawa is worthy of something more genuine. Apparently, however, he or his managers think that the public demands this sort of stuff, and so they continue to turn it out. It's a pity that they do not feel equal to another 'Bonds of Honor' or 'The Dragon Painter.' . . . The story becomes merely a fight between the hero and the villain for the possession of the heroine, with the victory of the former certain from the start. . . ."[69] The *MPW* noted, "Sessue Hayakawa's preference for the role of the self-sacrificing hero is asserted in much his usual style in 'Five Days to Live.' To some who have tired of his somewhat obvious art in impersonating the man who stands alone, the man who is capable of supreme acts of altruism, his latest offers little that is new or enterprising."[70] On *The Vermilion Pencil*, MPW stated, "His [Hayakawa's] addiction to self-sacrificing roles is once more evident. . . . Such melodramatic touches occur frequently and unless one is an abandoned admirer of Hayakawa, the picture will not register where realism is sought, and even where romanticism is preferred, there is scarcely enough novelty here to make a decided appeal."[71]

In accordance with the unfavorable tone in the reviews, Robertson-Cole and its cost-conscious studio managers reduced their efforts to promote Hayakawa as a star. As a result, when *Five Days to Live* was released, for the first time for his star vehicles MPW did not mention Hayakawa's name as "a sales point" in its "Exploitation Angles" for exhibitors.[72] The same thing happened when *The Vermilion Pencil* was released.[73]

After *The Vermilion Pencil*, Robertson-Cole originally planned to make three more Hayakawa films, including one titled *Thirteen Poppy Seeds*.[74] Hayakawa was expected to start shooting a film around 9 January 1922.[75] However, it never happened. A Japanese film magazine reported that Robertson-Cole fired Hayakawa to trim its wage bills.[76] There is no official record that Robertson-Cole fired Hayakawa, but in May 1922 Hayakawa sued Robertson-Cole, charging breach of contract.[77] In 1926, Hayakawa said that there was "a series of unsatisfactory pictures" and "a series of unsatisfactory incidents in dealing with the powers that be."[78] Hayakawa asserts in his autobiography that Robertson-Cole added more life insurance on him before shooting *The Vermilion Pencil*. Then, according to Hayakawa, during the production there was an attempt to take his life for the insurance. A stone wall was rigged to fall on him during an earthquake sequence.[79] Whether true or not, this episode clearly indicates Hayakawa's perception that Robertson-Cole had lost interest in Hayakawa as a star. Hayakawa tried to fight back against his employer in the lawsuit, but, obviously, the odds were heavily stacked against him.

Hayakawa's decline in popularity and the Hollywood film industry's loss of interest in him were also the results of the emergence of many new stars in the restructuring of the studio system in Hollywood. During the early 1920s, under the condition of political extremism, as a result of racial and ethnic resentment, anti-radical paranoia, economic dislocation, and cultural conservatism, the federal government, many states, and many cities established film censorship boards.[80] Hollywood film studios institutionally responded to such regulations by inviting Will H. Hays, the postmaster general in Harding's administration, to the Motion Picture Producers and Distributors of America (MPPDA) in 1922. The Hays Office, as the MPPDA came to be called, initiated a self-regulatory, or self-disciplinary, policy.

Under these more conservative industrial conditions, the typical star image of Hayakawa, the movable middle-ground position in the racial and cultural hierarchy between white and nonwhite, between the Americanized and the inassimilable, and between the refined and the primitive, was taken over by other actors who were not as threatening as Hayakawa in terms of race and sex. Rudolph Valentino was one of those stars who succeeded Hayakawa's star image.[81] Hayakawa wrote, "Valentino was among those who had applied for work when Haworth began production. I met him then, and liked him; but I did not hire him. The atmosphere of his personality was too similar to mine. And although his acting ability was less than skin deep, I sensed something of a rival in him. He once paid me the compliment of saying, 'I've always wanted to have something of the art you achieve in your performance in mine, so I could reproduce the sort of action and behavior the public associates with you.'"[82]

Valentino's first major role was in *The Four Horsemen of the Apocalypse* (Rex Ingram, 1920). Valentino's character had many things in common with Hayakawa's character in *The Cheat*. Both actors became overnight sensations right after these films. Valentino plays Julio, an Argentine playboy living in Paris. In the opening scene, Julio is characterized as a villainous and sensual gigolo in the vicious surroundings of a Buenos Aires dance hall. Julio wears a gaucho-style outfit, smokes cigarettes, stares at a woman with a sensual gaze, and dances a tango with the woman. However, in the next scene, set in Paris, Julio, in a European suit and with his hair neatly set, kisses a bunch of roses and gives it to a married white woman, who is attracted to Julio's refined manner. Later, Julio invites her into his studio, lets her take off her shoes, embraces her, and kisses her, whispering in her ear, "You are mine." When her husband appears on the scene, Julio is punished for his conduct. The ambivalent presentation of Julio, as both a sensual/threatening and refined/Westernized male, clearly followed that of Hayakawa in *The Cheat*.

In the end, Julio decides to become a soldier for the Allies and dies heroically for his love. Showing his self-sacrificial loyalty to the Allies, Julio is accepted into white American and European society for the first time, as was Hayakawa repeatedly in his star vehicles.

After signing a hugely publicized contract with Paramount, Valentino played the title role of *The Sheik* (George Melford, 1921), which helped to inaugurate the "Valentino craze."[83] The motif of the racial and cultural middle ground of the protagonist was used in *The Sheik*, as it was in many of Hayakawa's star vehicles.[84] A Frenchman (Adolphe Menjou) enlightens and Westernizes Valentino's character, especially in terms of romantic love and monogamy. When another Arabian tribe with its evil chief kidnaps a white woman, the sheik turns into a heroic nonwhite man, who sacrifices himself to protect the white heroine. The heroine prays to the Christian God for the sheik's recovery from his fatal wound, while the Arabian people pray to Allah. Eventually, the sheik is revealed to be a son of an English gentleman and his Spanish wife, who had been abandoned in the Sahara.[85] Thus, the sheik racially and religiously stands between European and Arab in the narrative.

The title role of *The Sheik*, a white European man raised by Arabian people, was first offered to Hayakawa, but he declined it, according to Hayakawa.[86] However, it was unlikely that Hayakawa was offered the role of the European-born Arab. In early 1920, he was severely criticized for his role as a Spanish matador in *The Brand of Lopez*, the "whitest" character in his whole career.[87] The unfavorable reviews of *The Brand of Lopez* confined Hayakawa and his star image to an Oriental milieu and regarded his Spanish role as too European and unsuitable for him. Matthew Taylor from *MPN* claimed, "The star hardly satisfies in his Spanish role. . . . Hayakawa is a typical Oriental, and it is difficult for an Oriental to register the hot passions, especially the diabolic revenge of a quick tempered Latin."[88] A reviewer from *Variety* wrote, "Let's hope he will confine himself to native roles and sidestep crude meller of a type set forth above."[89]

Moreover, the narrative device that identifies the sheik as a white male was impossible for Hayakawa. Even though Valentino became popular as an "ethnic" star ("Latin lover"), he was "white" enough, compared to the Asian star, to portray an Anglo-Saxon aristocrat who was raised in the Middle East. Valentino's sensuality and eroticism were allowed to unfold more completely, while Hayakawa's eroticism was curtailed for racial reasons. Valentino was "off white," but still white. Hayakawa came close to being white, but still was not white. Valentino was a "whiter" successor to Hayakawa's star image. Valentino was convincing enough to embody the middle-ground position of a racial and cultural hierarchy.

However, even Valentino was not white, or American, enough for a full-fledged star in the xenophobic and nativist culture and within the conservative tendency in the Hollywood film industry under the Hays Office. The film historian Alexander Walker argues, "Women were already beginning to turn away from the exotic foreign model and back to the staple American product represented by a new star like John Gilbert" by the mid-1920s.[90] By the mid-1920s, Caucasian stars such as Douglas Fairbanks Sr., "the smiling, clean-cut, genteel American hero," started playing nonwhite foreign heroes, even though they "rarely did, if ever—as a sexual being," compared with Hayakawa or Valentino.[91] Robertson-Cole followed this trend and released the film *The Sheik of Araby* in April 1922, which was a reedited version of *The Man Who Turned White*, starring a Caucasian actor named H. B. Warner.[92] As Gaylyn Studlar argues, these Caucasian stars "could satisfy female desire for erotic exoticism without threatening either American men or the nation's Nordic/Anglo-Saxon purity."[93]

According to Studlar, fan magazine discourse of the 1920s began to foster an appreciation of stars who were exemplars of "the fine, upstanding, typical American."[94] In this trend, there was barely any room left for Hayakawa. In the 1920s, the number of articles on Hayakawa in fan magazines decreased drastically. Even in the few articles about Hayakawa, his ultimate difference from American stars became emphasized, rather than his Americanized way of life. This shift of fan magazine discourse surely served to destroy the tense balance between Americanization and Japaneseness of Hayakawa's star image.

As early as 1919, Harry C. Carr from the *Motion Picture Classic* emphasized Hayakawa's cultural difference:

> In all his [Hayakawa's] customs and manners and conversation he is American to the finger-tips, but one always feels that in Hayakawa there is the soul of some stern old Samurai, who has returned to earth and got into the body of a very up-to-date young man of fashion by mistake. One always feels that this handsome, attractive young clubman is reaching back into dim mysteries of an old philosophy that we wot [*sic*] not of. I see him in spiffy neckties and vest-chains, with golf-sticks poking out of the tonneau of his car, but beyond I see old Samurai temples and queer Samurai swords, strange aromas of Oriental perfumes. Hayakawa is modern Japan. He is the proud old Samurai caste in patent leather shoes and spats. The spirit of the old Japan which met death with a contemptuous smile and killed any one who touched its sword. But the manners and thoughts of modern America. We think we have taught them a lot, but they call upon life forces of which we know nothing.[95]

Carr thus regarded Hayakawa as a descendent of the samurai class, no matter how Americanized his surface was.

The *Motion Picture Classic* published photos of Hayakawa wearing a Japanese-style kimono over a Western suit, and looking at a Japanese mask and a sword. One of the captions for these photos says, "Now and then he gets down the tragic mask and the centuries-old Samurai sword of the Japanese player. Then he forgets all about the Cooper-Hewitts and the fleeting fame of celluloid success."[96] When Hayakawa was at Lasky, his Americanized surface was regarded as the sign of his Americanization and assimilation to the American way of life, no matter how many Japanese traits he showed. The Japanese characteristics were viewed as his symbolical embodiment of Japanese Taste. However, after World War I, the same Japanese objects came to be used as examples of Hayakawa's inassimilable cultural and racial difference.

Other articles on Hayakawa in the 1920s also rearticulated Hayakawa's star image from the notion of racial and cultural difference. Adele Whitely Fletcher pointed out Hayakawa's "essential" Japaneseness in her article in *Motion Picture Magazine* in 1920. She wrote,

> I asked him [Hayakawa] if he would ever return to Japan to make pictures and he said he hoped to go there to make a great production, one which would have great beauty in its scenes and, in a certain sense, be spectacular. . . . Like those of the Far East he is essentially the fatalist. . . . And he is essentially a son of his native land, for even in a business office in Manhattan-on-the-Subway he suggested the far-away isle where he was born. Temple bells in a violet dusk; peaceful nights and dawns fragrant with cherry blossoms, which wake in pale rose to bird calls and the shuffle of sandaled footfalls along the quiet ways.[97]

In 1922 Leslie Bryers of *Motion Picture Magazine* also distinguished Hayakawa from American gentlemen, no matter how gently he behaves. Starting her article in an exotic mode, "The perfumed censers, purple shadows, solitudes and silences of your true Oriental fable were ostentatious in their absence. Thus I offer you a Nipponese *conte*." Bryers concludes, "One finds in Hayakawa that consistent courtesy, that deference to another's opinions which yet in no way sets his own at a disadvantage, which characterizes the majority of his race. It is impossible to observe whether his manner is concealing boredom or interest. It is always impassive. Only in the brief, brilliant flashes of his eyes does one catch the intense illumination within him. In his American experience and his American clothes he yet remains a splendid example of the Japanese gentleman."[98]

In the wrecked balance between Americanization and Japaneseness, all that seemed left for Hayakawa was his reputation among Japanese specta-tors. At a dinner held by Robertson-Cole to celebrate the completion of *The Vermilion Pencil* on 17 March 1922, Hayakawa declared that he would leave Hollywood because he was a patriot of Japan. According to his autobiography, Hayakawa said,

> The agitation against us [Japanese] was still prevalent, and those of small in-come, engaged in farming and small business in California, were having a hard time of it. . . . The other day, a public poll was taken concerning the current dis-crimination against Japanese in this country and the passage of legislation that will do them considerable harm. I have learned that this company has taken a position in favor of discrimination against the Japanese. Moreover, an attempt on my life was made during the filming of *The Vermilion Pencil*. Fortunately for me it was unsuccessful. I was warned. . . . If things have reached such a state, there is no longer any cause for me to remain in Hollywood. I am going to leave. This is my last day.[99]

Only a week after Hayakawa resigned, Robertson-Cole signed a contract with Harry Carey, an all-American type of star, and R. T. Thornby, who had di-rected Carey's films at Universal Pictures. Robertson-Cole's contract with Carey may not have had any direct relationship with Hayakawa's resignation, but it still indicated the move of Robertson-Cole, and the Hollywood film industry, toward white Americanism.

FOUR

Stardom and Japanese Modernity

Sessue Hayakawa in Japan

15

AMERICANIZATION AND
NATIONALISM

The Japanese Reception of Sessue Hayakawa

T he stardom of Sessue Hayakawa allowed the Japanese actor to be regarded as the representative of Japanese people not only by American audiences but also by Japanese spectators. Inevitably, Hayakawa
came to be positioned in the sociopolitical terrain between Japan and the
United States.

The Japanese American press in California played an important role in
articulating Hayakawa's stardom within broader sociopolitical discourses for
Japanese spectators in the United States. Right after *The Cheat* was released
in Los Angeles, the *Rafu Shimpo* started a strong campaign against Hayakawa's Japanese character. However, the *Rafu Shimpo*'s criticism of *The Cheat*
was contradictory. On the one hand, it criticized *The Cheat* "for the good of
the future of Japanese people in the U.S.," who were making every effort to
assimilate into American society. On the other hand, as for assimilation, the
Rafu Shimpo adopted the idea of the middle-ground position of Japanese
people in the racial and cultural hierarchy.

A series titled "Are the Japanese Assimilable?" by Sidney Gulick, a former
missionary in Japan and a pro-Japanese professor, most typically represented
the basic tone of argument in the *Rafu Shimpo*. Gulick insisted that there
were two types of assimilation, "biological" and "social," and Japanese immigrants were able to assimilate socially, but not biologically. Gulick wrote,
"Biological assimilation may touch upon the issue of miscegenation, but social assimilation is surely possible because it can be achieved by education
and surrounding conditions. The Japanese can learn our language, way of
thinking, and democracy."[1] Regarding miscegenation, Gulick argued, "The
result has not been well studied scientifically yet. Therefore, I do not recom-

mend it. Yet, at the same time, miscegenation must not be prohibited only because of temporary emotion or racial prejudice until the scientific result comes."[2]

Gulick's claim about miscegenation indicated his adherence to the idea of a racial hierarchy between white and nonwhite, based on pseudo-scientific social Darwinism, which was a part of the popular discourse of the period; and his insistence upon accepting Japanese immigrants into American society was a compromise. According to Gulick, if Japanese immigrants learned American language, thought, and democracy, and so long as they avoided causing anxiety over miscegenation, there could be a good chance for Japanese immigrants to assimilate into American life.

While supporting the notions of a racial hierarchy and of assimilation that located Japan in an inferior position, the *Rafu Shimpo*'s criticism of *The Cheat* placed a greater emphasis on the film's "insult of Japanese national pride." The *Rafu Shimpo* abhorred Hayakawa's show of "misery" at the climactic scene of the lynching as a "humiliation to Japanese people."[3] This nationalist standpoint could have easily been transformed into a racist assertion of inassimilability of the "Japanese race" and of the ultimate difference from Americans.

Curiously, the *Rafu Shimpo* did not consider *The Typhoon* as problematic as *The Cheat*, even though, in both films, Japanese characters played by Hayakawa brutally attack white women and participate in trials. When the film *Harakiri* (1917) was criticized for its presumed anti-Japanese content, the actor Aoyama Yukio, who appeared in the film, made an excuse in the *Rafu Shimpo* that the film "was more like *The Typhoon*, and less anti-Japanese than *The Cheat*."[4] Hayakawa's character in *The Typhoon* shows his brutality only when his nationality is insulted. He commits suicide for his honor and is not lynched or attacked by American people. Later, when *The Typhoon* was released in Japan, a Japanese film magazine called it "a superb film without any anti-Japanese flavor that rather shows the Japanese spirit splendidly."[5] The fact that *The Typhoon* was excused from severe criticism underscores the nationalist tone of argument of the *Rafu Shimpo*. The *Rafu Shimpo* did not react harshly toward anti-Japanese films as long as Japan was treated as an independent nation and the Japanese people were depicted with honor.

The *Rafu Shimpo*'s nationalistic inclination is observable in its reaction to Hayakawa's other star vehicles, *The Honorable Friend* and *Hashimura Togo*. These two films depicted an idealized process of Americanization of Japanese men, which seemed to be most suitable to Gulick's idea of "social," but not "biological," assimilation of Japanese immigrants. However, the *Rafu Shimpo* criticized *The Honorable Friend* in nationalist terms: "Its content is said to be about a Japanese merchant who forces a Japanese man to have a picture marriage in order to bring his mistress to the U.S. and deceives the Gentlemen's Agreement. If this is true, . . . many Americans may think that the Japanese people are immoral. . . . It must be a film that insults the Japanese race."[6] The writer of this article had not even watched the film and did not pay attention to the film's successful assimilation narrative. He or she simply cared about the respectability of the "Japanese race."

The *Rafu Shimpo* also criticized *Hashimura Togo* from a nationalist standpoint, neglecting the content of a Japanese immigrant's Americanization process: "Hayakawa appears as a comic protagonist, and he cannot present his [acting] ability. Many people will surely insist that Hayakawa cannot show his unique technique unless he plays an abhorrent villain. Consequently, there is no doubt that the motion picture company will use him in roles that will do harm to the Japanese people. Probably other Japanese actors will no longer have roles that will do good to the Japanese people."[7]

The establishment of Haworth, which symbolized a Japanese man's success in the United States, satisfied the *Rafu Shimpo*'s nationalist inclination. About the first four productions at Haworth, the *Rafu Shimpo* noted favorably, "Four films so far have been well received among both the Japanese and the Americans."[8] Another article stated, "All four films in which Hayakawa appeared [at his own production company] are propaganda films that introduce unique Japanese *bushido*. They are valuable attempts."[9] About *His Birthright*, a reviewer claimed, "The plot seems like a sequel to *Madame Butterfly*. . . . To me it was more delightful than any other recent films by Hayakawa. . . . The main issue here is that the Japanese people have appreciated mysterious beauty in revenge since ancient times, and it looks sarcastic compared with the white hypocrisy hidden behind the discourse of 'Love your enemy.' . . . Sessue should explore more about showing the essence of the Japanese people and making films with delightful acts."[10] While admitting the stereotypical content of *His Birthright* that referred to *Madame Butterfly*, the reviewer praised Hayakawa's characterization of the hero, who preserves his Japanese background and attains justice in the United States.

Contrary to American fan magazines, the *Rafu Shimpo* interpreted Hayakawa's display of Japanese traits in his lifestyle not as an embodiment of Japanese Taste but as a nationalist attitude. One report stated, "Motion picture actor Sessue Hayakawa is known to both American and Japanese people as one of the most Americanized Japanese people in the U.S. [Yet,] he appears to be an ultra-nationalist. This is obvious if we read what he has said to English magazine reporters. According to Sessue, it is very good for Japanese people to import Western culture, but it is completely wrong to change their clothes to American ones. He insists that Japanese clothes are most suitable for Japanese people."[11] The *Rafu Shimpo* also praised Aoki, especially for her "Japanese" way of playing the role of the faithful wife: "While Mrs. Tsuruko can speak fluent English to get along with the Americans, she can also become a faithful wife as a pure Japanese lady who does not speak English at all. In this sense, Mrs. Tsuruko is superior to the Japanese ladies who prefer to speak only in English."[12]

There were some Japanese intellectuals who were cautious of the nationalistic viewpoint of the *Rafu Shimpo*. Okina Kyuin criticized the *Rafu Shimpo*'s campaign against *The Cheat* for its "narrow-minded nationalism." Okina wrote in the *Nichibei Shinbun*, a Japanese newspaper published in San Francisco,

> Since the Kotoku Shusui incident, a strange tendency had risen in the Japanese community in the U.S.: narrow-minded nationalism.[13] Such a thought was not suitable to the New World where freedom and democracy were its ideal. . . . Vulgar journalists followed the trend and cried out, "Japanese men should do like this," or " God's People should do like that," etc. I did want to have pride as Japanese, but I hated such a vulgar tendency. . . . After watching [*The Cheat*], I thought that the performance of Sessue, who played a brilliant role with other white actors, was worth praising. The criticism that regarded this film as anti-Japanese considered the scene in which the Japanese man takes advantage of a white woman as humiliating to the Japanese. It is not bad to think that Japanese people should not behave rudely to white people, but *The Cheat* was only a movie. The author did not write the script with an intention of anti-Japanese propaganda, but just referred to the Japanese custom of stamping on everything. If that behavior enhances anti-Japanese sentiment, what about the cruel and brutal scenes in films with white actors? . . . Sessue's acting was realistic. He obtained a status of a star because of his acting skill. If he had been used only as a tool to enhance anti-Japanese sentiment, he would have been thrown away right after *The Cheat*. . . . The Japanese people were only suffering from and excited about a self-delusion. . . .[14]

In response, Yamaguchi Hikotaro of the *Rafu Shimpo* severely criticized Okina, even questioning Okina's Japanese nationality. Yamaguchi wrote, "If Okina is Japanese, he must support the *Rafu Shimpo*'s opinion that worries about *The Cheat*'s bad influence. . . . Since Okina scorns the action of the Japanese Association [against the exhibition of *The Cheat*] with his immature artistic point of view, he must not be Japanese but Chinese."[15] Yamaguchi's claim reveals the conspicuously nationalist tone of the *Rafu Shimpo*, which simultaneously and in a contradictory manner admitted the notion of racial hierarchy that distinguished Japanese from other Asians as well as from Caucasians.

The *Rafu Shimpo*'s vehement nationalist reaction against *The Cheat* and Hayakawa was not universally shared. There were calm and less political views like Okina's. In addition to Okina, the *Nyu Yoku Shimpo*, a Japanese newspaper published in New York that shared a certain nationalist tendency with the *Rafu Shimpo*, praised Hayakawa's and Aoki's efforts of Americanization in its review of *The Honorable Friend*. The report noted, "[In *The Honorable Friend*,] when the bride looks at a car on her way home from the Immigration Office, she thinks that a dog will pull it because she does not see any horse. If any Japanese women today look at such a scene in the film, they should be offended and furiously jump on the stage and tear down the screen. However, the two leading actors [Hayakawa and Aoki] are impressive. They are trained in America and completely Americanized in their facial expressions. Their expressions will never be mistaken whether they are happy or sad as other actors in films made in Japan have been. Moreover, their handsome and beautiful appearances enhance their abilities."[16] Nevertheless, the nationalist inclination of the *Rafu Shimpo* had a certain degree of influence on the emerging public discourse in the Japanese American community in Los Angeles, where Hayakawa resided and made his films.

Sessue Hayakawa's name first arrived in Japan in film magazines, but not as a matinee idol. No female fan attached an enthusiastic poem for Hayakawa in her letter to the editors. Nobody even thought about sending a fan letter to Hayakawa in the first place. Most of the Japanese film magazines, many of which were established in the mid- to late 1910s and whose primary readers in the beginning were intellectuals of the middle and upper middle classes, at first treated Hayakawa and his films using an unfavorable tone.[17] The Japanese government was making every effort to reach equal status with European countries and the United States in international relations and, along with this, supported Japanese communities in the United States in the attempt to abolish the legal inequality of Japanese immigrants.[18] Under these political conditions, Hayakawa was introduced to Japanese spectators as a "traitor" for appearing in films "insulting" Japan and enhancing anti-Japanese sentiment in the United States.

The film magazine *Katsudo Shashin Zasshi* reported that Hayakawa was "famous because he often causes problems."[19] *Katsudo no Sekai* provided an unfavorable caption to Hayakawa's photo, "Sessue Hayakawa, who aroused a heated discussion when he appeared in *The Cheat*, and his extremely ugly Japanese sword," despite the fact that the same photo was used in an American film fan magazine in a favorable tone.[20] The magazine also reported that Hayakawa and Aoki were thinking of retirement from the film industry very soon because of the severe criticism of their films from Japanese communities in the United States.[21] Sometimes, in Japanese film magazines, Hayakawa's name was intentionally spelled with a series of dashes for concealment, as if it had been too shameful to print his name.

The Cheat was not released in Japan. *The Wrath of the Gods* was released at the Fujikan Theater in Asakusa on 15 September 1918, but after several weeks it was banned from exhibition "because of its too primitive and disgraceful depiction of Japanese people."[22] *Alien Souls* was imported to Japan and the release date at Fujikan Theater in Asakusa was already set (1 August 1918); however it was eventually banned from exhibition because "the film would insult Japanese people and enhance anti-American thought."[23] The notorious rumors about *The Cheat* and other early Hayakawa films could not be substantiated or disproved without the release of the films themselves.

As a result, other than the infamous rumors, the name and face of Hayakawa was not well known until the end of the 1910s in Japan. The film magazine *Katsudo Kurabu* used photos of Hayakawa several times for "Who's this?" questions for a prize competition in 1919–20, which means that Hayakawa's face was not very familiar to Japanese audiences even then.[24] The famous kabuki actor Nakamura Utaemon had not heard of Hayakawa in 1920 despite the fact that Hayakawa often mentioned in American film fan magazines the influence on him of the kabuki actor Danjuro.[25]

After Hayakawa established his own company, the reception of Hayakawa and his films changed drastically in Japan, as it did in the Japanese communities in the United States. As all of Hayakawa's star vehicles at Haworth were widely advertised and released in Japan, the previous negative tone that had regarded Hayakawa as a national shame almost completely disappeared.[26]

Hayakawa became favorably introduced in some newspaper reports as if he had been "a Japanese national hero" in the United States.[27] A 1921 article by a female film critic, Saiki Junko, even reads like an open love letter to Hayakawa. Saiki writes:

> Sessue devotes himself to the Japanese people and he is not such a bad person as some newspaper[s] had reported. It's all misunderstanding. . . . The name of Sessue, a Japanese man, is brightly and clearly shining in the U.S., even during the anti-Japanese movements. . . . In such recent films as *The Temple of Dusk*, *His Debt*, and *The Gray Horizon*, Sessue always loves justice and is the ideal representative of Eastern morality who is generous to his enemy. His character, who is always brokenhearted and lonely in the end, is so unique in American films that I cannot help feeling sympathy with him all the time. . . . We must celebrate 10 June 1889 [*sic*], the birthday of the greatest person in the world, Sessue Hayakawa. . . . A person with Dustin Farnum's dignity, Warren Kerrigan's beauty, Francis X. Bushman's grace, and Charles Ray's beautiful youth still cannot match Sessue. . . . Mr. Sessue Hayakawa, Miss Jun Saiki will bless you with the earth that gave birth to you. . . . Mr. Hayakawa, please do not give up motion pictures until I become a great director. . . .[28]

Hayakawa thus finally became a matinee idol for some female fans in Japan.

Yet, in Japan, Hayakawa was not so much a matinee idol as a national hero. The establishment of Haworth was interpreted by the Japanese media as Hayakawa's effort "to make pro-Japanese films in order to dispel his shameful reputation" and as his display of a nationalistic attitude toward his native country.[29] Hayakawa came to be considered as a favorable representative of Japan. Hayakawa's success in a foreign country thus turned into a matter of national pride. As Hayakawa's early films were criticized in a nationalistic tone, the establishment of Haworth was praised nationalistically as "an honor for the Japanese people."[30] From then on, such characterizations as "Hayakawa always fights alone for Japanese people in California, the region which is filled with anti-Japanese sentiment" appeared in many film magazines and newspapers. In this sense, one aim of Hayakawa when he established Haworth, to appeal to Japanese spectators, was successfully accomplished.

However, even after 1918, Japanese reception of Hayakawa's stardom was not unanimously favorable but was ambivalent. Hayakawa was nationalistically praised as a representative of Japan, but, at the same time, he was regarded positively and negatively as a foreign star, or as an imported star from the United States. This twofold reception of Hayakawa's stardom had to do with the contradictory conditions of Japanese film culture in this period of modernity. Throughout the Taisho era (1912–26), the social definition of cinema was transforming in accordance with the transformation of Japanese society. Domestically, mass culture developed with the emergence of the working class in urban areas. Americanization was a keyword in the newly developed mass culture. Internationally, as one of the modernizing nation-states, Japan was imperialistically trying to obtain colonies. Both Hayakawa's star image and cinema itself obtained ambivalent statuses under these conditions of Americanization, modernization, and nationalism.

In the Taisho period, some Japanese intellectuals, ranging from film critics and filmmakers to government officials, attempted to modernize the production and exhibition practices of motion pictures in Japan. Their writings and subsequent experimental filmmaking are often noted as *jun'eigageki undo*, the Pure Film Movement. Even though the Pure Film Movement was not a coherent and monolithic movement, the advocates of the movement shared their desires to renovate film culture in Japan. The movement had ambivalent goals: Westernization and nationalization of cinema. According to the historian Takemura Tamio, in the Taisho era, "ordinary Japanese people were neurotically and madly trying to incorporate Americanism with their traditional lifestyles. . . . The essence of popular culture of the period was, in short, the attempted unity of American popular culture and the morality of traditional [Japanese] society."[31] The Pure Film Movement's ambivalent goals typically embodied the transitional conditions of Japanese popular culture of the period.

Hayakawa's career in American silent cinema from around 1914 until 1922 coincided with the period when the Pure Film Movement was most active in Japan both in theory and in practice. The ambivalent reception of Hayakawa's stardom in Japan was closely related to the Pure Film advocates' ambivalent goals toward modernizing cinema in Japan.

In the early 1910s, in such film journals as *Kinema Record*, primarily young intellectual figures began to criticize the production, exhibition, and reception of mainstream commercial films in Japan. According to Joanne Bernardi, the Pure Film Movement was "a loosely defined discourse-based 'movement' comprised of diverse paths leading to a single destination . . . . or common cause, [which] was the realization of culturally respectable film, endowed with both aesthetic legitimacy and contemporary realism, that theoretically would challenge a mainstream commercial product that had theatrical origins."[32] One of the goals of the Pure Film advocates was "the attainment of an internationally viable level of narrational clarity for films also endowed with a comprehensible and distinct national and cultural identity."[33] They criticized mainstream commercial Japanese motion pictures, which had appealed to "mass" audiences because, for the most part, they were merely reproducing stage repertories of *kyugeki* (period drama of kabuki style) and *shinpa* (new school or modern drama influenced by traditional kabuki styles). They found inspiration in imported films, American and European film magazines and instructional books on cinema, and news of the latest production techniques brought back by a number of filmmakers and producers who toured the Hollywood studios during the American film industry's sudden boom in production after World War I. They insisted on modernizing Japanese-made films with formal and narrative techniques, such as spoken titles (dialogue intertitles), more varied and complex camera work (in particular, close-up shots and moving camera techniques), artificial lighting, continuity editing, and a more natural style of acting.

There were various and contradictory standpoints in the Pure Film Movement, but there was a shared ideological and economic concern. There were nationalist (or historically teleological) discourses on cinema in the period that tried to distinguish the "cinematic" entity from other "uncinematic" forms of entertainment and spectacle, which were often connected to lower-class and juvenile spectators. The major goals of the Pure Film advocates included exporting Japanese-made films to foreign markets and affirming Japanese national identity internationally and domestically. In this sense, the major goals of the Pure Film Movement were motivated not so much artistically as politically, economically, and strategically. Such a technique as continuity editing was not necessarily perceived by the Pure Film advocates as simply the most "efficient" way of telling a story, but as part of the Americanism that they tried to incorporate with their political and economic concerns.[34]

The Pure Film advocates were well aware of the international popularity of films that depicted such stereotypical Japanese culture and landscape as dances of geisha girls, hara-kiri, cherry blossoms, and Mount Fuji in "tales of honor, revenge, self-sacrifice, and unrequited love" in the style of *Madame Butterfly*.[35] These intellectuals felt not only uncomfortable with the "inaccurate" depiction of Japan in these films, but also offended by the fact that Japanese landscape and culture, about which Japanese filmmakers should be making films and making profits, were "stolen" by foreign filmmakers.[36]

The *Kinema Record* criticized *The Wrath of the Gods* for its representation of Japanese people who "look very ugly," and stated, "We feel sick when we see [that] this kind of film is being made in foreign countries. We want to export films made purely by Japanese people as soon as possible."[37] *Katsudo Shashin Zasshi* similarly criticized *The Wrath of the Gods* and noted, "Even though the major characters are Japanese, it is a Japanese drama made out of Western people's minds and it has an extremely Westernized view. . . . It is a pity that this film introduces Japan without telling the truth of Japan."[38] Kaeriyama Norimasa, who was the leading theorist of the Pure Film Movement, also referred to *The Wrath of the Gods* and claimed, "Isn't it a huge loss that Japanese producers do not make any films for export and have all the greatly unique landscape of Japan stolen by foreigners?"[39] The critic Okura Kihachiro expressed his regret that no Japanese-made film had ever been exported to foreign markets, despite such attractions and artistic heritage as Mount Fuji and the Giant Buddha in Nara, which would surely capture the interest of foreign audiences. Okura thus requested of Japanese filmmakers that they "dedicate themselves to producing original Japanese films for export, films that would introduce Japanese landscape and culture, and export them" in order to develop cinema at once "nationally and internationally."[40]

The Pure Film advocates insisted on making Japanese-made films exportable right away not only to fight back against the pressure that the Hollywood market put on the home front, but also to regain the profits in international markets. An editorial in *Katsudo Shashin Zasshi* claimed, "Even scenic films of [Japanese] landscape were made by foreigners and introduced as 'authentic' Japan," and insisted that "the Monroe Doctrine should be applied to motion pictures" and "Japanese films must be made by Japanese people" and "expand its [Japan's] market share in the world."[41] In this sense, the Pure Film advocates were conscious about the idea of the market and recognized that Japanese images, tactically evocative and stereotypical ones, could be profitable and exportable. They were well aware of foreign audiences' expectations and the necessity of exoticization of their films. The *Kinema Record* insisted in its editorial that even though "the Japanese people imagined by foreign people" were misrepresented, "it is indispensable to play characters in an appropriate way for foreign audiences."[42]

The Pure Film advocates claimed that the only way Japanese-made film would become exportable to foreign markets was to imitate the forms and styles of foreign films. They believed that only the "unique characteristics of motion pictures distinguished from theatrical dramas or dances" would make films made in Japan become understandable to foreign audiences.[43] This is nothing but the posing of Japan's cinematic identity in Western terms, which in turn, strategically or not, presupposes and establishes the centrality of Western cinema as the universal point of reference.

Yet, the Pure Film advocates were not satisfied with slavishly imitating foreign products. Mukai Shunko of *Katsudo Gaho* insisted on making films that would use Western techniques but express *yamato damashii*, the pure Japanese spirit that he, and others, considered to represent Japan's power and strength as a nation.[44] Muromachi Kyoji, an editor-in-chief of *Katsudo Gaho*, emphasized the importance of imitating the techniques of foreign films "without losing the essence of Japanese cinema."[45] They insisted that the proper mixture of imitation of cinematic and technical innovations in the West and unique Japanese content would lead the Japanese cinema to attain an internationally viable level of narrational clarity and become an exportable and marketable product.

The issue was about the mutual development of Japanese cinema (nationalization of film culture) and Japanese national identity. In fact, the Pure Film advocates insisted that cinema was a national project and should serve the nation.[46] As of the 1910s, Japanese popular entertainment culture was not rendered nationally. Some reformist critics as well as governmental and educational elites who supported the Pure Film Movement desired to establish a national culture and stressed cinema's major role in it.[47] They also desired to lift cinema from its status as a working-class diversion to something worthy of respect. One way of promoting cinema's claims to legitimacy was to tie its fortunes to those of the nation, to articulate its value in nationalist and patriotic terms.[48] Kaeriyama stated in 1916 that the motion pictures "should work for the social education of Japan, serve the mental and intellectual progress of every single citizen, and contribute to individual improvement and to the people's awareness of their national ideals."[49] Kaeriyama tried to rearticulate the motion picture, which had been considered lower-class entertainment, as an art form that would be useful "not only for the edification of the individual, but also as a means of awakening the Japanese to a sense of national identity."[50] Notable intellectuals wrote articles that highly evaluated cinema's cultural, artistic, social, and pedagogical legitimacy for Japan's "national development." After visiting the United States and observing the degree of rationalization of its film industry, Baron Shibusawa Eiichi insisted that "cinema is not only entertainment but also has an important national and social mission . . . to boost the morals of the Japanese people."[51]

The nationalist attitude of the Pure Film Movement was in accordance with the governmental discourses of modernization in Japan, even though the movement was not directly under the control of the Japanese government. In order to obtain recognition as a nation in international relations, since the late nineteenth century the Japanese government had implemented policies showing Japan's achievement toward modernization in a European sense. The Japanese government tried to use Western standards and ideas and to Westernize the state in order to construct Japan's own national identity and to escape from being colonized by Western imperialism.[52] This contradictory attitude of the Japanese government between modernization and nationalism was indicated by its slogan, "Japanese Spirit and Western Culture" (*wakon yosai*). Using American and European styles of cinema, the Pure Film advocates insisted on the mutual development of Japanese cinema and Japanese national identity. This is the innate ambivalence of the Pure Film Movement: between Westernization and nationalism.

With regard to these notions of Westernization and nationalism, the Pure Film advocates responded ambivalently to Hayakawa's films from the outset. They criticized the stereotypical depiction of Japanese people in such films as *The Wrath of the Gods*, but they also highly valued Hayakawa's films. To them Hayakawa's films effectively used "cinematic" forms and techniques understandable to foreign audiences and exoticized, or Orientalized, the images of Japan to satisfy American audiences' expectations.

Kinema Junpo noted that Hayakawa's films were "international" and "possible to exhibit anywhere in the world" because they used "purely cinematic techniques."[53] The film critic Mori Iwao, who would later become a producer, argued that if *The Cheat* was "seen from an artistic point of view, it is not so problematic. . . . It is a pity that an artistically great piece was rejected only because of a trivial ethnic bias." Mori insisted in his book on Hayakawa that Hayakawa "satisfactorily introduced the true Japanese spirit worldwide using motion pictures" that "have a strong power to impress people" with their "international language."[54] *Katsudo Gaho* noted, "We cannot stop appreciating Hayakawa's efforts for the U.S.-Japan goodwill. He is doing his best to make them [foreign people] understand Japanese characteristics."[55] Even a member of the Diet, Mochizuki Kotaro, insisted that motion pictures would be useful to correct foreign people's misunderstanding of Japanese people with "the most understandable method," and he praised Hayakawa for his efforts of doing this in the United States.[56]

Even if Hayakawa's films were too stereotypical forms of representing

Japanese culture and people, the Pure Film advocates highly valued the fact that they became successful in the American market. Numata Yuzuru praised *Bonds of Honor* for its appeal to foreign audiences: "The plot seems hackneyed for Japanese audiences, but Western audiences may be interested in its depiction of Japanese people's self-control."[57] *Kinema Junpo* positively reviewed the use of stereotypical Japanese landscape in *His Birthright*: "It is clear from its opening shot of Mt. Fuji that this film was made to make for-eigners understand our country's culture and custom."[58] The film critic Koda Honami regarded *The Dragon Painter* as the ideal film that Japanese film-makers "should definitely refer to" because of "its utilizing Japanese dance, landscape, and so forth," despite the film's use of strange Japaneseque names and landscapes.[59]

When the Pure Film advocates praised the international understandability of Hayakawa's films, what they appreciated most was Hayakawa's expressive and natural acting style. Mori claimed that Hayakawa's "technique of facial expression is known as the most understandable international method," and it was "even praised by renowned American stage actors." Mori praised Haya-kawa's "extremely subtle and fluent" facial expression in *An Arabian Knight* and the "marvelous . . . clarity with which Hayakawa expresses the pro-tagonist's psychology" in *The First Born*.[60] *Kinema Junpo* noted Hayakawa's "humorous expression and very good command of body movement" in *An Arabian Knight*.[61] *Katsudo Gaho* praised *The Swamp* for Hayakawa's "perfect technique of delicate expression and calm action."[62] Consequently, general film audiences came to appreciate Hayakawa's acting capability. A fan praised *Five Days to Live* for Hayakawa's "matured technique."[63] When Hayakawa returned to Japan in 1922, *Tokyo Asahi Shinbun* reported with a headline, "Mr. and Mrs. Sessue return full of facial expression."[64]

From the beginning, the Pure Film Movement put emphasis on "pan-tomime" as "the crux of the motion pictures."[65] Kaeriyama insisted in 1915 that the "photoplay" should consist of three elements, "pantomime," "natural background," and "(inter)titles."[66] Osanai Kaoru of the Shochiku Kinema In-stitute, another central figure of the Pure Film Movement, insisted that "the essence of motion picture drama is pantomime and facial expressions."[67] An editorial of the *Kinema Record* emphasized, "Since the motion picture is pan-tomime, actors have to focus on showing their feelings only with their appar-ent expressions. They have to express their feelings such as anger, sorrow, joy, and surprise, clearly by moving their faces or their hands. However, Japanese actors are not interested in these things at all."[68] Another editorial of the

Kinema Record criticized the popular acting style in Japanese cinema that was "directly taken from the Japanese stage," which did not have "any expression and gesture."[69] The writer Matsumoto Ryukotsu also claimed, "Japanese cinema looks as if it is just a longer version of a stage play . . . with Japanese actors' empty way of expression and gesture."[70] Ide Tessho, the editor-in-chief of *Katsudo no Sekai*, even insisted, "Japanese actors do not have facial expressions . . . which is because Asian people do not tend to express outwardly their inner feelings."[71] Having these criticisms in mind, even stage actors, who were criticized by the Pure Film advocates for their "uncinematic" facial expressions when they appeared in motion pictures, came to admit what the Pure Film advocates problematized. Inoue Masao, who was one of the first *shinpa* actors to act in Japanese motion pictures, wrote that it would be indispensable for motion picture actors to study abroad.[72] The kabuki actor Ichikawa Sadanji said that one "cannot become a motion picture actor without practicing abroad."[73]

The Pure Film advocates praised Hayakawa's "naturalistic" acting style in gestures and facial expressions in particular. To them, Hayakawa's expressivity and naturalness were an embodiment of the successful deviation from Japanese people's lack of facial expressions and Japanese theatrical actors' stylized performances. They valued highly Hayakawa's conception of acting, which was described in articles in American film magazines. In these articles, Hayakawa claimed, "Japanese people are trained not to show their emotions in their expressions" and "it is a racial characteristic that they lack facial expressions." Hayakawa continued, "To act [in motion pictures] is not to act. . . . [Actors] have to think about their roles very carefully, study them closely, and get into their roles." Hayakawa then emphasized the importance of "subtle gestures" and "extreme use of eyes and lips" as the results of "careful observation and thinking of the roles" in motion pictures more than explicit words, dialogue, and stylized theatrical performance.[74] Following Hayakawa's opinions, Kaeriyama insisted on the importance of presenting "pure expressions and behaviors of actual lives" in motion pictures. Kaeriyama referred to Thomas Ince's words: "Motion picture actors' behavior should be natural."[75] For Kaeriyama, "purity" of motion picture acting meant its "naturalness."[76] *Katsudo Shashin Zasshi* also published Ince's idea on motion picture actors, which emphasized "natural expressions."[77]

Strategically or not, the Pure Film advocates did not question the validity of Hayakawa's opinion in the context of Japanese history and culture. They simply accepted Hayakawa's words. Consequently, Hayakawa's rather stereo-typical view on Japanese people was translated back into Japanese and en-hanced the monolithic view on Japanese culture and people. Here, Japanese-ness was articulated through Hayakawa's star image, which was shaped in America. That is, what American media reported about the successful Japa-nese figure outside of Japan became internalized as the standard of what Japanese people should be, no matter how stereotypical these reports were.

In addition to his acting style, the Pure Film advocates regarded Haya-kawa's body itself as more "cinematic" than those of other Japanese actors.[78] The Pure Film advocates considered that American stars' "cinematic" charac-teristics stemmed from their highlighted bodily features, expressions, sexu-ality, and/or the sense of everydayness.[79] Hayakawa was reportedly bigger than average in Japan and much closer to American actors in stature.[80] It was reported that Hayakawa was not only practicing facial expressions, but also training his body every day like other American actors.[81] Hanayagi Tamio of *Katsudo Zasshi* examined Hayakawa's face based on "phrenology" and stated that "his power" comes from "his cool eyes that could even make villains shrink." Hanayagi even wrote that Hayakawa's nose looked like that of a pros-perous Jewish man.[82]

In early twentieth-century Japan, "Caucasian complex" was observable in the discourse of physical appearances. Japanese bodies were considered to be "shameful," compared with well-built and well-balanced Western bodies.[83] The terms *nikutai-bi* (the beauty of the body) and *hyojo-bi* (the beauty of ex-pressions) gained wide currency as words in vogue. According to the film historian Fujiki Hideaki, from the late 1910s onward, general magazines and women's magazines in Japan began to recurrently feature essays about what beauty was and how one could become beautiful, and the commentators presupposed that Western white women were the ideal models for this matter.[84]

The preference of Western bodies was based on a colonialist idea that sus-tained Eurocentric worldviews that assumed "Western" and "Japanese" racial and cultural characteristics were visibly and physically separable. It corre-sponded to pseudo-scientific thoughts typified by social Darwinism, which had been influential in Japan since the 1880s.[85] At least thirty-two transla-tions of the works of Herbert Spencer (1820–1903), which explained the progress of human society, culture, and civilization in terms of Darwinism, were published in Japan between 1877 and 1890.[86] Social Darwinist thought was used to justify the Westernization policy of the Japanese government for "progress toward a good society" because Japan was placed on the evolutionary ladder below the more "advanced races" in Darwinist thought.

The "Racial Equality Clause" in the principles of the League of Nations that Japan requested in 1919 at the Paris Conference was based on Japan's "Caucasian complex." Japan requested the inclusion of a sentence, "Equality of nations being a basic principle of the League of Nations, the High Contracting Parties agree to accord as soon as possible to all alien nationals of states, members of the League, equal and just treatment in every respect making no distinction either in law or in fact, on account of their race and nationality." When Japan's request was not accepted at the conference, Makino Nobuaki, the ambassador plenipotentiary, openly expressed his "tremendous disappointment" at the fact that "the Japanese government's and Japanese people's lingering dissatisfaction" with racial inequality in international relations was not resolved.[87]

With the trashing of the Racial Equality Clause, Hayakawa's image of an Americanized body perceived as being detached from Japaneseness gave hope that the Japanese people could become physically equal to the perceived beauty of Western bodies. Hayakawa's body and acting style displayed a promising future for Japanese cinema that an American audience would also appreciate. Hayakawa's popularity in the United States became the symbol of Japanese men's successful social achievement of the Western standard. Hayakawa's body could even overcome Darwinism, or the presumption of naturally determined Western racial and social hegemony. Hayakawa was thus conceived as the ideal physical embodiment of modernization. *Kinema Junpo* noted, "It is really difficult for Japanese people, who are said to lack facial expressions, to depict psychology mainly by facial expressions. It is encouraging that Sessue does that perfectly."[88] Y. K. Kasagi wrote, "We are proud of Hayakawa, because Japanese people are considered to be poor at expressing feelings but Hayakawa is famous in the motion picture that requires expressing feelings at its core" for using his bodily language. Kasagi praised Hayakawa because he showed the "capability of progress" of Japanese people toward the foreign standard in terms of their ability to express their feelings.[89] Kaeriyama also insisted that the "beauty of the body" paralleled the progression of civilization, and that Hayakawa was favorably received in the United States because he embodied the universal standard of "male beauty," beyond the Japanese as an inferior race.[90]

Thus, Japanese spectators positively considered Hayakawa to be an American import to a certain degree. Hayakawa was even chosen as the most popular "foreign actor" in a popularity contest conducted by *Katsudo Shashin Zasshi* in 1921.[91] Both *Katsudo no Sekai* and *Katsudo Gaho* placed Hayakawa in the category of "popular American actors."[92] A fan praised Hayakawa by juxtaposing him with Chaplin and Fairbanks Sr. in 1919.[93] Another fan, in a more negative and ultra-nationalistic tone, claimed that Hayakawa's acting was good in an "Americanized" sense, but "not as Japanese."[94] However, in the same magazine, yet another fan criticized this negative view on Hayakawa's Americanization and positively appreciated his deviation from Japanese actors' lack of expression.[95]

In this sense, there was a clear gap in the reception of Hayakawa's stardom in Japan and in the United States. In Japan, where, according to Betty Willis of *Motion Picture Magazine*, he "smashed a national tradition," Hayakawa was a symbol of Americanization, no matter how much his success was praised in a nationalistic tone.[96] However, in the United States, Hayakawa was a representative of Japan no matter how Americanized his star image was. In the 1930s, Betty Willis wrote that in the United States, "The only things Western about Sessue Hayakawa that I could discover were the black-and-white American sport shoes emerging from beneath his two kimonos. He smokes Japanese cigarettes, has Japanese people around him, talks with a completely bewildering Japanese accent, looks Oriental, and above all, thinks with the Oriental's attitude."[97] Hayakawa himself was aware of the ambivalent reception of his stardom in Japan and in the United States. He confessed his distress in an interview for a Japanese film magazine, "Some Japanese people talk about me as if I were not Japanese, but white people regard me as Japanese."[98]

Even Hayakawa's acting style was praised for contrasting reasons in Japan and in the United States. In both countries, Hayakawa's acting style was received as "foreign." In Japan, Hayakawa was praised for his American acting style, which was detached from Japanese theatrical acting. In contrast, in the United States, Hayakawa's acting was praised for its deviation from the Western style of acting, no matter how much he had learned of the Western theatrical arts. It was explained as having come from Japaneseness, such as Danjuro's *haragei*, or "restrained" style.

As a result, two completely different manners of appreciating Hayakawa's body and his acting style came to coexist in Japanese film magazines, which often translated articles from American film magazines. As mentioned in the introduction of this book, in one case, the same Japanese film magazine that highly valued Hayakawa's Americanized acting style, which was full of gestures and facial expressions, simultaneously praised his expressionless face and restrained acting style, which American film magazines particularly noted.

This contradictory reception of Hayakawa's stardom in the United States and in Japan made the Pure Film advocates realize their own ambivalent position between Westernization and nationalism. As a result, they consciously articulated Hayakawa's acting as "Americanized Japaneseness" to justify their contradiction. They argued that the ambivalent reception of Hayakawa proved the need for Hayakawa's efforts to articulate Japaneseness for American spectators. Kondo Iyokichi claimed that Hayakawa had to accomplish a double-bound duty "to show Japanese characteristics vividly as a Japanese actor," and, at the same time, "he must be based on a worldly common, cosmopolitan acting style" that would be "understandable to any foreign audience." Kondo insisted that Hayakawa "extremely emphasized the local color, geisha, Japanese swords, and lack of facial expression that were known as Japanese characteristics at the same time as he was based on naturalistic acting that was the worldly common standard for motion pictures."[99]

While the Pure Film advocates highly valued Hayakawa's Americanized body and acting style, they simultaneously praised Hayakawa's patriotic and nationalistic attitude and tried to connect the two within the star image of Hayakawa. They called Hayakawa "the pride and honor of Japan because of his international fame as a great motion picture actor."[100] Oda Suezo, an executive of Teikoku Engei Kinema Company (Teikine), called Hayakawa "a patriot" because of his success in the American motion picture industry.[101] *Katsudo Kurabu* reported that Hayakawa proudly said that he recovered from his illness quickly not only because of his daily physical training but also "because of his Japanese spirit."[102]

In his book on Hayakawa, Mori wrote that despite Hayakawa's international fame as a Hollywood star "Sessue has a very profound relationship with Japan. Like Japanese cherry blossoms, Utamaro, and Mt. Fuji, Sessue is the representative of Japan." Mori even called Hayakawa "a unofficial diplomat" to the United States and insisted that "therefore, we have a responsibility to support him nationally." Mori intentionally picked up Truman B. Handy's article in *Photoplay Magazine*, which referred to Hayakawa's nationalist "ambition to epitomize the history of his country in films" that would show the entire history of Japan's foreign relations.[103] Mori concluded his book by asking Hayakawa "to express thoughts and emotions that are essential to Japanese people by his unique international performance" and demanding that the audience of Hayakawa's films "support him nationally."[104]

Taguchi Oson, a producer at Shochiku Kinema Company, who toured American film studios in 1920, claimed, "It is ignorant and anachronistic that the Japanese police are still misunderstanding Hayakawa's films despite the fact that Hayakawa is making every effort for Japanese people in Southern California, where anti-Japanese sentiment is very strong."[105] *Katsudo Gaho*, in a favorable tone, quoted Hayakawa saying, "I will never do such an immoral thing [as appearing in anti-Japanese films] because *I am Japanese*."[106] Seki Misao, a Japanese actor, praised Hayakawa for his "spirit of *bushido* as a Japanese man . . . . and his practice of purely Japanese sword fighting [even in America]."[107]

The Pure Film advocates praised Hayakawa's films, especially those made at Haworth, for their nationalistic attitudes. Mori regarded *His Birthright, His Debt*, and *The Gray Horizon* as Hayakawa's attempts to show "the Japanese spirit" and insisted that *The Temple of Dusk* was "a masterpiece that depicts the Japanese spirit, and it is a great pleasure to have this film for Sessue, for Japan, and for cinema."[108] *Kinema Junpo* stated that *The Temple of Dusk* would "regain Sessue's honor and credit" because the protagonist "completely has the unique Japanese spirit."[109] *Katsudo Gaho* praised *Black Roses* because Hayakawa, "who had been concentrated on making films of Chinese subject matters," finally played a Japanese role and "expressed the Japanese spirit against anti-Japanese sentiments."[110] Hayakawa's "calm attitudes" in *The Illustrious Prince* (Worthington, 2 November 1919) and *Black Roses* were noted as "the expression of the essence of Japanese people, the Japanese spirit."[111] Even Hayakawa's performance as a Mexican in *The Jaguar's Claws*, which was made at Lasky but released in Japan after the establishment of Haworth, was praised because "in his expression and behavior, there is Japanese uniqueness that is difficult to hide."[112] The *Tokyo Asahi Shinbun* even reported that Hayakawa said he was planning to make an expensive film about the Mongol invasion in the thirteenth century, in which a typhoon blew away the Mongolian army and protected Japan, a symbolic historical event of Japanese nationalism known as kamikaze, or the God's wind.[113]

The ambivalent reception of Hayakawa's stardom in Japan, torn between Americanization and nationalism, coincided with Japanese audiences' adoration of the "white race" and their hope of overcoming their "Caucasian complex." When Japan started expanding imperialistically in Asia during and after World War I, Japanese intellectuals began to praise the Japanese people as "a blessed race." They imagined "Japan" as "an alternative time and place outside of the 'logic of civilization' and the progressive history of modernity."[114] By the time the war in the Pacific started, such an argument had spread widely as a "myth" with the slogan "overcoming modernity" and had become the basis of Japan's own imperialism toward other Asian countries.[115] "Modernity" here was synonymous with Westernization. As the historian Yumiko Iida argues, in the notion of "overcoming modernity," "'Japan' was located in an ambiguous position between the West and Asia, both assuming itself to be a part of the spiritual virtue of Asia while equally playing the role of an imperial power attempting to put Asia under its control by reducing 'Asia' to a rhetorical site grounding Japan's counter hegemonic revolt against the modern West." This discourse on the uniqueness of Japanese civilization was an attempt to overcome Japan's complex toward the "superiority" of Europe and the United States, despite the fact that Japan had "continuing difficulties in coming to terms with the modernly configured world" but simultaneously adored the "white race."[116]

Under these conditions, Hayakawa was once again located in the middle-ground position with the reception of his stardom in Japan. Hayakawa was a perfect symbol of Americanization, but, simultaneously, Hayakawa's stardom was an ideal object to enhance the nationalist consciousness. In addition to Hayakawa's image of Americanization, Japanese spectators attributed his star image to a Japaneseness that was clearly understandable even to American audiences. This foreign version of Japaneseness in Hayakawa's star image became a catalyst for Japanese audiences to articulate the meaning of being Japanese, or to problematize what Japan was.[117]

The ambivalent reception of Hayakawa's stardom in Japan even foreshadowed the problematic transition of Japanese social discourses from the 1920s to the 1930s, from the Taisho era to the Showa (1926–89). In the 1920s, with the influential trend of Americanization in the field of urban consumer culture that flourished in Tokyo after the Great Kanto Earthquake in 1923, the display of Japaneseness tended to be suppressed in various media, such as numerous newly published magazines, popular songs, radio, and movie theaters. In the 1930s, in accordance with the advancement of imperialism, a nationalist tendency, "recurrence of tradition" or "invention of tradition," that revalued Japaneseness became observable.

However, in reality, there was no discontinuity between the 1920s and the 1930s. A binary view, with the 1920s as the decade of Americanization and the 1930s as that of Japanization, is likely to overlook the actual continuity of popular imagination and social discourses on race and nation between the two decades. Throughout the 1920s and 1930s Japanese intellectuals continuously discussed the concept of Americanism in relation to Japanese nationalism.[118] The praise of Hayakawa's body and acting for their embodiment of Americanism was based on strong Japanese nationalism.

Under these conditions, Hayakawa's return to Japan in 1922, for the first time since he had become a star in the United States, became a symbolic event that indicated Japanese audiences' ambivalent reception of his stardom. Hayakawa as an actual person suffered due to his twofold star images in Japan: the embodiment of Americanization and the representative of Japan. The Japanese reaction to Hayakawa's visit revealed the inherent contradiction in popular culture and social discourses in Japan in the 1910s to the 1920s.

On Hayakawa's arrival, the Pure Film advocates, Japanese film companies, and fans unanimously and nationalistically expressed their welcome for Hayakawa for his continuous efforts to introduce Japanese culture to American audiences and for "impressing them with his Japanese art for the U.S.-Japan goodwill."[119] Mori Tomita, the president of *Katsudo Kurabu*, wrote, "We cannot stop thanking Mr. Hayakawa for making [the] Japanese race understood by Americans."[120] Kokusai Katsuei Company (Kokkatsu), which distributed Robertson-Cole's films, widely publicized Hayakawa's visit to Japan. On 14 April 1922, the central figures of the Pure Film Movement, including Kaeriyama, Mori, Shibusawa, Osanai, Thomas Kurihara, and Henry Kotani formed a group to support Hayakawa.[121] Several biographical books of Hayakawa appeared and praised Hayakawa's success in the United States, in spite of anti-Japanese sentiments, as "the representative of Japanese people."[122] In these books, Hayakawa's innocence during the filming of the controversial film *The Cheat*, his high salary, and his popularity among American women were particularly emphasized.[123] *Kinema Junpo* reported that "on every face of those who welcomed Hayakawa at Yokohama port there was pride as Japanese."[124] Many fan letters were published in newspapers almost every day during Hayakawa's visit.[125]

At the same time, there were some people who did not welcome Hayakawa's return for the same nationalistic reasons. The "Hayakawa assassination group" or "unwelcoming Sesshu group" was formed right after Hayakawa left San Francisco for Japan.[126] This group and another nationalist group, Yamato Minro Kai, insisted that Hayakawa's appearance in anti-Japanese films was a "national disgrace" and he had to apologize at Meiji Jingu Shrine and Ise Jingu Shrine before he entered Japan.[127] (In fact, *Katsudo Zasshi* reported that Hayakawa and Aoki went to Meji Jingu Shrine and Nijubashi to pay their respects to the emperor.)[128] Contrary to the report in *Kinema Junpo*, some newspapers reported that Hayakawa landed at Yokohama and was guarded by the police because there was a demonstration against his return.[129] Even during the welcome party for Hayakawa on 4 July 1922, some men from the "assassination group" caused some problems.[130] These incidents indicate that Hayakawa was still received unfavorably among some Japanese audiences, even after the Pure Film advocates' positive reactions toward his films became widely shared by popular film audiences and readers of film magazines.

For the Pure Film advocates, Hayakawa's return was a grave opportunity to develop their nationalistically oriented activities to modernize cinema. They wanted Hayakawa to contribute to "the progress and improvement of Japanese cinema" with his skill and experiences in American-style filmmaking.[131] They expected Hayakawa to play an active role of "Americanizing" Japanese cinema.[132] Some film fans also suggested that Hayakawa make films "that introduce Japan to the world."[133]

Indirectly but certainly, Hayakawa played important roles in the Pure Film Movement, even before he arrived in Japan. Thomas Kurihara, a film director at Taisho Katsudo Shashin Company (Taikatsu), a film studio established in 1920, and Henry Kotani, a cinematographer at Shochiku's Kamata Studio, had been working with Hayakawa at Lasky and Haworth. Ushiyama Kiyohito, who introduced an American-style makeup technique into Japan in the 1920s, started his career in the United States thanks to Hayakawa's advice.[134] A Japanese film, *Reiko no chimata ni* [At the top of sacred light] (Hosoyama Kiyomatsu, 1922), was reported to have imitated Hayakawa's *The First Born* for its plot and editing style, and *Where Lights Are Low* for its choreography of the climactic fighting scene. Film critics praised *Reiko no chimata ni* for its deviation from the theatrical style of filmmaking.[135]

As for the industrial discourse, Hayakawa's stardom had a profound influence on the development of the star system in the Japanese film industry. A new star system had been developed in Japan with an increasing prevalence of American stars' images.[136] Before Hayakawa, the only stars that the Japanese film industry had were arguably the ones from kabuki. Yet, after Hayakawa, it was a different story. Suzuki Denmei, the first Japanese star in modern dramas, for instance, started his acting career in the Pure Film Movement and its experimental works, such as Murata Minoru's *Rojo no reikon* (*Souls on the Road*, 1921), an adaptation of Maxim Gorky's *The Lower Depths* in the style of Griffith's *Intolerance* (1916), but he became a star after he was hired by Shochiku. In addition to his big salary, Suzuki had a specific star persona, Americanized and athletic. Shochiku's star-making strategy toward Suzuki seemed to follow Hayakawa's star image.

Moreover, in Japan, there were not many motion picture actresses until arguably as late as 1918, when Hanayagi Harumi starred in *Sei no kagayaki* [Radiance of life], a product of the film modernization movement. Before this film, there were *onnagata*, female impersonators in kabuki, and only a few female actresses, including Morita Suzuko, Hanamura Nobuko, Miho Matsuko, and Hashimoto Yaeko, appeared in motion pictures in Japan. Therefore, Tsuru Aoki, Hayakawa's wife, was arguably one of the first female Japanese motion picture stars and became the template for actresses and stars in Japan.

A reporter emphasized Aoki's Americanized star image, noting that Aoki preferred playing golf and riding horses and she had difficulty in sitting on a Japanese tatami mat because she was so used to sitting on a chair.[137] Simultaneously, Aoki was an important element for the Pure Film advocates' nationalist goal. She was praised as an ideal Japanese housewife in spite of her Americanized appearance. Those who visited the Hayakawas in Hollywood praised the Hayakawas for entertaining them in a Japanese-style room with Japanese food prepared by Aoki.[138] Many articles in Japanese magazines were devoted to Aoki and her role as a wife, contrary to the U.S. film magazines, which mainly wrote about Hayakawa after 1916. The editor-in-chief of *Katsudo Kurabu* claimed, "Hayakawa's fame is not accidental but owes a lot to his wife Tsuruko. . . . She is a faithful wife who devotes herself to improving her husband's position."[139] In this sense, American film fan magazines and their Japanese counterparts played similar roles in the formation of Aoki's public image within different contexts. In the United States, Aoki was regarded as an ideal Victorian middle-class wife who created a refined domestic space with consumer goods, while in Japan she was an ideal housewife who devotedly supported her husband.

When Hayakawa and Aoki arrived in Yokohama, according to a newspaper report, Hayakawa said, "I came back to Japan to learn Japanese culture and customs, especially not to forget about *bushido*. . . . [Since *The Cheat*] I never appeared in films that would insult Japanese honor, . . . and I am planning to study and collect materials about Japanese unique fairy tales filled with philosophical thoughts [for his future films]."[140] *Katsudo Zasshi* also reported that

Hayakawa told the audience at the welcome party that he was "one of the re-spectable *Yamato* [Japanese] race" and started crying with joy over his return to his own country.[141] These words of Hayakawa corresponded to the ideal of the Pure Film Movement, and the Pure Film advocates expected Hayakawa to advance their movement substantially.

However, in reality, neither Hayakawa nor Aoki played active roles in the movement during their stay, partly because of some "unwelcome" activities. The Pure Film advocates criticized Japanese audiences "who did not under-stand the art of motion pictures" and formed the "Hayakawa assassination group" only because of *The Cheat*; consequently they did not provide Haya-kawa with any opportunity to work for improving Japanese cinema. *Kinema Junpo* stated, "It is a pity that newspapers have jokingly written annoying articles on Hayakawa."[142] *Katsudo Gaho* reported that Hayakawa had to go back to the United States because he was called "a national traitor" again in Japan.[143] The *Tokyo Asahi Shinbun* also reported that Hayakawa and Aoki had to go back to America "sadly by themselves, . . . as if they had to run away," be-cause of the unwelcome atmosphere.[144] In 1937, the *Los Angeles Times* recalled that fifteen years earlier, Hayakawa was "accused of being 'anti-Japanese,' [and] fled Tokio."[145]

The disappointment of the Pure Film advocates was great when Hayakawa was not able to fulfill their expectations. The favorable view of Hayakawa's Americanized stardom quickly turned into abhorrence from a nationalist standpoint. Even during Hayakawa's stay in Japan, the society for supporting Hayakawa held a meeting and condemned Hayakawa for not doing anything for it.[146] Sakamoto Shigetaro criticized Hayakawa for "behaving like an ordi-nary American actor" who "faked Japanese characters on screen based just on his rough childhood memories of Japan" and never acted like the Japanese in his "expression and attitude."[147] Ichikawa Sai wrote that they "tried to obtain a method that would enable the export of Japanese films" through Hayakawa and planned "to promote Japanese cinema to Japanese general audiences" with Hayakawa. According to Ichikawa, the Pure Film advocates made a list of propositions for Hayakawa:

1   Hayakawa should give a lecture to explain what he had done thus far.
2   Hayakawa should talk with people in the motion picture business, such as scenario writers, directors, actors, and technicians, about present conditions in Japan and in the United States.
3   Hayakawa should demonstrate how to direct films.[148]

4   Hayakawa should instruct the group in the appropriate methods with which to export Japanese films.

5   Hayakawa should donate a certain amount of money to Tokyo if possible.

Ichikawa insisted that these plans were never realized, even though Hayakawa listened to the requests of the Pure Film advocates. Ichikawa nationalistically condemned Hayakawa: "What he [Hayakawa] said and did were not suitable to Japanese customs."[149] *Kinema Junpo* published a fan's letter with similar requests to Hayakawa. The fan wanted Hayakawa to

1   talk with major governmental officials and the "Unwelcome Group" to clear up misunderstandings;

2   give a lecture for his audiences;

3   make a film as a demonstration in front of Japanese film actors; and

4   show how to direct a film in front of Japanese film directors.[150]

In the same article, Ichikawa angrily reported that when Hayakawa arrived in San Francisco, he "arrogantly" declared that "he would never go back to Japan because it was very uncomfortable." *Katsudo Zasshi* also reported on Hayakawa's public speech in San Francisco and noted that Hayakawa even said, "The very members of the society for supporting me were actually members of [the] anti-Hayakawa group" and "threatened me for money."[151] The same magazine also called him an "American nouveau riche" and unfavorably noted that "after spending as long as fifteen years in a foreign country," Hayakawa's speech sounded like "a non-eloquent foreigner who speaks Japanese a little."[152] If these reports were correct, the public speech that Hayakawa delivered in San Francisco was completely contradictory to what he had said when he left Japan. In Japan Hayakawa declared, according to the *Miyako Shinbun*, "When I come back to Japan again, I will work toward making a big film that will publicize Japan to the world. I want to make a film with a splendid international dramatic plot that will introduce Japan not by rickshaws or thatched cottages but by its culture and customs, industries, political system, unique landscape, huge buildings, and so forth."[153]

Even fans came to criticize Hayakawa's "Americanized attitude" from their nationalist perspectives. Yamauchi Uichi sent a letter to *Katsudo Kurabu*, criticizing Hayakawa's words, "Japanese do not understand art," and called Hayakawa a "Japanese-Westerner."[154] Noguchi Yonejiro, the father of the renowned sculptor Isamu Noguchi, published a poem that criticized Hayakawa in *Chuo Koron*, one of the most popular magazines in Japan. Noguchi insisted that Hayakawa should have learned "the true human nature" in Japan, which was not in Hollywood studios.[155]

In 1924, following the passage of the Immigration Act, which limited immigration to the United States, some intellectuals in Japan initiated a movement that insisted on rejecting the importation of American films. They regarded the "anti-Japanese" immigration act in the United States as "a good opportunity" to "produce Japanese cinema as good as American films," and to "develop our film enterprise safely."[156] Tsutsumi Tomojiro of Shochiku insisted that Japanese cinema was developing and "it is possible to exclude American films."[157] Under such conditions, Hayakawa's privileged middle-ground position during the height of the Pure Film Movement disappeared. In fact, anti-American sentiments caused by the 1924 Immigration Act easily turned to anti-Hayakawa, opposing the Americanized star. In the anti-American film movement that started in June 1924, Hayakawa's image in Japan went back to that of the Japanese actor who was "simply used by Americans to make *The Cheat* to enhance anti-Japanese fever."[158]

The anti-American film movement and the boycott of American films by some Japanese film companies lasted only about a month because, with the trend of Americanism in popular culture, many film audiences realized that they wanted to see American films. *Kinema Junpo* published fans' letters that opposed the anti-American film movement, saying that the movement ignored the demand from film fans.[159] By mid-July the four companies that had organized the boycott attempt returned to distributing and showing American films.[160]

However, Hayakawa never regained his popularity in Japan. He became regarded as too Japanese in the Japanese adoration for American culture in the mid- to late 1920s and too Americanized for the nationalist trend that followed. According to a report in *Katsudo Zasshi*, the books, trading cards, and postcards of Hayakawa, which were published in the summer of 1922, had not sold very well.[161] Consequently, Hayakawa became an exile because of his ambivalent middle-ground position between Japanese and American. The *Nyu Yoku Shimpo* reported in 1922 that Hayakawa left Japan "as if he had been running away."[162] Even when Hayakawa tried to open his own production company in Japan in 1925, supported by Teikoku Engei Kinema Company, very few people wanted to buy the stock. His nomadic life continued until the 1950s.

EPILOGUE

L eaving Hollywood in 1922, Sessue Hayakawa became an actor in exile. After his short visit to Japan, Hayakawa went to back to the United States and appeared in a stage play, *Tiger Lily*, a drama by Fred de Greasac, in January 1923.[1] *Tiger Lily* was not received well. It was cancelled after three weeks' performance in Pittsburgh, Washington, D.C., and Atlantic City, and did not play in New York.[2] Hayakawa did not regain his popularity even on the East Coast, where anti-Japanese sentiment was less than on the West Coast. After his appearance in *Tiger Lily*, it was reported that Hayakawa had signed a new contract with the "True Art" company to make twelve films in three years, but that did not happen.[3] Instead, Hayakawa received an offer from France to appear in a film called *La Bataille* (*The Danger Line*, E. E. Violet, 1923).[4]

Hayakawa decided to go to Europe, where audiences were still enthusiastic about him. *Katsudo Zasshi* claimed in 1924 that Hayakawa was "more popular than Chaplin in Europe."[5] A British producer, who visited Robertson-Cole in 1922, stated that Hayakawa was "the actors' actor" in England, and his "histrionic technique, and ability to 'put over' things in a subtle way are studied by those anxious to improve their own work upon the screen." He also said that Hayakawa's films were "great box office attractions with the masses" in Europe.[6]

La Bataille followed many devices in Hayakawa's star vehicles at Lasky, Haworth, and Robertson-Cole. The MPW noted that Hayakawa "once again" appeared in a "picturesque Japanese" film.[7] Stereotypical images of Japan are emphasized from the very beginning of the film. The opening title and credits use drawings of Mount Fuji, a Japanese lady in a kimono, a samurai with a large sword, the rising sun, cherry blossoms, and chrysanthemums, the symbol of the Japanese emperor. The opening scene of a night festival in Japan emphatically displays Japanese objects, including lines of paper lanterns, torii, and Japanese flags. In the following scene, Tsuru Aoki appears in a kimono, plays the koto (a Japanese harp), and dances a Japanese dance in a tatami room with *fusuma*, shoji, and Japanese flowers. There is even a character who commits hara-kiri at the end of the film.

The motif of racial hierarchy is also repeated. Japanese people in the film are clearly differentiated from Chinese people, who have darker skins and are mostly depicted as opium smokers. As in *The Soul of Kura San*, a white male painter seduces Aoki but regards her merely as a pictorial object, and Hayakawa's character tries to revenge the white man. In fact, Margaret Turnbull, who contributed to crystallizing Hayakawa's star image at Lasky with her screenplays, including *Alien Souls* and *The Victoria Cross* (William C. DeMille, 14 December 1916), wrote the screenplay of *La Bataille*.

La Bataille was a great opportunity for Hayakawa to revitalize his stardom, even though it was not in the United States. Hayakawa used many of the motifs standardized at Lasky and Robertson-Cole in order to make another star vehicle for himself. As a result, *La Bataille* became a critically and financially successful film in Paris and Hayakawa proudly proclaimed this in his autobiography.[8]

Hayakawa kept resorting to his existing star images after *La Bataille*. After appearing in three more films in France and in the United Kingdom in 1924—*Sen Yan's Devotion* (A. E. Coleby), *J'ai tué!* (*I Have Killed*, Roger Lion), and *The Great Prince Shan* (Coleby)—Hayakawa received offers to appear in the stage dramas *Knee of the God* in Paris and William Archer's one-act play, *Samurai*, in London. Again, both *Knee of the God* and *Samurai* were stereotypically about *bushido*, hara-kiri, and revenge.[9]

With these successes in Europe, Hayakawa returned to the United States and appeared in a stage drama, *The Love City*. After several performances in Pennsylvania, *The Love City* opened at the Little Theatre on Broadway on 25 January 1926. *The Love City*, set in China and London, was, according to its program booklet, "a colorful, clashing drama of east and west." Hayakawa played Chang Lo, a rich opium dealer who "commits murder as calmly as he drinks a cup of tea, . . . yet [he] has a tender appreciation of loveliness whether it be in a simple flower or a beautiful woman such as Tze-shi whom he holds caged in his house."[10] The exotic setting and the twofold characterization of Hayakawa's protagonist in *The Love City* imitate such Hayakawa star vehicles as *The Tong Man*. The Chinese heroine, Tze-shi, was played by a white actress, Margaret Mower.[11]

In the same year, Hayakawa went on a vaudeville tour with *The Bandit Prince*, a one-act play, that was a dramatized fragment of his own novel.[12] In *The Bandit Prince*, a story set in China, a young Harvard graduate who is a

Chinese prince turns out to be a bandit, a "Chinese Robin Hood," with the ambition to free his country from the tyranny of a despotic and monarchical rule. He falls in love with a modern Manchurian princess and self-sacrificially devotes himself to the good of the heroine and of his country.[13] Such characterization of the protagonist, a foreign educated high-class nonwhite with a self-sacrificing motive, clearly imitates the narrative structure of many of Hayakawa's vehicles. The *New York Times* noted that it was "as excellently tailored a role for Mr. Hayakawa as could be found anywhere."[14] Hayakawa self-consciously used his standardized star image and attempted to revitalize his popularity in the United States.

One fan magazine article reported, "Prejudices vanish like smoke. Today I find a broader, friendlier feeling. There is even a marked desire for Oriental pictures. . . . 'The Bandit Prince,' is the name of the story in which he [Hayakawa] will make his reappearance in pictures. Hayakawa himself wrote the novel."[15] However, the film version of *The Bandit Prince* was never produced. In spite of Hayakawa's strong desire to make films about "subdued romance" with "subtleties" that had made him a star a decade before, Hayakawa never had a chance to play leading roles in feature films in Hollywood.[16] Even though Hayakawa proudly announced in December 1926 that he had several offers from film companies and would decide soon, it took more than two years for him to reappear in films.[17]

In 1928, Hayakawa appeared in another stage play, *The Man Who Laughs Last* (aka *The Man Who Laughed*) at the Hillstreet Theater in Los Angeles (see fig. 22).[18] This vaudeville act by Hayakawa, which once again exploited the miscegenation issue, was filmed as one of the two-reel Vitaphone projects at Warner Bros. in 1929. However, this appearance in a short sound film did not lead Hayakawa to a leading role in a feature film. In 1931, after appearing in a few films in Japan, Hayakawa went back to Hollywood again but was only able to appear in Sax Rohmer's Fu Manchu story, *Daughter of the Dragon* (Lloyd Corrigan, 1931), as a supporting character for the heroine, Anna May Wong.[19] Yet, Hayakawa's role in the film was severely criticized. *Variety* noted that Hayakawa "never gives [plays] the role plausibly."[20]

In the same year, there was also an unfortunate incident in Hayakawa's real life. The incident seemed to imitate the theme of the anxiety of miscegenation in his star vehicles. On 26 August 1931, the *Los Angeles Times* reported that Hayakawa and his wife, Tsuru, legally adopted a two-year-old boy, Alexander Hayes, and renamed him Yukio Hayakawa.[21] Right after this report, a white actress asserted that she was the mother and Hayakawa the father of

22 *A still from* The Man Who Laughs Last.

the boy and filed a suit against Hayakawa to regain custody of her son. The reports in the *Los Angeles Times* emphasized the racial differences between the couple and were sympathetic to the white woman, "Miss Ruth Noble." One report stated: "She is of the Caucasian race. . . . Miss Noble said that after the child was born she feared she could not give him the opportunities in life he deserved and agreed to a pact with Hayakawa by which she surrender[ed] the boy to the actor. . . . Miss Noble said she met and was engaged and played with Hayakawa in a vaudeville act called 'The Bandit Prince,' prior to the birth of the baby and before the actor's return to Hollywood, during which she says a romance existed between them. Hayakawa could not be located yesterday."[22] Another report noted that Noble's suit against Hayakawa was simply "prompted by mother love and by the feeling the child will not receive opportunities to which he is entitled in the event he is taken to Japan."[23]

The *Los Angeles Times* kept reporting the "scandal" of the nonwhite star of the silent period in a melodramatic manner and, according to those reports,

Hayakawa did not play a heroic role in the melodrama.[24] When Hayakawa left for Japan to fulfill a contract with Shochiku, a film production company in Tokyo, the *Los Angeles Times* reported in an article titled, "East and West Part in Tears": "In bidding Hayakawa bon voyage, the actress [Ruth Noble] indicated she was saying farewell to love and to hopes of regaining custody of her son. . . . 'I just told him I was sorry if I had caused him any trouble,' the actress expressed."[25] In fact, Noble intended to follow Hayakawa to Japan and was on the boat from Los Angeles to San Francisco, where she gave up after reportedly receiving $7,000 in cash from Hayakawa, in addition to the $150 a month he had previously agreed to pay her.[26] Noble's act could be regarded as that of obsessed stalking and the *Los Angeles Times* reported that Noble's act surprised her attorneys.[27] However, in general, Noble was given the position of a sympathetic victim in this incident of miscegenation by the newspaper. Tsuru had to defend her husband from the perspectives of a loyal wife and a warm-hearted stepmother.[28] This real life incident, especially when it was scandalously reported in newspapers, hardened Hayakawa's decision to leave the United States once again.

In Japan, the Japanese audience's ambivalent attitude toward Hayakawa lingered on after his short visit in 1922. There was a certain gap between the audience's nationalist expectations toward Hayakawa as a representative of Japan and Hayakawa's Westernized image. An editorial in *Katsudo Zasshi* claimed that "Hayakawa cleared out his past infamous reputation in Japan, but his success [in *La Bataille*] was still based on the film's depiction of Westernized Japanese characters compromising for foreign audiences."[29]

When *La Bataille* was released in Japan, some praised the film for its "depiction of strong patriotism of Japanese people."[30] The Japanese Ministry of Foreign Affairs praised Hayakawa as "a new pride of Japan," for he was able to freely use as many as eleven French battleships for the shooting of his film and consequently received a French national award for the success of *La Bataille*.[31] The Ministry of the Navy also praised the film enthusiastically. It was even reported that Togo Heihachiro, the hero of the Russo-Japanese War, was very impressed by the film.[32]

Yet, at the same time, *La Bataille* was criticized for its story, which was "opposed to Japanese women's proper behavior and *bushido*," and Hayakawa and Aoki were called "national traitors" again.[33] The *Tokyo Nichinichi Shinbun* noted, "Sessue really causes problems very often."[34] The Metropolitan Police Department tried to ban the film from exhibition because it "would violate public morals."[35] This ambivalent reaction to *La Bataille* indicated the eagerness of Japanese policymakers to control visual images that would represent Japanese national identity in international relations in the post–World War I era. Hayakawa was not necessarily a perfect candidate for their goal.

Hayakawa's return to Japan in the 1930s revealed the Japanese audience's lingering ambivalent attitude toward him. Some Japanese investors regarded Hayakawa as the savior of Japanese cinema, as the Pure Film advocates did in the 1910s and 1920s. They planned to establish a film company for Hayakawa, Hayakawa Sesshu Kokusai Eiga Company, "in order to make films for export and to introduce our Japanese civilization."[36] The actor Kamiyama Sojin insisted that Hayakawa achieved his success in the United States because of his "deep, keen, and clever eyes of the Japanese race" and called Hayakawa "a successful figure that Japanese people should be proud of."[37]

Simultaneously, Hayakawa was still considered to be a foreign import. *Kinema Junpo* noted that *The Man Who Laughs Last* was a film for American audiences with its use of stereotypical Japanese images like jiu-jitsu and ninja.[38] The same magazine criticized Hayakawa's acting in *Daughter of the Dragon* for looking like an "anachronistic period drama style."[39] Japanese magazines sensationally reported Hayakawa's popularity among foreign women and his preference for American women.[40]

In fact, when Hayakawa appeared in films and stage dramas in Japan for the first time in the 1930s, most of these films and plays were translations of imported Western productions. Hayakawa played Westernized characters or foreigners in them. The first such stage drama was *Appare Wong* (*The Honourable Mr. Wong*, a play written by Achmed Abdullah and David Belasco, September 1930), which was performed at Teikoku Gekijo Theater.[41] Hayakawa toured around Japan with this stage drama. *Appare Wong*, a story about a Chinese American enforcer (Hayakawa) who marries the daughter of his friend whom he executes, is set in San Francisco's Chinatown and is filled with exoticism: Chinese gangsters, Buddhism, self-sacrifice, and so on. Subsequently, Hayakawa appeared in *Dr. Jekyll and Mr. Hyde* (June 1933) and *Cyrano de Bergerac* (January 1934).

The first Japanese film in which he appeared was *Taiyo wa higashi yori* [The sun rises from the east] (Shochiku, 1932), a remake of Frank Borzage's *Seventh Heaven* (1927). Shochiku's Kamata studio, where *Taiyo wa higashi yori* was made, was the studio that was established to pursue the goals of the Pure Film Movement: overcoming the theatrical tradition in Japanese-made films and pursuing an American-style filmmaking method under the producer system initiated by Kido Shiro. The films made at Shochiku Kamata aimed at depicting modernized urban lives in Japan. Hayakawa's image as a foreign import seemed a perfect fit to the Shochiku Kamata style (*Kamata-cho*). Shochiku let Hayakawa direct *Taiyo wa higashi yori*. It was a fulfillment of the Pure Film advocates' original request to Hayakawa in 1922 to direct a film to demonstrate American-style filmmaking, "the method that did not exist in Japanese cinema."[42]

However, once *Taiyo wa higashi yori* was released, both Hayakawa's acting and direction were severely criticized.[43] A review in *Kinema Junpo* stated, "Hayakawa's acting is not impressive at all because it is an absolutely exaggerated American method."[44] Despite Shochiku Kamata's modernization policy of filmmaking, Hayakawa's prefixed star image was too Americanized for Japanese spectators in the 1930s. As militarism seized the political hegemony and an ultra-nationalist atmosphere became intensified in Japan, Americanization was questioned. The Manchurian incident in September 1931 marked the escalation of nationalism and authoritarian imperialism. It was reported that a Japanese railway in Manchuria was bombed by the Chinese army, and the Japanese army declared the occupation of Manchuria in retaliation for the attack.

Under such sociopolitical conditions, the Japanese film industry turned to making films that praised militarism and imperialistic expansion to China. Even the films made at Shochiku's Kamata studio, with their Americanized surface, came to incorporate pro-nationalist senses of value. Suzuki Denmei, "the most Americanized star" of Shochiku, began to play stoic Japanese men who punish flippant youngsters wearing Americanized clothes in such star vehicles as *Kare to denen* [He and countryside] (Ushihara Kiyohiko, 1928).

After the failure of *Taiyo wa higashi yori*, Hayakawa consciously, or inevitably, began to play roles of national-hero types and challenged the foreign star image of himself. As early as 1928, when Hayakawa was still in the United States, he said in a Japanese American newspaper interview, "I will faithfully devote myself to the Japanese nation and do my best when I start working [in Japan]."[45] In 1933 Hayakawa appeared for the first time in a *jidaigeki*, a period film, *Nanko fushi* [Father and son of Honorable Kusunoki] (Ikeda Tomiyasu, 1933).[46] Hayakawa played Kusunoki Masashige, one of the most popular figures in Japanese history, who devoted his life to the emperor in the fourteenth century. In the tendency toward ultra-nationalism, so-called modern nationalistic *jidaigeki* put more emphasis on displaying Japanese cultural heritage and samurai warriors' loyalty to the Japanese emperor than on the spectacle of speedily choreographed sword fighting, which was more influenced by the sensitivity of modernity and American action films.[47] *Nanko fushi* was one such "modern nationalistic *jidaigeki*" film. Kishi Matsuo of *Kinema Junpo* claimed that "nationalistically devoted Japanese people will be deeply moved by this talkie."[48] It was even publicized that *Nanko fushi* was also shown to the emperor, Hirohito.[49]

However, *Nanko fushi* did not succeed at the box office.[50] Many audiences still regarded Hayakawa as a foreign import. One newspaper report noted that it might be "contradictory" for Hayakawa, "who had established his fame as an actor in the U.S.," to play such a heroic character in Japanese history.[51] *Nanko fushi* was released in theaters that usually showed foreign films, together with an American horror-thriller, *Murders in the Zoo* (Edward Sutherland, 1933).

Yet, Hayakawa's attempt to transform his star image into a nationalistic one continued. Following *Nanko fushi*, Hayakawa appeared in three nationalist propaganda films that were meant for the "formation of the Japanese spirit": *Bakugeki hiko tai* [Bomber pilots] (Saegusa Genjiro, 1934), a patriotic war film about the pilots of the Japanese air force; *Araki Mataemon: Tenka no Iga goe* [Araki Mataemon: Beyond the nationally famous Iga] (Katsumi Yotaro, 1934), another "modern nationalistic *jidaigeki*"; and *Kuni o mamoru Nichiren* [Nichiren, who protects Japan] (Sone Chiharu, 1935), a period film about a Buddhist who devoted his life to protect Japan and its people.[52]

In the spring of 1935 Hayakawa also went on a vaudeville tour to entertain the Japanese colonizers, playing *Appare Wong*, *Seventh Heaven*, and some other dramas in Manchuria, Korea, and Shanghai. Later in the 1960s, articles in *Coronet* and *Newsweek* depicted Hayakawa and his family as heroic victims of primitive and villainous Japanese militarism. Richard Hubler wrote in *Coronet*, "In 1932, during the prewar tension between China and Japan, he [Hayakawa] went on a lecture tour of the Orient, his speeches stressing the need for peace in the Far East. This made him unpopular with Japan's hot-headed militarists."[53] *Newsweek* stated, "Many members of his [Hayakawa's] family were executed in Tokyo by Premier Tojo for their opposition to the war."[54] However, Hayakawa's trip was not a lecture tour for peace but one with a propagandistic purpose for Japanese nationalism. In 1935 Hayakawa even said that he wanted to make a film that would praise the efforts of the Japanese army and Japanese colonizers in Manchuria and Korea.[55] Hayakawa's cross-cultural star image seemed to fit the promotion of Japan's "cosmopolitan" imperialism in Asia, or pan-Asianism, which was based on the idea of ethnic ambiguity in Asia.[56] There is no record that "many of his friends and family were murdered by pro-war fanatics," as Hubler claimed.[57]

However, Hayakawa's foreign star image was not easily displaced. For instance, his sword fighting in *Araki Mataemon: Tenka no Iga goe* was criticized as "fencing-like."[58] Ironically, when Hayakawa ended up playing Consul Townsend Harris, an American in Japan who wanted "to know the true character of Japan," according to the script, in *Tojin Okichi* [Okichi the China girl] (Fuyusima Taizo, 1935), his performance was praised as "appropriate" and his English as "good and fluent."[59]

When a diplomatic agreement was established between Japan and Germany on 25 November 1936, a film that incorporated Hayakawa's foreign image with nationalist filmmaking appeared: *Atarshiki tsuchi* (*Die Tochter des Samurai*, 1937), co-produced by Germany and Japan under the initiative of Kawakita Nagamasa of Towa Shoji Company.[60] *Atarashiki tsuchi* was called the "film for export" and "the first international cultural film in Japan" with a political goal to introduce Japanese culture to German audiences, in particular.[61] In order to enhance the "international" quality of the film, internationally renowned personnel were invited. The internationally known composer Yamada Kosaku was announced as the composer of the score for the film. The German director Arnold Fanck, who was famous for his mountain films, co-directed the film with Itami Mansaku, a renowned Japanese director, even though the two eventually split after severe conflicts and two different versions of the film were completed. Hayakawa, listed at the top of the film's cast, was appointed to play the father of the heroine (Hara Setsuko).

Atarashiki tsuchi turned out to be a catalogue of stereotypical Japanese images. Fanck's version, which begins with a subtitle, "The film is about Japan seen by a foreigner," especially emphasizes exotic Japanese objects, landscapes, and culture, including Mount Fuji, a volcano, earthquakes, the famous statue of the Buddha in Kamakura, a Japanese garden with torii and stone lanterns, paper lanterns, shrines, temples, tea ceremonies, flower ceremonies, a flower festival, sumo wrestling, kabuki, noh, and geisha in kimono.[62] The opening score is played by koto, Japanese harps, and drums. The father of the heroine, played by Hayakawa, emphasizes that their family descends from samurai and recommends that the heroine not wear a Western dress to see her fiancé. Hayakawa and the heroine even demonstrate Japanese archery and Japanese sword fighting. When the brokenhearted heroine climbs up a volcano at the climax of the film, a shot of cherry blossoms overlaps her face, and she hears a song "Sakura, sakura" [Cherry blossoms] sung by children. She sees an image of a statue of the Buddha at the edge of the volcano and ritualistically changes her clothes to a wedding gown. At this point, the volcano erupts. As in *The Wrath of the Gods*, the Japanese landscape is connected to the images of ritualistic religion.

Atarashiki tsuchi became a huge hit when it was released in February 1937. Despite the rather stereotypical images of Japanese landscape and cultural objects, Japanese audiences highly valued Fanck's film and favorably pointed out the Japanese spirit represented by the protagonist, Yamato Teruo. His name means "a shining Japanese man." Teruo, who has studied in Europe and has begun to despise his nationality, remembers his cultural background, national identity, and the "blood of ancestors in him" by revisiting Japanese customs and culture, including his talk with a Buddhist monk at a temple. The final sequence in the Japanese mountains, where the hero saves the heroine, was considered to be the climactic moment of the manifestation of "the Japanese spirit" and it was widely stated that "all the Japanese people must watch it."[63] The film critic Uchida Kimio praised Fanck's version for its clarity in showing how the protagonist eventually "re-discovers Japan in him" after experiencing Japanese arts and culture.[64]

Hayakawa's stereotypical representation of Japaneseness in this film was acceptable only because the film's goal was to publicize Japanese culture to foreign viewers in an understandable manner. Other than this exceptional film, Hayakawa's Americanized star image had very limited space in which to fit into Japanese films of the mid- to late 1930s, whose major function was to support the ultra-nationalistic state policy.[65] In March 1934, the Home Ministry established the Committee for Film Regulation. The Japanese government thus began to intervene directly in cinema. In 1935, Dainihon eiga kyokai [Great Japanese association for cinema] was established by the government and studio executives to "improve" Japanese cinema. In July 1937, when the Japanese army invaded China with full force, the Japanese film industry intensified, making pro-war films to promote Japanese national unity. In 1939, *Eiga ho* (film law) was enacted to "contribute to the development of national culture," following the Nazi example, and placed production, distribution, and exhibition of films under governmental regulation. The law recommended making educational propaganda films that would "enhance the spirit and intelligence of Japanese people," and *kokusaku eiga* (national policy film) was born as a result. Censorship under this law prohibited films in which Hayakawa's star image might fit: over-the-top American-style comedies, themes with American-style individual happiness, films that used foreign language, and kissing scenes or scenes showing a man and a woman walking hand in hand.[66]

Hayakawa left Japan once again and went to France. He stayed there until 1949. In France, Hayakawa appeared in *Yoshiwara* (Max Ophuls, 1937), a tragic love story between a Japanese geisha and a French lieutenant.[67] Hayakawa played a Japanese spy, who falls in love with the geisha. Obviously, *Yoshiwara* exploits some popular traits in Hayakawa's silent star vehicles: a narrative of the type of *Madame Butterfly* and the spy motif with deceitful Japanese men. *Variety* reported that both the Japanese government and film industry criticized *Yoshiwara* for its "racial discriminatory views."[68] Japanese media called Hayakawa an "insult to the nation" again.[69] Since Japan became allied with Germany in November 1937, Hayakawa's appearances in French films were not welcomed by Japanese spectators. Hayakawa stayed in Paris during World War II and made nine films after *Yoshiwara*, including *Forfaiture* (Marcel L'Herbier, 1937), which was a remake of *The Cheat*, and *Macao, L'enfer du jeu* (*Gambling Hell* aka *Mask of Korea*, Jean Delannoy, 1939) with Erich von Stroheim, who was also exiled in France.[70]

Even when the war was over, Hayakawa did not go back to Japan, where his wife Tsuru Aoki and his children were waiting for him. Begged by the independent producer-actor Humphrey Bogart, Hayakawa went to Hollywood to appear in *Tokyo Joe* (Stuart Heisler, 1949), a star vehicle for Bogart, who plays "one of those bulletproof, slightly shady but golden-hearted American soldiers of misfortune," and, then, in *Three Came Home* (Jean Negulesco, 1949), starring Claudette Colbert.[71] In both films, Hayakawa played roles befitting his popular image during the silent film period: a middle-ground position between civilized and "Oriental menace."[72] Especially in the latter film, this twofold characterization of Hayakawa is clear.

On the one hand, Hayakawa's Japanese camp commandant in *Three Came Home*, Colonel Michio Suga, is the representative of the Japanese army that brutally invades a peaceful island. Japanese soldiers in this film are savages who hit women, threaten children with their swords, laugh at corpses, wear dirty kimonos, try to rape the heroine, and silence her by torture. When Suga first appears in the film he strikes a white British man who says he is a civilian unreasonably hard on the face.

On the other hand, Suga is clearly differentiated from other Japanese soldiers. He is a gentle, humane, and Americanized family man. In the scene immediately following the one in which he strikes the British man, Suga, with a gentle voice, offers a cigarette to the American heroine (Colbert), the wife of a British colonial officer in Borneo. He then talks about his four years of education at the University of Washington, his experience on a football team there, his admiration of the book that she wrote, and his two sons and a daughter living in Japan. He gently but determinedly requests her autograph, too. The heroine is scared, though, because she hears some gunshots outside of the room while she is listening to Suga. Later, he humanely protects the heroine, like a savior, when she is about to be tortured because she refuses to retract the charges of an attack by a Japanese soldier. Suga apologizes to her for what other soldiers have done. He then offers fruits and biscuits (not Japanese sweets) to British children at his Westernized flowery garden terrace. Moreover, after Japan's surrender, Suga is depicted as a victim of the Japanese militarism that caused the war. He sadly tells the heroine about the death of his wife and children in Hiroshima and wishes her the best for her and her son. (His eight-year-old daughter's name is Cho Cho.) The first medium close-up of Suga in the film emphasizes his devastated expression in front of a portrait of Tojo Hideki, the Japanese prime minister, on the wall.[73] The heroine imagines Suga's revenge when she sees him taking her son and other children into his car. However, all Suga does in the end is to show his gently patriarchal but victimized characteristics. Suga thus represents an ideal patriarchal figure, by Western standards, who values families.

The reception of these films in the United States was ambivalent, again with regard to Americanization and nationalism. Hayakawa's return was welcomed by such critics as Edwin Schallert of the *Los Angeles Times*, who noted, "The Hayakawa performances, notably in 'The Cheat' with Fannie Ward are a legend."[74] Schallert highly rated Hayakawa's acting in *Three Came Home*: "The performance by Sessue Hayakawa, as a strangely contrary Japanese officer, is bound to appeal to the discriminating. He probably more truly represents the jangled philosophy and theories that pervaded Nippon during the war days than the crude villains so often seen."[75]

In contrast, according to a report in a Japanese magazine, some Americans criticized Hayakawa because "he did not obtain American citizenship when he was an American star during the silent period, and brought American money to Japan."[76] In fact, the *New York Times* stated in its report of Hayakawa's return, "He [Hayakawa] is still a Japanese citizen. . . . His activity during the German occupation of Paris came into question when Columbia [Pictures] applied for a visa to bring him to the United States." The report even sarcastically described how Hayakawa obtained the role in *Tokyo Joe*, implying his different cultural origin and his brutality:

The first question Robert Lord, producer of the picture [*Tokyo Joe*], wanted answered was: "Is Hayakawa too old and feeble to stage a good fight with Bogart?"

The Japanese actor says that Columbia's French representative called on him to ask the question.

"I said to him, 'Attack me.' At first he wouldn't, but finally he swung at my chin. I grabbed his arm and twisted his wrist until he cried, 'Oh, oh, oh.' I know jiu jitsu. We negotiated a salary and I signed the contract."

Hayakawa didn't explain whether he had stopped twisting the studio representative's wrist before or after the deal was concluded.[77]

Across the Pacific, Hayakawa's ambivalent status as an American star and a representative of Japan lingered on in the period of postwar reconstruction of Japanese national identity. Persuaded by Nagata Masaichi, the president of Daiei Company, Hayakawa returned to Japan in 1949 for the first time in twelve years. Hayakawa was expected to become a representative of Japan, not with his Japanese nationality but with his foreign-made star image, in order to gain recognition of Japanese cinema by international audiences. Nagata was planning to cast Hayakawa as the American consul Townsend Harris in a film version of *Tojin Okichi*, a 1935 theatrical drama in which Hayakawa had played the same role.[78] Hayakawa himself declared in 1949 that he intended to "make a Japanese film really targeting foreign audiences. . . . I want to create a new style that would go beyond the framework of Japanese cinema so far."[79] Hayakawa also said, "If I work in Japan, I am only working in films with international perspectives."[80]

Hollywood studios and American audiences were interested in films with Japanese subjects at that time. The background of *Tokyo Joe* was shot in Tokyo. It was the first time after World War II that an American company cleared rights with army authorities for filming in Japan.[81] It should have been perfect timing to make films targeting American audiences with an internationally renowned star.

Hayakawa's international fame was also considered to be a safety valve for the occupation government in Japan, which was trying to reestablish the Japanese film industry.[82] The goal of the occupation was to abolish the militarism and ultra-nationalism that had prevailed in Japanese politics and culture before and during the war and to educate Japanese people with American-style liberalism and democracy. The occupation government tried to use Japanese films to promote democratization. As early as September 1945, the occupation government met with the executives of Japanese film studios to communicate the government's interest in the film industry. The occupation government highly valued Hayakawa's role as a Japanese officer who defends international laws, family values, and the white American heroine in *Three Came Home*, even though it did not permit the release of the film in Japan because it depicted "Australians, the U.S. ally, villainously."[83]

After the war, Hayakawa's international star image, which did not fit well into wartime ultra-nationalist films, became the symbol of Japan's deviation from the militarist past and the transplantation of democracy from abroad. Not only Hayakawa, but also actors from *shingeki*, which had attempted since the 1920s to introduce modern foreign dramas, including those of Ibsen, increasingly appeared in films.[84] Hayakawa played a Japanese immigrant in South America in *Harukanari haha no kuni* [Far away mother's country] (Ito Daisuke, 1950), and a Japanese Jean Valjean in *Re Mizeraburu* [*Les Misérables*] (Part 1 "Kami to akuma [God and devil]" directed by Ito, and Part 2 "Ai to jiyu no hata [Flag of love and liberty]" by Makino Masahiro, 1950).[85] In both films, Hayakawa's characters come from outside of the communities and help people victimized under feudalistic oppression.[86] Such roles clearly emphasized Hayakawa's foreign image as a feudalism-buster. In fact, studios publicized Hayakawa as an international star. A one page leaflet of *Harukanari haha no kuni*, a promotional piece published by Daiei, did not use Chinese characters to spell "Sessue Hayakawa" but *katakana*, the characters usually used for foreign names.[87] A newspaper report on *Re Mizeraburu* emphasized Hayakawa's foreign image not only by suggesting his "Westernized" accent but also by noting that *Re Mizeraburu* was able to use Eastman film stock, instead of Japanese-made film stock, "because Sessue will bring a print when he goes back to America."[88]

In some interview articles in magazines, Hayakawa played the role of an instructor of the American way of life. It is ironic because, in the past, in American magazines, he had played the role of a master of Japanese thought. In one article in a Japanese magazine, Hayakawa told a renowned actress, Tanaka Kinuyo, Hayakawa's co-star in *Taiyo wa higashi yori*, who was about to go on a trip to the United States, how to behave there. He said, "You must forget the Japanese way of thinking and behave confidently. . . . You might be surprised how frankly American people speak and behave, but once you get used to it, you will feel comfortable. . . . [In Hollywood,] all staff members make their efforts to create the best atmosphere for the actors to perform as they want, and vice versa. This harmony, this morality is what you should learn from them."[89]

However, Hayakawa's prestigious position in the postwar Japanese film industry did not last long, once again because his star image was too Westernized. After the success of *Rashomon* (Kurosawa Akira, 1950) at the Venice International Film Festival, international distribution of their films became a prevalent aspiration of Japanese film studios. Yet, the strategy to appeal to international audiences drastically changed from Westernization in style and content to such cultural motifs as noh and kabuki drama, Zen Buddhism, samurai, and geisha, which were self-consciously marked as "traditional Japanese." Thus, exotic Japaneseness became a commodity for foreign audiences and a symbol of a national identity of Japan that would be approved internationally.[90]

Under such conditions, Daiei, the studio that initiated the exoticization of Japanese cinema under the producer Nagata, originally cast Hayakawa in a period film, *Shishi no za* [An heir's place] (Ito, 1953), that would depict the world of noh theater.[91] Eventually, Hayakawa's role was taken over by Hasegawa Kazuo, a matinee idol in Japan since the 1930s, whose background was kabuki. This replacement of stars indicates the inclination of the Japanese industry toward Japanese traditionality. Even though Hasegawa had appeared in modern-day dramas, the kabuki-influenced Japanese star was considered to be more appropriate to play the character of a noh actor. Hayakawa's international image was considered less fit for the period piece.

Hayakawa was aware of this trend. He said, "[Japanese cinema] will never be successful by merely imitating American films. Without using the unique Japanese tradition, such as *haragei* acting style, American audiences will not welcome Japanese films."[92] In several interviews, Hayakawa strategically started emphasizing how deeply his acting style and his way of thinking were rooted in the philosophy of Zen Buddhism and kendo, Japanese sword fighting.[93] However, eventually, Hayakawa left Japan again. In the United States, he began again to play roles that imitated his popularly remembered star image: the racial and cultural middle ground between civilized and primitive, or the "honorable bad guy." The most famous role for Hayakawa during this period was that in David Lean's anti-war film, *The Bridge on the River Kwai* (1957). In the story set in a Japanese prison camp in the jungles of Southeast Asia during World War II, Hayakawa played a refined but merciless Japanese commander, Colonel Saito.

The characterization of Saito amazingly imitates that of Tori in *The Cheat*: gentle and refined but culturally different and often brutal. A long shot shows Saito in a blue Japanese kimono sitting tight on the tatami floor of an organized and clean room. Behind him, there are flowers arranged in a Japanese style and a Japanese scroll painting. His language to his soldier who knocks on his door is very gentle, "Haitte yoroshii. Gokuro." [You may come in. Thank you.] Saito is even characterized as Westernized. Eating English corned beef, drinking Scotch whisky, and smoking a cigar later in the narrative, he says, "I spent three years in London. I studied at London Polytechnic." There is even a *Playboy*-style calendar with a glamorous blonde woman on the wall of his office. He also gives away packets from the Red Cross to the prisoners, insisting "All work and no play makes Jack a dull boy," as Tori gives a party for the Red Cross Fund in *The Cheat*.

However, a skinny black man keeps fanning him, which implies a despotism hidden behind his gentle surface. When he first appears in front of the prisoners, his authoritative and foreign nature is emphasized: a low angle shot shows his legs in his leather boots dominantly standing on the porch. He comes out of a dark shadow to the front and speaks to them in a decisive tone, "In the name of his Imperial Majesty, I welcome you. . . . The Japanese army does not have idle mouths to feed. If you do not work hard, you will be punished. . . . General Togo's motto: Be happy in your work!" When Saito goes back to his room, thunder roars (see fig. 23).

Saito brutally tortures Major Nicholson (Alec Guinness), locking him up in a small cell under the sun, "an oven," when Nicholson refuses his order to do manual labor, insisting that the code of the Geneva Convention prohibits officers from being forced to do it. Saito's barbarous act is specifically connected to Japanese militarism. He says to Nicholson, "What do you know of the soldiers' code, *Bushido*? Nothing! You are unworthy of command!" Saito does have his own principle, in the form of *bushido*, but it is not understandable to British and American soldiers. In the end, a British doctor murmurs, "Madness, madness, madness. . . ." Thus, despite his apparent gentleness, refinement, and Westernization, Saito is characterized as despotic, uncivilized, and inassimilable, like Tori in *The Cheat*.

When Nicholson wins the silent battle against Saito and obtains permission to work not as a manual laborer but as a commander to build a bridge over the River Kwai, a high angle long shot shows the back of Saito, who is crying severely alone in his room. This is the last emotional outburst of Saito that the viewers witness in the film. After this shot, Saito turns into a com-

23   *A still from* The Bridge on the River Kwai.

pletely receptive, meek, and defeated character. In *The Cheat*, Tori is deprived
of his right to speak and to make facial expressions to convey his emotional
states after being shot by Edith. Like Tori, Saito, who has been very eloquent
and determined, becomes a passive man who is not even allowed to speak
out or make facial expressions, except slight frowning, after being defeated
by Nicholson.

   During the meeting about reorganizing the plan for constructing the
bridge under the British command, all Saito can do is to accept all the requests from Nicholson without questioning anything: afternoon tea, dinner,
change of schedules, change of construction sites, and regrouping of the
laborers. At the construction site, Saito looks at the progress without any
words. When Nicholson recruits British soldiers from a hospital ward against
regulations, a medium shot of Saito in a Japanese kimono, standing in his
room without any words or particular facial expressions, is inserted and emphasizes his impotent existence.

When the construction is completed, the two happen to meet up on the bridge. Saito, observing the bridge and the sunset over the jungle, has only two lines: "Beautiful," and "Yes, a beautiful creation." When Nicholson eloquently starts talking about the feat that he accomplished and about his twenty-eight-year career with the British army, Saito merely stays silent and expressionless, even in the two medium close-ups of him. He is a passive listener, particularly when his back is captured in the right edge of the frames in the long shots that center on Nicholson talking.

That night, Nicholson makes his speech at a party that celebrates the completion of the bridge, stressing how "honorable" the British soldiers are who "survived in wilderness and turned defeat into victory." The shot of Nicholson is cross-cut to a high angle long shot that captures the back of Saito as he completes a document in Japanese and ritualistically cuts a few of his hairs with his knife. The scene does not clarify what the document is, but it looks like his suicide note, because he says earlier in the narrative "I'll have to kill myself" if he fails to accomplish his mission.

Eventually, the next morning, when Nicholson finds a wire that is connected to explosives, Saito simply follows him until a young Canadian soldier stabs him in the back. When he argues with Nicholson earlier in the narrative, Saito excitedly takes his knife out of his pocket, violently sticks it onto the table, ands eloquently shouts, "I hate the British. You are defeated, but have no shame. You are stubborn, but have no pride. You endure, but you have no courage. I hate the British!" However, when he is murdered, he cannot say a word and cannot even find his knife to fight back. Hayakawa's character in *Kwai* is eventually deprived of his right to speak and to fight. He turns into an expressionless, powerless, receptive, and mute object, in opposition to the white male characters.

Thus, Hayakawa's role in *Kwai* brought him back into the decades-old stereotypical image of twofold characteristics, such as those possessed by Tori in *The Cheat*: the middle-ground image between civilized but primitive, refined but brutal, authoritative but vulnerable, masculine and feminine, Westernized and Japanese.

Kwai worked as *The Cheat* did in Hayakawa's early career. Hayakawa's performance in the film was sensationally received and he was nominated for Best Supporting Actor by the Motion Picture Academy. His role as Saito was so impressive to the spectators that Hayakawa was offered similar roles over and over again. Hayakawa was cast as a mute Japanese soldier, who is left alone with an American pilot on a small Pacific island, in a television drama set during the period of World War II, *The Sea Is Boiling Hot* (1958). Hayakawa played Kimura, a Japanese soldier with ambivalent characteristics in *Kataki* (Alan Schneider, 1959), a stage drama at the Ambassador Theater on Broadway. He is menacing and violent toward an American GI in the first part, but becomes friendly with the GI, cultivates a flower garden on the Pacific Island on which they are marooned alone, and sheds a few tears in the second part.[94] In *The Geisha Boy* (Frank Tashlin, 1958), Hayakawa even played a parodied version of his role in *Kwai*. The Japanese character, played by Hayakawa, lives in the United States and builds a bridge over his swimming pool. The marching song from *Kwai* is used in the soundtrack of the film. In *Hell to Eternity* (Phil Karlson, 1960), another World War II drama and Hayakawa's last film with his wife, Tsuru Aoki, Hayakawa played a commanding Japanese general in Saipan who commits hara-kiri and made "a virtual career of his 'Kwai' type-casting."[95]

The decades-old strategy to Americanize Hayakawa's popular image also returned. In the *New York Times*, Brooks Atkinson reported how Americanized Hayakawa was even in a Japanese-style play, "Evening of Rare Pleasures," which opened at the Academy Theatre of the Seven Arts Center in New York, and regarded Hayakawa as a representative of an American actor rather than a Japanese one, despite his cultural origin. Atkinson argued, "He has been too far away from Japan too long. Being by experience a Western actor, he is vague, sluggish and heavy in the Oriental style. . . . As a despotic military officer in 'The Bridge on the River Kwai,' Mr. Hayakawa is excellent. He is unique in that sort of role. But Japanese birth is not enough to prepare him for the pantomimes and portraits of an evening in the Japanese manner. The elaborate style of Oriental acting is more than a drawing-room accomplishment."[96]

Some newspaper reports even started to repeat the structures of fan magazine articles about Hayakawa in the 1910s in order to emphasize Hayakawa's cultural and racial middle-ground position. A report in the *New York Post* on 29 December 1957 began almost exactly like the fan magazine articles on Hayakawa in the 1910s: "Sessue Hayakawa takes tea at cocktail time at the Astor. But, in his streamlined, air-conditioned American home with traditional Japanese furnishings in Tokyo, he said (over tea at the Astor), 'I have hot cakes and coffee every morning for breakfast. I still keep to many of the nice customs I picked during my years in the United States.' . . . The Oriental actor is bipartisan in food habits (he lived throughout the World War II period in Paris, painting Japanese watercolors on silk), and is multilingual."

After indicating Hayakawa's Americanized or cosmopolitan characteristics, the report emphasizes his Japanese cultural traits: "He is a deeply religious man, an ordained Bhuddist [sic] priest who does not preach from pulpit, but makes the rounds, lecturing on the philosophy of religion. During his brief stay in town, he attended Bhuddist [sic] meditation services."[97]

A report in the *New York Herald Tribune* had the same tone:

> "Sessue Hayakawa double character," said Mr. Hayakawa tapping his head. "Very, very complicated." . . . He divides his time between two houses. One is a Japanese-style eleven-room house where he sits on the floor when he eats (with chop sticks, of course) and sleeps on a mattress on the floor. The other is an American-style five-room house which has air-conditioning, oil heat, and electric refrigerator and a vacuum cleaner and where he eats at a table with a knife and fork and sleeps in a big bed. He has a Japanese cook for the one and an American cook for the other. . . . In Tokyo on certain ceremonial occasions Mr. Hayakawa puts on his red and purple robes with the yellow hat and conducts a service at the Rinzai Temple [as a Zen Buddhist priest]. . . . For his night club expedition Mr. Hayakawa was dressed sharply in American style: blue coat with a white handerchief [sic] in the breast pocket, blue shirt with a maroon tie, gray socks and black shoes with a high gloss.[98]

Similarly, the *New Yorker* started its article on Hayakawa: "In person, Hayakawa looks more like an off-duty samurai than a villain. His cheekbones are every bit as aristocratic and his eyes just as penetrating as they appear on the screen, but he himself proved to be easygoing and a cosmopolite whose career has embraced American, Japanese, French, and German films, as well as stages of London, Paris, Tokyo, and New York."[99]

In Japan, Hayakawa became a celebrity again after *Kwai*. Yet, many magazine articles emphasized Hayakawa's twofold image once again. *Shukan Asahi* [Weekly Asahi] used two photos in an article entitled, "Sessue Still in Good Health," one of which showed a half-naked Hayakawa sitting in Zen meditation. In the other photo, Hayakawa sits on a sofa and reads a book written in English with a cigar in his right hand.[100] Another magazine, *Shukan Yomiuri* [Weekly Yomiuri] noted, "For Hayakawa Japan is not a place to 'come back' but to 'visit,'" and emphasized his foreign image. Simultaneously, the article included Hayakawa's own words, "American people think that there is something mysterious in me, and so I wrote a book on my spiritual journey for an American publisher."[101] An article in the same magazine concludes with exactly the same hope expressed by the Pure Film advocates decades earlier: "We hope he will appear in at least one film a year for the development of Japanese cinema."[102]

By that point, one aspect of Hayakawa's star image, the strong emphasis on his Japanese cultural or national identity, had become outdated. When Hayakawa insisted that he had tried to be like a samurai when he had to display dignity in his films, an unconvinced interviewer asked, "Didn't you feel odd?" Moreover, the same article introduced an unfavorable comment from a person in the Japanese film industry: "He [Hayakawa] requests too much salary. As high as a Hollywood star. If he wants to live in Japan from now on, he should sometimes appear in Japanese films without asking too much salary. He talks about Zen or Buddhism, but he is like a money-seeking kid."[103]

Even after his stardom during the period of silent cinema, in transforming global political relations, Hayakawa represented the ambivalent images of Japan and Japanese people on and off the screen both in Japan and in the United States. In the United States, Hayakawa embodied the century-long contradictory but coexisting stereotypes of Japan and Japanese people: lovable and villainous, refined and threatening, civilized and primitive, Japanese Taste and the yellow peril. In Japan, Hayakawa was an embodiment of Americanization, whether a symbol of modernization or that of deviation from the imagined Japanese sense of values. Simultaneously, as one of a few internationally famous figures, Hayakawa was regarded as a representative of the Japanese people for foreign and domestic audiences. Hayakawa's star image, then, caused ambivalent reactions in both countries on different levels.

On 23 November 1973, Hayakawa died in Tokyo. In his obituary, Paul L. Montgomery wrote, "He [Hayakawa] starred as lover and villain in come [sic] than 120 films."[104] A Japanese magazine, Shukan Bunshun [Weekly Bunshun], published a brief article titled, "The ex-Hollywood actor, Sessue Hayakawa, died with a big question: Was he really an international star?" This article included comments about Hayakawa from various Japanese intellectuals, who expressed their ambivalent feelings toward him. They highly valued Hayakawa's financial success in the United States and his popularity among "beautiful blond women" in the middle of racial discrimination, while they questioned the value of those films of Hayakawa in which Japan was depicted with an image of "an evil, mysterious, and grotesque country." The article thus criticized the manner in which Hayakawa publicized Japan in his films. The article also questioned Hayakawa's acting ability. Despite Hayakawa's international fame and his own claim that such actors as Charlie Chaplin, Lawrence Olivier, and Jean Gabin were inferior to him, the article indicated, based on the comments by the intellectuals, that Hayakawa was not a capable actor and that all he could do was to stand still without any movement on his face, which was like a noh mask.[105]

Sessue Hayakawa's transnational stardom was a site of constant conflicts and struggles over the ownership of the image of Japan (and America). It casts light on the historical trajectory of American images of Japan and of Japanese self-images in the world and on the volatile social and cultural interactions between Japan and the United States.

NOTES

INTRODUCTION

The epigraph is from Nogami, *Seirin no o Hayakawa Sesshu* [King of Hollywood, Sessue Hayakawa], 14. All translations of Japanese books, leaflets, and newspaper and magazine articles in this book are by the author unless otherwise noted.

1   "Star's Large Female Following Will Like This," *Wid's Daily* 9.12 (13 July 1919): 5.

2   Hanayagi, "Katsukai enma cho" [Evaluation book of the motion picture world], 75.

3   Studlar, *This Mad Masquerade*, 91.

4   Ross, "Sessue Hayakawa Prefers the Wicked Oriental Roles," 1, 4. Newspapers and magazines sometimes rendered Hayakawa's words as fluent English and sometimes in dialect.

5   "A Tribute to Sessue Hayakawa," *Motion Picture* (October 1917): n.p., in *Sessue Hayakawa: Locke Collection Envelope* 659, the New York Public Library for the Performing Arts, Robinson Locke Collection (*SHE*).

6   Bodeen, "Sessue Hayakawa," 196.

7   Studlar, "Discourses of Gender and Ethnicity," 19.

8   Hansen, *Babel and Babylon*, 287.

9   "Vote for the Picture of Your Favorite Player," *Chicago Tribune* (14 May 1916): n.p., in *SHE*.

10 "Hayakawa, Hart and Chaplin at the Madison," *Detroit Journal* (29 October 1917): n.p., in *SHE*.

11 Goll, "Amerikanisches Kino," 164–65 (translation by Don Reneau).

12 Yutkevich and Eisenstein, "The Eighth Art: On Expressionism, America and, of course, Chaplin," 3.

13 Delluc, "Beauty in the Cinema," 138–39.

14 Delluc, "Beauty in the Cinema," 138–39, original emphasis.

15 "Pretty French Actress Gives Sphinx Tribute," *Los Angeles Times* (1 June 1924): I-14.

16 Delluc, "Beauty in the Cinema," 138–39.

17 Thompson and Bordwell, *Film History*, 89.

18 Clair, *Cinema*, 63.

19 Ad in *Moving Picture World* 32.11 (16 June 1917): 1712.

20 In the Ozawa case (260 U.S. 189), Ozawa Takao was denied naturalization on the grounds that he was not a "white person." Even though Ozawa was born in

Japan, he was raised in Hawaii and California, studied at Berkeley High School and the University of California, was fluent in English, and was a Christian. The Supreme Court ruled that "the Japanese race is not Caucasian. The determination that the words 'white persons' are synonymous with the words 'persons of the Caucasian race' simplifies the problem although it does not entirely dispose of it. . . . But it establishes a 'zone' . . . outside of which (an applicant) is clearly ineligible." Conroy, "Concerning the Asian-American Experience," 158–59.

21 Yoshihara, *Embracing the East*, 10.

22 "The Japanese Invasion," *Moving Picture World* 6.21 (28 May 1910): 873.

23 "Japanese Actor Dies at 87," *New York Post* (24 November 1973): 7.

24 Zhang, "'An Amorous History of the Silver Screen,'" 22.

25 Dyer, *Stars*, 30, 95.

26 Hansen, "Fallen Women, Rising Stars, New Horizons," 13.

27 By the end of the nineteenth century, the term "middle class" became used by American writers without definition or explanation. The historian Stuart M. Blumin maintains that there was a sufficient convergence of personal and social experience in at least five categories—work, consumption, residential location, formal and informal voluntary association, and family organization— to give credence to the idea of an emerging middle-class way of life and the establishment of a significant degree of middle-class consciousness in early nineteenth-century northeastern American cities. Blumin, "The Hypothesis of Middle-Class Formation in Nineteenth-Century America," 299–338.

28 Harris, *Cultural Excursions*, 29, 40.

29 Cook, "Beds and Tables, Stools and Candlesticks-III," 494.

30 Griffis, "Japan and the United States," 721, 730.

31 Kano, *Acting Like Woman in Modern Japan*, 94.

32 Yoshihara, "Women's Asia," 59.

33 Kurtz, *Official Illustrations from the Art Gallery of the World's Columbian Exposition*, 12.

34 Yoshihara, "Women's Asia," 68.

35 In other buildings at the Chicago fair, such as the Palace of Manufactures and Liberal Arts and the Fine Arts Palace, Japan also made extensive exhibits that focused more on its modernization, which was also Westernization, including photographs of railroad lines, telegraph systems, and so forth. Harris, *Cultural Excursions*, 41–44.

36 Iida, *Rethinking Identity in Modern Japan*, 14.

37 Yoshihara, "Women's Asia," 63.

38 Kano, *Acting Like Woman in Modern Japan*, 94.

39 According to Neil Harris, in the late nineteenth century, having anxiety about the menacing character of modernization and the effects of industrialization, the American people could identify with Japan's national dilemma between accepting Westernization and maintaining national customs. Harris, *Cultural Excursions*, 34, 39–40, 55.

40 Lowe, *Immigrant Acts*, ix.

41 Hanayagi, "Katsukai enma cho" [Evaluation book of the motion picture world], 74.

42 Katano, "Meiyu no shohyo" [Trademarks of famous actors], 107.

43 Du Bois, *The Souls of Black Folk*, 45.

44 Zhang, "'An Amorous History of the Silver Screen,'" 30; Hansen, *Babel and Babylon*, 76–89.

1. A STAR IS BORN

1 "Lasky and DeMille Enter Picture Field," *Motion Picture News* (MPN) (20 December 1913): 15; "Fannie Ward to Star for Lasky," *Moving Picture World* (MPW) 23.9 (6 March 1915): 1455; Holland, "Fannie Ward," 590–95.

2 *Wid's Daily* noted in 1918, "'The Cheat,' in which this talented star [Hayakawa] began to acquire an individual following, proved an unusual box-office attraction at that time." *Wid's Daily* 5.66 (14 July 1918): 29.

3 "Lasky May Releases," MPW 28.6 (6 May 1916): 959.

4 "Fannie Ward as a Movie Tragedienne," in *The New York Times Film Reviews 1913–1968*, vol. 1, *1913–1931* (New York: Arno, 1970), 8.

5 *Variety* (17 December 1915): 18.

6 "Sessue Hayakawa," MPW 26.10 (4 December 1915): 1810.

7 Hayne, *The Autobiography of Cecil B. DeMille*, 150.

8 *New Orleans Times* (26 February 1916): n.p., in SHE.

9 *Wid's Films and Film Folk Independent Criticisms of Features* 1.17 (30 December 1915): 4.

10 *Exhibitor's Herald* (EH) 1.4 (4 December 1915): 18; MPN 12.23 (11 December 1915): 76; *Motography* 14.24 (11 December 1915): 1223.

11 MPN 13.15 (15 April 1916): 2209. As early as January 1916, MPN published a list of actors and actresses, and Hayakawa was listed under the category of "leads," not "supports." MPN 13.4 (29 January 1916): 44.

12 Numerous articles and books on Hayakawa were published in Europe, including "Sessue Hayakawa," *Invicta Cine* (Portugal) 3 (1 June 1923): 4–5, and "Um morto vivo: Sessue Hayakawa," *Cinefilo* (Portugal) 24 (2 February 1929): 11, 22. Leaflet magazines entirely dedicated to Hayakawa were published in Spain (Ferry and Moreno, "Sessue Hayakawa") and Russia (Ovanesov, *Sessue Hayakawa*).

13 Hammond and Ford, "French End Games," 330.

14 Colette, *Colette at the Movies*, 18.

15 Colette, *Colette at the Movies*, 19–20.

16 Abel, *French Film Theory and Criticism*, 110.

17 Doane, "The Close-Up," 89.

18 Thompson and Bordwell, *Film History*, 89, 92.

19 Léon Moussinac, "Cinématographie," 229–35. In 1932, Germaine Dullac emphasized the importance of *The Cheat* as the first American film that used the editing style based on "a psychological, emotive, and rhythmical logic." Before

The Cheat, according to Dullac, "the pictures (tableaux) follow one after another independently from each other, bundled by one subtitle." Dullac, *Écrits sur le cinéma (1919–1937)*, 184, translation by Chika Kinoshita.

20 The Kawakami troupe started as "a purveyor of bitingly satirical antigovernment burlesques," which was called *oppekepe*. With his politically satirical dramas (*soshi shibai*), Kawakami supported *jiyu minken undo*, the people's rights movement, which was aimed at prevailing Western-style liberalism in Japan. The Kawakami troupe is often considered as a part of the *shingeki* movement, Japan's response to Ibsen and his contemporaries' realist reforms in Europe. Kawakami tried to modernize Japanese theaters with his original dramas that depicted the everyday lives of ordinary people and with his adopted European dramas, including *Othello* and *Hamlet*. In Kawakami's theater, Sadayakko, an actress, appeared on stage while female roles were played by an *onnagata*, a male impersonator, in most of the theaters in Japan. Y. Hayakawa, "Tsuru Aoki," 3–5, 16–18; Downer, *Madame Sadayakko*, 94–96, 113–14; Muramatsu, *Kawakami Otojiro (Jo)*, 160–61, 251–347; Muramatsu, *Kawakami Otojiro (Ge)*, 48–95; R. Yamaguchi, *Joyu Sadayakko* [The actress Sadayakko], 121–28.

21 In the United States, however, their tour was not financially successful. There was a strict regulation that prohibited a child from appearing on stage. Consequently, it became difficult for Kawakami to take Tsuru with them.

22 Fescourt and Bouquet, *L'Idée et l'écran*, 374.

23 Crisp, *Genre, Myth, and Convention in the French Cinema, 1929–1939*, 42. *The Cheat* was also remade in America in 1923, starring Pola Negri, and in 1931, starring Tallulah Bankhead. Hayakawa did not appear in either.

24 Stanley, *The New Grove Dictionary of Opera*, 68.

25 Colette, *Colette at the Movies*, 35–36. Later, Hayakawa produced his own play based on *The Cheat* in France in 1944. He did not play the role as mute, though.

26 Sessue Hayakawa, *Zen Showed Me the Way*, 136.

27 "Hainichi no tane o maku katsudo shashin" [Motion pictures that will cause anti-Japanese sentiment], *Rafu Shimpo* 3694 (23 December 1915): 3.

28 "Kyo ka oroka hainichi haiyu Hayakawa Sesshu" [Crazy or stupid, anti-Japanese actor Sessue Hayakawa], *Rafu Shimpo* 3695 (24 December 1915): 3.

29 "Nihon jin ashiki ka keisatsu muno ka" [Are the Japanese people bad, or the police incapable?], *Rafu Shimpo* 3698 (28 December 1915): 3; "Akudo no hainichi bodo" [Anti-Japanese riot by bad boys], *Rafu Shimpo* 3697 (26 December 1915): 1.

30 *Rafu Shimpo* 3699 (29 December 1915): 3.

31 *Osaka Mainichi Shinbun*, 23 February 1916, in *Shinbun shusei Taisho hennenshi*, 1916, vol. 1, (1980): 346.

32 *Katsudo no Sekai* 1.4 (April 1916): 41; SZO, "Katsudo omochabako" [Toy box of motion picture], 48.

33 *Katsudo Zasshi* 9.4 (April 1923): 147.

34 Aoyama, "Aren kun no Nihon kan" [Mr. Allen's view on Japan], 88.

35 Several Hayakawa films made at Lasky were released in Japan, including *Each to His Kind* (Edward Le Saint, 5 February 1917), *The Bottle Imp* (Marshall Neilan, 26 March 1917), *The Jaguar's Claws* (Neilan, 11 June 1917) in 1919, and *Forbidden Paths* (Robert T. Thornby, 5 July 1917), *The Victoria Cross* (William C. DeMille, 14 December 1916), and *The Hidden Pearls* (George H. Melford, 18 February 1918) in 1920. Most of them were the films in which Hayakawa did not play Japanese roles, except *Forbidden Paths*.

36 Okina, "Hayakawa Sesshu to Kamiyama Sojin" [Sessue Hayakawa and Sojin Kamiyama], 225.

37 Barber, "The Roots of Travel Cinema," 68–84.

38 Lee, *Orientals*, 88, 99–105.

39 "Shiro bijin Nihon jin koibito o jusatsu su" [A white beautiful woman shot a Japanese lover to death], *Rafu Shimpo* 3564 (20 July 1915): 3.

40 "Shiro bijin doho jofu goroshi zokkou kohan 4" [A white beautiful woman who killed her Japanese lover in court 4], *Rafu Shimpo* 3723 (28 January 1916): 3.

41 "Nihon jin no shufu gokan jiken shinso" [Truth about the rape of a housewife by Japanese], *Rafu Shimpo* 3725 (30 January 1916): 3.

42 S. Higashi, "Ethnicity, Class, and Gender in Film," 130.

43 J. Brown, "The 'Japanese Taste,'" 134.

44 See Noteheler, *Japan through American Eyes*.

45 J. Brown, "'Fine Arts and Fine People,'" 123.

46 La Farge, "Bric-a-Brac," 427–29.

47 J. Brown, "The 'Japanese Taste,'" 1, 155; Lears, *No Place of Grace*, 42–43.

48 J. Brown, "The 'Japanese Taste,'" 337; Coontz, *The Social Origins of Private Life*, 224–36; Lee, *Orientals*, 86.

49 Mahan, *The Problem of Asia and Its Effect upon International Policies*, 108, 110.

50 Niiya, *Japanese American History*, 362. Beginning in 1900, the number of Japanese immigrants to the United States rose to more than ten thousand a year. Until 1906, the numbers were under 15,000 (except 1903), but in 1907 the number increased to 30,226. Commissioner General of Immigration, *Annual Report*, quoted in Iino, "Beikoku niokeru hainichi undo to 1924 nen iminho seitei katei" [Anti-Japanese movement in the U.S. and the enactment process of the 1924 immigration law], 32. In 1920, Japanese people owned approximately 16 percent of cultivated land for agriculture, which was obtained between 1910 and 1920. In 1910, the amount was only 0.4 percent, when the *San Francisco Chronicle* criticized Japanese immigrants by insisting that they were "not earnest" and "buying lands." State Board of Control of California, *California and the Oriental*, 8; U.S. Bureau of the Census, *Chinese and Japanese in the United States*, 43–44; Tupper and McReynolds, *Japan in American Public Opinion*, 22.

51 The term "yellow peril" was originally used by Kaiser Wilhelm II of Germany in 1898.

52 Quoted in Daniels, *The Politics of Prejudice*, 25. See also Daniels, *Asian America*, 109.

53 McClatchy, *Four Anti-Japanese Pamphlets*, 45.

54 Jacobs, "Belasco, DeMille and the Development of Lasky Lighting," 416. These lighting effects were marketed as "Lasky lighting" and associated with the work of DeMille, his cameraman Alvin Wyckoff, and the art director Wilfred Buckland, in the trade press.

55 Script of *The Cheat*, University of Southern California, Cine-TV Library, Special Collection.

56 According to Sumiko Higashi, this handwriting was DeMille's. S. Higashi, *Cecil B. DeMille and American Culture*, 108.

57 Staiger, *Bad Women*, 164, 179.

58 Yoshihara, *Embracing the East*, 15–43.

59 Veblen, *The Theory of the Leisure Class*; Mason, *Conspicuous Consumption*, 8–10.

60 Mason, *Conspicuous Consumption*, 12.

61 Trimberger, "The New Woman and the New Sexuality," 98–115.

62 Staiger, *Bad Women*, 170.

63 Emphasis in the original.

64 Tori in a tuxedo looks like a vampire figure in a black coat that approaches the white woman from the back. Diane Negra argues, "*Dracula* and other vampire myths represent the vampire first and foremost as a liminal figure, caught between an old world and a new one, at first a welcomed visitor but ultimately a new arrival who comes to be seen as a menace." Negra, "Immigrant Stardom in Imperial America," 168. Tori as a "liminal figure" from Japan can be located in this context of the vampire myths. In fact, the Canadian filmmaker Guy Muddin's film, *Dracula: Pages from a Virgin's Diary* (2002) depicts vampires as "immigrants" from "the East" and an Asian dancer and actor, Zhang Wei-Qiang, plays Count Dracula. Several "vampire" films had been released in the United States by the time *The Cheat* was released. *The Vampire* (Kalem, 1910) and *The Vampire* (Selig, 1913) were inspired by the "Vampire Dance" popularized in the early teens by Alice Eis and Bert French. Staiger, *Bad Women*, 151. In 1915, *A Fool There Was*, the film that made Theda Bara a sensational "vamp" star, was released. The vamp's iconography was characterized by her "pale skin and heavily made-up lips and eyes." Negra, "Immigrant Stardom in Imperial America," 183. Hayakawa's character, with "heavily made-up" eyebrows and pale skin, is similar to the vamp. The vampire image of Tori may enhance the fear of mixing blood and the destructive influence that he brings into America despite his superficially assimilated image.

65 For feminist film critics, these scenes in the shoji room "can be looked at as a fulfillment of secret, forbidden desires for the pleasures and freedoms [of women] promised by a love affair with a man of another race." Marchetti, *Romance and the "Yellow Peril,"* 22; S. Higashi, *Cecil B. DeMille and American Culture*, 107.

66 The ambiguous sexuality of Tori refers to that of Dr. Fu Manchu, the universally recognized early Oriental villain in pulp fiction created by Sax Rohmer (Arthur Sarsfield Ward). The first three novels, *The Insidious Dr. Fu Manchu* (1913), *The*

Return of Fu Manchu (1916), and *The Hand of Fu Manchu* (1917), became popular in the United States in almost the same period when Hayakawa's stardom was being created. Fu Manchu's threat comes partly from his ability to shift his Chinese appearance to that of other nationalities. Also, Fu Manchu's power to incite the fevered imagination lies in his ambiguous sexuality, which combines a masochistic vulnerability marked as feminine and a sadistic aggressiveness marked as masculine.

67 S. Higashi, *Cecil B. DeMille and American Culture*, 104.

68 S. Higashi, *Cecil B. DeMille and American Culture*, 107.

69 Whissel, "The Gender of Empire," 141–42.

70 The script indicates that after Richard confirms that he shot Tori, a close-up of a group of three women in the audience, "who gossip pointing toward Edith," is to be inserted.

71 S. Higashi, *Virgins, Vamps, and Flappers*, 58.

72 Brooks, *The Melodramatic Imagination*, 56–80.

73 Staiger, *Bad Women*, 173.

74 Cavell, "What Photography Calls Thinking," 20–21.

75 *Photoplay* 9.4 (March 1916): n.p., in SHE.

76 MPN 22.10 (28 August 1920): 1755.

77 "Sessue Hayakawa to Support Ina Claire," MPW 23.11 (20 March 1915): 1779.

78 S. Higashi, "Cecil B. DeMille and the Lasky Company," 184–85. Cecil did not have a spectacular stage career, but the DeMilles are a distinguished Broadway family. S. Higashi, *Cecil B. DeMille and American Culture*, 1.

79 S. Higashi, "Touring the Orient with Lafcadio Hearn and Cecil B. DeMille," 332.

80 S. Higashi, "Cecil B. DeMille and the Lasky Company," 182–83.

81 MPN 9.22 (6 June 1914): 30.

82 MPW 23.3 (16 January 1915): 353.

83 "Japanese Customs in Motion Pictures," *Paramount Magazine* (March 1915): 7.

84 The conditions under which *The Typhoon* was made were complicated and unclear. The Paramount ad in MPN noted that the producer of *The Typhoon* was Paramount. MPN 10.13 (3 October 1914): 12. The review of *The Typhoon* in *Variety* ignored NYMPC and wrote that this film was "released by the Paramount, with no name of the manufacturing company given." *Variety* 36.13 (28 November 1914): 24. *Reel Life*, the promotional magazine of the Mutual, did not mention *The Typhoon* as its film at all. Yet, the NYMPC put an ad in MPW on 25 April 1914 announcing that the company would present the film "in the very near future, under the direction of Thomas H. Ince, The Imperial Japanese Company in Charles Swickard's version of The Typhoon." MPW 20.4 (25 April 1914): 549. According to Hayakawa, Paramount "bought" *The Typhoon*. "Popular Arts Project," Hayakawa-13. Paramount was adopting the Hodkinson system, which provided cash advances for production costs and guaranteed a minimum return to the producer. In exchange, Paramount received 35 percent of the proceeds for the right to distribute.

85 "Celestial" is an outdated slang for a Chinese person. *New York Dramatic Mirror* (*NYDM*) 73.1911 (21 July 1915): 27.

86 *Variety* 37.10 (6 February 1915): 23.

87 *EH* 1.4 (4 December 1915): 18; *MPN* 12.23 (11 December 1915): 76; *Motography* 14.24 (11 December 1915): 1223.

88 *MPN* 13.18 (6 May 1916): 2705. According to the dates written on the original scripts, the filming of *Temptation* started on 27 July 1915 and finished on 10 August 1915. It was released on 2 January 1916. The filming of *The Cheat* started on 20 October 1915 and finished on 10 November 1915, but it was released on 4 December 1915, earlier than *Temptation*. Script of *Temptation*, University of Southern California, Cine-TV Library, Special Collection.

89 91 *MPW* 28.15 (15 July 1916): 357; *MPN* 14.9 (2 September 1916): 1349. Famous Players and Lasky merged into Famous Players-Lasky Corporation in June 1916. Paramount Pictures Corporation had been a distributor of the productions of Lasky, the Famous Players Film Company, the Oliver Morosco Photo Play Company, and Pallas Pictures since 1914.

90 Sixteen films starring Hayakawa were made at Lasky starting with *Alien Souls*, but I do not consider *The Victoria Cross* (William C. DeMille, 14 December 1916) as a Hayakawa star vehicle. *The Victoria Cross* features Lou Telligan as the star, and Hayakawa as an Indian conspirator in a supporting role.

2. SCREEN DEBUT

1 Sessue Hayakawa, *Zen Showed Me the Way*, 104–24.

2 Oba, "Kotani Fuku to Kariforunia no awabi gyogyo" [Fuku Kotani and abalone fishing in California], 299–332; Oba, "Hayakawa Kintaro (Sesshu) no tobei kankyo to ryoken nituite" [About the circumstances before Kintaro (Sessue) Hayakawa went to the U.S., and about Hayakawa's passport], 57–58.

3 According to the biography of Hayakawa that was published in a Japanese magazine, *Fujin Gaho*, in 1930, Mr. Ono, a bookstore owner, took care of Hayakawa when he first arrived in San Francisco, his first stop in the United States. Then, Hayakawa went to Los Angeles to join a theater group, Futabakai, and appeared in some Japanese plays. T. Azuma (or Higashi), "Kaigai ni odoru hiro Sesshu Hayakawa to Aoki Tsuruko" [International heroes, Sessue Hayakawa and Tsuru Aoki], 153.

4 *Variety* 33.2 (12 December 1913): 12. Fred Mace (1878–1917) was a stage comedian and worked for Mack Sennet. After appearing in the Keystone comedies with Ford Sterling and Mabel Normand, he quit and opened his own company. An editor of the Japanese film magazine *Katsudo Zasshi* noted in 1922 that Hayakawa started his film career as a "part-time extra" for Fred Mace comedies, earning five dollars a week, and met Aoki there. *Katsudo Zasshi* 8.8 (August 1922): 64. The *MPW* claimed that the character in *The Oath of O'Tsuru San*, in which O'Tsuru San (Aoki) falls in love with a young American on whom she has

been ordered to spy, is as "dainty and attractive as Madame Butterfly." *MPW* 18.6 (3 November 1913): 613.

5 "Tom Ince of Inceville," *NYDM* 70.1827 (24 December 1913): 34.

6 Aoyama, *Hariuddo eiga okoku no kaibo* [Anatomy of Hollywood film kingdom], 279.

7 Oba, "Shokan kara mita Hayakawa Sesshu no kunan" [Sessue Hayakawa's hardship indicated in his letters], 50.

8 "Release Record," Harry and Roy Aitken Papers, 1909–1940, box 45, vol. 33, State Historical Society of Wisconsin, Archives Division; T. Yamanaka, "Umi no kanata yori" [From overseas], 91; Aoyama, *Hariuddo eiga okoku no kaibo* [Anatomy of Hollywood film kingdom], 279.

9 Carl Wilmore, "Sessue Hayakawa—Himself," *Photoplay Journal* 30 (August 1919): n.p., in *SHE*; "Release Record," Harry and Roy Aitken Papers, 1909–1940, box 45, vol. 33, State Historical Society of Wisconsin, Archives Division. Hayakawa later said, "I entered pictures in 1913. . . The first pictures I made were two-reelers and I sometimes played Indians." "Hayakawa Reveals Film Past in Letter," *Los Angeles Times* (20 July 1960): A6.

10 *MPW* 19.6 (7 February 1914): 678.

11 Suleri, *The Rhetoric of English India*, 108. For a historical overview of the notion of the picturesque, see Hussey, *The Picturesque*; Price, "The Picturesque Moment," 259–92; Copley and Garside, *The Politics of the Picturesque*.

12 Orvell, *The Real Thing*, 155.

13 Lears, *No Place of Grace*, 5.

14 Savada, *The American Film Institute Catalog of Motion Pictures Produced in the United States*, 350; Hanson and Gevinson, *The American Film Institute Catalog of Motion Pictures Produced in the United States*, 338.

15 Waller, "Historicizing, a Test Case," 13.

16 "The Japanese Invasion," *MPW* 6.21 (28 May 1910): 873.

17 Dizikes, *Opera in America*, 205–6; Baily, *The Gilbert and Sullivan Book*, 281–84.

18 The synopsis is in accordance with the print available at the George Eastman House, Rochester, New York.

19 Bakhtin, *The Dialogic Imagination: Four Essays*, 225–26.

20 *MPW* 19.6 (7 February 1914): 722. Whereas the emperor comes from the royal family in Japan, which is traditionally considered to have been founded in the year 660 B.C., the shogun, an abbreviation of *Seii-Tai-Shogun*, is originally a title conferred by the royal court upon the chief military commander, who should defend the royal family. The shogun overpowered the emperor and started to govern Japan for the first time in 1192. The shogun became a hereditary title, and several governments under different shogun families ruled Japan until 1867.

21 *The Mikado; or The Town of Titipu*, in Sullivan, *The Complete Plays of Gilbert and Sullivan*, 299–345.

3. CHRISTIANITY VERSUS BUDDHISM

1 *Toledo Blade*, in the New York Public Library for Performing Arts, Robinson Locke Collection, Scrapbook, vol. 255: 29; NYDM 71.1832 (28 January 1914): 30.

2 *New York Clipper* 59.51 (31 January 1914): 15.

3 MPW 20.7 (16 May 1914): 957.

4 Pratt, "'See Mr. Ince . . . ,'" 108.

5 MPN 9.20 (23 May 1914): 57.

6 Bowser, *The Transformation of Cinema 1907–1915*, 251; Thompson and Bordwell, *Film History*, 58.

7 MPW 19.5 (31 January 1914): 554. An article with exactly the same content appeared in the above-mentioned *Toledo Blade*, the *New York Clipper* of the same day, and in MPN 9.5 (7 February 1914): 20.

8 Oba, "Shokan kara mita Hayakawa Sesshu no kunan" [Sessue Hayakawa's hardship indicated in his letters], 50.

9 *Reel Life* 4.7 (2 May 1914): 21.

10 MPN 9.18 (9 May 1914): 48.

11 "Japanese Film Actress Marries," *New York Clipper* 62.14 (9 May 1914): 16.

12 It is also recorded in a document in the Japanese community in Los Angeles that Aoki had been a chorus girl in the Shornverg theater group in San Diego. Nanka Nikkeijin shogyo kaigi sho, *Nanka shu Nihonnjin shi* [History of Japanese in Southern California], 242. Cari Beauchamp writes that the popular screenwriter Frances Marion "had known and liked" Aoki "at St. Margaret's Hall" according to Marion's biographical writing, but Beauchamp does not clarify whether St. Margaret's Hall was a school or something else. Beauchamp, *Without Lying Down*, 31.

13 *New York Clipper* 62.1 (14 February 1914): 18.

14 MPW 20.9 (30 May 1914): 1216.

15 MPW 20.11 (13 June 1914): 1496.

16 MPW 20.7 (16 May 1914): 929; 20.12 (20 June 1914): 1643; MPN 9.19 (16 May 1914): 7.

17 MPN 9.18 (9 May 1914): 48.

18 The Strand, which opened at Forty-seventh Street on 11 April of the same year, was a prestigious theater that was "devoted exclusively to the projection of motion pictures." In "the heart of the so-called 'white light' district, in the home of the 'legitimate' drama, putting itself in actual daily competition with the world's greatest speaking stars, this theater is facing close competition." "Million-Dollar Theater Opens," MPN 9.15 (18 April 1914): 23.

19 MPN 9.24 (20 June 1914): 53.

20 MPW 20.12 (20 June 1914): 1643.

21 MPW 21.6 (8 August 1914): 793. The Opera House at Cleveland also showed the film for a week beginning 7 July 1914. The New York Public Library, Robinson Locke Scrapbook, vol. 25: 31.

22 MPW 21.2 (11 July 1914): 156; MPN 10.1 (4 July 1914): 12.

23 *MPN* 9.24 (20 June 1914): 53.

24 In 1862, when a Japanese mission visited London, the people in London regarded the kimonos worn by samurai as female clothes. In this sense, Japanese men were considered as more feminine than European men because of their clothes. Conte-Helme, *Japan and the North East of England*, 53–54.

25 It was popular in American motion pictures at that time to show a vengeful Buddha, as we see in such films as *The God of Vengeance* (April 1914).

26 Ince later confessed that he had made a mistake in Hayakawa's makeup and the beard was not good. "Kebi monogatari" [A Kay-Bee story], *Katsudo Shashin Zasshi* 5.5 (May 1919): 54.

27 K. McDonald, *Japanese Classical Theater in Films*, 43, 330.

28 *Variety* 35.2 (12 June 1914): 21. Since a prologue introducing the actors was a frequent device in feature films from about 1914 to 1917, this does not in itself indicate these films are theatrical. Yet, in the case of *The Wrath of the Gods*, the black curtains that appear in the beginning and at the end are so obvious that they create a sense of closure.

4. DOUBLENESS

1 Savada, *The American Film Institute Catalog of Motion Pictures Produced in the United States*, 439; Hanson and Gevinson, *The American Film Institute Catalog of Motion Pictures Produced in the United States*, 304, 406–7.

2 Savada, *The American Film Institute Catalog of Motion Pictures Produced in the United States*, 320.

3 Savada, *The American Film Institute Catalog of Motion Pictures Produced in the United States*, 350; Hanson and Gevinson, *The American Film Institute Catalog of Motion Pictures Produced in the United States*, 338.

4 Savada, *The American Film Institute Catalog of Motion Pictures Produced in the United States*, 152.

5 Kleine Optical Company Catalog (November 1905): 339.

6 *MPW* 7.13 (24 September 1910): 701.

7 Deacon, *Kempei Tai*, 84.

8 Lieut.-Gen. Sir Ian Hamilton, *A Staff Officer's Scrapbook during the Russo-Japanese War* (London: Arnold, 1907), quoted in Deacon, *Kempei Tai*, 53.

9 Deacon, *Kempei Tai*, 60.

10 "Chinamen as Spies," *Harper's Weekly* 11.2637 (6 July 1907): 995.

11 Hayakawa played spy roles in at least five silent films. Before *The Typhoon*, Hayakawa appeared as a Japanese spy in a two-reeler, *The Ambassador's Envoy* (Ince?, 28 May 1914).

12 "The Typhoon," *Milwaukee News*, no date available, in *SHE*.

13 *Reel Life* 4.11 (30 May 1914): 23.

14 *San Diego Union*, 24 October 1914: n.p., in Sessue Hayakawa Scrapbook, Hirasaki National Resource Center, Japanese American National Museum.

15 "Popular Arts Project," Hayakawa-11.

16 *The Typhoon* was based on a stage drama, *Taifun*, which was written in 1909 by a Hungarian, Menyhert (or Melchior) Lengyel, and had been successful in Berlin (1910), Paris (1911), London (1913), and in the United States. The Berlin version appeared at the Irving Place Theater in New York on 4 December 1911, and the American adaptation by Emil Nyitray and Byron Ongley, *Typhoon*, opened at the Fulton Theater in New York on 11 March 1912. The latter ran for ninety-six performances. Gergely, "Hungarian Drama in New York," 76, 186. Hayakawa said that he saw the play "20 or 30 times" in Chicago when he was at the University of Chicago and that he could "remember even the lines." According to Hayakawa, he performed in *Typhoon* in theaters in Los Angeles for a Japanese audience. "Popular Arts Project," Hayakawa-10. There is no official record that confirms his appearance in it. *Rafu Shimpo* reported that *Taifun* (Berlin version) was popular at the Court Theater in Los Angeles but did not mention Hayakawa. *Rafu Shimpo* 3688 (16 December 1915): 2.

17 Translation by the author.

18 Deacon, *Kempei Tai*, 55, 79.

19 McConaughy, *The Typhoon*, 168.

20 Probably, Hayakawa saw Danjuro IX, not Danjuro I.

21 H. C. Carr, "Sessue of the Samurai," 68.

22 The motif of a Japanese man murdering a white woman was presented in an earlier short film in which Hayakawa appeared. *A Relic of Old Japan* (Barker, 11 June 1914) depicts another tragedy of interracial love, and in it the Japanese man kills a white woman for revenge. MPW 20.11 (13 June 1914): 1600.

5. NOBLE SAVAGE AND VANISHING RACE

1 Quoted in Staiger, "Dividing Labor for Production Control," 22.

2 Bowser, *The Transformation of Cinema 1907–1915*, 175. According to Gregory S. Jay, about fifty one-reelers with Native American topics were released in 1909 and between one hundred and two hundred such films in each subsequent year through 1914. Jay, "'White Man's Book No Good,'" 5–6.

3 Steven Higgins, personal interview, 9 November 2000. Ince's films, especially his films under the trademark of Bison Films, were advertised as "the most spectacular and beautiful re-creations of the Old West yet seen." MPW 7.15 (8 October 1910): 843.

4 Higgins, personal interview, 9 November 2000.

5 Elliot, "Hollywood's Yellow Streak," 76.

6 Brooks, *The Melodramatic Imagination*, 4–5, 15.

7 Jay, "'White Man's Book No Good,'" 6–7.

8 Jay, "'White Man's Book No Good,'" 7–8.

9 The MPN noted, "Several realistic knife fights are staged which materially heighten the interest of this tale of Indians." MPN 10.12 (26 September 1914): 65.

10 MPW 22.13 (26 December 1914): 1842.

11 Hearne, "'The Cross-Heart People,'" 181–97.

12 Higgins, personal interview, 9 November 2000.

13 Ince was making three two-reelers a week at the end of 1913. Higgins, "The Wrath of the Gods," 1.

14 *Reel Life* 5.20 (30 January 1915): 16; *MPW* 23.7 (13 February 1915): 1048.

15 Higgins, personal interview, 9 November 2000. Hayakawa never played a Native American after 1914. The Indian genre itself was losing its popularity after 1914.

6. THE MAKING OF AN AMERICANIZED JAPANESE GENTLEMAN

1 DeCordova, "The Emergence of the Star System in America," 28.

2 Field, "A Japanese Idol on the American Screen," 23.

3 P. McDonald, *The Star System*, 33.

4 Ross, "Sessue Hayakawa Prefers the Wicked Oriental Roles," 4.

5 Koszarski, *An Evening's Entertainment*, 299. Even Douglas Fairbanks Sr., whose skin was far darker than that of the conventional leading men of the period, was using makeup to lighten his skin, in order to embody white Americanness. Cohen, *Silent Film and the Triumph of the American Myth*, 146.

6 Gleason, "American Identity and Americanization," 34–37.

7 Abramson, "Assimilation and Pluralism," 150–53.

8 Gleason, "American Identity and Americanization," 38–39.

9 Dumenil, *The Modern Temper*, 20.

10 Gleason, "American Identity and Americanization," 40.

11 Y. Matsumoto, "Amerika jin de arukoto, Amerika jin ni suru koto" [Being American, making American], 52–75.

12 Winokur, "Improbable Ethnic Hero," 7.

13 *Motography* 15.21 (20 May 1916): 1168.

14 *Philadelphia Telegraph* (16 May 1916): n.p., in *SHE*.

15 *Motography* 1521 (20 May 1916): 1168; *The Bioscope* 516.32 (31 August 1916): 806.

16 Negra, *Off-White Hollywood*, 13.

17 *Motion Picture* (October 1916): n.p., in *SHE*.

18 *MPN* 13.20 (20 May 1916): 3091.

19 Sessue Hayakawa, *Zen Showed Me the Way*, 139.

20 *Variety* 43.13 (25 August 1916): 25.

21 *MPN* 14.4 (29 July 1916): 623.

22 *MPN* 14.10 (9 September 1916): 1549.

23 In 1917 the *Literary Digest* published a cartoon that depicts a man named "Japan" villainously observing a woman named "Europe" who is skiing and in danger of falling off a cliff. "Japan" has Fu Manchu's signature appearance, a catfish-like mustache, in the cartoon. *Literary Digest* 54.13 (31 March 1917): 803.

24 All of the original scripts of Hayakawa's films at Lasky used in this book, except

those of *The Cheat* and *Temptation*, are at Paramount Script Collection, Center for Motion Picture Study, Margaret Herrick Library.

25 Grimsted, *Melodrama Unveiled*, 177.

26 Neu, *An Uncertain Friendship*, 163–80; Nihon Gaimusho, *Nihon gaiko bunsho* [Japanese diplomatic documents], Taisho era, vol. 24, 243–334.

27 U.S. Congress, House Committee on Immigration and Naturalization, *Hearings on Japanese Immigration*, 66th Congr., 2nd sess. (Washington: 1921): pt. 2, p. 717, quoted in Ichioka, "*Amerika Nadeshiko*," 343; Kato Shinichi, *Beikoku nikkeijin hyakunen shi* [Hundred-year history of the Japanese in the U.S.], 16.

28 Nihon Gaimusho, *Nihon gaiko bunsho*, 1917, vol. 1, 79. See also Masubuchi, "1910 nendai no hainichi to 'shashin kekkon'" [Anti-Japanese and "picture bride" in the 1910s], 300.

29 Modell, *The Economics and Politics of Racial Accommodation*, 6. In 1910, 719 Japanese babies were born in California, equaling only 2.24 percent of all the births in the state, but in 1919 the number rose to 4,378, or 7.82 percent. In the same period, Chinese births accounted for only 0.86 percent in 1910 and 0.77 percent in 1919 and African American births only 0.72 percent in 1910 and 0.46 percent in 1919. E. G. Mears, *Resident Orientals on the American Pacific Coast* (1978): 35, quoted in Masubuchi, "1910 nendai no hainichi to 'shashin kekkon'" [Anti-Japanese and "picture bride" in the 1910s], 303.

30 In 1920, according to the historian Ronald Takaki, the agricultural production of Japanese farms was valued at $67,000,000, approximately 10 percent of the total value of California's crops. Takaki, *Strangers from a Different Shore*, 270.

31 Ichioka, "*Amerika Nadeshiko*," 347.

32 *Motography* 16.11 (9 September 1916): 612.

33 *MPW* 29.11 (9 September 1916): 1685.

34 "The Japanese Immigrant Appraised," *Nation* 101.26 (9 September 1915): 316.

35 Jordan, "Japan and the United States," 63.

36 "Can We Assimilate the Japanese?" *Literary Digest* 47.5 (2 August 1913): 166.

37 Griffis, "Our Honor and Shame with Japan," 569, 571.

38 Tully C. Knoles, "What Is Nationality?" *Annual Publications of Historical Society of Southern California* 10 (1917), quoted in Y. Matsumoto, "Amerika jin de aru koto, Amerika jin ni suru koto" [Being American, making American], 54.

39 Irwin, *Hashimura Togo, Domestic Scientist*, 105–12.

40 Irwin, *Letters of a Japanese Schoolboy*, 352–53, 357–58, 362.

41 Irwin, *Hashimura Togo, Domestic Scientist*, 158, 161–62.

42 Irwin, *Letters of a Japanese Schoolboy*, 7. Togo's inassimilable Japaneseness and his ignorance of customs in middle-class white American homes, however, often function as a social criticism of the extreme cult of domesticity in the genteel tradition. Most housewives who hire Togo are depicted as unreasonable figures who stick to the cult of domesticity too much. For instance, Mrs. Fill-ups, who spends "all day long cleaning up," tells her husband "Don't" all the time. "Don't track snow on rug," "Don't leave hat and coat on sofa," "Don't lay

cigars on mahogany table," "Don't dry your thumbs on clean towels," "Don't eat salad with oyster fork," "Don't spill ash on fine velvet furniture," and so forth. Togo says to her, "If you would be less careful of his comfort, maybe he would be more comfortable. Many husbands quit home because it is too beautiful. . . . Husbands should not be furniture for the home—Home should be furniture for the Husband." Mrs. Fillups fires him immediately. Irwin, *Mr. Togo, Maid of All Work*, 39–48.

43 *MPW* 33.8 (25 August 1917): 1152. See also *MPN* 16.9 (1 September 1917): 1349; *Exhibitor's Trade Review* (*ETR*) 2.12 (25 August 1917): 885.

44 *MPN* 16.9 (1 September 1917): 1349.

45 *MPN* 16.9 (1 September 1917): 1491.

46 *MPN* 16.9 (1 September 1917): 1459.

47 *MPW* 33.9 (1 September 1917): 1386.

48 *The Bioscope* 37.582 (6 December 1917): 32; *ETR* 2.12 (25 August 1917): 885.

49 Easterfield, "The Japanese Point of View," 34–35.

50 Koszarski, *An Evening's Entertainment*, 176.

51 Albert McLean, *American Vaudeville as Ritual*, 121–22.

7. MORE AMERICANIZED THAN THE MEXICAN

1 Italics original. Williams, *Playing the Race Card*, xiv, xv; Williams, "Melodrama Revised," 58.

2 Williams, *Playing the Race Card*, xiv, 6, 8, 9, 26.

3 Sklar, *F. Scott Fitzgerald*, 20.

4 Sklar, *The Plastic Age (1917–1930)*, 3.

5 Santayana, "The Genteel Tradition in American Philosophy (1911)," 37–64.

6 Sklar, "A Leap into the Void," 45.

7 K. McDonald, *Japanese Classical Theater in Films*, 72.

8 "Japanese Customs in Motion Pictures," *Paramount Magazine* (March 1915): 7.

9 Lears, *No Place of Grace*, 149.

10 *MPW* 33.1 (7 July 1917): 78.

11 Psychoanalytically, the Japanese brush could be read as a phallic symbol.

12 Gérard Genette defines focalization as the "angle of vision, from which the life or the action is looked at." Genette, *Narrative Discourse*, 161–211. Shlomith Rimmon-Kenan expands Genette's definition of focalization in a "purely visual sense" to include "cognitive, emotive and ideological orientation," in addition to the optical one. Rimmon-Kenan, *Narrative Fiction*, 71.

13 Griffis, "Our Honor and Shame with Japan," 574.

14 *NYDM* 77.2010 (30 June 1917): 30.

15 *MPN* 16.1 (7 July 1917): 118. *Forbidden Paths* was not favorably reviewed unanimously. Those who wanted Hayakawa to play more villains criticized the film. *Variety* noted, "One does not expect to see him in a role that calls for sympathy after the heavies he has been in the habit of playing." *Variety* 47.8 (20 July

1917): 31. The film obtained only "34%" of "pleased patrons" out of five reports. *Wid's Independent Reviews of Feature Films* 3.38 (20 September 1917): 608.

8. SYMPATHETIC VILLAINS AND VICTIM-HEROES

1 These reports continued until *Wid's Daily* 5.143 (29 September 1918).
2 *Wid's Independent Reviews of Feature Films* 3.5 (1 February 1917): 65.
3 *Wid's Independent Reviews of Feature Films* 3.20 (17 May 1917): 306; *Wid's Independent Reviews of Feature Films* 3.27 (5 July 1917): 427.
4 *Wid's Independent Reviews of Feature Films* 2.51 (21 December 1916): 1178.
5 *New York Times* (15 May 1916): 7.
6 NYDM 76.1976 (4 November 1916): 27.
7 Since the prints of these films are no longer extant, the following discussion on the films is primarily based on their original scripts.
8 The MPN noted that *The Call of the East* had a strong similarity to *The Cheat*. MPN 16.16 (20 October 1917): n.p.
9 MPN 14.19 (11 November 1916): 2909.
10 MPW 34.5 (3 November 1917): 707.
11 No matter how imaginary the overall configuration of the Japanese space, Lasky tried to make the Japanese sets as authentic as possible. Even though there is no constructional instruction for the sets of Hakoshima in the original script of *The Call of the East*, there is one for a set of a Japanese store in the original script of *The Bravest Way* (George H. Melford, 16 June 1918). The instruction is practical, and its intention to make the set as realistically Japanese looking as possible is clear. The instruction suggests following the furnishings of actual Japanese stores: "Small Japanese store, catering to Japs only—selling candy, tea, notions, 'kalulus' (rice cakes) put up in round cartons, 'Most Dainty' wafers, manufactured by 'Ojama & Co. Tokyo,' Jap books with Jap title—candy featured, candy images of fish, balls on vines, etc.—original parcel of tea and matches—Jap ads. Formed of small beans of rice. (See stores of Mikaway, 365 E. 1st St.; Ishimitsu, 336 E. 1st St.; Hattori & Co., 123 North San Pedro St.; Matsunoya, 129 N. San Pedro.)"
12 MPN 16.18 (3 November 1917): 2992.
13 MPW 34.5 (3 November 1917): 707.
14 Hubler, "Honorable 'Bad Guy,'" 148.
15 In *The Honor of His House*, Count Ito Onato (Hayakawa), a famed Japanese scientist, attracts white women with his refined appearance. After marrying a half-Japanese, half-white heroine, Onato begins to show his inassimilable aspect of Japaneseness. Out of jealousy, Onato poisons his wife. Eventually, his murderous thought is offset by his repentant and self-sacrificial act. Onato transplants his blood to his wife. After Onato's death, the heroine gives birth to Onato's son and marries an American man. The American husband, who has been introduced in the film as a drunken racist, learns to become an appropriate American father, being moved by Onato's self-sacrificial act.

16 Holmes, "The Hollywood Star System and the Regulations of Actors' Labour, 1916–1934," 98.

17 *The Honor of His House, The Bravest Way,* and *The City of Dim Faces* use the device of mixed blood in order to unite Hayakawa's character with white-looking women without causing serious fear of miscegenation.

18 In 1922 an article in *Photoplay* stated, "Will Pola [Negri] escape the standardization process?" Howe, "The Real Pola Negri," 19.

19 *MPN* 17.24 (15 June 1918): 3599.

20 *Variety* 51.2 (7 June 1918): 32.

21 *MPW* 36.12 (15 June 1918): 1615; *ETR* 4.2 (17 May 1918): 126.

22 Easterfield, "The Japanese Point of View," 34–35.

9. SELF-SACRIFICE IN THE FIRST WORLD WAR

1 *Nation* 105.2733 (15 November 1917): 528.

2 *Outlook* 117 (10 October 1917): 200.

3 What the United States wanted to prevent was a German-Japanese alliance. Germany would have only to abandon its relatively minor ambitions in the Far East and to give Japan a free hand there; then Japan would support Germany's expansion in Latin America in return. There was an incident known as "the Zimmermann telegram of 1917," which became one reason for the U.S. entry into World War I in April 1917. The German foreign secretary, Arthur Zimmermann, suggested an alliance between Germany, Mexico, and Japan in order to deflect the attention of the United States southward and westward and to prevent a U.S. military commitment in Europe. Part of the German plot involved a Japanese invasion of the United States via Mexico. "Germany Flirting with the Orient," *Literary Digest* 54.12 (24 March 1917): 808. See also, Mehnert, "German *Weltpolitik* and the American Two-Front Dilemma," 1476.

4 *MPW* 36.7 (11 May 1918): 898.

5 The credit published in *MPW* still noted Hayakawa as "Tori (one of Long Island's Smart Set)." *MPW* 38.9 (30 November 1918): 990.

6 *Katsudo Shashin Zasshi* 5.4 (April 1919): 65.

7 Easterfield, "The Japanese Point of View," 119.

8 "Sessue Hayakawa as Mediator," *Los Angeles Times* (30 May 1917): II3.

9 *Variety* 49.2 (7 December 1917): 50.

10 *ETR* 2.22 (3 November 1917): 1753.

11 *MPW* 34.11 (15 December 1917): 1643.

12 The emphasis is original in the intertitles.

13 *Wid's Independent Reviews of Feature Films* 3.49 (6 December 1917): 775.

14 *Wid's Independent Reviews of Feature Films* 3.49 (6 December 1917): 775.

15 There is an African American janitor in this film. Nara-Nara, in a three-piece suit, treats him as a lower-class character. When Nara-Nara gives him a tip, the janitor smiles ridiculously, showing his white teeth, and bows to Nara-Nara over

and over again. A racial hierarchy is observable between the Japanese spy and the African American janitor. This racial and class hierarchy positions Hayakawa's character as "whiter" and more Americanized than the African American character.

16   "Exhibitors' Box Office Reports," MPN 17.3 (19 January 1918): 395.

10. THE COSMOPOLITAN WAY OF LIFE

1   DeCordova, *Picture Personalities*, 12; Studlar, "The Perils of Pleasure?" 264; Lounsbury, *Origins of American Film Criticism, 1909–1939*, xvi.

2   P. McDonald, *The Star System*, 32; deCordova, *Picture Personalities*, 28.

3   Two million copies of *Photoplay* circulated nationally by 1922. Slide, *The Idols of Silence*, 109.

4   Kingsley, "That Splash of Saffron," 139–41. "Shoki" does not mean "destruction," but it is a name in Japanese myths.

5   For example, see MPN 13.4 (29 January 1916): 44; *New York Times* (6 February 1916): 18; *Los Angeles Times* (19 August 1917): III-3.

6   EH 3.10 (2 September 1916): 25, emphasis by the author. Even in the late 1920s, when Hayakawa appeared in several stage plays, this fictional biography of Hayakawa playing Shakespeare, and so forth, was used to enhance the authenticity of his stage appearances in the United States and in Europe. See, for instance, "Former Japanese Film Star Credited with Introduction of Shakespeare to Orient," *Los Angeles Times* (19 December 1926): C27; "Hayakawa on Bill in Stage Play," *Los Angeles Times* (16 January 1927): C13.

7   Kingsley's emphasis on Hayakawa's Americanized star image set the tone of future articles on Hayakawa in magazines and newspapers. See "Japanese Stars Like Americans," *Toledo Times* (13 August 1916): n.p., in SHE; "Mixture of Nations," *Cleveland Plain Dealer* (19 August 1916): n.p., in SHE; "Japanese Actor and Bride Have California Bungalow," *Brooklyn Eagle* (29 April 1917): n.p., in SHE; "Mr. and Mrs. Hayakawa and Their New Shoji," *Photoplay* (November 1917): n.p., in SHS: 153–54.

8   Kingsley, "That Splash of Saffron," 140. Even before Kingsley's article was published, the *New York Times* reported, "Hayakawa has discovered that in speaking Japanese he cannot get the proper facial expression, so even in his Japanese company he speaks broken English in dramatic scenes." *New York Times* (6 February 1916): 18. Most Japanese people learn English, but only a limited number of them have full command of it even now.

9   Gaddis, "The Romance of Nippon Land," 18–20.

10   Reed, "The Tradition Wreckers," 62–65.

11   *Madame Butterfly* became widely popular among middle-class Americans after January 1898, when a Japanophile lawyer named John Luther Long published the novella, based on the French writer Pierre Loti's 1887 novella *Madame Chrysanthème*, in the *Century* magazine. The renowned dramatist David Belasco adapted Long's story as a single-set one-act stage production, which opened at

the Herald Square Theater in New York in March 1900. Then, this American version of *Japonisme* was re-imported to Europe. Giacomo Puccini created his opera version, *Madama Butterfly*, in 1904. This opera made the hardly original story of a victimized Japanese woman the most popular one among other similar works. It was first performed in the United States in 1906 in Washington, D.C. At New York's Metropolitan Opera House, *Madama Butterfly*, with Geraldine Farrar as Cio-Cio-San, was performed 106 times in sixteen seasons after 1906. The Savage English Grand Opera Company took *Madama Butterfly* on a national tour in 1907–8. This *Madama Butterfly* tour was the most comprehensive, for one opera, of any in the history of American touring up to that time. As a result, *Madama Butterfly* had become one of the most popular operas and one of the most popular narratives about Japan in the United States by the mid-1910s. Dizikes, *Opera in America*, 317. *Madame Butterfly*, a story between a U.S. naval officer named Pinkerton and a Japanese geisha named Cio-Cio-San, not only depicts Japan as a premodern space but also functions as an archetypal morality tale between West and East, civilized and primitive, masculine and feminine, and good and evil. Cio-Cio-San, who is faithful to her husband and gives birth to a child, is an ideal embodiment of the latter. *Madame Butterfly* provided a basic narrative structure for many films with Japanese subjects. Hayakawa and Aoki had appeared in short films with the *Madame Butterfly* narrative, including *The Geisha* (10 April 1914), even though the one who commits suicide is not the Japanese woman (Aoki) but the American man when he realizes his mistake in marrying "outside of his race." MPN 9.14 (11 April 1914): 50.

12 According to Yukio Hayakawa, Hayakawa's son, Aoki made her debut in Hollywood in 1912 in a film directed by George Osbourne, in which she portrayed a Native American. Hayakawa, "Tsuru Aoki," 3.

13 *Variety* 33.2 (12 December 1913): 12.

14 "Japanese Actress in This Film," *Variety* 34.10 (8 May 1914): 19.

15 *Reel Life* 3.21 (7 February 1914); *Reel Life* 4.14 (20 June 1914).

16 *Reel Life* 3.7 (1 November 1913).

17 MPW 19.6 (7 February 1914): 701; MPN 9.5 (7 February 1914): 5.

18 "Miss Tsura Aoki, Japanese Actress," MPW 19.7 (14 February 1914): 825.

19 MPN 9.18 (9 May 1914): 48.

20 "Tsuru Aoki," *Reel Life* 4.7 (2 May 1914): 21.

21 "How to Hold a Husband: Mr. and Mrs. Hayakawa, in an Oriental Lesson in Four Chapters," *Photoplay* (November 1918): n.p., in SHS: 165.

22 Reed, "The Tradition Wreckers," 65.

23 Ibid.; Gaddis, "The Romance of Nippon Land," 20.

24 Bourne, *The Radical Will*, 248, 256, 258.

25 "Sessue Hayakawa: Japanese Film Star Decided to Become a Great Actor Even as a Boy," *Los Angeles Times* (2 December 1917): III-15.

26 DeCordova, *Picture Personalities*, 22.

27 NYDM 75.1951 (13 May 1916): 29.

28 Field, "A Japanese Idol on the American Screen," 22–25, 72–73.

29 Field, "A Japanese Idol on the American Screen," 72–73.

30 "Hayakawa, Japanese Screen Star," 70.

31 Exactly the same quote is in Easterfield, "The Japanese Point of View," 34–35; and in "His Best Work Is Seen in Repression," *San Antonio Light* (4 November 1917): n.p., in *SHE*.

32 "Is the Higher Art of the Movies to Come from Japan?" 30–31.

33 Harootunian, "Introduction," 17.

34 Gluck, *Japan's Modern Myths*, 273.

35 *Tokyo Nichinichi Shinbun* (20 May 1917), in *Shinbun shusei Taisho hennenshi*, 1917, vol. 1, 736.

36 "Katsudo shashin to shumi no kojo (Jou)" [Motion picture and the improvement of taste (1)], *Katsudo Shashin Kai* 4 (January 1910): 2–3.

37 Gonda, "Minshu goraku mondai" [Issues of mass entertainment] (1921), *Gonda Yasunosuke Chosaku shu dai 1 kan*, 69–70.

38 Gerow, "Writing a Pure Cinema," 203.

39 "Sokan ni nozomite," *Katsudo no Sekai* 1.1 (January 1916): 2–3.

40 Kamata, "Zento tabo naru katsudo shashin kai" [Promising motion picture world], 96–99.

41 Quoted in Gerow, "Writing a Pure Cinema," 170.

42 Numata, "Posuta no machi ni tachite" [Standing in a city filled with posters], 112–15.

43 *Yorozu Choho* (25 May 1917), in *Shinbun shusei Taisho hennenshi*, 1917, vol. 1, 764. There was an argument that dramas played by Japanese people were more influential on Japanese audiences than dramas played by foreigners. As a result, Hayakawa's films were censored more strictly than any other foreign films. *Rafu Shimpo* 5401 (8 March 1921): 3. It was also reported that Hayakawa's films drew close attention by the Tokyo Metropolitan Police Department because Hayakawa once criticized Japanese censorship, saying "the Japanese people who censor motion pictures are all idiots without any knowledge about them, and films should not be censored by such people." *Tokyo Asahi Shinbun* (4 February 1921), in *Shinbun shusei Taisho hennenshi* 1921, vol. 1, 342–43.

44 Makino, *Nihon eiga kenetsu shi* [History of motion picture censorship in Japan], 78–80.

45 The National Board noted more specifically in 1916, "No comedy which in effect holds up to ridicule any religious sect, religion generally, or the popular characteristics of any race of people should be shown." The National Board of Review of Motion Pictures, *The Standards and Policy of the National Board of Review of Motion Pictures*, 8, 14.

46 The National Board stated more specifically in 1916, "Marital infidelity, degeneracy, and sex irregularities are notable examples. . . . [The National Board] *should not and will not pass any pictures containing incidentally or extensively the female nude, dating from January 1, 1917*," italics original. The National Board of Review of Motion Pictures, *The Standards and Policy of the National Board of Review of Motion Pictures*, 8, 17.

47 The National Board also noted in 1916, "Arson is a difficult crime to present in photoplays in such a manner that the suggestion be not a menace to the public." The National Board of Review of Motion Pictures, *The Standards and Policy of the National Board of Review of Motion Pictures*, 10–11.

48 The National Board of Review of Motion Pictures, *Report Regarding Pictures Reviewed and a Financial Statement*, New York, 1 January 1917, quoted in Feldman, *The National Board of Censorship (Review) of Motion Pictures, 1909–1922*, 122.

49 "National Board of Review of Motion Pictures Records, 1906–1971," Box 140: Publicity Articles 1916–17, the New York Public Library.

50 "National Board of Review of Motion Pictures Records, 1906–1971," Box 84: Foreign Correspondence Japan, the New York Public Library.

51 The National Board of Review of Motion Pictures, *The Standards and Policy of the National Board of Review of Motion Pictures*, 5; Barrett, "The Work of the National Board of Review," 178.

52 Feldman, *The National Board of Censorship (Review) of Motion Pictures, 1909–1922*, 5–6, 211–12.

53 Jowett, *Film*, 127–29.

54 "National Board of Review of Motion Pictures Records, 1906–1971," Box 9: Correspondence with Film Companies, Paramount Pictures, 1914–22, the New York Public Library. The National Board also chose Hayakawa's 1921 vehicle, *The First Born* (Colin Campbell, 30 January 1921), a love story set in San Francisco's Chinatown, as one of the "Exceptional Photoplays during 1921." "National Board of Review of Motion Pictures Records, 1906–1971," Box 140: Press Releases 1921–34, the New York Public Library.

11. BALANCING JAPANESENESS AND AMERICANIZATION

1 The financial background of the establishment of Haworth Pictures Corporation is not clear. According to Hayakawa's autobiography, William Connery, Hayakawa's college friend, introduced Hayakawa to the president of A. B. C. Dohrman, a china and glassware company in San Francisco, who was willing to pay one million dollars to establish Hayakawa's own company. Also, a new distribution company, Robertson-Cole, was planning to distribute films of independent productions. Sessue Hayakawa, *Zen Showed Me the Way*, 141–42. Hayakawa also said that Connery himself was "the son of a multimillionaire here, owns the coal mine," and his parents provided the one million dollars. "Popular Arts Project," Hayakawa, 27.

2 Kingsley, "That Splash of Saffron," 139.

3 Higham, *Cecil B. DeMille*, 45.

4 *Cleveland Daily*, 12 May 1916: n.p., in *SHE*.

5 *Rafu Shimpo* 3699 (29 December 1915): 3.

6 *Rafu Shimpo* 3970 (16 July 1916): 3.

7 Already in December 1915 the *Rafu Shimpo* reported that Hayakawa had tried

to introduce *kyugeki*, a period stage drama influenced by kabuki, to film producers. *Rafu Shimpo* 3683 (10 December 1915): 3.

8   *Picture-Play* (January 1917): n.p., in *SHE*.

9   *MPN* 14.15 (14 October 1916): 2359; "Foreign Film World," *Kinema Record* 42 (10 December 1916): 556. According to a report in the *EH*, a "wealthy Japanese of Los Angeles presented Hayakawa with a theater where he appears from time to time." *EH* 3.10 (2 September 1916): 25.

10   *Rafu Shimpo* 4203 (19 April 1917): 3.

11   *St. Louis Democrat* (11 December 1917): n.p., in *SHE*; Aoyama, *Hariuddo eiga okoku no kaibo*, 281–82; *Katsudo Shashin Zasshi* 3.3 (March 1917): 59. As early as 2 December 1914, the Japanese Photoplayers' Club had been organized and headed by Hayakawa. Nanka nikkeijin shogyo kaigi sho, *Nanka shu nihonnjin shi*, 291.

12   Yoneyama, "Rafu Nihonjin kai kiroku" [Record of Rafu Nihonjin kai], n.p.; "Senji kibun no beikoku kinema kai" [U.S. cinema world in a war mood], *Katsudo no Sekai* 3.11 (November 1918): 66–67.

13   Hayakawa also invited many famous Japanese people who visited Los Angeles, including Dr. Nitobe Inazo and the opera singer Miura Tamaki, to his house "to recover his reputation." *Miyako Shinbun* 12322 (22 April 1922): 10.

14   "Haworth Pictures Signs Hayakawa," *MPW* 35.10 (16 March 1918): 1497; "Hayakawa Names First Two Productions," *MPW* 36.15 (6 July 1918): 76; Aoyama, "Beikoku katsudo shashin no miyako yori (12)" [From the capital of the American motion picture], 35.

15   "Popular Arts Project," Hayakawa-28–29; Aokusasho, "Kamome tobu Korea-maru no kanpan de" [On the deck of the *Korea* where seagulls fly], 50.

16   Aoyama, "Beikoku katsudo shashin no miyako yori (12)," 35.

17   "Hayakawa Names First Two Productions," *MPW* 36.15 (6 July 1918): 76.

18   "Kamome tobu Korea-maru no kanpan de" [On the deck of the *Korea* where seagulls fly], 51.

19   Watkins, "Sessue Hayakawa Today," 391.

20   Sessue Hayakawa, *Zen Showed Me the Way*, 138–39, 143.

21   *MPN* 17.14 (6 April 1918): 2061.

22   *Katsudo Gaho* 3.1 (January 1919): 14.

23   Sessue Hayakawa, *Zen Showed Me the Way*, 143. William Worthington studied stage technique with an opera company in Germany.

24   Bowser and Spence, *Writing Himself into History*, xix.

25   "How Sessue Hayakawa Leaned to Smile," *Photoplay Journal* (June 1919): n.p., in *SHS*: 176.

26   Sessue Hayakawa, *Zen Showed Me the Way*, 105.

27   Du Bois, *The Souls of Black Folk*, 45.

28   The idea of "trans-position" is borrowed from Ota, *Toransupojishon no shiso* [Thoughts of trans-position].

29   Barbas, "The Political Spectator," 217–30.

30   Parker and Sedgwick, *Performativity and Performance*, 2.

31 Butler, *Gender Trouble*, 146–47.

32 Regarding this twisted, contradictory relationship between mimicry and authority, see Bhabha, *The Location of Culture*, 85–92.

33 Japanese people in the United States and in Japan certainly had different thoughts on their national identities. The former had to balance themselves between assimilation to the United States and association with Japan. Some people in Japan criticized Japanese immigrants who stuck to their Japanese customs and did not adapt to the new environments. Yanaihara, "Jinko mondai to imin" [Problems of population and immigration], 75–112.

34 *MPW* 35.9 (9 March 1918): 1332.

35 *MPW* 35.10 (16 March 1918): 1467.

36 *MPW* 36.8 (18 May 1918): 960.

37 Handy, "Kipling Was Wrong!" 51, 124.

38 *Katsudo no Sekai* [Active world, or Motion picture world] 3.6 (June 1918): 168.

39 The print of *His Birthright* has been preserved by Nederlands Filmmuseum.

40 *MPW* 37.8 (24 August 1918): 1153.

41 *Kinema Junpo* 51 (21 December 1920): 7. See also Koda, *Sesshu*, 65.

42 *ETR* 4.19 (12 October 1918): 1615.

43 *MPW* 38.2 (12 October 1918): 254. Exactly the same sentences are found in *EH* 7.16 (12 October 1918): 54.

44 Authentic Japanese atmosphere was emphasized in the following films at Haworth. According to the reviews in trade journals, the opening scenes of *The Temple of Dusk* are set in Japan. *MPN* 18.14 (5 October 1918): 2259. *Variety* noted about *Bonds of Honor* (Worthington, 19 January 1919), "The locale is laid in Japan, and picturesque scenery from that country has been reproduced." *Variety* 53.11 (7 February 1919): 53. A one-page ad of *A Heart in Pawn* (Worthington, 10 March 1919) in *MPW* displays a photo, cropped in the shape of a Japanese shrine, in which Hayakawa and Aoki, both in appropriate Japanese kimono, look at each other under cherry blossoms. *MPW* 39.13 (22 March 1919): 1596. According to Japanese film magazines, *A Heart in Pawn* was a screen version of Nakamura Shunu's *Ichijiku* [A fig] and Hayakawa appeared in the stage version of it ("Shadows") before. *Katsudo Shashin Zasshi* 4.12 (December 1918): 42–43; "Kamome tobu Korea-maru no kanpan de" [On the deck of the *Korea* where seagulls fly], *Katsudo Gaho* 4.6 (June 1920): 50.

45 *Variety* 52.4 (20 September 1918): 45.

46 Aoyama, "Beikoku katsudo shashin no miyako yori (13)" [From the capital of the American motion picture], 59, 63.

47 *MPW* 37.8 (14 September 1918): 1612.

48 Studlar, *This Mad Masquerade*, 33.

49 Quoted in Studlar, *This Mad Masquerade*, 34.

50 Studlar, *This Mad Masquerade*, 34.

51 *ETR* 4.12 (24 August 1918): 1006.

52 "Hayakawa Holds Samurai Sword of His Ancestors," *ETR* 4.12 (24 August 1918): 1004.

53   *ETR* 4.12 (24 August 1918): 1018.

54   *MPW* 38.3 (19 October 1918): 340–41.

55   "Screen Players in Loan Drive," *MPW* 36.7 (18 May 1918): 985; "Hayakawa Makes Film for Next Loan Drive in Thirty-six Hours," *EH* 7.11 (7 September 1918): 39.

56   *Popular Art* (April 1918): n.p., in *SHE*; "Sesshu naito seiko" [Sessue night successful], *Rafu Shimpo* 4823 (26 April 1919): 3.

57   *NYDM* 79.2076 (5 October 1918): 519.

58   Studlar, *This Mad Masquerade*, 176.

12. RETURN OF THE AMERICANIZED ORIENTALS

1   Slide, *The American Film Industry*, 291–92; Fernett, *American Film Studios*, 193; Beauchamp, *Without Lying Down*, 157.

2   "Robertson-Cole Buying Productions on Merit," *MPW* 38.13 (28 December 1918): 1546.

3   "Robertson-Cole Company Gets Close to Exhibitor," *MPW* 39.5 (1 February 1919): 612.

4   *EH* 9.18 (25 October 1919): 57. Robertson-Cole not only developed rapidly in the domestic market but also expanded to "every civilized country in the world." "Robertson-Cole Sells Universally," *MPW* 41.5 (2 August 1919): 693. In Japan, the Nippon Katsudo Shashin Company (Nikkatsu) obtained the rights to distribute Robertson-Cole films after 1918. After that time, Hayakawa's films were released regularly in Japan.

5   "Robertson-Cole Films in Big Houses," *MPW* 40.7 (17 May 1919): 1036.

6   I. Mori, *Hayakawa Sesshu*, 35.

7   "Robertson-Cole Units Start Big Production Drive," *MPW* 40.6 (10 May 1919): 927.

8   *MPW* 41.1 (5 July 1919): 118. According to *AFI Catalog*, Exhibitors Mutual distributed Hayakawa's films produced at Haworth until *The Tong Man* (Worthington, 14 December 1919). Hanson and Gevinson, *The American Film Institute Catalog of Motion Pictures Produced in the United States*, 55, 940. Robertson-Cole attempted to cancel its contract with Mutual in July 1919, but the U.S. District Court decided against the cancellation, and Robertson-Cole had to continue its cooperation with Mutual until *The Tong Man*. "Robertson-Cole and Mutual Agree," *MPW* 41.6 (9 August 1919): 789.

9   *MPN* 18.13 (28 September 1918): 1946–47; *MPW* 41.9 (30 August 1919): 1234.

10 *MPW* 41.12 (20 September 1919): 1963; "In a Class by Himself Hayakawa," *EH* 9.13 (20 September 1919): 41.

11 "Superior Pictures Show Hayakawa: Robertson-Cole Will Present Japanese Star Solely in Series of Exacting Standards by Way of Production," *MPW* 41.11 (13 September 1919): 1660.

12 "Robertson-Cole to Add Three Stars," *EH* 9.12 (13 September 1919): 54.

13 Robertson-Cole published these press books at least for *Li Ting Lang* (Charles

Swickard, July 1920) and *An Arabian Knight* (Swickard, 22 August 1920). "Robertson-Cole Prepares Elaborate Press Book on Sessue Hayakawa's 'Li Ting Lang,'" *MPW* 45.3 (17 July 1920): 364; "Robertson-Cole Issues Elaborate and Helpful Press Book on Hayakawa Film," *MPW* 45.7 (14 August 1920): 928.

14   *EH* 8.26 (21 June 1919): 7–8; *MPN* 40.11 (14 June 1919): 3916.

15   *MPW* 42.7 (6 December 1919): 652.

16   "'The Courageous Coward' Goes Big in Washington," *MPW* 40.4 (26 April 1919): 559.

17   *Wid's Daily* 5.128 (15 September 1918): 23.

18   *MPN* 19.17 (26 April 1919): 2711.

19   McKelvie, "Playing with Fire in Hawaii," 14, 46.

20   *Wid's Daily* 7.19 (26 January 1919): 23.

21   *Photoplay Journal* (July 1919): n.p., in *SHE*.

22   Koszarski, *An Evening's Entertainment*, 261.

23   *MPW* 38.3 (19 October 1918): 452.

24   *Rafu Shimpo* 4655 (6 October 1918): 2. Hayakawa liked *The Temple of Dusk* very much. In 1957, when he was nominated for an Academy Award as best supporting actor in *The Bridge on the River Kwai*, he said in an interview, "I should very much like . . . to do a new version of the picture which was my first for my own company in 1919, after I had finished a Paramount contract. It is called 'The Temple of Dusk.'" Thirer, "Sessue Hayakawa—Then and Now," n.p.

25   *EH* 7.15 (5 October 1918): 36.

26   In *The Courageous Coward*, Suki (Hayakawa), a young Japanese American law student, succeeds in American sports. His girlfriend Rei decides to convert herself into an up-to-date American girl to please Suki. Suki, who still worships the customs of his country, is disappointed in Rei's change and in her being escorted by Tom Kirby, the son of a rich politician. Later, Tom kills one of the servants who works in his father's gambling house. Suki, now a district attorney, finds himself confronted with the confession of Tom while he is prosecuting the wrong man. To keep Tom's secret for Rei's sake and not to execute the wrong man, Suki allows himself to be displaced as district attorney and branded a coward. Finally, Tom makes a confession in public, and Suki is saved from his bad name.

27   *MPW* 40.9 (31 May 1919): 1391. In *His Debt*, Hayakawa plays Goro Moriyama, a young Japanese gambling house owner in an American city. Moriyama gives poor people the money that is collected from the rich. Whitcomb, a drunk American, shoots Moriyama in rage because he has lost all of his money. Whitcomb's girlfriend is a nurse and takes care of Moriyama without knowing what has happened. Moriyama falls in love with her. When Moriyama avenges himself on Whitcomb by giving him up to the police, the girl pleads to Moriyama. He gives up his vengeful thought and his love for her.

28   *MPW* 41.6 (16 August 1919): 1019. In *The Gray Horizon*, Hayakawa plays Yano Masata, a young Japanese artist in the United States. An art expert praises Yano's paintings and asks him to tint some bonds, which are counterfeits.

Yano's sister arrives from Japan and recognizes the counterfeiter as her faithless American husband. Yano's sister is shot dead during the fight between Yano and the counterfeiter. Yano kills the counterfeiter. Later, Yano falls in love with a woman who was kind to his sister. When she asks him to paint a portrait of her late husband, he realizes that she was the counterfeiter's wife. She does not know that her husband was a criminal. Rather than destroying her memory of her husband, Yano burns all the evidence of the man's crimes and leaves her.

29 Miyake, "Insho eiga tanpyo" [Short impressions on films], 161.

30 *EH* 8.5 (25 January 1919): 14. The *New York Times* chose *Bonds of Honor* as one of "The Year's Best," *New York Times* (11 January 1920): VIII-3.

31 *EH* 9.4 (19 July 1919): 13; *MPW* 41.4 (26 July 1919): 463.

32 *Wid's Daily* 9.12 (13 July 1919): 5; *MPW* 41.1 (5 July 1919): 391. In *The Man Beneath*, Hayakawa plays Dr. Chindi Ashutor, a young Hindu scientist. Ashutor loves a white woman. He tries to prove his love by rescuing her sister's fiancé from gangsters, but she refuses his love because of their racial differences. It is a story of "the tragic situation created by a race barrier blocking the gates of love." Margaret I. MacDonald, review of *The Man Beneath*, *MPW* 41.1 (5 July 1919): 111.

33 *MPN* 21.22 (22 May 1920): 4404.

34 George T. Pardy, review of *The Man Beneath*, *ETR* 7.9 (31 January 1920): 905.

35 The only exception was *Black Roses* (Colin Campbell, 22 May 1921).

36 *Photoplay* 9.5 (April 1916): n.p., in *SHE*.

37 *MPN* 21.22 (22 May 1920): 4404.

38 *EH* 9.18 (25 October 1919): 57–58.

39 "Robertson-Cole Celebrates Its First Birthday; Resume of Year's Activities," *MPW* 42.7 (13 December 1919): 818.

40 *MPW* 43.5 (31 January 1920): 770.

41 *Current Biography*, 195.

42 *MPW* 41.13 (27 September 1919): 1943.

43 *EH* 9.15 (4 October 1919): 33–34.

44 Margaret I. MacDonald, review of *The Dragon Painter*, *MPW* 42.1 (4 October 1919): 161.

45 "'The Dragon Painter' Is a New Hayakawa Picture," *MPW* 41.13 (27 September 1919): 1975.

46 *Kinema Junpo* 59 (1 April 1922): 12.

47 Fenollosa, *The Dragon Painter*.

48 The name of Fenollosa's son was also Kano.

49 *Katsudo Kurabu* 5.5 (May 1922): 61, 125. The Japanese critic Kasumi Ura Jin claims that the passionate embrace between a husband and a wife and their kissing in a public space in *The Dragon Painter* follow American customs because they are not usually seen in Japan. Kasumi Ura Jin, *Hayakawa Sesshu*, 208.

50 Kasumi Ura Jin, *Hayakawa Sesshu*, 208.

51 This motif of a dream maiden was used in *Death Mask*.

52 *EH* 9.17 (18 October 1919): 62.

53 *EH* 9.18 (25 October 1919): 57–58.

54 Helen Rockwell, review of *The Dragon Painter*, *ETR* 6.18 (4 October 1919): 1585.

55 *New York Times* (11 January 1920): VIII-3. The only negative review of *The Dragon Painter* was not about the film itself; the reviewer simply wanted Hayakawa to play another villainous role. A reviewer in *Wid's Daily* wrote, "It seems a pity that they don't put Hayakawa into some big vital drama where he can play the heavy. His one great success was 'The Cheat.' He is a very capable actor and with the right opportunity could undoubtedly score a bigger success as a heavy than he ever has in a sympathetic character." *Wid's Daily* 10.12 (12 October 1919): 3.

56 *ETR* 7.3 (20 December 1919): 275.

57 *MPW* 44.12 (19 June 1920): 1622.

58 Taguchi, "Nanjino yatoinin wa dareka" [Who's your servant?], 51.

59 The National Board of Review of Motion Pictures also "requested a change" in *The Tong Man*, according to the letter from the executive secretary to Robertson-Cole dated 28 October 1920, but Robertson-Cole carried out no change in the film. "National Board of Review of Motion Pictures Records, 1906–1971," Box 11: Correspondence with Film Companies—Robertson-Cole Distributing Corporation, the New York Public Library.

60 Gong, "Zen and the Art of Motion Picture Making," 14.

61 *EH* 10.2 (10 January 1920): 62.

62 *Leslie's Illustrated Newspaper* (17 December 1887): 296. *Leslie's Illustrated Newspaper* often published anti-Chinese cartoons, too. See Choy, Dong, and Hom, *The Coming Man*.

63 *MPW* 42.9 (20 December 1919): 1009.

64 Tom Hamlin, review of *The Tong Man*, *MPN* 20.26 (20 December 1919): 4533.

65 Kepley, "Griffith's *Broken Blossoms* and the Problem of Historical Specificity," 40–41.

66 For an example of the kidnap narrative, see *Leslie's Illustrated Newspaper* (19 May 1883): 204.

67 "Sesshu wo miru ki" [Record of watching Sessue], *Rafu Shimpo* 4782 (11 March 1919): 2.

68 Epstein, *Écrits sur le Cinéma 1921–1953*, 143, translation by Brian Price.

69 In order for Hayakawa to edit the film by himself, a "special projection machine, such as was used during the war in military and naval hospitals for the benefit of service men, was placed in Mr. Hayakawa's room." *NYDM* 83.2216 (4 June 1921): 978. It was reported later that *The Swamp* was written, or co-written, by Jack Abe, another Japanese man working with Hayakawa. Tamura, "Chikagoro no watashi" [About me recently], 81.

70 K. Hayakawa, "Sesshu zatsuwa" [Hayakawa talks], 8.

71 *MPW* 45.8 (21 August 1920): 968.

72 Lant, "The Curse of the Pharaoh, or How Cinema Contracted Egyptomania," 98.

73 Richard White, "Sun, Sand and Syphilis: Australian Soldiers and the Orient, Egypt 1914," *Australian Cultural History* 9 (1990): 50, quoted in Lant, "The Curse of the Pharaoh, or How Cinema Contracted Egyptomania," 98.

74 *MPW* 45.8 (21 August 1920): 968.

75 Hayakawa displayed his chivalrous actions in his other star vehicle, *Li Ting Lang*. In *Li Ting Lang*, a Chinese student (Hayakawa) who falls in love with an American woman protects her from rebellious Chinese groups, especially in a climactic fighting scene on a dark staircase in a Chinese temple ornamented with shoji screens and paper lanterns.

76 Studlar, "'Out-Salomeing Salome,'" 103.

77 *MPW* 43.13 (27 March 1920): 2058.

78 Hansen, *Babel and Babylon*, 277, 282.

79 Studlar, *This Mad Masquerade*, 92.

80 Studlar, "The Perils of Pleasure?" 288–89.

81 Studlar, *This Mad Masquerade*, 101.

82 Kern, *The Culture of Love*, 101.

83 Studlar, *This Mad Masquerade*, 115.

84 Hansen, "Pleasure, Ambivalence, Identification," 12.

13. THE MASK

1 Geraghty, "Re-examining Stardom," 190–91.

2 Hansen, "The Mass Production of the Senses," 64.

3 "Actors and Stars," *New York Times* (25 April 1920), n.p., in G. Brown, *New York Times Encyclopedia of Film 1896–1928*, n.p.

4 "Is the Higher Art of the Movies to Come from Japan?" 30–31.

5 Brewster and Jacobs, *Theatre to Cinema*; Keil, *Early American Cinema in Transition*; Pearson, *Eloquent Gestures*; Staiger, "The Eyes Are Really the Focus," 14–23.

6 Blum, *American Film Acting*, 8.

7 Brewster and Jacobs, *Theatre to Cinema*, 88.

8 Pearson, *Eloquent Gestures*, 8.

9 Pearson, *Eloquent Gestures*, 15–16.

10 Staiger, "The Eyes Are Really the Focus," 20; Louis Reeves Harrison, "Eyes and Lips," *MPW* 8.67 (18 February 1911): 348–49.

11 Pearson, "'O'er Step Not the Modesty of Nature,'" 9, 21.

12 *NYDM* (3 December 1913): 36.

13 Pearson, *Eloquent Gestures*, 5. In 1919, a Japanese film journal, *Katsudo Hyoron*, published an essay by Kasamori Sennosuke, in which he examined in detail the facial expressions of the actress Vivian Martin, who had appeared in films

with Hayakawa. Kasamori attached ten close-up photographs of Martin in his article and labeled them "joy," "contemplation," "hesitation," "understanding," "ridicule," "fear," "anxiety," and so forth, and explained how clearly the skilled motion picture actors in Hollywood could represent "the motion of emotion" in their facial expressions. Kasamori, "Hyojo no suii" [Transition of facial expressions], 34–35.

14 Pearson, "'O'er Step Not the Modesty of Nature,'" 9, 21–22.

15 Brewster and Jacobs, *Theatre to Cinema*, 81.

16 Yoshiyuki, "Sekai ni kakeru Nihon no hashi" [The Japanese bridge over the world], 48.

17 Field, "A Japanese Idol on the American Screen," 22–25, 72–73.

18 Noguchi, "Sekai no heiwa to waga katsudo gyosha no susumubeki michi" [World peace and the way that our motion picture industry should take], 46.

19 Field, "A Japanese Idol on the American Screen," 72.

20 K. McDonald, *Japanese Classical Theater in Films*, 43.

21 Ihara Toshiro, *Ichikawa Danjuro*, quoted in Imao, *Kabuki no rekishi* [History of kabuki], 165–66. The *haragei* technique was "the acting style that denies stylized movement or words and attempts to express human emotions or psychological development in silence, only by static facial expressions and eyes." Imao, *Kabuki no rekishi*, 166.

22 "Hayakawa, Japanese Screen Star," 70.

23 The same quote was used in Easterfield, "The Japanese Point of View," 34.

24 Doane, "The Close-Up," 98.

25 *Photoplay* 9.4 (March 1916): n.p., in SHE.

26 Epstein, "Grossissement," 235–41.

27 The emphasis is in the original.

28 Staiger, "The Eyes Are Really the Focus," 15, 20.

29 Card, *Seductive Cinema*, 222.

30 Benjamin, "A Short History of Photography," 240–57; Benjamin, "The Work of Art in the Age of Mechanical Reproduction," 235–37. See also Hansen, "The Mass Production of the Senses," 70–71.

31 Kracauer, *Theory of Film*, 71–72.

32 Cavell, "What Photography Calls Thinking," 14.

33 "Feature Films as Wid Sees Them," *Wid's Films and Film Folk Independent Criticisms of Features* 1.15 (16 December 1915): n.p.

34 "Feature Films of the Week: Lasky Was Right When He Selected 'The Cheat' as His Best Picture—Christmas Spirit in 'The Old Homestead' and Pathe's 'Life of Our Savior,'" NYDM 74.1931 (25 December 1915): 40.

35 Leed, review of *Five Days to Live*, *Variety* 65.8 (13 January 1922): 42. George Arliss was a British stage actor who came to America in 1902 and appeared in many Broadway productions. Onstage, Arliss established himself in historical roles, or as eminent statesmen, kings, and rajahs, or as eccentric millionaires. At the age of fifty-three, he debuted on film in *The Devil* (1921), in which he had

appeared onstage in 1906. Also in 1921, Arliss reprised his stage work in the title role of the silent film *Disraeli*. He won an Academy Award for his work in the sound version of *Disraeli* (1929).

14. THE STAR FALLS

1 "The Motion Picture Hall of Fame," *Motion Picture Story Magazine* 16.11 (December 1918): 12; "Popular Contest Closes," *Motion Picture Story Magazine* 20.11 (December 1920): 94.

2 "Suggestions," *MPN* 24.3 (9 July 1921): 407. Also in 1921, Robert E. Sherwood of *Life* mentioned Hayakawa as one of "the stars who neither gained nor lost much ground." Robert E. Sherwood, "A Fan Paper Critic Says—This Film Year Has Been a Fan's Year," *MPN* 25.2 (31 December 1921): 218.

3 "Sesshu ga futsukoku de tsukutta shin eiga Nihongeki ze batsutoru" [*La Bataille*, a new film about Japan that Sessue made in France], *Katsudo Kurabu* 7.5 (May 1924): 38. Hayakawa's decline in popularity did not occur very quickly, though. Even in March 1922, when Hayakawa left Robertson-Cole, exhibitors reported the reception of Hayakawa's films in favorable tones. *Where Lights Are Low* was reported by an exhibitor in Maryland to have "pleased 100 per cent" of the audience and Hayakawa was "in a class by himself." *The Swamp* was called a "very good picture" and Hayakawa was "well liked" by an exhibitor in Illinois. "Straight from the Shoulder Reports," *MPW* 55.2 (11 March 1922): 196. The novelized story of the final Hayakawa star vehicle with Robertson-Cole, *The Vermilion Pencil* (Norman Dawn, 19 March 1922), appeared in a film fan magazine. Peter Andrews, "The Vermilion Pencil," *Motion Picture Magazine* 23.4 (April 1922): 49–53, 102. Robertson-Cole claimed that *The Vermilion Pencil* was "big bookings," the biggest ever in Hayakawa's films. "Big Bookings on 'Vermilion Pencil,'" *MPW* 55.7 (15 April 1922): 723. Of course, Robertson-Cole's report had a publicity purpose. It never officially announced in trade journals that Hayakawa had left the company.

4 Negra, "The Fictionalized Ethnic Biography," 182.

5 Quoted in Negra, "The Fictionalized Ethnic Biography," 182.

6 Michaels, *Our America*, 2, 8–9, 11.

7 Kellor, *The Federal Administration and the Alien*, 70, 72.

8 Daniels, *The Politics of Prejudice*, 77.

9 "Fox Films Show How American and Japanese Interests May Cross and What Might Happen," *MPW* 54.8 (25 February 1922): 824.

10 McClatchy, *Four Anti-Japanese Pamphlets*, 13–14, 25–26.

11 Lothrop Stoddard, *The Rising Tide of Color against White World Supremacy* (New York, 1920): 297–303, quoted in Daniels, *The Politics of Prejudice*, 67. There were pro-Japanese intellectuals on the East Coast who opposed such an anti-Japanese tendency. See Kawakami, *The Real Japanese Question*.

12 "Japan and Ourselves," 166–67.

13 Bliven, "The Japanese Problem," 172.

14 Tupper and McReynolds, *Japan in American Public Opinion*, 114.

15 Daniels, *Asian America*, 151.

16 Takaki, *Strangers from a Different Shore*, 208.

17 Daniels, *Asian America*, 149.

18 Daniels, *The Politics of Prejudice*, 65.

19 *Readers' Guide to Periodical Literature*, 3:126; Sherwood and Painter *Readers' Guide to Periodical Literature*, 4:92; Sherwood and Goodman, *Readers' Guide to Periodical Literature*, 5:77.

20 Gevinson, *American Film Institute Catalog*, 1284.

21 *Katsudo Zasshi* 7.2 (February 1921): 79.

22 Yamamoto, "Renai geki ni akita beikoku eiga kai" [The American motion picture world got tired of love stories], 42–43; Yamamoto, "Beikoku seigeki tsushin" [News about American silent films], 65.

23 Aoyama, "Beikoku katsudo shashin kai [American motion picture world]," 15.

24 *Katsudo Zasshi* 8.5 (May 1922): 104.

25 The film was based on Julian Johnson's stereotypically exotic stage play, "Harakiri." Aoyama, "Nanji no yatoinin wa dareka no shutsuen ni tsuite" [About appearing in *Who's Your Servant?*], 82.

26 ETR 7.14 (6 March 1920): 1442.

27 *Wid's Daily* 12.1 (14 March 1920): 17. The MPW also compared *Who's Your Servant?* with *The Cheat.* "'Who's Your Servant?' Acclaimed a Winner; Release Plan Not Announced," MPW 43.3 (17 January 1920): 430.

28 Thomas Kurihara (Kurihara Kisaburo) went back to Japan in 1918 and Henry Kotani (Kotani Soichi) in 1920. Kurihara and Kotani worked with Hayakawa when they were at the NYMPC. Both Kurihara and Kotani played important roles in the modernization of cinema in Japan when they returned.

29 Kamiyama Sojin, the only Japanese actor who took an active part in Hollywood after Hayakawa left, never played any Japanese roles. It was his strategic and nationalistic choice. Kamiyama wrote in 1930, "I will not appear in any films if I have to play Japanese. I do not want to dishonor Japan even indirectly. . . . [For Americans] since Japan is an imaginary enemy, there won't be any favorable Japanese characters. Never." Many American audiences believed that Kamiyama was Chinese. Kamiyama, *Sugao no Hariuddo* [Hollywood without makeup], 189. As opposed to Hayakawa, Kamiyama had a career as an actor in Japan before he arrived in the United States in 1919. Kamiyama was a renowned actor in *shingeki*, modern drama, the Japanese response to modernization of theater in Europe by Ibsen and others. In *The Thief of Bagdad* (Raoul Walsh, 1924), a star vehicle for Douglas Fairbanks Sr., Kamiyama played the role of a conspiring Mongolian prince and became famous.

30 Aoyama, "Beikoku katsudo shashin kai" [American motion picture world], 15.

31 *Rafu Shimpo* 4846 (23 July 1919): 2.

32 Inoue, "Nichibei shinzen wa mazu nisshi gaiko yori" [Japanese-Chinese relationship is firstly important for U.S.-Japan goodwill], 25.

33 *Katsudo Gaho* 6.3 (March 1922): 58.

34 "Straight from the Shoulder Reports," MPW 53.5 (3 December 1921): 584.

35 "Straight from the Shoulder Reports," MPW 55.6 (8 April 1922): 659.

36 *EH* 14.23 (3 June 1922): 70.

37 Studlar, "The Perils of Pleasure?" 274.

38 *MPW* 36.12 (15 June 1918): 1615.

39 *ETR* 8.8 (24 July 1920): 843. There is an amazing close-up of Hayakawa in *Li Ting Lang*. When Li Ting Lang (Hayakawa) suddenly wakes up in a cabin on a ship to China, as a result of a conspiracy of a rebellious Chinese group, he displays in a close-up a facial expression of tremendous shock and horror: his eyes wide open, his mouth half-opened, and his teeth revealed. This close-up emphasizes Hayakawa's well-publicized acting styles that used the power of his eyes.

40 *Variety* 63.11 (5 August 1921): 26. In *Where Lights Are Low*, based on the short story "East Is East" by Lloyd Osbourne, which appeared in *Metropolitan Magazine* in April 1920, a Chinese prince, T'Su Wong Shih (Hayakawa), who loves a gardener's daughter, goes to America to study at a college. Later, when he finds his loved one in a prostitute auction in San Francisco's Chinatown, he fights against gangsters to rescue her.

41 *EH* 13.16 (15 October 1921): 20; Hart, review of *The Swamp*, *Variety* 64.11 (4 November 1921): 43.

42 *EH* 14.13 (25 March 1922): 59.

43 Quoted in Kakii, *Hariuddo no nihonjin* [Japanese people in Hollywood], 94.

44 Nogami, *Seirin no o Hayakawa Sesshu*, 95–96. Hayakawa also appeared as himself in the film *Night Life in Hollywood* (Fred Caldwell and Jack Pratt, 1922) to publicize his luxurious lifestyle.

45 *Rafu Shimpo* 4804 (4 April 1919): 3.

46 *Rafu Shimpo* 4801 (1 April 1919): 3; *Rafu Shimpo* 5663 (14 January 1921): 3.

47 *Katsudo Zasshi* 7.2 (February 1921): 69; *Katsudo Zasshi* 7.3 (March 1921): 74.

48 *Rafu Shimpo* 5265 (24 September 1920): 3.

49 *Rafu Shimpo* 5418 (29 June 1921): 3; "Sessue Hayakawa's 'Recuperative Trip' Develops into a Mighty Busy Vacation," MPW 51.2 (9 July 1921): 212.

50 *Nyu Yoku Shimpo* 736 (25 June 1921): 4.

51 *Nyu Yoku Shimpo* 739 (6 July 1921): 1.

52 In *The Vermilion Pencil*, Tse Chan (Hayakawa), a Chinese man, believing his wife to be unfaithful, condemns her to the sentence of *Ling Chee*, a terrible execution of jumping into a volcano, the Vermilion Pencil. He learns her innocence later. Her son, Li Chan (Hayakawa, in a dual role), returns from America and falls in love with Hyacinth, but she is kidnapped by a viceroy. Li Chan rescues her and seeks refuge in the caverns of the Sleeping Dragon, an active volcano. Li Chan is caught and faces the same torture as his mother, but an unknown hermit, in fact Tse-Chan, who has been missing, self-sacrificially helps them. During an eruption of the volcano, the lovers escape.

53 "Thrills in R-C Attractions," MPN 25.9 (18 February 1922): 1140.

54 Reeve, "What Happened to Hayakawa," 90.

55 *MPW* 51.2 (9 July 1921): 163. In December 1921, Robertson-Cole completed its "largest and most beautiful" studio on Melrose Avenue in Hollywood. "Beautiful Studios for R-C Completed," *MPW* 53.7 (17 December 1921): 814; *Katsudo Zasshi* 7.6 (June 1921): 66. Robertson-Cole's film production failed by the end of 1922 because of the poor quality of the company's work. Robertson-Cole was reorganized and its name changed to Film Booking Office of America. The FBO, the Radio Corporation of America, and the Keith-Albee-Orpheum vaudeville circuit merged into RKO Radio Pictures, Inc. in the 1920s.

56 "Sessue Hayakawa Signs Four Year Contract Renewal with Robertson-Cole," *MPW* 43.13 (27 March 1920): 2170; *EH* 11.26 (25 December 1920): 156; A. H. Giebler, "Los Angeles News Letter," *MPW* 44.2 (10 April 1920): 247.

57 Kingsley, "Flashes: Hayakawa Solus [*sic*]," III-4; I. Mori, *Hayakawa Sesshu*, 35.

58 *NYDM* 83.2196 (15 January 1921): 136; *EH* 11.3 (17 July 1920): 41.

59 Sessue Hayakawa, *Zen Showed Me the Way*, 150.

60 "Popular Arts Project," Hayakawa-30.

61 *NYDM* 81.2156 (10 April 1920): 704; Kingsley, "Flashes: Hayakawa Solus [*sic*]," III-4.

62 H. Carr, "Son of the Samurai," 81. Carr was not satisfied with *The First Born*, while highly valuing the original play and praising Hayakawa as an actor. Carr, "'First Born' Is Weakling," III-1. In *The First Born*, Chang Wang (Hayakawa) is forced by his father to give up a woman he loves and to marry a woman he does not love. When his wife dies, Wang goes to America and becomes a wood peddler to take care of his son. He finds out that the woman he once loved is now a slave of a notorious man. The man knows of Wang's romance in China. In order to avoid Wang's revenge, the man kidnaps Wang's son and threatens Wang. Wang rescues the woman in the end but his son dies falling out of a window. *The First Born* was adapted from a stage play written and acted in by Francis Powers and produced in San Francisco by Fred Belasco, who came from a family well known in theater. It is assumable that Robertson-Cole tried to enhance the "Super-Special" quality of the film by adapting a renowned theater production.

63 "Nineteen Exceptional Pictures Selected in 1921," *EH* 14.4 (21 January 1922): 26. A Japanese film magazine reported that *The First Born* was chosen as the fifth best film in 1920. *Katsudo Kurabu* 4.6 (June 1921): 84.

64 "'The First Born' Has a Large Number of Exploitation Angles," *MPW* 49.2 (12 March 1921): 177.

65 *MPW* 44.7 (15 May 1920): 916.

66 "Sessue Hayakawa Talks of His Future Productions While Visiting New York," *MPW* 44.9 (29 May 1920): 1184.

67 "Jidai shicho ni tekigo suru katsudo shashin no seiryoku" [Power of motion picture that corresponds to zeitgeist], *Rafu Shimpo* 5645 (19 December 1921): 1.

68 *Rafu Shimpo* 5684 (8 February 1921): 3; *Katsudo Kurabu* 5.3 (March 1922): n.p.

69 *New York Times* (1 August 1921): 12.

70 *MPW* 54.3 (21 January 1922): 319.

71 MPW 55.3 (18 March 1922): 299.

72 MPW 54.3 (21 January 1922): 319.

73 MPW 55.3 (18 March 1922): 299.

74 "Twenty-six R-C Pictures Scheduled for Year Beginning on September 1," MPW 51.7 (13 August 1921): 719; EH 13.7 (13 August 1921): 42.

75 "R-C Statement Denies Plan to Close Hollywood Studios," EH 14.2 (7 January 1922): 35.

76 "Sesshu no songai baisho yokyu" [Sessue's request for damages], Katsudo Gaho 6.7 (July 1922): 138.

77 "Japanese Star Sues Picture Corporation," Los Angeles Times (5 May 1922): II-10.

78 Lipke, "Films Lure Hayakawa," C25.

79 Sessue Hayakawa, Zen Showed Me the Way, 154–55.

80 Stoloff, "Normalizing Stars," 167.

81 Erich von Stroheim was another. Stroheim's character in Foolish Wives (Stroheim, 1921), who masquerades as Count Karamazin, a Russian aristocrat, was very similar to Hayakawa's character in The Cheat, except that Hayakawa was Japanese and Stroheim was European. In these films, both Stroheim and Hayakawa attract married women of leisure by their rich and refined appearances, but their hidden savage sexual desires are revealed in the middle of the film. In the end, white men punish both of them. See Staiger, Interpreting Films, 124–38.

82 Sessue Hayakawa, Zen Showed Me the Way, 144.

83 "Valentino to Star for Paramount," EH 14.5 (28 January 1921): 77.

84 Hayakawa's character in An Arabian Knight and Valentino's in The Sheik and The Son of the Sheik (George Fitzmaurice, 1926) are named Ahmed.

85 Valentino was born in Italy to an Italian father and a French mother.

86 Nogami, Seirin no o Hayakawa Sesshu, 103.

87 In The Brand of Lopez, Lopez (Hayakawa) loves Lola. When Lola flirts with an opera singer, Lopez brands the back of her neck with a lighted cigarette, out of jealousy. When Lola's mother objects to their marriage, Lopez becomes angry and kidnaps Lola's younger sister and her child. Though Lola's sister dies, her child runs away to Lola. Lopez and his outlaw gangs try to destroy Lola's home. When the nurse tells him that the child is actually his and Lola's, Lopez turns remorseful. The Brand of Lopez refers to the branding scene in The Cheat. Since trade journals criticized the scene for its lack of necessity in the narrative, the meaning of its existence seems only to be that of a reference to The Cheat. According to MPN, "The branding incident has little to do with the story." MPN 21.16 (10 April 1920): 3367. Wid's Daily claimed that "the branding trick was evidently introduced merely for its sensationalism." Wid's Daily 12.4 (4 April 1920): 6. In Blood and Sand (Fred Niblo, 1922), Valentino played the role of a Spanish matador, very similar to Hayakawa's role in The Brand of Lopez. Valentino was not criticized for playing a Spaniard.

88 MPN 21.16 (10 April 1920): 3367.

89   *Variety* 58.6 (2 April 1920): 95.

90   Walker, *Rudolph Valentino*, 118–19.

91   Sklar, *Movie-Made America*, 99.

92   *MPN* 25.17 (15 April 1922): 2212.

93   Studlar, *This Mad Masquerade*, 194.

94   Studlar, "The Perils of Pleasure," 269, 289.

95   H. C. Carr, "Sessue of the Samurai," 68.

96   McGaffey, "The Man from Japan," 58–59, 90.

97   Fletcher, "The Orient on the Subway," 53, 99.

98   Bryers, "The Gentleman from Japan," 54, 109.

99   Sessue Hayakawa, *Zen Showed Me the Way*, 154–56. Hayakawa also sent a letter explaining the anti-Japanese movement in California to his home in Japan on 22 May 1921. Oba, "Shokan kara mita Hayakawa Sesshu no kunan" [Sessue Hayakawa's hardship indicated in his letters], 49–51. Yet, at that point, Hayakawa did not imply any possibility of leaving Hollywood.

15. AMERICANIZATION AND NATIONALISM

1   Gulick, "Nihonjin wa douka shiuruya" [Are the Japanese assimilable?] (1), 2.

2   Gulick, "Nihonjin wa douka shiuruya (2)," 2.

3   "Gokuaku naru hainichi katsudo shashin jikken ki" [A record of watching an extremely evil anti-Japanese motion picture], *Rafu Shimpo* 3696 (25 December 1915): 3.

4   "Harakiri no katsudo ni tsuite" [About the film *Harakiri*], *Rafu Shimpo* 4318 (1 September 1917): 3. *Harakiri* turned into *Who's Your Servant?* in 1920, against which Aoyama himself engaged in an action to ban its release. *Rafu Shimpo* 5031 (1 May 1920): 3.

5   *Kinema Junpo* 120 (11 December 1922): 9.

6   "Hainichi katsudo saien setsu" [Rumor about another anti-Japanese film], *Rafu Shimpo* 3968 (14 July 1916): 3.

7   "Katsuhai o seisai seyo" [Sanction motion picture actors], *Rafu Shimpo* 4312 (25 August 1917): 3.

8   "Sesshu no shingeki" [Sessue's new drama], *Rafu Shimpo* 4782 (9 March 1919): 2. The ad of the film with Hayakawa's portrait appeared every day from the day of its release. *Rafu Shimpo* 4627–4634 (1–7 September 1918): all in p. 2.

9   "Katsudo dayori" [Motion picture report], *Rafu Shimpo* 4741 (21 January 1919): 2.

10   "Tsukai na katsudo" [Delightful motion picture], *Rafu Shimpo* 4627 (3 September 1918): 3.

11   "Yoso no Nihonjin dai-kirai" [I hate the Japanese in Western clothes], *Rafu Shimpo* 4682 (8 November 1918): 2.

12   Shigoro, "Rafu todai fujin arubamu (1)" [Album of famous ladies in Los Angeles 1], *Rafu Shimpo* 4764 (16 February 1919): 3.

13   Kotoku Shusui (1871–1911) was one of the founders of the socialist movement

in Japan at the turn of the century. Kotoku started a newspaper called the *Heimin Shinbun* [Newspaper for ordinary people] in 1903, and translated Karl Marx's and Frederick Engels's *The Communist Manifesto* (1848). In the Japanese government's suppression of the socialist movement, Kotoku was accused of conspiring to assassinate the emperor in 1910 and was sentenced to death.

14 According to Okina, the *Nichibei Shinbun* had been read widely in southern California. The *Rafu Shimpo*, which started as a local paper, tried to increase its popularity by degrading the value of the *Nichibei Shinbun* and by attacking Sessue and Okina. Okina, *Okina Kyuin zenshu* [Okina Kyuin's complete works], 108–12. Okina's claim about the *Rafu Shimpo*'s attitude was probably correct because the *Nichibei Shinbun* was also taking a position that criticized anti-Japanese films, even though it reported in a less nationalistic tone. One article in the *Nichibei Shinbun* noted, "It is good for actors to introduce beautiful Japanese characteristics, but they should stop showing cruel behaviors and helping to enhance anti-Japanese sentiment among white people." *Nichibei Shinbun* 5778 (25 December 1915): 5. Another article reported, "The Association of Tokyo People is conducting an investigation to do something against motion picture actor Sessue Hayakawa who caused anti-Japanese sentiment by appearing in an ugly motion picture." *Nichibei Shinbun* 5780 (27 December 1915): 5. Later in 1917, Okina was invited by Hayakawa to his house when he visited Los Angeles. Okina was impressed by his "dignified attitude as a renowned actor" and his house, "similar to those of upper-class white Americans." Itsumi, *Okinna Kyuin to imin shakai 1907–1924* [Okina Kyuin and immigrant communities 1907-1924], 259–69.

15 H. Yamaguchi, "Okina Rokkei ni kuyu [I regret about Okina], 7.

16 *Nyu Yoku Shimpo* 268 (9 September 1916): 4.

17 Newly started film magazines included *Film Record* (October 1913), the pioneer magazine that exerted a strong influence on subsequent publications in their formats and tone (it changed its name to *Kinema Record* in December 1913); *Katsudo Shashin Zasshi* [Motion picture magazine] (May 1915); *Katsudo no Sekai* [Active world, or Motion picture world] (January 1916); *Katsudo Gaho* [Motion picture graphic] (January 1917); *Katsudo Hyoron* [Motion picture review] (November 1918), which changed its name to *Katsudo Kurabu* [Motion picture club] in September 1919; *Katsudo Zasshi* [Movie magazine] (September 1919; and *Kinema Junpo* (aka *The Movie News*, July 1919).

18 Ichioka, "Japanese Associations and the Japanese Government," 409–37.

19 *Katsudo Shashin Zasshi* 3.1 (January 1917): 207.

20 *Katsudo no Sekai* 1.9 (September 1916): 4.

21 "Beikoku de daininki no nihon joyu Aoki Tsuruko" [Tsuru Aoki, a very popular Japanese actress in the U.S.], *Katsudo no Sekai* 2.1 (January 1917): 93.

22 *Katsudo Kurabu* 3.11 (November 1920): 30; I. Mori, *Hayakawa Sesshu*, 69; Makino, *Nihon eiga kenetsu shi* [History of motion picture censorship in Japan], 150–51. Some Japanese religious groups were said to protest against the film's

depiction of a Japanese god. "Mondo yuyo" [It is useful to question and answer], *Shukan Asahi* 31 August 1952: 22.

23 *Katsudo Gaho* 3.1 (January 1919): 14.

24 *Katsudo Kurabu* 2.8 (August 1919): 95; *Katsudo Kurabu* 3.1 (January 1920): 84.

25 Nonomiya, "From Rice Curry to Sessue," 7.

26 It was also because of Robertson-Cole's strategy to increase its international market.

27 *Osaka Mainichi Shinbun* (17 February 1918), in *Shinbun shusei Taisho hennenshi* 1918, vol. 1, 456.

28 Saiki, "Awabi romansu" [Abalone romance], 38–40. Hayakawa was born in 1886, according to his passport.

29 Aoyama, "Zaibei Nihonjin katsudo haiyu hatten shi" [History of progress of Japanese photoplay actors in the U.S.], 10.

30 Aoyama, "Beikoku katsudo shashin no miyako yori" [From the capital of the American motion picture], 46; Aoyama, "Beikoku katsudo shashin no miyako yori (12)," 35.

31 Takemura, *Taisho bunka* [Taisho culture], 135–36.

32 Bernardi, *Writing in Light*, 22.

33 Bernardi, *Writing in Light*, 13.

34 Hansen, "The Mass Production of the Senses," 61.

35 Bernardi, *Writing in Light*, 133.

36 Gerow, "Writing a Pure Cinema," 306–12.

37 "The World's Latest News," *Kinema Record* 3.15 (10 September 1914): 18.

38 *Katsudo Shashin Zasshi* 4.11 (November 1918): 174.

39 Kaeriyama, "Jiko o shireriya?" [Do we know ourselves?], 2.

40 Okura, "Ware mo mata shutsuba semu" [I will also run], 17–18.

41 "Eiga puropaganda ron" [An idea of film propaganda], *Katsudo Shashin Zasshi* 5.5 (May 1919): 38–39.

42 "Obei gekidan to toyo no geki" [European and American stage and dramas of the East], *Kinema Record* 2.9 (15 March 1914): 2–3.

43 Numata, "Katsudo shashin no geijutsu bi" [Artistic beauty of motion picture], 142.

44 Mukai Shunko, "Katsudo shashin kai no shin keiko: Kigeki no zensei jidai kuru" [A new tendency in motion pictures: The golden period of comedy has come], *Katsudo Gaho* (March 1917), quoted and translated in Bernardi, *Writing in Light*, 192.

45 Muromachi, "Furukushite atarshiki tsuneni tayumanu taido" [An old but new, consistent attitude], 4.

46 Gerow, "Writing a Pure Cinema," 300–2.

47 Gerow, "One Print in the Age of Mechanical Reproduction," n.p.

48 Rhodes, "'Our Beautiful and Glorious Art Lives,'" 308–9.

49 *Kinema Record* (November 1916): 479, quoted and translated in Gerow, "Writing a Pure Cinema," 123. Kaeriyama repeated his nationalistic vision on cinema,

using the same terms in his article of 1917, in another film magazine, *Katsudo Gaho*. Kaeriyama, "Katsudo shashin kogyo ni tsuite" [About the motion picture industry], 45.

50 Kakeisanjin (Kaeriyama), "Geijutsu to shite no katsudo shashin" [Motion picture as an art], 15–16; Kakeisanjin, "Katsudo shashin ga atauru chishiki" [Knowledge that motion picture can provide], 16; Kakeisanjin, "Katsudo shashin geijutsu ron" [Theory of motion picture art], 4. See also Bernardi, *Writing in Light*, 192.

51 Shibusawa, "Odorokubeki beikoku no katsudo shashin kai" [Amazing world of motion picture in America], 62–65. Contributors to *Katsudo no Sekai* wrote in abundance about the "national and social mission" of cinema, stressing educational and military applications. Kamata Eikichi, the president of Keio University, suggested an application of the motion picture for education and "for the national interests." Kamata, "Zento tabo naru katsudo shashin kai" [Promising motion picture world], 96–99. Nagai Ryutaro, a lecturer at Waseda University, wrote, "Cinema and national education are inextricably related." Nagai, "Waseda no kodo kara" [From the hall of Waseda University], 24.

52 S. Tanaka, *Japan's Orient*, 182.

53 *Kinema Junpo* 104 (1 July 1922): 3.

54 I. Mori, *Hayakawa Sesshu*, 15–17, 72.

55 "Hayakawa Sesshu shi to Keraman jo" [Mr. Sessue Hayakawa and Miss Kellerman], *Katsudo Gaho* 3.11 (November 1919): 47.

56 Mochizuki, "Beikokujin no rikai" [American people's understanding], 2–3. Mochizuki highly valued *Madame Butterfly* for its "understandable" treatment of a Japanese subject. Another critic writing for women's magazines also regarded Cio-Cio-San not as shameful but as favorable for her loyalty. Terada, "Teiso no kuni no onna Ocho fujin" [Cio-Cio-San, the woman of faithful country], 70.

57 Numata, "Rafu no eiga kai kara" [From cinema world in Los Angeles], 40.

58 *Kinema Junpo* 51 (21 December 1920): 7.

59 Koda, *Sesshu*, 99.

60 I. Mori, *Hayakawa Sesshu*, 40, 58–59, 90, 95, 128, 131. Mori highly valued *The Swamp* because it was written by Hayakawa and was based on a famous Japanese story, "Shidehara Tasuke." Mori wrote, "It is pleasurable that the Japanese story told in a different form moved the American audience." I. Mori, *Hayakawa Sesshu*, 141.

61 *Kinema Junpo* 71 (11 July 1921): 9.

62 *Katsudo Gaho* 6.9 (September 1922): 50–51.

63 *Tokyo Asahi Shinbun* (22 July 1922): 3.

64 *Tokyo Asahi Shinbun* (1 July 1922): 2.

65 "Saikin ni okeru eiga keiko yori" [From the recent tendency of cinema], *Kinema Record* 38 (10 August 1916): 336.

66 Kaeriyama, "Katsudo shashin geki kyakushoku jo no kenkyu (2)" [A study of directing photoplays], 4.

67 *Tokyo Asahi Shinbun* (5 February 1921), in *Shinbun shusei Taisho hennenshi* 1921, vol. 1, 330.

68 "Gujin no gugo ka aruiwa Nihon eiga no ketten ka" [Foolish words from a fool, or the weak point of Japanese cinema], *Kinema Record* 39 (10 September 1916): n.p.

69 "Beijin no waga katsudo shashin kan ni tsuite" [About the American view of our motion picture], *Kinema Record* 41 (10 November 1916): 478.

70 R. Matsumoto, "Nihon eiga no shinro" [Japanese cinema's direction], 9.

71 Ide, "Eiga geki no honshitsu to enshutsu ho no icchi" [Correspondence between the essence of photoplay and the directing method], 4.

72 Inoue, "Chikaku tobei shitai" [I want to visit America soon], 38–39. In 1930, Inoue appeared in a stage drama, *Appare Wong* (*The Honourable Mr. Wong*), with Hayakawa.

73 Ichikawa Sadanji, "Katsudo yakusha to naru niwa" [To become a motion picture actor], 35.

74 Y. Kasagi, "Ikyo no eiga kai ni katsuyaku seru Hayakawa Sesshu no hyoban" [The reputation of Sessue Hayakawa, who is popular in a foreign film world], 84–87, 109–10; Hayakawa Sesshu, "Katsudo shashin ni yakusha toshite seiko suru yoso" [Elements (needed) to become successful as a motion picture actor], 117. All the words by Hayakawa quoted in Kasagi's article are translations of those in Easterfield, "The Japanese Point of View," 33–35.

75 Kaeriyama, "Eiga geki to haiyu dosa (Sono 1)" [Photoplay and acting (1)], 5.

76 Kaeriyama, "Eiga geki to haiyu dosa (Sono 2)," 5.

77 "Daredemo katsudo yakusha ni nareru" [Anybody can become a motion picture actor], *Katsudo Shashin Zasshi* 2.8 (August 1920): 56–59.

78 Kaeriyama, "Sesshu no seiko bunseki" [An analysis of Sessue's success], 2–5.

79 Fujiki, "American Cinema Reshaping Japanese Culture," n.p.

80 I. Mori, "Eiga haiyu no hanashi (2)" [A story about film actors], 72. Hayakawa was reported to be 172 centimeters (5 feet 8 inches) tall. This was taller than the average for Japanese men of the Taisho period because, according to the novelist Yoshiyuki Junnosuke, at that time a height of 165 centimeters (5 feet 6 inches) was considered to be tall. Yoshiyuki, "Sekai ni kakeru Nihon no hashi" [The Japanese bridge over the world], 46. However, there is a prevalent term, "Sesshu suru" [Do Sessue], among Japanese filmmakers, which means to use a stepladder to make an actor look taller on the screen. If this expression is based on fact, Hayakawa was not a tall man.

81 "Hayakawa Sesshu shi no chikagoro no seikatsu" [Sessue Hayakawa's life these days], *Katsudo Gaho* 3.10 (October 1919): 75; I. Mori, *Hayakawa Sesshu*, 37–38. Articles in American trade journals publicized Hayakawa's physical training when he started Haworth. "Hayakawa Keeps in Physical Trim with Bicycle in His Attic," *ETR* 4.12 (24 August 1918): 1005.

82 Hanayagi, "Katsukai enma cho" [Evaluation book of the motion picture world], 75.

83 Deguchi, "Nani ga hakujin konpurekkusu o umidashitaka" [What caused white complex?], 104–23. In the 1930s, a female Japanese star, Hara Setsuko, became popular for her face and body, which "detached from Japaneseness." Yomota, *Nihon no joyu* [Actresses of Japan], 13.

84 Fujiki, "American Cinema Reshaping Japanese Culture," n.p.

85 Watanabe, "Meiji shoki no Dawinizumu" [Darwinism in the early Meiji period], 85.

86 J. Thomas, "Naturalizing Nationhood," 117.

87 Gaimu sho [The Ministry of Foreign Affairs], *Nihon gaiko bunsho: Pari kowa kaigi gaiyo* [Japanese Documents of Foreign Affairs: Abstract of the Paris Conference], 203, quoted. in Ichinokawa, "Koka ron to Yusei gaku" [The yellow peril and eugenics], 136. Since the Racial Equality Clause was based on Japan's "Caucasian complex" and its desire to obtain equal status with Caucasian nations in international relations, Japan did not question its own colonialism that racially discriminated against China and Korea. The Japanese government suppressed independence movements in China and Korea that occurred during the conferences.

88 *Kinema Junpo* 106 (21 July 1922): 14.

89 Y. K. Kasagi, "American News," *Kinema Record* 47 (15 May 1917): 226.

90 Kaeriyama, "Hatashite jinshu kankei kara kangaeruto sekaiteki ni nariuru ya" [Is it going to be worldwide if we think of racial relations?], 40–43. Also quoted and translated in Fujiki, "American Cinema Reshaping Japanese Culture," n.p.

91 *Katsudo Shashin Zasshi* 3.12 (December 1921): 83.

92 *Katsudo no Sekai* 4.1 (January 1919): 95; "Beikoku ninki haiyu oyobi kaisha mei ichiran" [A list of popular American actors and film companies], *Katsudo Gaho* 3.4 (April 1919): 96.

93 Imura Shigeru, letter to the editor, *Katsudo Gaho* 3.3 (March 1919): 168.

94 T. Nagai, "Nihonjin Hayakawa Sesshu wa shieseri" [A Japanese Sessue Hayakawa is dead], 97.

95 Kataoka, "Sesshu nitsuite Toshimichi san e" [To Toshimichi about Sessue], 98.

96 Willis, "Famous Oriental Stars Return to the Screen," 90.

97 Willis, "Famous Oriental Stars Return to the Screen," 44.

98 Nanbu, "Hayakawa Sesshu shi to kataru" [A talk with Mr. Sessue Hayakawa], 32–33.

99 I. Kondo, "Sesshu Hayakawa no engi" [Sessue Hayakawa's acting], 6–14.

100 *Katsudo Gaho* 6.7 (July 1922): 100.

101 Oda, "Beikoku katsudo kai kenbutsu miyage" [After visiting American motion picture world], 100.

102 Y. Sato, "Amerika eiga haiyu no tanaorosi" [News of American film actors], 53.

103 Handy, "Kipling Was Wrong!" 124.

104 I. Mori, *Hayakawa Sesshu*, 8, 17, 51–52, 151–52, 154, 166–68.

105 O. Taguchi, "Hariuddo kenbun roku," 32.

106 Amano, "Beikoku katsudo shashin no chimata yori" [News from American motion pictures], 164, emphasis in the original.

107 Seki, "Shitashiki Hayakawa Sesshu shi yori eta watashi no kangeki" [I was impressed by Mr. Sessue Hayakawa, my good friend], 33–34.

108 I. Mori, *Hayakawa Sesshu*, 93, 96, 104, 109.

109 Koda, *Sesshu*, 60; *Kinema Junpo* 50 (11 December 1920): 7.

110 *Katsudo Gaho* 6.1 (January 1922): 48–49.

111 Tsukimura, "Setsumeisha kara mitaru Sesshu geki" [Sessue's films viewed by benshi], 26.

112 *Katsudo Gaho* 3.6 (June 1919): 78.

113 *Tokyo Asahi Shinbun* (21 August 1922): 3.

114 Iida, *Rethinking Identity in Modern Japan*, 4.

115 Hashikawa, *Oka monogatari* [Story of yellow peril], 187, 200.

116 Iida, *Rethinking Identity in Modern Japan*, 4.

117 In 1918, Kita Sadakichi was launching a new academic journal, *Minzoku to Rekishi* [Ethnos and history], which posed a question, "Who are the Japanese people?" Kita, "'Minzoku to rekishi' hakkan shuisho," 1–8.

118 Shillony, "Friend or Foe," 187–211.

119 *Kinema Junpo* 101 (1 June 1922): 15; *Katsudo Zasshi* 8.8 (August 1922).

120 T. Mori, "Hayakawa Sesshu fusai o mukaete" [Welcoming Mr. and Mrs. Sessue Hayakawa], 28–29.

121 *Kinema Junpo* 97 (21 April 1922): 11; "Senpu no gotoku okorishi Taisho Katsudo Shashin Kabushiki Kaisha" [Taikatsu company, which rose like a hurricane], *Katsudo Zasshi* 6.5 (May 1920): 92–93; Kurihara, "Katsudo shashin to boku" [Motion picture and I], 22.

122 I. Mori, *Hayakawa Sesshu*; Ichikawa Sai, *Sekaiteki meiyu ni naru made* [Before he became an international great actor]; Koda, *Sesshu*; Kasumi Ura Jin, *Hayakawa Sesshu*.

123 Kasumi Ura Jin, *Hayakawa Sesshu*, 1–76.

124 *Kinema Junpo* 105 (11 July 1922): 4.

125 *Tokyo Asahi Shinbun* (15, 16, 19, 20, 21, 23, 24, 27 June); (9, 10, 11, 13, 15, 18 July 1922): all in page 3.

126 *Tokyo Asahi Shinbun* (14 June 1922): 3.

127 *Nichibei Shinbun* 8140 (7 July 1922): 3; *Katsudo Zasshi* 8.9 (September 1922): 85.

128 *Katsudo Zasshi* 8.8 (August 1922): 65.

129 *Nichibei Shinbun* 8134 (1 July 1922): 5. It was also reported in a newspaper that Japanese communities in America did not want Hayakawa to come back to the United States because of Hayakawa's cooperation with anti-Japanese movements. *Manshu Nichinichi Shinbun* (1 July 1922): 1.

130 *Tokyo Asahi Shinbun* (5 July 1922): 5.

131 *Kinema Junpo* 104 (1 July 1922): 3.

132 "Beikoku mubi kai no iro iro" [Various news about American movie world],

Katsudo Gaho 7.4 (April 1923): 106. Already in 1920, Hayakawa was reported to be the adviser of Shochiku Kinema Company, which intended to pursue the Pure Film Movement. *Katsudo Zasshi* 6.11 (November 1920): 113; *Tokyo Nichi-nichi Shinbun* (26 February 1920), quoted in Tsuzuki, *Shinema ga yattekita!* [Cinema has come!], 186.

133 *Tokyo Asahi Shinbun* (28 June 1922): 3; *Tokyo Asahi Shinbun* (18 August 1922): 3.

134 Ushiyama started a fashion school in Japan in 1925. See the Hollywood Fashion and Beauty College website, http://www.hollywood.ac.jp/d/d.html (accessed Nov. 17, 2006).

135 *Katsudo Gaho* 6.11 (November 1922): 35–38.

136 Fujiki, "American Cinema Reshaping Japanese Culture," n.p.

137 Y. Azuma (or Higashi), "Aoki Tsuruko to gyunabe o kakomu" [Having beef for a dinner with Aoki Tsuruko], 44–46.

138 Y. Suzuki, "Shinsetsu na Hayakawa Sesshu to Tsuruko fujin" [Kind Sessue Hayakawa and Mrs. Tsuruko], 16–20.

139 Shigeno Yukiyoshi, "Beikoku dewa Nihongeki ga donnna kankyo de torareruka" [Why films about Japan were made in the U.S.]," 28.

140 *Tokyo Asahi Shinbun* (1 July 1922): 2; *Miyako Shinbun* 12392 (1 July 1922): 11; *Tokyo Nichinichi Shinbun* (1 July 1922), in *Taisho nyusu jiten* 5:564–65; *Rafu Shimpo* 5808 (2 July 1922): 1.

141 *Katsudo Zasshi* 8.8 (August 1922): 66–67.

142 *Kinema Junpo* 108 (11 August 1922): 8.

143 "Beikoku mubi kai no iro iro" [Various news about American movie world], *Katsudo Gaho* 7.4 (April 1923): 106.

144 *Tokyo Asahi Shinbun* (28 August 1922): 3; *Tokyo Asahi Shinbun* (29 August 1922): 2.

145 "Fifteen Years Ago in Hollywood," *Los Angeles Times* (1 August 1937): D1.

146 *Kinema Junpo* 110 (1 September 1922): 14.

147 Sakamoto, "Sesshu ni atauru sho" [A letter to Sessue], 96.

148 Mori mentioned in his book that many Americans highly valued Hayakawa's directing ability in addition to his acting. I. Mori, *Hayakawa Sesshu*, 164.

149 Ichikawa Sai, "Aa awarenaru Sesshu yo" [Ah, poor Sessue], 60–63.

150 *Kinema Junpo* 106 (21 July 1922): 15.

151 "Kibei shita Hayakawa Sesshu fusai wa ko nihon taizai no shinso o katatta" [The returned Mr. and Mrs. Sessue Hayakawa talked about the truth of their stay in Japan like this], *Katsudo Zasshi* 8.12 (December 1922): 74–75. A Japanese fan pointed out that several welcome parties were held only for obtaining money from Hayakawa. *Tokyo Asahi Shinbun* (21 July 1922): 3. Japanese spectators, in-cluding the advocates of Pure Film, believed that Hayakawa was a millionaire because it was reported in a Japanese film magazine that Hayakawa had told Nitobe Inazo that he was earning $20,000 a week. *Katsudo Kurabu* 5.6 (June 1922): 93. However, it became clear later that Hayakawa received $20,000 per film, not per week, when Hayakawa sued Robertson-Cole. That is, according to

Aoyama, Hayakawa received only $1,538 a week. Aoyama, "Gimon datta Haya-kawa Sesshu no kyukin" [Sessue Hayakawa's salary, which had been unknown], 50–54. Later, Mori and Aoyama corrected Hayakawa's salary to $3,500 a week when he made an initial contract with Robertson-Cole. I. Mori, *Hayakawa Sesshu*, 55; Aoyama, *Hariuddo eiga okoku no kaibo*, 249.

152 *Katsudo Zasshi* 8.8 (August 1922): 67–68.

153 *Miyako Shinbun* 12449 (27 August 1922): 10.

154 Yamauchi, "Sesshu san!" [Mr. Sessue!], 108.

155 Noguchi, "Hayakawa Sesshu," 81–82. There were a few fans who sympathized with Hayakawa. Ayase, "Waga Sesshu o noroeru hitora e" [To those who curse on Sessue], 154–55.

156 Morioka, "Ko kikai" [A good opportunity], 40; Ishimaki, "Kongo no eiga haikyu mondai" [The issue of film distribution from now on], 47.

157 Tsutsumi, "Nihon mono to Oshu mono to o motte" [By Japanese and European films], 38.

158 "Beikoku eiga fujoei mondai" [The issue of not showing American films], *Katsudo Zasshi* 10.8 (August 1924): 36.

159 *Kinema Junpo* 163 (21 June 1924): 24; *Kinema Junpo* 164 (1 July 1924): 27.

160 "Japan's Film Boycott Given Up as Failure," *New York Times* (13 July 1924): section 2-1; K. Thompson, *Exporting Entertainment*, 141.

161 *Katsudo Zasshi* 8.9 (September 1922): 92–93.

162 *Nyu Yoku Shimpo* 864 (16 September 1922): 3.

EPILOGUE

1 *New York Times* (14 January 1923): n.p.; *Atlantic City Union* (16 January 1923): n.p.; *Variety* (19 January 1923): n.p., in *Tiger Lily Clipping*, The New York Public Library for the Performing Arts, Robinson Locke Collection. According to Aoyama Yukio, Hayakawa signed a contract with Lee Shubert (1871–1953), the Broadway theater owner and producer, in early May 1922, right after he left Robertson-Cole. Aoyama, "Beikoku sukurin geppo" [American screen monthly], 136.

2 The *New York Times* reported, "Sessue Hayakawa and 'Tiger Lily' seem to have been unaccountably lost en route to the Metropolis." *New York Times* (4 February 1923): xi. There is no listing of *Tiger Lily* in the Internet Broadway Data Base. When Hayakawa appeared in another stage drama, *The Love City*, in 1926, its program note stated, "May we introduce to you a new actor on the American stage. . . . None of you have ever seen him on stage before." Program of *The Love City*, in sHE.

3 Aoyama, "Gimon datta Hayakawa Sesshu no kyukin" [Sessue Hayakawa's salary, which had been unknown], 54

4 *La Bataille* was based on an exotic novel by Claude Farrere. Iijima, "Hayakawa Sesshu ga furansu de satsuei suru" [Sessue Hayakawa shoots a film in France], 19.

5   "Oshu butai de oatari no Hayakawa Sesshu" [Sessue Hayakawa's big success on European stages], *Katsudo Zasshi* 10.5 (May 1924): 40–43.

6   "British Producer Praises R-C Stars and Tells of Handicaps in England," MPW 54.1 (7 January 1922): 56.

7   MPW 68.4 (24 May 1924): 409.

8   Another thing that Hayakawa relates about *La Bataille* in his autobiography is the shooting of the climactic naval war scene, which used actual French battleships borrowed from the French navy. When Hayakawa was a child, he gave up his dream of becoming a naval officer because of an accident. For Hayakawa, *La Bataille* was also a chance to realize his broken dream of taking command of a navy vessel. Sessue Hayakawa, *Zen Showed Me the Way*, 171–72.

9   Takada, "Butai no Hayakawa Sesshu" [Sessue Hayakawa on stage], 25–26.

10 Program of *The Love City*, in SHE.

11 Hayakawa's performance in *The Love City* was poorly reviewed for the same reason that he was praised on the silent screen, the "rigid" facial expression. *The Billboard* 38.6 (6 February 1926): 10; *Theatre Magazine* 43.301 (April 1926): 16. A critic at the *New York Times* praised Hayakawa's acting, but only in reference to his early film career: "Mr. Hayakawa is a good enough actor, held down, by the nature of the play, when he plays a death scene with genuine emotion. It was a moment that atoned for much of the monotony of his earlier work." "'The Love City' Blends Drama and Fantasy," *New York Times* (26 January 1926): 18.

12 Busby, "Hayakawa Plays Suave Oriental," A9; "Chinese Robin Hood," *New York Times* (2 January 1927): BR12.

13 Sessue Hayakawa, *The Bandit Prince*.

14 *New York Times* (27 July 1926): 15.

15 Reeve, "What Happened to Hayakawa," 33, 90, 91.

16 Lipke, "Films Lure Hayakawa," C25–26.

17 Lipke, "Films Lure Hayakawa," C26.

18 "Sessue Hayakawa Heading Hillstreet Vaudeville Bill," *Los Angeles Times* (12 August 1928): C13.

19 Kingsley, "Romantic Vehicle Serves Star," A9.

20 *Variety* 103.11 (25 August 1931): 14.

21 "Japanese Actor Adopts Heir," *Los Angeles Times* (26 August 1931): A1.

22 "Mother Fights Hayakawa Adoption," *Los Angeles Times* (17 October 1931): A16.

23 "Hayakawa Served in Child Suit," *Los Angeles Times* (18 October 1931): A5.

24 Hayakawa was believed to be a womanizer and was responsible for this incident, though. See Nogami, *Seirin no o Hayakawa Sesshu* [King of Hollywood, Sessue Hayakawa], 136–43.

25 "East and West Part in Tears," *Los Angeles Times* (11 December 1931): A2.

26 "When East and West Came to Parting: But Twain May Meet Again," *Los Angeles Times* (12 December 1931): 3.

27 "East and West Part in Tears," *Los Angeles Times* (11 December 1931): A2.

28 Mrs. Sessue Hayakawa, "Mrs. Sessue Hayakawa Talks," A2.

29 "Taisho 13 nendo no waga eigakai" [Our film world in 1924], *Katsudo Zasshi* 11.1 (January 1925): 75–76.

30 "Sesshu ga futsukoku de tsukutta shin eiga nihongeki Ze Batsutoru" [*La Bataille*, a new film about Japan that Sessue made in France], *Katsudo Kurabu* 7.5 (May 1924): 39.

31 *Katsudo Zasshi* 10.12 (December 1923): 49–56.

32 *Eiga Shincho* 1.1 (May 1924): 78–79.

33 "Hayakawa Sesshu no Ra Bataiyu geki no joei zengo" [Before and after the exhibition of Sessue Hayakawa's *La Bataille*], *Katsudo Zasshi* 10.12 (December 1924): 49–56.

34 *Tokyo Nichinichi Shinbun* (1 October 1924), in *Shinbun shusei Taisho hennenshi* 1924–3 [Periodical history of Taisho through newspapers], 12.

35 *Yomiuri Shinbun* (28 September 1924), in *Shinbun shusei Taisho hennenshi* 1924–2, 1205.

36 Iwamoto and Makino, *Eiga nenkan Showa hen 1–4, Showa 5 nen ban* [Annual report of cinema: Showa period 1-4, Showa 5 edition] [1930], 19, 756–57; *Miyako Shinbun* (13 April 1930), in *Shinbun shusei Showa hennenshi*, 5: 240. According to Nogami, Hayakawa did not agree with the plan, but this plan developed without Hayakawa and resulted in the establishment of Toho, one of the largest studios in Japan. Nogami, *Seirin no o Hayakawa Sesshu*, 140.

37 Kamiyama, *Sugao no Hariuddo* [Hollywood without makeup], 219.

38 *Kinema Junpo* 371 (11 July 1930): 24.

39 *Kinema Junpo* 424 (21 January 1932): 44.

40 Yamanaka, "Hayakawa Sesshu 'onna' o kataru" [Sessue Hayakawa talks about "women"], 118–21; Hayashi, "Sesshu to Itari garu" [Sessue and Italian girls], 40–42; Abe, "Appare 'Wongu' no koi" [Love of great Wong], 124–28.

41 *The Honourable Mr. Wong* was made into the film *The Hatchet Man* (William Wellman, 1932) with Edward G. Robinson and Loretta Young.

42 Takahashi, "Sekaiteki meiyu no eiga toshite" [As a film of the world famous actor], 124.

43 *Kinema Junpo* 442 (21 July 1932): 53.

44 *Kinema Junpo* 443 (1 August 1932): 71. The print of *Taiyo wa higashi yori* is not extant.

45 *Nichibei Jiho* (29 December 1928): 3.

46 This was the first talking picture in Japan in which Hayakawa appeared.

47 For a more detailed discussion on the historical transformation of *jidaigeki*, see Yoshimoto, *Kurosawa*, 205–22.

48 *Kinema Junpo* 475 (1 July 1933): 74.

49 *Kinema Junpo* 473 (11 June 1932): 6.

50 *Kinema Junpo* 477 (21 July 1933): 10.

51 *Keijo Nippo* (24 April 1935): n.p., *Sessue Hayakawa Scrapbook*, Hirasaki National Resource Center, Japanese American National Museum.

52 Hayakawa Sesshu, "Kicho geidan" [Talk on art on his return], 26. Another film about Nichiren, *Kokuchu Nichiren daishonin* [The great Nichiren, the pillar of

Japan] (Nakajima Jitsuzo, 1935), was made at Daito studio in the same year. After *Nichiren*, Hayakawa even established the Japan Buddhist Theater Group and appeared in a play that depicted the life of the Buddha, written by Hayakawa himself. "Hayakawa Sesshu: Jijo shoden (jo) [Sessue Hayakawa: A short autobiography (1)]," *Sande Mainichi* (20 November 1949): 16.

53 Hubler, "Honorable 'Bad Guy,'" 149.

54 "Enter the 'Villain,'" *Newsweek* (17 March 1958): 62.

55 *Pyongyang Mainichi* (20 April 1935), evening edition, n.p., in *Sessue Hayakawa Scrapbook*, Hirasaki National Resource Center, Japanese American National Museum.

56 The Japanese actress Ri Koran (aka Li Xianglan, aka Shirley Yamaguchi), who disguised herself as a Chinese star in propaganda films for Japanese imperialism, existed as such a pan-Asian star, especially in the 1930s and 1940s. See Stephenson, "'Her Traces Are Found Everywhere,'" 222–45.

57 Hubler, "Honorable 'Bad Guy,'" 148–49.

58 *Kinema Junpo* 513 (1 August 1934): 105.

59 *Kinema Junpo* 530 (1 February 1935): 110.

60 Towa shoji had imported German and French films since 1928. Kawakita was willing to export Japanese films to Europe and the United States.

61 *Kinema Junpo* 597 (1 January 1937): 238.

62 Some audiences opposed the film's "anachronistic" depiction of the Japanese family system, "insulting" description of Japanese men, and "ignorant" characterization of Japanese women. "Gijutsu hihyo no hitsuyo" [Necessity for criticism on techniques], *Kinema Junpo* 603 (1 March 1937): 11. A fan criticized Fanck's "infantile point of view on Japan" and his "primitivist" view of Japanese people. *Kinema Junpo* 604 (11 March 1937): 83.

63 *Kinema Junpo* 588 (21 September 1936): 24; *Kinema Junpo* 600 (1 February 1937): 27–28.

64 Uchida, "Futatsu no *Atarashiki tsuchi*" [Two *Die Tochter des Samurai*], 10.

65 Even the heroine of the film, Hara Setsuko, who played Hayakawa's daughter, was criticized for her Westernized image in the late 1930s after she came back to Japan from the promotional tour in Germany. Like Hayakawa, her Westernized image, which had been used for the fascist propaganda film, was used for a completely different purpose after World War II: promoting American-style democracy in films, including Kurosawa Akira's controversial film *Waga seishun ni kui nashi* (*No Regrets for Our Youth*, 1949). Hara later appeared in many films by Ozu Yasujiro and played roles that were considered as "typically Japanese."

66 Okudaira, "Eiga no kokka tosei" [The state regulation of cinema], 238–55.

67 "Honra Japonesa," *Cine-Journal* (Portugal) 122 (14 February 1938): n.p.

68 *Variety* 126.9 (12 May 1937): 15.

69 *Tokyo Nichinichi Shinbun* (13 March 1937), in *Shinbun shusei Showa hennenshi* 12-I, 757. *Yoshiwara* was not released in Japan until 1946.

70 Other films were *Tempête sur l'Asia* (*Storm over Asia*, Richard Oswald, 1938),

Patrouille blanche (Christian Chamborant, 1942), *Le Soleil de minuit* (Bernard Roland, 1943), *Malaria* (Jean Gourguet, 1943), *Quartier chinois* (René Sti, 1946), *Le Cabaret du grand large* (René Jayet, 1946). *Macao, L'enfer du Jeu* was banned in France because it was not pro-Nazi. It was released in 1950 in the United States, when the Korean War drew more interest in Asia, with two different new titles, *Mask of Korea* and *Gambling Hell. Variety* 179.9 (9 August 1950): 9.

71 *Newsweek* (14 November 1949): 91. Hayakawa regarded himself as stars of these films. He praised Bogart because Bogart let him act as he wanted. In contrast, Hayakawa criticized Colbert for being afraid of losing her star status in the film and for being irritated with Hayakawa's "restrained" performance. "Hariuddo konjaku: Hayakawa Sesshu miyage banashi" [Hollywood, the past and the present: Sessue Hayakawa talks], *Shukan Asahi* 1554 (23 October 1949): 22. In *Tokyo Joe*, Hayakawa's fiendish Japanese smuggler, who pretends to be an entrepreneur of a commercial airline but, in fact, tries to bring back a trio of Japanese ex-generals to Japan from post–World War II Korea, was "typical Japanese malevolence" but simultaneously "suave." *New York Times* (27 October 1949): 35; *Variety* 176.5 (12 October 1949): 6.

72 *Newsweek* (14 November 1949): 92.

73 Edwin Schallert, "Women's War Story Inspired," A8; *Motion Picture Herald* 178.6 (11 February 1950): 185.

74 Schallert, "Hal Roach Television Plans Move into High; Hayakawa Will Return," 7.

75 Schallert, "Women's War Story Inspired," A8.

76 *Kinema News* (10 May 1949): 2.

77 "In This Corner, Sessue Hayakawa," *New York Times* (9 January 1949): X5. In 1949 at a gallery in Los Angeles there was an exhibition that showed the paintings Hayakawa had done in France. The report of it in the *Los Angeles Times* again emphasized the ambivalent characteristic of Hayakawa's work between Japaneseness and Westernization: "His [Hayakawa's] style infuses into traditional Chinese-Japanese brush drawings [a] charming delicacy of tone and color evidently learned from French Impressionism." "Oriental Style Works Shown by Hayakawa," *Los Angeles Times* (27 February 1949): D4.

78 *Sukurin Suteji* 174 (6 September 1949): n.p.

79 Quoted from an unidentified newspaper clipping. *Ito Daisuke Bunko* [Ito Daisuke Collection], Box 20, Kyoto Bunka Hakubutsukan.

80 "Hayakawa Sesshu: Jijo shoden (Ge)" [Sessue Hayakawa: A short autobiography (2)], *Sande Mainichi* (27 November 1949): 22.

81 *Hollywood Reporter* (10 December 1948): 5.

82 The period of postwar occupation of Japan began with the Japanese surrender to the Allies in August 1945 and continued until signing of the San Francisco Peace Treaty in April 1952. Australia, the Soviet Union, China, and the United States officially administered the occupation, but for all intents and purposes it was a U.S.-run operation.

83 Nogami, *Seirin no o Hayakawa Sesshu*, 192.

84 Mori Masayuki, who played the husband in *Rashomon*, and Sugimura Haruko, who appeared in Ozu's films many times, were among them.

85 The director Ito Daisuke, who initiated the rise of *jidaigeki* after 1923 with his modern techniques, had been a big fan of Hayakawa. T. Saiki, *Eiga dokuhon* [Cinema reader], 135.

86 Hayakawa's Japanese character in *Harukanari haha no kuni*, Joe Hayami, commits a crime in December 1915. Because of the crime, Hayami leaves Japan for Latin America and does not come back to Japan for twenty years. When he finally comes back, his former sweetheart has been married to another man and has a daughter. Hayami protects them from gangsters. After the fight he decides to leave Japan, where there is no place for him. The story of Hayami consciously incorporates Hayakawa's own life story. When *The Cheat* was released in December 1915, Japanese spectators treated Hayakawa as if he had committed a crime. He was not able to stay in Japan when he came back twenty years later and so left for France.

87 *Daiei Kyoto sakuhin annai*, 193, in *Ito Daisuke Bunko*, Box 14, Kyoto Bunka Hakubutsukan.

88 *Jiji Shinpo* (2 November 1950): 4.

89 "Amerika orai" [To and from America], *Mainichi Gurafu* (15 November 1949): 20–21.

90 These exotic films were not necessarily popular among domestic audiences. Ironically, films by Ozu or Naruse Mikio that were set in contemporary Japan were regarded as "too Japanese" and were not exported eagerly but rather retained within the domestic market. There was a double standard or two different forms of Japaneseness here: Japaneseness for foreign audiences and Japaneseness for domestic audiences.

91 *Shishi no za*, production plan, *Ito Daisuke Bunko*, Box 29, Kyoto Bunka Hakubutsukan.

92 "Hariuddo konjaku: Hayakawa Sesshu miyage banashi" [Hollywood, the past and the present: Sessue Hayakawa talks], *Shukan Asahi* 1554 (23 October 1949): 23.

93 Hayakawa Sesshu, "Kicho geidan," 27–28.

94 Ross, "Sessue Hayakawa Prefers the Wicked Roles," n.p., in *SHE*.

95 *Variety* 219.10 (3 August 1960): 7.

96 Atkinson, "Theatre," 26.

97 Thirer, "Sessue Hayakawa—Then and Now," n.p.

98 Ross, "Sessue Hayakawa Prefers the Wicked Roles," n.p., in *SHE*.

99 "Risen Sun," *New Yorker* 35 (1 August 1959): 16.

100 "Kenzainari Sesshu" [Sessue still good in health], *Shukan Asahi* (30 March 1958): 47–49.

101 "Sekai o butai ni suru otoko Hayakawa Sesshu shi" [The man who plays in the world: Mr. Sessue Hayakawa], *Shukan Yomiuri* (20 September 1959): 43, 47.

102 "Anata e adobaisu" [Advice to you], *Shukan Yomiuri* (2 March 1958): 90.

103 "Anata e adobaisu" [Advice to you], *Shukan Yomiuri* (2 March 1958): 90.

104   Paul L. Montgomery, "Sessue Hayakawa Is Dead at 83 [sic]; Silents Star Was in 'River Kwai,'" *New York Herald Tribune* (25 November 1973): n.p., in SHE.

105   "Moto Hariuddo haiyu, Hayakawa Sesshu, shishite ichidai gimon: Kare wa hontoni kokusai suta dattanoka" [The ex-Hollywood actor, Sessue Hayakawa, died with a big question: Was he really an international star?], *Shukan Bunshun* 756 (17 December 1973): 176, 181–82.

FILMOGRAPHY

NEW YORK MOTION PICTURE COMPANY
(1914–15)

O Mimi San (Domino, Reginald Barker, 5 February 1914)
The Courtship of O San (Domino, Barker, 26 February 1914)
The Geisha (Kay-Bee, Barker, 10 April 1914)
Love's Sacrifice (Kay-Bee, George Osborne, 1 May 1914) (Tsuruko Aoki only)
The Ambassador's Envoy (Ince?, 28 May 1914)
A Tragedy of the Orient (Broncho, Barker, 10 June 1914)
A Relic of Old Japan (Domino, Barker, 11 June 1914)
The Wrath of the Gods (aka *The Destruction of Sakurajima*, Domino Special, Barker, 22 June 1914)
Star of the North (Domino, Jay Hunt, 16 July 1914)
The Curse of Caste (Domino, Barker, 30 July 1914)
The Village 'Neath the Sea (Domino, Hunt, 27 August 1914)
Death Mask (Kay-Bee, Hunt, 25 September 1914)
The Typhoon (NYMPC/Paramount, Barker, 8 October 1914)
Nipped (Domino, Osborne, 19 November 1914)
The Vigil (Domino, Osborne, 3 December 1914)
The Last of the Line (aka *Pride of Race*, Domino, Hunt, 24 December 1914)
The Famine (Kay-Bee, Osborne, 29 January 1915)
The Chinatown Mystery (Broncho, Barker, 10 February 1915)

JESSE L. LASKY FEATURE PLAY COMPANY
(1915–18)

After Five (Oscar Apfel and Cecil B. DeMille, 28 January 1915)
The Clue (James Neill and Frank Reicher [credited as Frank Reichert], 8 July 1915)
The Secret Sin (Frank Reicher, 21 October 1915)
The Cheat (Cecil B. DeMille, 4 December 1915)
Temptation (Cecil B. DeMille, 30 December 1915)
Alien Souls (Reichert, 11 May 1916)
The Honorable Friend (Edward J. Le Saint, 24 August 1916)
The Soul of Kura San (Le Saint, 30 October 1916)
The Victoria Cross (William C. DeMille, 14 December 1916)
Each to His Kind (Le Saint, 5 February 1917)

The Bottle Imp (Marshall Neilan, 26 March 1917)
The Jaguar's Claws (Neilan, 11 June 1917)
Forbidden Paths (Robert T. Thornby, 5 July 1917)
Hashimura Togo (William C. DeMille, 19 August 1917)
The Call of the East (George H. Melford, 15 October 1917)
The Secret Game (William C. DeMille, 3 December 1917)
The Hidden Pearls (Melford, 18 February 1918)
The Honor of His House (William C. DeMille, 1 April 1918)
The White Man's Law (James Young, 6 May 1918)
The Bravest Way (Melford, 16 June 1918)
The City of Dim Faces (Melford, 15 July 1918)

HAWORTH PICTURES CORPORATION (1918–20)
HAYAKAWA FEATURE PLAY COMPANY (1921)
R-C PICTURES (1922)

His Birthright (William Worthington, 1 or 8 September 1918)
Banzai (1918)
The Temple of Dusk (Young, 13 or 20 October 1918)
Bonds of Honor (Worthington, 19 January 1919)
A Heart in Pawn (Worthington, 10 March 1919)
The Courageous Coward (Worthington, 14 April 1919)
His Debt (Worthington, 25 May 1919)
The Man Beneath (Worthington, 6 July 1919)
The Gray Horizon (Worthington, 18 August 1919)
The Dragon Painter (Worthington, 28 September or 4 October 1919)
The Illustrious Prince (Worthington, 2 November 1919)
The Tong Man (Worthington, 14 December 1919)
The Beggar Prince (Worthington, 25 January 1920)
The Brand of Lopez (Joseph De Grasse, April 1920)
The Devil's Claim (Charles Swickard, 2 May 1920)
Li Ting Lang (Swickard, July 1920)
An Arabian Knight (Swickard, 22 August 1920)
The First Born (Colin Campbell, 30 January 1921)
Black Roses (Campbell, 22 May 1921)
Where Lights Are Low (Campbell, 4 September 1921)
The Swamp (Campbell, 30 October 1921)
Five Days to Live (Norman Dawn, 8 January 1922)
The Vermilion Pencil (Dawn, 19 March 1922)

1922 AND AFTER

Night Life in Hollywood (Fred Caldwell and Jack Pratt, 1922)
La Bataille (*The Danger Line*, E. E. Violet, 1923)

Sen Yan's Devotion (A. E. Coleby, 1924)

J'ai tué! (*I Have Killed*, Roger Lion, 1924)

The Great Prince Shan (Coleby, 1924)

The Man Who Laughs Last (aka *The Man Who Laughed*, 1929)

Daughter of the Dragon (Lloyd Corrigan, 1931)

Around the World in 80 Minutes with Douglas Fairbanks (Douglas Fairbanks and Victor Fleming, 1931)

Taiyo wa higashi yori [The sun rises from the east] (Shochiku, Hayakawa Sesshu, 1932)

Nanko fushi [Father and son of Honorable Kusunoki] (Uzumasa Hassei, Ikeda Tomiyasu, 1933)

Bakugeki hiko tai [Bomber pilots] (Uzumasa Hassei, Saegusa Genjiro, 1934)

Araki Mataemon: Tenka no Iga goe [Araki Mataemon: Beyond the nationally famous Iga] (Uzumasa Hassei, Katsumi Yotaro, 1934)

Tojin Okichi [Okichi the China girl] (Shinko Tokyo, Fuyusima Taizo, 1935)

Kuni o mamoru Nichiren [Nichiren, who protects Japan] (Shinko Tokyo, Sone Chiharu, 1935)

Atarshiki tsuchi (*Die Tochter des Samurai*, Arnold Fanck and Itami Mansaku, 1937)

Yoshiwara (Max Ophuls, 1937)

Forfaiture (Marcel L'Herbier, 1937)

Tempête sur l'Asia (*Storm over Asia*, Richard Oswald, 1938)

Macao, L'enfer du jeu (*Gambling Hell*, aka *Mask of Korea*, Jean Delannoy, 1939)

Patrouille blanche (Christian Chamborant, 1942)

Tornavara (Jean Dreville, 1943)

Le Soleil de minuit (Bernard Roland, 1943)

Malaria (Jean Gourguet, 1943)

Quartier chinois (René Sti, 1946)

Le Cabaret du grand large (René Jayet, 1946)

Tokyo Joe (Stuart Heisler, 1949)

Three Came Home (Jean Negulesco, 1949)

Harukanari haha no kuni [Far away mother's country] (Daiei, Ito Daisuke, 1950)

Re Mizeraburu [*Les Miserables*] (Toyoko, Part 1 "Kami to akuma" [God and devil] by Ito Daisuke, and Part 2 "Ai to jiyu no hata" [Flag of love and liberty] by Makino Masahiro, 1950)

Akoroshi [The royal forty-seven samurai] (Toei, Sasaki Yasushi, 1953)

Higeki no shogun Yamashita Hobun [The tragic general, Yamashita Hobun] (Toei, Saeki Kiyoshi, 1953)

Kurama Tengu to Katsu Kaishu [Kurama Tengu and Katsu Kaishu] (Shintoho, Ikeda Toyoyasu, 1953)

Nihon yaburezu [Japan did not lose] (Shintoho, Abe Yutaka, 1954)

The House of Bamboo (Samuel Fuller, 1955)

Yarodomo omote e dero [Guys, get out] (Toei, Kobayashi Tsuneo, 1956)

Ikare! Rikidozan [Get angry! Rikidozan] (Toei, Kobayashi Shigehiro, 1956)

The Bridge on the River Kwai (David Lean, 1957)

The Geisha Boy (Frank Tashlin, 1958)
Green Mansions (Mel Ferrer, 1959)
Hell to Eternity (Phil Karlson, 1960)
Swiss Family Robinson (Ken Annakin, 1960)
The Big Wave (Ted Danielewski, 1962)
Daydreamer (Jules Bass, 1962)
Bosu wa ore no kenju de [With my gun, Boss] (Toei, Murayama Shinji, 1966)
Junjo nijuso [Naïve duet] (Shochiku, Umezu Meijiro, 1967)

BIBLIOGRAPHY

ARCHIVAL MATERIALS

Cecil B. DeMille Scrapbook. The New York Public Library for the Performing Arts, Robinson Locke Collection.

Harry and Roy Aitken Papers, 1909–1940. State Historical Society of Wisconsin, Archives Division.

Ince/Reed Collection. The Museum of Modern Art, New York.

Ito Daisuke Bunko [Ito Daisuke Collection]. Kyoto Bunka Hakubutsukan [The Museum of Kyoto].

The Motion Picture Commission of the State of New York File. New York State Archives, Cultural Education Center, Albany.

National Board of Review Records, 1907–1971. The New York Public Library, Special Collections.

Paramount Script Collection. Center for Motion Picture Study, Margaret Herrick Library, Beverly Hills.

"Popular Arts Project: Sessue Hayakawa." Oral History Research Office, Columbia University, 1959.

Script of *The Cheat* and *Temptation*. University of Southern California, Cine-TV Library, Special Collection.

Script of *The Cheat* (1931). New York State Archives, Cultural Education Center, Albany.

Sessue Hayakawa File. Japanese American National Museum, Los Angeles.

Sessue Hayakawa File. The Museum of Modern Art, New York.

Sessue Hayakawa: Locke Collection Envelope 659. The New York Public Library for the Performing Arts, Robinson Locke Collection.

Sessue Hayakawa: Scrapbook. The New York Public Library for the Performing Arts, Robinson Locke Collection. Abbreviated in the "Books and Articles" section of the bibliography as *SHS*.

Synopses of Productions Made by Thomas H. Ince During the Period of April 1912 to August 1915. UCLA Research Library, Special Collections.

Thomas H. Ince Scrapbook. The New York Public Library for the Performing Arts, Robinson Locke Collection.

SELECTED PERIODICALS

Bioscope, 3 February 1916–26 October 1922.

Exhibitor's Herald (*Exhibitor's Film Exchange*; *Exhibitor's Herald and Motography*; *Motion Picture Herald*), 24 June 1915–3 June 1922.

Exhibitor's Trade Review, 16 December 1916–25 March 1922.

Katsudo Gaho [Motion picture graphic], January 1917–September 1922.

Katsudo Kurabu [Motion picture club], September 1919–July 1925.

Katsudo no Sekai [Active world, or Motion picture world], January 1916–April 1919.

Katsudo Shashin Zasshi [Motion picture magazine], May 1915–December 1921.

Katsudo Zasshi [Movie magazine], September 1919–December 1925.

Kinema Junpo (aka *The Movie News*), July 1919–present.

Kinema News, 10 May 1949–31 May 1949.

Kinema Record, December 1913–November/December 1917 (formerly *Film Record*, October–November 1913).

Los Angeles Times, 30 April 1915–22 December 1957.

Motion Picture Classic, December 1916–May 1926.

Motion Picture Magazine, January 1915–April 1922.

Motion Picture News, 10 January 1914–15 April 1922.

Motography, 19 November 1911–23 March 1918.

Moving Picture World, 14 March 1908–15 April 1922.

New York Clipper, 15 December 1906–1 August 1914.

New York Dramatic Mirror, 2 November 1910–March 1922.

New York Times Film Reviews 1913–1968. Vol. 1: 1913–1931. New York: Arno, 1970.

Nichibei Shinbun (*Japanese American News*), 25 December 1915–16 September 1922.

Nyu Yoku Shimpo, 18 September 1915–6 September 1924.

Picture Progress (*Paramount Magazine*), January 1915–May 1917.

Rafu Shimpo, 8 December 1914–26 January 1923.

Reel Life, 23 August 1913–9 June 1917.

Shinbun shusei Taisho hennenshi [Periodical history of Taisho through newspapers]. Tokyo: Meiji Taisho Showa Shinbun Kenkyukai, 1980–1987.

Shinbun shusei Showa hennenshi [Periodical history of Showa through newspapers]. Tokyo: Meiji Taisho Showa Shinbun Kenkyukai, 1958–1990.

Taisho nyusu jiten [Taisho news encyclopedia]. 8 vols. Tokyo: Mainichi komyunike-shonzu, 1988.

Tokyo Asahi Shinbun [Tokyo Asahi newspaper], 18 February 1919–29 August 1922.

Variety, 2 February 1907–12 November 1960.

Wid's Daily (formerly *Wid's Films and Film Folk Independent Criticisms of Features* and *Wid's Independent Reviews of Feature Films*), 9 September 1915–15 August 1920.

BOOKS AND ARTICLES

Abe, Yu. "Appare 'Wongu' no koi" [Love of great Wong]. *Fujin Saron* 4.9 (September 1932): 124–28.

Abel, Richard. *French Film Theory and Criticism: A History/Anthology 1907–1939*. Volume 1, *1907–1929*. Princeton, N.J.: Princeton University Press, 1988.

Abramson, Harold J. "Assimilation and Pluralism." *Harvard Encyclopedia of American Ethnic Groups*, ed. Stephen Thernstorm, 150–60. Cambridge, Mass.: Harvard University Press, 1980.

Affron, Charles. *Lillian Gish: Her Legend, Her Life*. New York: Scribner's, 2001.

———. *Star Acting: Gish, Garbo, Davis*. New York: Dutton, 1977.

Amano, Chugi. "Beikoku katsudo shashin no chimata yori" [News from American motion pictures], *Katsudo Gaho* 3.9 (September 1919): 164–65.

"Amerika orai" [To and from America]. *Mainichi Gurafu* (15 November 1949): 20–21.

Andrews, Peter. "The Vermilion Pencil." *Motion Picture Magazine* 23.4 (April 1922): 49–53, 102.

Aokusasho. "Kamome tobu Korea-maru no kanpan de" [On the deck of the *Korea* where seagulls fly], *Katsudo Gaho* 4.6 (June 1920): 50–51.

Aoyama, Yukio. "Aren kun no Nihon kan" [Mr. Allen's view on Japan]. *Katsudo Shashin Zasshi* 3.12 (December 1917): 88–89.

———. "Beikoku katsudo shashin kai" [American motion picture world]. *Rafu Shimpo* 5951 (18 December 1922): 15.

———. "Beikoku katsudo shashin no miyako yori" [From the capital of the American motion picture]. *Katsudo Shashin Zasshi* 3.10 (October 1917): 44–47.

———. "Beikoku katsudo shashin no miyako yori (12)." *Katsudo Shashin Zasshi* 4.7 (July 1918): 35–41.

———. "Beikoku katsudo shashin no miyako yori (13)." *Katsudo Shashin Zasshi* 4.8 (August 1918): 58–65.

———. "Beikoku no eiga to Hirai Yoshitaka kun" [American films and Mr. Yoshitaka Hirai]. *Katsudo Zasshi* 8.5 (May 1922): 116–21.

———. "Beikoku sukurin geppo" [American screen monthly]. *Katsudo Zasshi* 8.8 (August 1922): 136–40.

———. "Gimon datta Hayakawa Sesshu no kyukin" [Sessue Hayakawa's salary, which had been unknown]. *Katsudo Zasshi* 10.1 (January 1924): 50–54.

———. *Hariuddo eiga okoku no kaibo* [Anatomy of Hollywood film kingdom]. Tokyo: Hakubundo, 1929.

———. "Haro Tomasu" [Hello, Thomas]. *Katsudo Zasshi* 9.11 (November 1923): 68–71.

———. "Nanji no yatoinin wa dareka no shutsuen ni tsuite" [About appearing in *Who's Your Servant?*]. *Katsudo Zasshi* 6.11 (November 1920): 78–82.

———. "Zaibei nihonjin katsudo haiyu hatten shi" [History of progress of Japanese photoplay actors in the U.S.]. *Katsudo Shashin Zasshi* 4.4 (April 1918): 5–11.

Atkinson, Brooks. "Theatre: Japanese Style." *New York Times* (4 June 1959): 26.

Ayase, Hideko. "Waga Sesshu o noroeru hitora e" [To those who curse on Sessue]. *Katsudo Zasshi* 8.12 (December 1922): 154–55.

Azuma (or Higashi), Takeo. "Kaigai ni odoru hiro Sesshu Hayakawa to Aoki Tsuruko" [International heroes, Sessue Hayakawa and Tsuruko Aoki]. *Fujin Gaho* 290 (June 1930): 152–55.

Azuma, Yonosuke (or Higashi). "Aoki Tsuruko to gyunabe o kakomu" [Having beef for a dinner with Tsuruko Aoki]. *Katsudo Kurabu* 3.8 (August 1920): 44–46.

Baily, Leslie. *The Gilbert and Sullivan Book*. London: Spring, 1952.

Bakhtin, M. M. *The Dialogic Imagination: Four Essays*. Ed. Michael Holquist. Trans. Caryl Emerson and Michael Holquist. Austin: University of Texas Press, 1981.

Barbas, Samantha. "The Political Spectator: Censorship, Protests and the Movie-going Experience, 1912–1922." *Film History* 11.2 (1999): 217–230.

Barber, X. Theodore. "The Roots of Travel Cinema: John L. Stoddard, E. Burton Holmes and the Nineteenth-Century Illustrated Travel Lecture." *Film History* 5.1 (1993): 68–84.

Bardèche, Maurice, and Robert Brasillach. *The History of Motion Pictures*, trans. and ed. Iris Barry. New York: Norton, 1938.

Barrett, Wilton. A. "The Work of the National Board of Review." *Annals of the American Academy of Political and Social Science* 128 (November 1926): 175–86.

Bartlett, Randolph. "The Star Idea Versus the Star System." *Motion Picture Magazine* 18.7 (August 1919): 36–37.

Beauchamp, Cari. *Without Lying Down: Frances Marion and the Powerful Women of Early Hollywood*. Berkeley: University of California Press, 1997.

Bell, Michael. *Primitivism*. London: Methuen, 1972.

Benjamin, Walter. "A Short History of Photography." In *One Way Street and Other Writings*, trans. Edmund Jephcott and Kingsley Shorter, 240–57. London: Verso, 1985.

———. "The Work of Art in the Age of Mechanical Reproduction." In *Illuminations*, ed. Hannah Arendt, trans. Harry Zohn, 217–51. New York: Schocken, 1969.

Bernardi, Joanne. *Writing in Light: The Silent Scenario and the Japanese Pure Film Movement*. Detroit: Wayne State University Press, 2001.

Bhabha, Homi K. *The Location of Culture*. London: Routledge, 1994.

"Biographical Brevities: Sessue Hayakawa." *Picturegoer* (February 1921): 39.

Bliven, Bruce. "The Japanese Problem." *Nation* 112.2900 (2 February 1921): 171–72.

Blum, Richard A. *American Film Acting: The Stanislavski Heritage*. Ann Arbor: UMI Research Press, 1984.

Blumin, Stuart M. "The Hypothesis of Middle-Class Formation in Nineteenth-Century America: A Critique and Some Proposals." *American Historical Review* 90 (1985): 299–338.

Bodeen, Dewitt. "Sessue Hayakawa: First International Japanese Star." *Films in Review* 27.4 (April 1976): 193–208.

Bourne, Randolph. *The Radical Will: Selected Writings 1911–1918*. New York: Urizen, 1977.

Bowser, Eileen. *The Transformation of Cinema 1907–1915*. New York: Scribner's, 1990.

Bowser, Pearl, and Louise Spence. *Writing Himself into History: Oscar Micheaux, His Silent Films, and His Audiences*. New Brunswick, N.J.: Rutgers University Press, 2000.

Brewster, Ben, and Lea Jacobs. *Theatre to Cinema: Stage Pictorialism and the Early Feature Film*. Oxford: Oxford University Press, 1997.

Brock, Alan. "Sessue Hayakawa: American Style." *Classic Film Collector* 27.12 (spring/summer 1970): 12–13.

Brooks, Peter. *The Melodramatic Imagination: Balzac, Henry James, Melodrama, and the Mode of Excess*. 1976. Reprint, New Haven: Yale University Press, 1995.

Brown, Gene, ed. *New York Times Encyclopedia of Film 1896–1928*. New York: New York Times, 1984.

Brown, Jane Converse. "'Fine Arts and Fine People': The Japanese Taste in the American Home, 1876–1916." *Making the American Home: Middle-Class Women and Domestic Material Culture 1840–1940*, ed. Marilyn Ferris Motz and Pat Browne, 121–39. Bowling Green, Ohio: Bowling Green State University Popular Press, 1988.

———. "The 'Japanese Taste': Its Role in the Mission of the American Home and in the Family's Presentation of Itself to the Public as Expressed in Published Sources: 1876–1916." Ph.D. diss., University of Wisconsin, Madison, 1987.

Browne, Nick. "Orientalism as an Ideological Form: American Film Theory in the Silent Period." *Wide Angle* 11.4 (1989): 23–31.

———. "The Undoing of the Other Woman: Madame Butterfly in the Discourse of American Orientalism." *The Birth of Whiteness: Race and the Emergence of U.S. Cinema*, ed. Daniel Bernardi, 227–56. New Brunswick, N.J.: Rutgers University Press, 1996.

Brownlow, Kevin. *Behind the Mask of Innocence: Sex, Violence, Prejudice, Crime: Films of Social Conscience in the Silent Era*. Berkeley: University of California Press, 1990.

Bryers, Leslie. "The Gentleman from Japan." *Motion Picture Magazine* 23.3 (March 1922): 54–55, 109.

Busby, Marquis. "Hayakawa Plays Suave Oriental." *Los Angeles Times* (20 December 1926): A9.

Butler, Judith. *Gender Trouble: Feminism and the Subversion of Identity*. London: Routledge, 1990.

"Can We Assimilate the Japanese?" *Literary Digest* 47.5 (2 August 1913): 165–66.

Card, James. *Seductive Cinema: The Art of Silent Film*. New York: Knopf, 1994.

Carr, Harry. "'First Born' Is Weakling," *Los Angeles Times* (6 February 1921): III-1.

———. "Son of the Samurai." *Motion Picture Classic* 14.7 (July 1922): 31–33, 81.

Carr, Harry C. "Sessue of the Samurai: Hayakawa Is the Proud Old Japanese Caste with the Manners of Modern America." *Motion Picture Classic* 7 (January 1919): 22–23, 68.

Carroll, David. *The Matinee Idols*. New York: Arbor, 1972.

Cavell, Stanley. "What Photography Calls Thinking." *Raritan: A Quarterly Review* 4.4 (spring 1985): 1–21.

Choy, Philip P., Lorraine Dong, and Marlon K. Hom. *The Coming Man: Nineteenth-Century American Perceptions of the Chinese*. Hong Kong: Joint, 1994.

Clair, René. *Cinema: Yesterday and Today*. Trans. Stanley Appelbaum. Ed. R. C. Dale. New York: Dover, 1972.

Cohen, Paula Marantz. *Silent Film and the Triumph of the American Myth*. Oxford: Oxford University Press, 2001.

Colette. *Colette at the Movies: Criticism and Screenplays*. Trans. Sarah W. R. Smith. Ed. Alain Virmaux and Odette Virmaux. 1970. Reprint, New York: Frederick Ungar, 1980.

Conroy, Hilary. "Concerning the Asian-American Experience." In *Ethnic Images in American Film and Television*, ed. Randall M. Miller, 157–69. Philadelphia: Balch Institute, 1978.

Conte-Helme, Marie. *Japan and the North East of England: From 1862 to the Present Day*. London: Althone, 1989.

Cook, Clarence. "Beds and Tables, Stools and Candlesticks-III." *Scribner's Monthly* 11 (1875): 494.

Coontz, Stephanie. *The Social Origins of Private Life: A History of American Families*. London: Verso, 1988.

Copley, Stephen, and Peter Garside, eds. *The Politics of the Picturesque: Literature, Landscape and Aesthetics since 1770*. Cambridge: Cambridge University Press, 1994.

Cortés, Carlos E. "Hollywood Interracial Love: Social Taboo as Screen Titillation." In *Beyond the Stars II: Plot Conventions in American Popular Film*, ed. Paul Loukides and Linda K. Fuller, 21–35. Bowling Green: Bowling Green State University Popular Press, 1991.

Crisp, Colin. *Genre, Myth, and Convention in the French Cinema, 1929–1939*. Bloomington: Indiana University Press, 2002.

Current Biography. New York: H. W. Wilson, 1962.

Daniels, Roger. *Asian America: Chinese and Japanese in the United States since 1850*. Seattle: University of Washington Press, 1988.

———. *The Politics of Prejudice: The Anti-Japanese Movement in California and the Struggle for Exclusion*. Berkeley: University of California Press, 1962.

Deacon, Richard. *Kempei Tai: A History of the Japanese Secret Service*. New York: Beaufort, 1983.

deCordova, Richard. "The Emergence of the Star System in America." In *Stardom: Industry of Desire*, ed. Christine Gledhill, 17–29. London: Routledge, 1991.

———. *Picture Personalities: The Emergence of the Star System in America*. Urbana: University of Illinois Press, 1990.

Deguchi, Takehito. "Nani ga hakujin konpurekkusu o umidashitaka" [What caused white complex?]. In *Nihon eiga to Modanizumu 1920–1930*, ed. Iwamoto Kenji, 104–23. Tokyo: Riburopoto, 1991.

Delluc, Louis. "Beauty in the Cinema." *Le Film* 73 (6 August 1917): 4–5. Translated in Richard Abel, *French Film Theory and Criticism: A History/Anthology 1907–1939*. Vol. 1, *1907–1929*, 137–39. Princeton, N.J.: Princeton University Press, 1988.

Dixon, Royal. *Americanization*. New York: Macmillan, 1916.

Dizikes, John. *Opera in America: A Cultural History*. New Haven, Conn.: Yale University Press, 1993.

Doane, Mary Ann. "The Close-Up: Scale and Detail in the Cinema." *Differences: A Journal of Feminist Cultural Studies* 14.3 (2003): 89–111.

Downer, Lesley. *Madame Sadayakko: The Geisha Who Seduced the West*. London: Review, 2003.

Du Bois, W. E. B. *The Souls of Black Folk*. 1903. Reprint, New York: Penguin, 1982.

Dullac, Germaine. *Écrits sur le cinéma (1919–1937)*. Paris: Paris Experimental, 1994.

Dumenil, Lynn. *The Modern Temper: American Culture and Society in the 1920s.* New York: Hill, 1995.

Dyer, Richard. *Stars.* London: BFI, 1979.

Easterfield, Harry Carr. "The Japanese Point of View: And Incidentally a Chat with Hayakawa." *Motion Picture Story Magazine* (15 April 1918): 33–35, 119.

Elliot, Harvey. "Hollywood's Yellow Streak." *After Dark* (September 1977): 76–78.

"Enter the 'Villain.'" *Newsweek* (17 March 1958): 62.

Epstein, Jean. *Écrits sur le Cinéma 1921–1953.* Vol. 1, *1921–1947.* 1957. Reprint, Paris: Seghers, 1974.

———. "Grossissement." In *Bonjour Cinema*, 93–108. Paris: Editions de la sirène, 1921. Translated and reprinted in *October* 3 (spring 1977): 9–15. Reprinted, with changes, in Richard Abel, *French Film Theory and Criticism: A History/Anthology 1907–1939.* Vol. 1, *1907–1929*, 235–41. Princeton, N.J.: Princeton University Press, 1988.

———. "Magnification and Other Writings." Trans. Stuart Liebman. *October* 3 (spring 1977): 9–25.

———. "The Senses I (b)." In *Bonjour Cinema*, 27–44. Paris: Editions de la sirène, 1921. Translated and reprinted in *After Image* 10 (autumn 1981): 9–16. Reprinted in Richard Abel, *French Film Theory and Criticism: A History/Anthology 1907–1939.* Vol. 1, *1907–1929*, 241–46. Princeton, N.J.: Princeton University Press, 1988.

"Ethnological Basis of the Japanese Claim to Be a White Race." *Current Opinion* 55 (July 1913): 38–39.

Evans, Delght. "West Is East." *Photoplay* 20.4 (October 1921): 30.

Feldman, Charles Matthew. *The National Board of Censorship (Review) of Motion Pictures, 1909–1922.* New York: Arno, 1977.

Fenollosa, Mary McNeil. *The Dragon Painter.* Boston: Little, Brown, 1906.

Fernett, Gene. *American Film Studios: An Historical Encyclopedia.* Jefferson, N.C.: McFarland, 1988.

Ferry, J., and Y. Moreno. "Sessue Hayakawa." *Tras La Pantalla: Galeria de Artistas Cinematograficos* 21 (16 April 1921): 1–16.

Fescourt, Henri, and Jean-Louis Bouquet. *L'Idée et l'écran: Opinions sur le cinéma*, vol. 1. Paris: Haberschill and Sergent, 1925.

Field, Charles K. "A Japanese Idol on the American Screen: A 'Close-up' of the Hayakawas on the New Rialto." *Sunset* 37 (July 1916): 22–25, 72–73.

Fletcher, Adele Whitely. "The Orient on the Subway." *Motion Picture Magazine* 20.9 (October 1920): 52–53, 99.

Fox, Dennis. "Silent Film Star Guided by Zen." *Japan Times* (21 June 1987): 8.

"From Out the Flowery Kingdom." *Motion Picture Classic* (November 1918: n.p.). In *SHS*: 167–68.

Fujiki, Hideaki. "American Cinema Reshaping Japanese Culture: The Beauties of the Body and Expressions, and Tanizaki Junichiro." Paper presented at the annual meeting of the Society for Cinema and Media Studies, 6 March 2004, Atlanta.

Fuller, Karla Rae. "Hollywood Goes Oriental: CaucAsian Performance in American Cinema." Ph.D. diss., Northwestern University, 1997.

Funahashi, Kazuo. "Hayakawa Sesshu, Oini kataru" [Sessue Hayakawa talks a lot].
    Shinario [Scenario] 49.12 (December 1993): 58–61.
Gaddis, Pearl. "The Romance of Nippon Land." *Motion Picture Classic* (December
    1916): 18–20.
Geltzer, George. "The Complete Career of Reginald Barker." *Griffithiana* 32/33 (Sep-
    tember 1988): 245–51.
Genette, Gérard. *Narrative Discourse: An Essay in Method.* Ithaca, N.Y.: Cornell Uni-
    versity Press, 1980.
Geraghty, Christine. "Re-examining Stardom: Questions of Texts, Bodies and Perfor-
    mance." In *Reinventing Film Studies*, ed. Christine Gledhill and Linda Williams,
    183–201. London: Arnold, 2000.
Gergely, Emro Joseph. "Hungarian Drama in New York: American Adaptations
    1908–1940." Ph.D. diss., University of Pennsylvania, 1947.
"Germany Flirting with the Orient." *Literary Digest* 54.12 (24 March 1917): 808.
Gerow, Aaron. "One Print in the Age of Mechanical Reproduction: Film Industry
    and Culture in 1910s Japan," http://www.latrobe.edu.au/screeningthepast/
    firstrelease/fr1100/agfr11e.rtf. Accessed 20 June 2006.
————. "Writing a Pure Cinema: Articulations of Early Japanese Film." Ph.D. diss.,
    University of Iowa, 1996.
Gevinson, Alan, ed. *American Film Institute Catalog: Within Our Gates: Ethnicity in
    American Feature Films, 1911–1960.* Berkeley: University of California Press,
    1997.
Gleason, Philip. "American Identity and Americanization." *Harvard Encyclopedia
    of American Ethnic Groups*, ed. Stephen Thernstorm, 31–58. Cambridge, Mass.:
    Harvard University Press, 1980.
Gluck, Carol. *Japan's Modern Myths: Ideology in the Late Meiji Period.* Princeton, N.J.:
    Princeton University Press, 1985.
Goll, Claire. "Amerikanisches Kino." *Die neue Schaubühne* 2.6 (1920): 164–65.
Gonda, Yasunosuke. "Minshu goraku mondai" [Issues of mass entertainment] (1921).
    In *Gonda Yasunosuke chosaku shu dai 1 kan* [Gonda Yasunosuke collection vol. 1].
    Tokyo: Bunwa shobo, 1974.
————. *Katsudo shashin no genri oyobi oyo* [Principles of motion pictures and their
    application]. Tokyo: Uchida rokakuho, 1914.
Gong, Stephen. "Zen and the Art of Motion Picture Making." *Program of 1982 Asian-
    American International Film Festival* (June 1982): 9–18.
————. "Zen Warrior of the Celluloid (Silent) Years." *Asian American Perspectives/
    Bridge* 8.2 (winter 1982–83): 37–41.
Greene, Daniel Crosby. "Anti-Japanese Prejudice." *Outlook* (9 July 1910): 539.
Griffis, William Elliot. "Japan and the United States: Are the Japanese Mongolian?"
    North American Review 197 (June 1913): 721–33.
————. "Our Honor and Shame with Japan." *North American Review* 200 (October
    1914): 566–75.
Grimsted, David. *Melodrama Unveiled: American Theater and Culture 1800–1850.*
    Berkeley: University of California Press, 1968.

Gulick, Sidney L. *American Democracy and Asiatic Citizenship*. New York: Scribner's, 1918.

———. *The American Japanese Problem: A Study of the Racial Relations of the East and the West*. New York: Scribner's, 1914.

———. "Nihonjin wa douka shiuruya (1)" [Are the Japanese assimilable?]. *Rafu Shimpo* 3581 (8 August 1915): 2.

———. "Nihonjin wa douka shiuruya (2)." *Rafu Shimpo* 3582 (10 August 1915): 2.

Hammond, Robert M., and Charles Ford. "French End Games: For Some American Silent Stars a Trip Abroad Was a Tonic for Ailing Careers." *Films in Review* 34.6 (June–July 1983): 329–33.

Hanayagi, Tamio. "Katsukai enma cho: Hayakawa Sesshu no maki" [Evaluation book of the motion picture world: Sessue Hayakawa]. *Katsudo Zasshi* 8.9 (September 1922): 74–75.

Handy, Truman B. "Kipling Was Wrong!: West Isn't West, nor Is East East, as Far as the Hayakawas Are Concerned." *Photoplay* 17.1 (December 1919): 51, 124.

Hansen, Miriam. *Babel and Babylon: Spectatorship in American Silent Film*. Cambridge, Mass.: Harvard University Press, 1991.

———. "Fallen Women, Rising Stars, New Horizons: Shanghai Silent Film as Vernacular Modernism." *Film Quarterly* 54.1 (2000): 10–22.

———. "The Mass Production of the Senses: Classical Cinema as Vernacular Modernism." *Modernism/Modernity* 6.2 (1999): 59–77.

———. "Pleasure, Ambivalence, Identification: Valentino and Female Spectatorship." *Cinema Journal* 25.4 (summer 1986): 6–32.

Hanson, Patricia King, and Alan Gevinson, eds. *The American Film Institute Catalog of Motion Pictures Produced in the United States: Feature Films, 1911–1920*. Berkeley: University of California Press, 1989.

Harootunian, H. D. "Introduction: A Sense of an Ending and the Problem of Taisho." In *Japan in Crisis: Essays on Taisho Democracy*, ed. Bernard Silberman and H. D. Harootunian, 3–28. Princeton, N.J.: Princeton University Press, 1974.

Harris, Neil. *Cultural Excursions: Marketing Appetites and Cultural Tastes in Modern America*. Chicago: University of Chicago Press, 1990.

Harrison, Louis Reeves. "Eyes and Lips." *MPW* 8.67 (18 February 1911): 348–49.

Hashikawa, Bunzo. *Oka monogatari* [Story of yellow peril]. 1976. Reprint, Tokyo: Iwanami, 2000.

"Hayakawa, Japanese Screen Star." *Literary Digest* (3 November 1917): 70, 72.

Hayakawa, Kintaro. "Sesshu zatsuwa" [Hayakawa talks]. *Nichibei Jiho* [Japanese-American commercial weekly] 1044 (16 July 1921): 8.

Hayakawa, Sesshu. "Katsudo shashin ni yakusha toshite seiko suru yoso" [Elements (needed) to become successful as a motion picture actor]. *Katsudo Gaho* 2.11 (November 1918): 117.

———. "Kicho geidan" [Talk on art on his return]. *Eiga Hyoron* (March 1950): 24–31.

Hayakawa, Sessue. *The Bandit Prince*. New York: Macaulay, 1926.

———. *Zen Showed Me the Way . . . to Peace, Happiness and Tranquility*. Indianapolis: Bobbs-Merrill, 1960.

Hayakawa, Sessue, Mrs. "Mrs. Sessue Hayakawa Talks; Loyal to Actor in Woe." *Los Angeles Times* (14 December 1931): A2.

Hayakawa, Yukio. "Heaven and Hell: The Legend of Hollywood Star—Sessue Hayakawa (1)." *The Rafu Magazine* 1.8 (14 August 1998): 3–4, 10.

———. "Heaven and Hell: The Legend of Hollywood Star—Sessue Hayakawa (2)." *Shinshokurin* 18 (July 1997): 84–101.

———. "Heaven and Hell: The Legend of Hollywood Star—Sessue Hayakawa (3)." *Shinshokurin* 19 (November 1997): 82–99.

———. "Heaven and Hell: The Legend of Hollywood Star—Sessue Hayakawa (4)." *Shinshokurin* 20 (March 1998): 34–49.

———. "Heaven and Hell: The Legend of Hollywood Star—Sessue Hayakawa (5)." *Shinshokurin* 22 (November 1998): 76–84.

———. "Heaven and Hell: The Legend of Hollywood Star—Sessue Hayakawa (6)." *Shinshokurin* 23 (August 1999): 44–57.

———. "Tsuru Aoki: A Flower of Japan." *The Rafu Magazine* 1.4 (19 June 1998): 3–5, 16–18.

"Hayakawa Sesshu: Jijo shoden (Jo)" [Sessue Hayakawa: A short autobiography (1)]. *Sande Mainichi* (20 November 1949): 14–16.

"Hayakawa Sesshu: Jijo shoden (Ge)" [Sessue Hayakawa: A short autobiography (2)]. *Sande Mainichi* (27 November 1949): 22–24.

Hayashi, Hisao. "Sesshu to Itari garu" [Sessue and Italian girls]. *Bungei Shunju* 8.14 (December 1930): 40–42.

Hayne, Donald, ed. *The Autobiography of Cecil B. DeMille*. Englewood Cliffs, N.J.: Prentice-Hall, 1959.

Hearn, Lafcadio. *Glimpses of Unfamiliar Japan*. 1894. Reprint, Tokyo: Tuttle, 1976.

Hearne, Joanna. "'The Cross-Heart People': Race and Inheritance in the Silent Western." *Journal of Popular Film and Television* 30.4 (winter 2003): 181–97.

Herman, David George. "Neighbors on the Golden Mountain: The Americanization of Immigrants in California." Ph.D. diss., University of California, Berkeley, 1981.

Higashi, Sumiko. *Cecil B. DeMille and American Culture: The Silent Era*. Berkeley: University of California Press, 1994.

———. "Cecil B. DeMille and the Lasky Company: Legitimating Feature Film as Art." *Film History* 4.3 (1990): 181–97.

———. "Ethnicity, Class, and Gender in Film: DeMille's *The Cheat*." In *Unspeakable Images: Ethnicity and the American Cinema*, ed. Lester D. Friedman, 112–39. Urbana: University of Illinois Press, 1991.

———. "Melodrama, Realism, and Race: World War II Newsreels and Propaganda Film." *Cinema Journal* 37.3 (spring 1998): 38–61.

———. "Touring the Orient with Lafcadio Hearn and Cecil B. DeMille: Highbrow versus Lowbrow in a Consumer Culture." In *The Birth of Whiteness: Race and the Emergence of U.S. Cinema*, ed. Daniel Bernardi, 329–53. New Brunswick, N.J.: Rutgers University Press, 1996.

———. *Virgins, Vamps, and Flappers: The American Silent Movie Heroine*. St. Albans, Vt.: Eden Press Women's Publications, 1978.

Higgins, Steven. "I film di Thomas H. Ince." *Griffithiana* 7.18–21 (October 1984): 155–203.

———. "The Wrath of the Gods." *The Museum of Modern Art Program Note* (1986): 1–2.

Higham, Charles. *Cecil B. DeMille*. New York: Scribner's, 1973.

Higham, John. *Strangers in the Land: Patterns of American Nativism, 1860–1925*. 1955. Reprint, New Brunswick, N.J.: Rutgers University Press, 1983.

Hirakawa, Sukehiro. *Wakon yosai no keifu: Uchi to soto karano meiji nihon* [Genealogy of Japanese spirit and Western knowledge: Meiji Japan from inside and outside]. 1971. Reprint, Tokyo: Kawade shobo shinsha, 1987.

Hirano, Kyoko. *Mr. Smith Goes to Tokyo: Japanese Cinema under the American Occupation, 1945–1952*. Washington,: Smithsonian, 1992.

Holland, Larry Lee. "Fannie Ward." *Films in Review* 36.12 (December 1985): 590–95.

Holmes, Sean P. "The Hollywood Star System and the Regulations of Actors' Labour, 1916–1934," *Film History* 12.1 (2000): 97–114.

"How Sessue Hayakawa Learned to Smile." *Photoplay Journal* (June 1919): n.p., in SHS: 176.

"How to Hold a Husband: Mr. and Mrs. Hayakawa, in an Oriental Lesson in Four Chapters." *Photoplay* 14.6 (November 1918): n.p., in SHS: 165.

Howe, Hergert. "The Real Pola Negri." *Photoplay* 22.6 (November 1922): 59.

Howe, Daniel Walker. "American Victorianism as a Culture." *American Quarterly* 27 (1975): 507–32.

Hubler, Richard. "Honorable 'Bad Guy.'" *Coronet* 50 (May 1961): 146–50.

Hussey, Christopher. *The Picturesque: Studies in a Point of View*. London: G. P. Putnam's Sons, 1927.

Ichikawa, Sadanji. "Katsudo yakusha to naru niwa" [To become a motion picture actor]. *Katsudo no Sekai* 1.4 (April 1916): 34–40.

Ichikawa, Sai. "Aa awarenaru Sesshu yo" [Ah, poor Sessue]. *Katsudo Kurabu* 6.1 (January 1923): 60–63.

———. *Sekaiteki meiyu ni naru made* [Before he became an international great actor]. Tokyo: Sesshu kurabu, 1922.

Ichinokawa, Yasutaka. "Koka ron to yusei gaku: Dai ich ji taisen zengo no baiopori-thikusu" [The yellow peril and eugenics: Bio-politics before and after World War I]. In *Hensei sareru nashonarizumu 1920 nendai—30 nendai 1* [Nationalism being organized: 1920s–30s, vol. 1], ed. Komori Yoichi, Sakai Naoki, Shimazono Susumu, Chino Kaori, Narita Ryuichi, and Yoshimi Shunya, 119–65. Tokyo: Iwanami shoten, 2002.

Ichioka, Yuji. "*Amerika Nadeshiko*: Japanese Immigrant Women in the United States, 1900–1924." *Pacific Historical Review* 49.2 (1980): 339–57.

———. "Japanese Associations and the Japanese Government: A Special Relationship, 1909–1926." *Pacific Historical Review* 46 (August 1977): 409–37.

Ide, Tessho. "Eiga geki no honshitsu to enshutsu ho no icchi" [Correspondence between the essence of photoplay and the directing method]. *Katsudo no Sekai* 2.9 (September 1917): 2–5.

Iida, Yumiko. *Rethinking Identity in Modern Japan: Nationalism as Aesthetics*. London: Routledge, 2002.

Iijima, Tadashi. "Hayakawa Sesshu ga furansu de satsuei suru" [Sessue Hayakawa shoots a film in France]. *Kinema Junpo* 141 (1 August 1923): 19.

Iino, Masako. "Beikoku niokeru hainichi undo to 1924 nen iminho seitei katei" [Anti-Japanese movement in the U.S. and the enactment process of the 1924 immigration law]. *Tsudajuku Daigaku Kiyo* 10 (1978): 1–41.

Imao, Tetsuya. *Kabuki no rekishi* [History of kabuki]. Tokyo: Iwanami, 2000.

Ince, Thomas H. "The Early Days at Kay Bee." *Photoplay* 7.4 (March 1915): 41–45.

———. "Troubles of a Motion Picture Producer." *Motion Picture Magazine* (May 1915): 113–15.

Inoue, Masao. "Chikaku tobei shitai" [I want to visit America soon]. *Katsudo no Sekai* 1.3 (March 1916): 38–39.

———. "Nichibei shinzen wa mazu nisshi gaiko yori" [Japanese-Chinese relationship is firstly important for U.S.-Japan goodwill]. *Katsudo Kurabu* 3.11 (November 1920): 24–25.

Irwin, Wallace. *Hashimura Togo, Domestic Scientist*. New York: Hearst's International, 1914.

———. *Letters of a Japanese Schoolboy ("Hashimura Togo")*. New York: Doubleday, 1909.

———. *Mr. Togo, Maid of All Work*. New York: Duffield, 1913.

———. *Seed of the Sun*. 1921. Reprint, New York: Arno, 1978.

"Is the Higher Art of the Movies to Come from Japan?: Japanese Actors, Obtaining Remarkable Emotional Effects Without Moving a Face Muscle, Astound Our Masters of the Craft." *Current Opinion* 64 (January 1918): 30–31.

"Is There Danger of a Japanese Invasion?" *Nation* 101.2634 (23 December 1915): 5.

Ishimaki, Yoshio. "Kongo no eiga haikyu mondai" [The issue of film distribution from now on]. *Katsudo Zasshi* 10.9 (September 1924): 42–47.

Itami Mansaku Zenshu: Dai 1 kan [Hansaku Itami Works, vol. 1]. Tokyo: Chikuma, 1961.

Itsumi, Kumi. *Okinna Kyuin to imin shakai 1907–1924: Zaibei ju-hachi nen no kiseki* [Okina Kyuin and immigrant communities 1907–1924: The record of eighteen years of stay]. Tokyo: Bensei shuppan, 2002.

Iwamoto, Kenji, and Makino Mamoru, eds. *Eiga nenkan Showa hen I-1, Taisho 15 nen ban* [Annual report of cinema: Showa period I-1, Taisho 15 edition]. 1926. Reprint, Tokyo: Nihon tosho senta, 1994.

———. *Eiga nenkan Showa hen I-4, Showa 5 nen ban* [Annual report of cinema: Showa period I-4, Showa 5 edition]. 1930. Reprint, Tokyo: Nihon tosho senta, 1994.

———. *Fukkokuban Kinema Junpo* [Reprinted edition of *Kinema Junpo*]. 19 vols. Tokyo: Yushodo, 1994–1996.

Jacobs, Lea. "Belasco, DeMille and the Development of Lasky Lighting." *Film History* 5.4 (1993): 405–18.

"Japan and Ourselves." *Nation* 112.2900 (2 February 1921): 166–67.

"Japanese Actor Dies at 87." *New York Post* (24 November 1973): 7.

"Japanese Customs in Motion Pictures." *Paramount Magazine* (March 1915): 7.

"The Japanese Immigrant Appraised." *Nation* 101.26 (9 September 1915): 316–17.

"The Japanese Method of Preserving Cut Flowers and Fruit." *Picture Progress* (August 1916): 12.

"A Japanese Play. And Morals." *Life* 35.904 (15 March 1900): 212.

Jauss, Hans Robert. *Toward an Aesthetic of Reception.* Trans. Timothy Bahti. Minneapolis: University of Minnesota Press, 1982.

Jay, Gregory S. "'White Man's Book No Good': D. W. Griffith and the American Indian." *Cinema Journal* 39.4 (summer 2000): 3–26.

Jordan, David Starr. "Japan and the United States." *Sunset* 28 (January 1912): 62–63.

Jowett, Garth. *Film: The Democratic Art.* Boston: Little, Brown, 1976.

Kaburagi, Kiyokata. "Nihon hirumu no oomote" [Huge popularity of films about Japan]. *Katsudo no Sekai* 1.4 (April 1916): 11.

Kaeriyama, Norimasa. "Eiga geki to haiyu dosa (Sono 1)" [Photoplay and acting (1)]. *Katsudo Gaho* 3.7 (July 1919): 2–7.

———. "Eiga geki to haiyu dosa (Sono 2)." *Katsudo Gaho* 3.8 (August 1919): 2–6.

———. "Hatashite jinshu kankei kara kangaeruto sekaiteki ni nariuru ya" [Is it going to be worldwide if we think of racial relations?]. *Katsudo Kurabu* 5.11 (November 1922): 40–43.

———. "Jiko o shireriya?" [Do we know ourselves?] *Kinema Record* 4.19 (10 January 1915): 2–3.

———. "Katsudo shashin geki kyakushoku jo no kenkyu (2)" [A study of directing photoplays]. *Kinema Record* 5.28 (10 October 1915): 3–7.

———. "Katsudo shashin kogyo ni tsuite" [About the motion picture industry]. *Katsudo Gaho* 1.9 (September 1917): 45.

———. "Sesshu no seiko bunseki" [An analysis of Sessue's success]. In *Sesshu*, ed. Honami Koda, 2–5. Tokyo: Shin jidai sha, 1922.

Kakeisanjin (Norimasa Kaeriyama). "Geijutsu to shite no katsudo shashin" [Motion picture as an art]. *Katsudo Shashin Kai* 19 (February 1911): 15–16.

———. "Katsudo shashin ga atauru chishiki" [Knowledge that motion picture can provide]. *Katsudo Shashin Kai* 20 (March 1911): 16–17.

———. "Katsudo shashin geijutsu ron" [Theory of motion picture art]. *Katsudo Shashin Kai* 26 (September 1911): 4.

Kakii, Michihiro. *Hariuddo no Nihonjin: eiga ni arawareta nichibei bunka masatsu* [Japanese people in Hollywood: The U.S.-Japan cultural conflict seen in films]. Tokyo: Bungei shunju, 1992.

Kamata, Eikichi. "Zento tabo naru katsudo shashin kai" [Promising motion picture world]. *Katsudo no Sekai* 1.1 (January 1916): 96–99.

Kamiyama, Sojin. *Sugao no Hariuddo* [Hollywood without makeup]. Tokyo: Jitsugyo no nihon sha, 1930.

Kano, Ayako. *Acting Like Woman in Modern Japan: Theater, Gender, and Nationalism.* New York: Palgrave, 2001.

Kasagi, Y. K. "American News." *Kinema Record* 47 (15 May 1917): 226–27.

————. "American News." *Kinema Record* 48 (15 June 1917): 287.

Kasagi, Yasusaburo. "Ikyo no eiga kai ni katsuyaku seru Hayakawa Sesshu shi no hyoban" [Reputation of Sessue Hayakawa, who is popular in a foreign film world]. *Katsudo Gaho* 2.11 (November 1918): 84–87, 109–10.

Kasamori, Sennosuke. "Hyojo no suii" [Transition of facial expressions]. *Katsudo Hyoron* 2.8 (August 1919): 34–35.

Kasumi Ura Jin. *Hayakawa Sesshu.* Tokyo: Haruedo, 1922.

Katano, Hakuro. "Meiyu no shohyo" [Trademarks of famous actors]. *Katsudo Gaho* 3.6 (June 1919): 104–7.

Kataoka, Kunio. "Sesshu nitsuite Toshimichi san e" [To Toshimichi about Sessue]. *Katsudo Gaho* 5.11 (November 1921): 98.

Kato, Shinichi, ed. *Beikoku nikkeijin hyakunen shi* [Hundred-year history of the Japanese in the U.S.]. Tokyo: Shin nichibei shimbun sha, 1961.

Kato, Shuichi. "Taisho Democracy as the Pre-Stage for Japanese Militarism." In *Japan in Crisis: Essays on Taisho Democracy*, ed. Bernard Silberman and H. D. Harootunian, 217–36. Princeton, N.J.: Princeton University Press, 1974.

Kawada, Kyokukei. "Nihon eiga to gaikoku eiga no hikaku kenkyu" [A comparative study of Japanese cinema and foreign cinema]. *Katsudo Gaho* 3.3 (March 1919): 162–63.

Kawakami, Kiyoshi Karl. *The Real Japanese Question.* 1921. Reprint, New York: Arno, 1978.

Keil, Charlie. *Early American Cinema in Transition: Story, Style, and Filmmaking, 1907–1913.* Madison: University of Wisconsin Press, 2001.

Kellor, Frances. *The Federal Administration and the Alien.* New York: Doran, 1921.

Kennan, George. "Are the Japanese Honest?" *Outlook* 100 (31 August 1912): 1011–16.

————. "Are the Japanese Moral?" *Outlook* 102 (14 September 1912): 79–83.

————. "Can We Understand the Japanese?" *Outlook* 97 (10 August 1912): 815–22.

Kepley, Vance, Jr. "Griffith's *Broken Blossoms* and the Problem of Historical Specificity." *Quarterly Review of Film Studies* 3.1 (winter 1978): 37–47.

Kern, Stephen. *The Culture of Love: Victorians to Moderns.* Cambridge: Harvard University Press, 1992.

Kerr, Catherine E. "Incorporating the Star: The Intersection of Business and Aesthetic Strategies in Early American Film." *Business History Review* 64 (autumn 1990): 383–410.

Kingsley, Grace. "Flashes: Hayakawa Solus [*sic*]." *Los Angeles Times* (24 March 1920): III-4.

————. "Romantic Vehicle Serves Star." *Los Angeles Times* (14 May 1931): A9.

————. "That Splash of Saffron: Sessue Hayakawa, a Cosmopolitan Actor, Who for Reasons of Nativity, Happens to Peer from Our White Screens with Tilted Eyes." *Photoplay* 9.4 (March 1916): 139–41.

Kipling, Rudyard. *The Writings in Prose and Verse of Rudyard Kipling: Verses 1889–.* New York: Scribner's, 1907.

Kirihara, Donald. "The Accepted Idea Displaced: Stereotype and Sessue Hayakawa."

The Birth of Whiteness: Race and the Emergence of U.S. Cinema, ed. Daniel Bernardi, 81–99. New Brunswick, N.J.: Rutgers University Press, 1996.

Kishi, Yoshio. "Final Mix: Unscheduled." In *Moving the Image: Independent Asian Pacific American Media Arts*, ed. Russel Leong, 157–70. Los Angeles: Visual Communications and UCLA Asian American Studies Center, 1991.

Kita, Sadakichi. "'Minzoku to rekishi' hakkan shuisho" [The reasons for publishing "Ethnos and history"]. *Minzoku to Rekishi* 1.1 (January 1918): 1–8.

Klump, Inez, and Helen Klump. *Screen Acting: Its Requirements and Rewards*. New York: Falk, 1922.

Kobayashi, Kisaburo. "Katsudo shashin no shimei to togyosha no sekinin" [Motion pictures' mission and responsibilities of people in film business]. *Katsudo no Sekai* 1.4 (April 1916): 29–31.

Koda Honami, "Ikoku ni saku obara" [A male rose blossoms in a foreign country]. In *Sesshu*, ed. Koda Honami, 32–40. Tokyo: Shin jidai sha, 1922.

———, ed. *Sesshu*. Tokyo: Shin jidai sha, 1922.

Kodama, Sanehide. *Amerika no Japonizumu: Bijutsu, kogei o koeta nihon shiko [Japonisme in America: A tendency toward Japan beyond arts and crafts]*. Tokyo: Chuo koron sha, 1995.

Kondo, Iyokichi. "Sesshu Hayakawa no engi" [Sessue Hayakawa's acting]. In *Sesshu*, ed. Koda Honami, 6–14. Tokyo: Shin jidai sha, 1922.

Kondo, Keiichi. "Eiga okoku no junrei o oete" [After the pilgrimage of film kingdom]. *Katsudo Kurabu* 7.11 (November 1924): 38–41.

Kondo, Masami. "Hayakawa Sesshu." In *Haha o Kataru* [Talking about mother], 149–55. Tokyo: Kyoiku koho sha, 1954.

Koszarski, Richard. *An Evening's Entertainment: The Age of the Silent Feature Picture*. New York: Scribner's, 1990.

Kracauer, Siegfried. *Theory of Film: The Redemption of Physical Reality*. 1960. Reprint, Princeton, N.J.: Princeton University Press, 1997.

Kurihara, Tomasu. "Katsudo shashin to boku" [Motion picture and I]. *Katsudo Kurabu* 3.6 (June 1920): 22–23.

Kurtz, Carles M., ed. *Official Illustrations from the Art Gallery of the World's Columbian Exposition*. 1st ed. Philadelphia: George Barrie, 1893.

Kyne, Peter B. *The Pride of Palomar*. New York: Cosmopolitan, 1921.

La Farge, John. "Bric-a-Brac: An Artist's Letters from Japan." *Century* 46.24 (1893): 427–29.

Lahue, Kalton C. *Gentlemen to the Rescue: The Heroes of the Silent Screen*. South Brunswick, N.J.: A. S. Barnes, 1972.

Lant, Antonia. "The Curse of the Pharaoh, or How Cinema Contracted Egyptomania." *October* 53 (winter 1992): 87–112.

Lasky, Jesse L. "How to Win Screen Success." *Photoplay* 17.3 (February 1920): 32–33, 131.

Lea, Homer. "The Legacy of Commodore Perry." *North American Review* 197 (June 1913): 741–60.

Lears, T. J. Jackson. *No Place of Grace: Antimodernism and the Transformation of American Culture, 1880–1920*. Chicago: University of Chicago Press, 1981.

Lee, Robert G. *Orientals: Asian Americans in Popular Culture*. Philadelphia: Temple University Press, 1999.

"The Life of Thomas Harper Ince 1882–1924." *The Silent Picture* 14 (spring 1972): 4–6.

Lindsay, Vachel. *The Art of the Moving Picture*. 1915. Reprint, New York: Modern, 2000.

Lipke, Katherine. "Films Lure Hayakawa," *Los Angeles Times* (26 December 1926): C25–26.

Long, John Luther. *Madame Butterfly, Purple Eyes, Etc.* 1898. Reprint, New York: Garrett, 1969.

Loomis, H. "Is There Danger of a Japanese Invasion?" *Nation* 101.2634 (23 December 1915): s-5.

López, Ana M. "Are All Latins from Manhattan? Hollywood, Ethnography, and Cultural Colonialism." *Unspeakable Images: Ethnicity and the American Cinema*, ed. Lester D. Friedman, 404–24. Chicago: University of Illinois Press, 1991.

Louise, Helen Morris. "Hayakawa Sesshu shi ni au" [Meeting Mr. Sessue Hayakawa]. *Kinema Junpo* 412 (11 September 1931): 56.

Lounsbury, Myron Osborn. *Origins of American Film Criticism, 1909–1939*. New York: Arno, 1973.

Lowe, Lisa. *Immigrant Acts: On Asian American Cultural Politics*. Durham, N.C.: Duke University Press, 1996.

Mahan, A. T. *The Influence of Sea Power upon History 1660–1783*. Boston: Little, Brown, 1890.

———. *The Problem of Asia and Its Effect upon International Policies*. Boston: Little, Brown, 1900.

Makino, Mamoru. *Nihon eiga kenetsu shi* [History of motion picture censorship in Japan]. Tokyo: Gendaishokan/Pandora, 2003.

———, ed. *Fukkokuban Katsudo Shashin Kai*. 3 vols. Facsimile edition of *Katsudo Shashin Kai* (June 1909–May 1911), nos. 1–21; (November 1911), no. 26. Tokyo: Kokusho kanko kai, 1999.

———, ed. *Fukkokuban Kinema Rekodo*. Vol. 1. Facsimile edition of *Film Record* (1 October 1913–11 November 1913), vol. 1, nos. 1–4; *Kinema Record* (10 December 1913–10 May 1915), vol. 1, no. 5–vol. 4, no. 23. Tokyo: Kokusho kanko kai, 1999.

———, ed. *Fukkokuban Kinema Rekodo*. Vol. 2. Facsimile edition of *Kinema Record* (10 January 1916–10 December 1916), vol. 4, nos. 31–42; (10 January 1917–1 December 1917), vol. 5, nos. 43–51. Tokyo: Kokusho kanko kai, 2000.

———, ed. *Nihon eiga shoki shiryo shusei* [A collection of research material from the early days of Japanese cinema]. Vols. 1–9. Facsimile edition of *Katsudo Shashin Zasshi* (June–December 1915), vols. 1–2; *Katsudo no Sekai* (January–December 1916), vols. 3–5; *Katsudo Gaho* (January–December 1917), vols. 6–9. Tokyo: Sani-chi shobo, 1990–1991.

———, ed. *Nihon eiga shoki shiryo shusei*. Vols. 10–14. Facsimile edition of *Katsudo*

Hyoron (December 1918–August 1919), vols. 10–11; *Katsudo Kurabu* (September 1919–December 1920), vols. 12–14. Tokyo: Sanichi shobo, 1992.

Marchetti, Gina. *Romance and the "Yellow Peril": Race, Sex, and Discursive Strategies in Hollywood Fiction*. Berkeley: University of California Press, 1993.

Mason, Roger S. *Conspicuous Consumption: A Study of Exceptional Consumer Behaviour*. Westmead, England: Gower, 1981.

Masubuchi, Rumiko. "1910 nendai no hainichi to 'shashin kekkon'" [Anti-Japanese and "picture bride" in the 1910s]. In *Japanese American: Iju kara jiritsu eno ayumi* [Process from immigration to independence], ed. Togami Munetake, 293–318. Tokyo: Mineruva shobo, 1986.

Masui, Keiji. *Opera o shitteimasuka* [Do you know about opera?]. Tokyo: Ongaku no tomo sha, 1995.

Masumoto, Kiyoshi. "Riarizumu no eiga" [Cinema of realism]. *Katsudo Kurabu* 4.5 (May 1921): 28–29.

Matsui, Suisei. "Tokino hito: Nihon ga unda dai suta" [People of the time: The big star from Japan]. *Goraku Yomiuri* [Entertainment Yomiuri] (17 January 1958): 16.

Matsumoto, Ryukotsu. "Nihon eiga no shinro" [Japanese cinema's direction]. *Katsudo Gaho* 1.12 (December 1917): 2–11.

Matsumoto, Yuko. "Amerika jin de arukoto, Amerika jin ni suru koto: 20 seiki shoto no 'Amerika ka' undo ni okeru jenda, jinshu, kaikyu" [Being American, making American: Gender, class, and race in the "Americanization" movement in the early twentieth century]. *Shiso* [Thoughts] 884 (February 1998): 52–75.

Matsuura, Kozo. *Nihon eiga shi taikan: Eiga torai kara gendai made — 86 nenkan no kiroku* [Encyclopedia of Japanese film history: Since the arrival of cinema until now — Record of eighty-six years]. Tokyo: Bunka shuppan kyoku, 1982.

McClatchy, Valentine Stuart. *Four Anti-Japanese Pamphlets*. 1919, 1921, 1921, 1925. Reprint, New York: Arno, 1978.

McConaughy, J. W. *The Typhoon: A Story of New Japan*. New York: H. K. Fly, 1912.

McDonald, Keiko I. *Japanese Classical Theater in Films*. London: Associated University Press, 1994.

McDonald, Paul. *The Star System: Hollywood's Production of Popular Identities*. London: Wallflower, 2000.

McGaffey, Kenneth. "The Man from Japan." *Motion Picture Classic* (September 1921): 58–59, 90.

McKelvie, Martha Grover. "Playing with Fire in Hawaii." *Photoplay Journal* (November 1919): 14, 46.

McLean, Adrienne L. "'I'm a Cansino': Transformation, Ethnicity, and Authenticity in the Construction of Rita Hayworth, American Love Goddess." *Journal of Film and Video* 44.3–4 (fall–winter 1992–1993): 8–26.

McLean, Albert F., Jr. *American Vaudeville as Ritual*. Lexington: University Press of Kentucky, 1965.

Mehnert, Ute. "German *Weltpolitik* and the American Two-Front Dilemma: The 'Japanese Peril' in German-American Relations, 1904–1917." *The Journal of American History* 82.4 (March 1996): 1452–77.

Michaels, Walter Benn. *Our America: Nativism, Modernism, and Pluralism*. Durham, N.C.: Duke University Press, 1995.

Mitry, Jean. "Thomas H. Ince: His Esthetic, His Films, His Legacy." *Cinema Journal* 22.2 (winter 1983): 2–25.

Miyake, Kafu. "Insho eiga tanpyo" [Short impressions on films]. *Katsudo Zasshi* 7.6 (June 1921): 161.

Mizumachi, Seiji. "Bonsaku *Atarashiki tsuchi* no shokon" [The merchants' spirit in the mediocre film *Die Tochter des Samurai*]. *Kinema Junpo* 604 (11 March 1937): 12–13.

Mizusawa, Tsutomu. "The Artists Start to Dance: The Changing Image of the Body in Art of the Taisho Period." *Being Modern in Japan: Culture and Society from the 1910s to the 1930s*, ed. Elise K. Tipton and John Clark, 15–24. Honolulu: University of Hawai'i Press, 2000.

Mochizuki, Kotaro. "Beikokujin no rikai" [American people's understanding]. *Katsudo no Sekai* 3.2 (February 1918): 2–3.

Modell, John. *The Economics and Politics of Racial Accommodation: The Japanese of Los Angeles, 1900–1942*. Urbana: University of Illinois Press, 1977.

"Mondo yuyo" [It is useful to question and answer]. *Shukan Asahi* (31 August 1952): 22.

Mori, Iwao. "Eiga haiyu no hanashi (2)" [A story about film actors]. *Katsudo Kurabu* 5.7 (July 1922): 72–73.

———. *Hayakawa Sesshu*. Tokyo: Toyo shuppan sha, 1922.

———. "Shorai no nihon eiga no tameni sono 1" [For Japanese cinema in the future (1)]. *Katsudo Gaho* 6.2 (February 1922): 69–71.

———. "Shorai no nihon eiga no tameni sono 2." *Katsudo Gaho* 6.3 (March 1922): 74–75.

Mori, Iwao, and Tomonari Yozo. *Katsudo shashin taikan* [A survey of the motion pictures]. 4 vols. Supplement to *Nihon eiga shi soko* [Notes on Japanese film history], ed. Okabe Ryu. Tokyo: Tokyo Film Library Council, 1976.

Mori, Tomita. "Hayakawa Sesshu fusai o mukaete" [Welcoming Mr. and Mrs. Sessue Hayakawa]. *Katsudo Kurabu* 5.8 (August 1922): 28–29.

Morioka, Kakuo. "Ko kikai" [A good opportunity]. *Katsudo Kurabu* 7.7 (July 1924): 40–41.

"Moto hariuddo haiyu, Hayakawa Sesshu, shishite ichidai gimon: Kare wa hontoni kokusai suta dattanoka" [The ex-Hollywood actor, Sessue Hayakawa, died with a big question: Was he really an international star?]. *Shukan Bunshun* 756 (17 December 1973): 176, 181–82.

Moussinac, Léon. "Cinématographie: Le Lys brisé." *Mercure de France* (1 February 1921): 797–804. Translated and reprinted in Richard Abel, *French Film Theory and Criticism: A History/Anthology 1907–1939*. Vol. 1, *1907–1929*, 229–35. Princeton, N.J.: Princeton University Press, 1988.

Munden, Kenneth W., ed. *The American Film Institute Catalog of Motion Pictures Produced in the United States: Feature Films, 1921–30*. Berkeley: University of California Press, 1997.

Muramatsu, Shofu. *Kawakami Otojiro (Jo)*. Tokyo: Taiheiyo shuppan, 1952.
———. *Kawakami Otojiro (Ge)*. Tokyo: Taiheiyo shuppan, 1952.
Muromachi, Kyoji. "Furukushite atarshiki tsuneni tayumanu taido" [An old but new, consistent attitude]. *Katsudo Gaho* 3.4 (April 1919): 2–5.
Nagai, Ryutaro. "Waseda no kodo kara" [From the hall of Waseda University]. *Katsudo no Sekai* 1.4 (April 1916): 24–28.
Nagai, Toshimichi. "Nihonjin Hayakawa Sesshu wa shieseri" [A Japanese Sessue Hayakawa is dead]. *Katsudo Gaho* 5.10 (October 1921): 97.
Naimu sho keiho kyoku, ed. *Katsudo shashin "firumu" kenetsu nenpo* [Annual report of moving picture, "film," censorship]. 1927–1943. Tokyo: Ryukei sho sha, 1984.
Nanbu, Kunihiko. "Hayakawa Sesshu shi to kataru" [A talk with Mr. Sessue Hayakawa]. *Katsudo Gaho* 5.4 (April 1921): 30–33.
Nanka Nikkeijin shogyo kaigi sho. *Nanka shu nihonnjin shi* [History of Japanese in Southern California], Los Angeles: Nanka Nikkeijin shogyo kaigi sho, 1955.
Naremore, James. *Acting in the Cinema*. Berkeley: University of California Press, 1988.
The National Board of Review of Motion Pictures. *The Standards and Policy of the National Board of Review of Motion Pictures*. New York: The National Board of Review of Motion Pictures, 1 October 1916.
Naylor, Simpson. "Richard Barthelmess: An Impression." *Motion Picture Magazine* 19.1 (February 1920): 56–57, 93.
Negra, Diane. "The Fictionalized Ethnic Biography: Nita Nardi and the Crisis of Assimilation." In *American Silent Film: Discovering Marginalized Voices*, ed. Gregg Bachman and Thomas J. Slater, 176–200. Carbondale: Southern Illinois University Press, 2002.
———. "Immigrant Stardom in Imperial America: Pola Negri and the Problem of Typology." *Camera Obscura* 48 (2001): 159–95.
———. "Introduction: Female Stardom and Early Film History." *Camera Obscura* 48 (2001): 1–7.
———. *Off-White Hollywood: American Culture and Ethnic Female Stardom*. London: Routledge, 2001.
Neu, Charles E. *An Uncertain Friendship: Theodore Roosevelt and Japan, 1906–1909*. Cambridge: Cambridge University Press, 1967.
Nihon Gaimusho. *Nihon gaiko bunsho: Taisho-hachi-nen dai-issatsu* [Japan diplomatic documents 1917, vol. 1]. Tokyo: Nihon Gaimusho, 1969.
———. *Nihon gaiko bunsho: Taibei imin mondai keika gaiyo* [Japan diplomatic documents: Abstract of issues of immigration to the U.S.], Taisho-ki dai 24 satsu [Taisho era, vol. 24]. Tokyo: Nihon Gaimusho, 1972.
Niiya, Brian, ed. *Japanese American History: An A-to-Z Reference from 1868 to the Present*. New York: Facts on File, 1993.
Nitobe, Inazo. *Bushido: The Soul of Japan*. 1900. Reprint, London: G. P. Putnam's Sons, 1906.
Nogami, Hideyuki. *Seirin no o Hayakawa Sesshu* [King of Hollywood, Sessue Hayakawa]. Tokyo: Shakai shiso sha, 1986.

Noguchi, Yonejiro. "Hayakawa Sesshu." *Chuo Koron* 37.9 (August 1922): 81–82.

———. "Sekai no heiwa to waga katsudo gyosha no susumubeki michi" [World peace and the way that our motion picture industry should take]. *Katsudo Shashin Zasshi* 5.2 (February 1919): 44–47.

Nonomiya, Suihei. "From Rice Curry to Sessue." *Katsudo Kurabu* 5.11 (November 1922): 62–64.

Noteheler, F. G., ed. *Japan through American Eyes: The Journal of Francis Hall Kanagawa and Yokohama 1859–1866*. Princeton, N.J.: Princeton University Press, 1992.

Numata, Yuzuru. "Katsudo shashin no geijutsu bi" [Artistic beauty of motion picture]. *Katsudo Gaho* 1.6 (June 1917): 141–45.

———. "Posuta no machi ni tachite" [Standing in a city filled with posters]. *Katsudo Gaho* 1.4 (April 1917): 112–15.

———. "Rafu no eiga kai kara" [From cinema world in Los Angeles]. *Katsudo no Sekai* 4.4 (April 1919): 40–42.

Oba, Toshio. "Hayakawa Kintaro (Sesshu) no tobei kankyo to ryoken nituite" [About the circumstances before Kintaro (Sessue) Hayakawa went to the U.S., and about Hayakawa's passport]. *Boso no kyodo shi* 22 (1995): 57–58.

———. "Kotani Fuku to Kariforunia no awabi gyogyo" [Fuku Kotani and abalone fishing in California]. *Kamogawa Fudoki* (1980): 299–332.

———. "Shokan kara mita Hayakawa Sesshu no kunan" [Sessue Hayakawa's hardship indicated in his letters]. *Boso no kyodo shi* 24 (1997): 49–51.

Oda, Suezo. "Beikoku katsudo kai kenbutsu miyage" [After visiting American motion picture world]. *Katsudo Zasshi* 7.1 (January 1921): 98–101.

Odell, George C. D. *Annals of the New York Stage*, vol. 12 (1882–1885). 1940. Reprint, New York: AMS, 1970.

Oehling, Richard A. "The Yellow Menace: Asian Images in American Film." In *The Kaleidoscopic Lens: How Hollywood Views Ethnic Groups*, ed. Randall M. Miller, 182–206. Englewood, N.J.: Ozer, 1980.

Ogawa, Seiji. "Sennendo no katsudo shashinkai zakkan" [Some thoughts about the film world last year]. *Kinema Record* 2.6 (1 January 1914): 8–11.

Okabe, Ryu. "Amerika jidai no Henri Kotani" [Henry Kotani of the American period]. *Eiga Shi Kenkyu* [The study of the history of cinema] 2 (1973): 15–29.

———. "Tomasu Kurihara Kisaburo ni tsuite" [About Thomas Kurihara Kisaburo]. *Eiga Shi Kenkyu* 6 (1975): 22–26.

Okina, Kyuin. "Hayakawa Sesshu to Kamiyama Sojin" [Sessue Hayakawa and Sojin Kamiyama]. *Chuo Koron* 45.5 (May 1930): 223–31.

———. *Okina Kyuin zenshu: Waga issho dai 1 kan: Konjiki no sono* [Okina Kyuin's complete works: My life volume 1: Garden of gold]. Toyama: Okina Kyuin zenshu kanko kai, 1972.

Okudaira, Yasuhiro. "Eiga no kokka tosei" [The state regulation of cinema]. In *Koza Nihon eiga 4: Senso to Nihon eiga* [Lecture on Japanese cinema 4: War and Japanese cinema], ed. Imamura Shohei, Sato Tadao, Shindo Kaneto, Tsurumi Shunsuke, and Yamada Yoji, 238–55. Tokyo: Iwanami, 1986.

———. "Eiga to kenetsu" [Cinema and censorship]. In *Koza Nihon eiga 2: Musei eiga no kansei* [Lecture on Japanese cinema 2: Completion of silent cinema], ed. Imamura Shohei, Sato Tadao, Shindo Kaneto, Tsurumi Shunsuke, and Yamada Yoji, 302–18. Tokyo: Iwanami, 1986.

Okura, Kihachiro. "Ware mo mata shutsuba semu" [I will also run]. *Katsudo no Sekai* 1.3 (March 1916): 17–18.

Orvell, Miles. *The Real Thing: Imitation and Authenticity in American Culture*. Chapel Hill: University of North Carolina Press, 1989.

Ota, Yoshinobu. *Toransupojishon no shiso* [Thoughts of trans-position]. Tokyo: Sekai-shiso-sha, 1995.

Ovanesov, K. *Sessue Hayakawa*. Moscow: Kinopechat, 1926.

Owens, Gina. "The Making of the Yellow Peril." In *Cultural Difference, Media Memories: Anglo-American Images of Japan*, ed. Phil Hammond, 27–47. London: Cassell, 1997.

"Oya Soichi no oshaberi dochu michizure wa Hayakawa Sesshu" [Soichi Oya's chatting trip with Sessue Hayakawa]. *Shukan Goraku Yomiuri* [Weekly entertainment Yomiuri] (7 November 1958): 44–48.

Parish, James Robert, and Michael R. Pitts. *The Great Spy Pictures*. Metuchen, N.J.: Scarecrow, 1974.

Parker, Andrew, and Eve Kosofsky Sedgwick, eds. *Performativity and Performance*. London: Routledge, 1995.

Pearson, Roberta. *Eloquent Gestures: Transformation of Performance Style in the Griffith Biography Films*. Berkeley: University of California Press, 1992.

———. "'O'er Step Not the Modesty of Nature': A Semiotic Approach to Acting in the Griffith Biographs." In *Making Visible the Invisible: An Anthology of Original Essays on Film Acting*, ed. Carole Zucker, 1–27. Metuchen, N.J.: Scarecrow, 1990.

Pratt, George. "'See Mr. Ince. . .'" *Image* 5.5 (May 1956): 100–11.

Price, Martin. "The Picturesque Moment." In *From Sensibility to Romanticism: Essays Presented to Frederick Pottle*, ed. Frederick Hilles and Harold Bloom, 259–92. New York: Oxford University Press, 1965.

Puccini, Giacomo. *Puccini's Madama Butterfly*. Trans. and ed. Stanley Appelbaum. New York: Dover, 1983.

Quinn, Michael J. "Paramount and Early Feature Distribution: 1914–1921." *Film History* 11.1 (1999): 98–114.

Radaway, Janice A. *Reading the Romance: Women, Patriarchy, and Popular Literature*. Chapel Hill: University of North Carolina Press, 1984.

Readers' Guide to Periodical Literature. Vol. 3, *1910–1914 (A–K)*. New York: Wilson, 1915.

Redway, Sara. "Old Pictures in New Frames." *Motion Picture Classic* 23.5 (May 1926): 54–55, 78, 86.

Reed, Warren. "The Tradition Wreckers: Two People Who Became Famous, Though Few People without Almond Eyes Can Pronounce Their Names." *Picture-Play Magazine* 4.1 (March 1917): 61–65.

Reeve, Winnifred Eaton. "What Happened to Hayakawa: This Japanese Gentleman

Reveals Why He Forsook the American Screen." *Motion Picture Magazine* 36 (January 1929): 33, 90–91.

Rhodes, John David. "'Our Beautiful and Glorious Art Lives': The Rhetoric of Nationalism in Early Italian Film Periodicals." *Film History* 12.3 (2000): 308–22.

Richie, Donald. "Sessué Hayakawa." In *Public People, Private People: Portraits of Some Japanese*, 98–100. Tokyo: Kodansha, 1996.

Rimmon-Kenan, Shlomith. *Narrative Fiction: Contemporary Poetics*. London: Methuen, 1983.

"Risen Sun." *New Yorker* 35 (1 August 1959): 16–18.

Rogers, Allison. "A Potential Madame Butterfly." *Motion Picture Magazine* 17.3 (April 1919): 64–65, 108.

Rogin, Michael. "Making America Home: Racial Masquerade and Ethnic Assimilation in the Transition to Talking Pictures." *Journal of American History* 79.3 (December 1992): 1050–77.

Rony, Fatimah Tobing. *The Third Eye: Race, Cinema, and Ethnographic Spectacle*. Durham, N.C.: Duke University Press, 1996.

Ross, Don. "Sessue Hayakawa Prefers the Wicked Oriental Roles." *New York Herald Tribune* (5 April 1959): 1, 4.

Said, Edward. *Culture and Imperialism*. New York: Knopf, 1993.

———. *Orientalism*. New York: Vintage, 1978.

Saiki, Junko. "Awabi romansu: Kantoku to natte" [Abalone romance: Being a director]. *Katsudo Hanagata* 1.4 (April 1921): 38–41.

Saiki, Tomonori, ed. *Eiga dokuhon: Ito Daisuke* [Cinema reader: Daisuke Ito]. Tokyo: Firumuato sha, 1996.

Sakamoto, Shigetaro. "Sesshu ni atauru sho" [A letter to Sessue]. *Katsudo Kurabu* 5.11 (November 1922): 96–98.

Sakurabashi, Hanjin. "Eiga geki tsuji seppo" [A lecture on cinema]. *Katsudo Gaho* 6.12 (December 1922): 118–23.

Santayana, George. "The Genteel Tradition in American Philosophy (1911)." *The Genteel Tradition: Nine Essays by George Santayana*, ed. Douglas L. Wilson, 37–64. Lincoln: University of Nebraska Press, 1967.

Sato, Tadao. *Nihon eiga shi 1 1896–1940* [History of Japanese cinema]. Tokyo: Iwanami, 1995.

Sato, Yasuo. "Amerika eiga haiyu no tanaorosi" [News of American film actors]. *Katsudo Kurabu* 4.11 (November 1921): 52–53.

Savada, Elias, comp. *The American Film Institute Catalog of Motion Pictures Produced in the United States: Film Beginnings, 1893–1910: A Work in Progress*. Metuchen, N.J.: Scarecrow, 1995.

Schallert, Edwin. "Hal Roach Television Plans Move into High; Hayakawa Will Return." *Los Angeles Times* (25 December 1948): 7.

———. "Women's War Story Inspired." *Los Angeles Times* (22 April 1950): A8.

Seikanji, Ken. "Eiga suta oitachi hiwa: Unmei no chugaeri" [Secret stories of film stars' biographies: Somersault of fate]. *Kingu* 31.1 (January 1955): 136–41.

Seki, Misao. "Shitashiki Hayakawa Sesshu shi yori eta watashi no kangeki" [I was impressed by Mr. Sessue Hayakawa, my good friend]. *Katsudo Kurabu* 5.6 (June 1922): 32–34.

"Sesshu hodan" [Sessue talks freely]. *KRT Chosa Joho* 19 (June 1960): 30–33.

"Sessue Hayakawa." *Invicta Cine* (Portugal) 3 (1 June 1923): 4–5.

Sherwood, Elizabeth J., and Dorothy Goodman, eds. *Readers' Guide to Periodical Literature*. Vol. 5, *1919–1921*. New York: Wilson, 1922.

Sherwood, Elizabeth J., and Estella E. Painter, eds. *Readers' Guide to Periodical Literature*. Vol. 4, *1915–1918*. New York: Wilson, 1919.

Sherwood, Robert E. "A Fan Paper Critic Says—This Film Year Has Been a Fan's Year." *MPN* 25.2 (31 December 1921): 218.

Shibusawa, Eiichi. "Odorokubeki beikoku no katsudo shashin kai" [Amazing world of motion picture in America]. *Katsudo no Sekai* 1.2 (February 1916): 62–65.

Shigeno, Yukiyoshi. "Beikoku dewa Nihon geki ga donnna kankyo de torareruka" [Why films about Japan were made in the U.S.]. *Katsudo Kurabu* 3.2 (February 1920): 26–29.

Shigeno, Yumeji. "Gaikoku gaisha no utsushita Nihon geki [Films about Japan made by foreign companies]." *Film Record* 1.3 (November 1913): 6.

———. "Gaikoku gaisha no utsushita Nihon geki (2)." *Kinema Record* 1.5 (10 December 1913): 4.

Shigoro. "Rafu todai fujin arubamu (1)" [Album of famous ladies in Los Angeles 1]. *Rafu Shimpo* 4764 (16 February 1919): 3.

Shillony, Ben-Ami. "Friend or Foe: The Ambivalent Images of the U.S. and China in Wartime Japan." In *The Ambivalence of Nationalism: Modern Japan between East and West*, ed. James W. White, Michio Umegaki, and Thomas R. H. Havesn, 187–211. Lanham, Md.: University Press of America, 1990.

Shimizu, Chiyota. "*Atarashiki tsuchi* no koseki" [The achievement of *Die Tochter des Samurai*]. *Kinema Junpo* 603 (1 March 1937): 13.

Singal, Daniel Joseph. "Toward a Definition of American Modernism." *American Quarterly* 39.1 (spring 1987): 7–26.

Singer, Ben. *Melodrama and Modernity: Early Sensational Cinema and Its Contexts*. New York: Columbia University Press, 2001.

———. "Modernity, Hyperstimulus, and the Rise of Popular Sensationalism." *Cinema and the Invention of Modern Life*, ed. Leo Charney and Vanessa R. Schwartz, 72–99. Berkeley: University of California Press, 1995.

Sklar, Robert. *Film: An International History of the Medium*. New York: Abrams, 1993.

———. *F. Scott Fitzgerald: The Last Laocoon*. New York: Oxford University Press, 1967.

———. "A Leap into the Void: Frank Capra's Apprenticeship to Ideology." In *Frank Capra: Authorship and the Studio System*, ed. Robert Sklar and Vito Zagarrio, 37–63. Philadelphia: Temple University Press, 1998.

———. *Movie-Made America: A Cultural History of American Movies*. 1975. Reprint, New York: Vintage, 1994.

————, ed. *The Plastic Age (1917–1930)*. New York: Braziller, 1970.

Slide, Anthony. *The American Film Industry: A Historical Dictionary*. New York: Greenwood, 1986.

————. *The Idols of Silence*. South Brunswick, N.J.: A. S. Barnes, 1976.

Stacey, Jackie. *Star Gazing: Hollywood Cinema and Female Spectatorship*. London: Routledge, 1994.

Staiger, Janet. *Bad Women: Regulating Sexuality in Early American Cinema*. Minneapolis: University of Minnesota Press, 1995.

————. "Dividing Labor for Production Control: Thomas Ince and the Rise of the Studio System." *Cinema Journal* 38.2 (spring 1979): 16–25.

————. "The Eyes Are Really the Focus: Photoplay Acting and Film Form and Style." *Wide Angle* 6.4 (1985): 14–23.

————. *Interpreting Films: Studies in the Historical Reception of American Cinema*. Princeton, N.J.: Princeton University Press, 1992.

Stanley, Sadie, ed., *The New Grove Dictionary of Opera*. Vol. 2, *E-Lom*. New York: Macmillan, 1992.

State Board of Control of California. *California and the Oriental*. Sacramento: State Board of Control of California, 1920.

Steiner, Jesse Frederick. *The Japanese Invasion: A Study in the Psychology of Inter-Racial Contacts*. 1917. Reprint, New York: Arno, 1978.

Stephenson, Shelley. "'Her Traces Are Found Everywhere': Shanghai, Li Xianglan, and the Greater East Asia Film Sphere." In *Cinema and Urban Culture in Shanghai, 1922–1943*, ed. Yingjin Zhang, 222–45. Stanford, Calif.: Stanford University Press, 1999:.

Stoloff, Sam. "Normalizing Stars: Roscoe 'Fatty' Arbuckle and Hollywood Consolidation." In *American Silent Film: Discovering Marginalized Voices*, ed. Gregg Bachman and Thomas J. Slater, 148–75. Carbondale: Southern Illinois University Press, 2002.

Studlar, Gaylyn. "Dialogue." *Cinema Journal* 26.2 (winter 1987): 51–53.

————. "Discourses of Gender and Ethnicity: The Construction and De(con)struction of Rudolph Valentino as Other." *Film Criticism* 13 (winter 1989): 18–35.

————. "'Out-Salomeing Salome': Dance, the New Woman, and Fan Magazine Orientalism." In *Visions of the East: Orientalism in Film*, ed. Matthew Bernstein and Gaylyn Studlar, 99–129. New Brunswick, N.J.: Rutgers University Press, 1997.

————. "The Perils of Pleasure?: Fan Magazine Discourse as Women's Commodified Culture in the 1920s." In *Silent Film*, ed. Richard Abel, 263–97. New Brunswick, N.J.: Rutgers University Press, 1996.

————. *This Mad Masquerade: Stardom and Masculinity in the Jazz Age*. New York: Columbia University Press, 1996.

Suleri, Sara. *The Rhetoric of English India*. Chicago: University of Chicago Press, 1992.

Sullivan, Arthur. *The Complete Plays of Gilbert and Sullivan*. Garden City, N.Y.: Garden City Publication Co., 1941.

Sumida, Alice, "The Truth about Hayakawa's Past." *Nisei Vue* (February 1949): 8–9.

Suzuki, Akira. "Oriental Exclusion in the United States, 1850s–1920s: Its Logic and Practice." *Ajia Kenkyu* 34.3 (January 1988): 92–141.

Suzuki, Yo. "Shinsetsu na Hayakawa Sesshu to Tsuruko fujin" [Kind Sessue Hayakawa and Mrs. Tsuruko]. In *Sesshu*, ed. Honami Koda, 16–20. Tokyo: Shin jidai sha, 1922.

SZO. "Katsudo omochabako" [Toy box of motion picture]. *Katsudo no Sekai* 1.7 (July 1916): 42–48.

Tagawa, Daikichiro. "Kuwazu girai no hitobito" [People who are prejudiced against new things]. *Katsudo no Sekai* 1.5 (May 1916): 10–11.

Taguchi, Oson. "Hariuddo kenbun roku" [A record of visiting Hollywood]. *Katsudo Gaho* 4.8 (August 1919): 29–33.

———. "Idainaru pantomaimu" [Great pantomime]. *Katsudo Gaho* 6.9 (September 1922): 76–77.

———. "Nanjino yatoinin wa dareka" [Who's your servant?]. *Katsudo Gaho* 4.8 (August 1920): 48–52.

Taguchi, Ryokusui. "Nihon eiga gaikoku eiga no hikaku kenkyu (3)" [A comparative study of Japanese cinema and foreign cinema (3)]. *Katsudo Gaho* 3.3 (March 1919): 77–79.

Takada, Masao. "Butai no Hayakawa Sesshu: *Kami no gozen e* to *Samurai*" [Sessue Hayakawa on stage: *Knee of the God* and *Samurai*]. *Shukan Asahi* 11 (9 March 1924): 25–26.

Takahashi, Toshio. "Sekaiteki meiyu no eiga toshite" [As a film of the world famous actor]. *Kamata* 11.7 (July 1932): 124.

Takaki, Ronald. *A Different Mirror: A History of Multicultural America*. Boston: Little, Brown, 1993.

———. *Strangers from a Different Shore: A History of Asian Americans*. New York: Penguin, 1989.

Takemura, Tamio. *Taisho bunka* [Taisho culture]. Tokyo: Kodansha, 1980.

Tamura, Yoshihiko. "Chikagoro no watashi" [About me recently]. *Katsudo Gaho* 7.7 (July 1923): 80–81.

Tanaka, Jun'ichiro. *Nihon eiga hattatsu shi* [A history of the development of Japanese cinema]. 5 vols. Tokyo: Chuo koron sha, 1985.

Tanaka, Saburo. "Beikoku eiga haiseki mondai ichigen" [A word about the issue of American film exclusion]. *Kinema Junpo* 163 (21 June 1924): 7.

Tanaka, Stefan. *Japan's Orient: Rendering Pasts into History*. Berkeley: University of California Press, 1993.

Tanizaki, Jun'ichiro. "Katsudo shashin no genzai to shorai" [The present and the future of motion pictures] (1917). In *Jun'ichiro rabirinsu XI: Ginmaku no kanata* [Jun'ichiro labyrinth: Beyond the silver screen], ed. Chiba Shunji, 251–62. Tokyo: Chuo koron sha, 1999.

Terada, Shiro. "Teiso no kuni no onna Ocho fujin" [Cho-Cho-San, the woman of faithful country]. *Fujin Koron* 64 (April 1921): 66–70.

Thirer, Irene. "Sessue Hayakawa—Then and Now." *New York Post* (29 December 1957): n.p. In Sessue Hayakawa Clippings, the Museum of Modern Art, Film Study Center.

Thomas, Julia Adeney. "Naturalizing Nationhood: Ideology and Practice in Early Twentieth-Century Japan." In *Japan's Competing Modernities: Issues in Culture and Democracy 1900–1930*, ed. Sharon A. Minichiello, 114–32. Honolulu: University of Hawaii Press, 1998.

Thomas, Nicholas, ed. *International Dictionary of Films and Filmmakers—3: Actors and Actresses*. Detroit: St. James, 1992.

Thompson, Kristin. *Exporting Entertainment: America in the World Film Market 1907–34*. London: BFI, 1985.

Thompson, Kristin, and David Bordwell. *Film History: An Introduction*. New York: McGraw-Hill, 1994.

Thompson, Richard Austin. *The Yellow Peril, 1890–1924*. 1957. Reprint, New York: Arno, 1978.

Tipton, Elise K., ed. *Society and the State in Interwar Japan*. London: Routledge, 1997.

Tipton, Elise K., and John Clark, eds. *Being Modern in Japan: Culture and Society from the 1910 to the 1930s*. Honolulu: University of Hawaii Press, 2000.

"Tokyo Joe." *Newsweek* 34 (14 November 1949): 90–93.

Tompkins, J. M. S. *The Art of Rudyard Kipling*. London: Methuen, 1959.

Trimberger, Ellen Kay. "The New Woman and the New Sexuality: Conflict and Contradiction in the Writings and Lives of Mabel Dodge and Neith Boyce." In *1915, the Cultural Moment: The New Politics, the New Woman, the New Psychology, the New Art, and the New Theatre in America*, ed. Adele Heller and Lois Rudnick, 98–115. New Brunswick, N.J.: Rutgers University Press, 1991.

Tsubaki, Shogo. "Itami Mansaku no tachiba" [Mansaku Itami's position]. *Kinema Junpo* 602 (21 February 1937): 16.

Tsukimura, Uhoku. "Setsumeisha kara mitaru Sesshu geki" [Sessue's films viewed by benshi]. In *Sesshu*, ed. Koda Honami, 24–26. Tokyo: Shin jidai sha, 1922.

Tsukuba, Hachiro. "Shin no Nippon towa" [What is the true Japan?]. *Kinema Junpo* 568 (1 March 1936): 77.

Tsutsumi, Tomojiro. "Nihon mono to Oshu mono to o motte" [By Japanese and European films]. *Katsudo Kurabu* 7.7 (July 1924): 38–39.

Tsuzuki, Masaaki. *Shinema ga yattekita!: Nihon eiga kotohajime* [Cinema has come!: The beginning of Japanese cinema]. Tokyo: Shogakukan, 1995.

Tupper, Eleanor, and George E. McReynolds, *Japan in American Public Opinion*. New York: Macmillan, 1937.

"Two Delights from Nippon." *Photoplay Journal* (February 1919): n.p., in SHS: 175.

Uchida, Kimio. "*Atarashiki tsuchi*" [*Die Tochter des Samurai*]. *Kinema Junpo* 601 (11 February 1937): 53.

———. "Futatsu no *Atarashiki tsuchi*" [Two *Die Tochter des Samurai*]. *Kinema Junpo* 602 (21 February 1937): 10.

"Um morto vivo: Sessue Hayakawa." *Cinefilo* (Portugal) 24 (2 February 1929): 11, 22.

U.S. Bureau of the Census. *Chinese and Japanese in the United States*. 13th Census Bulletin 127. Washington: Government Printing Office, 1914.

Utagawa, Wakaba. "Meikin no kichi ni funshitaru guresu kanado jo ni menkai suru ki" [Meeting Grace Carnard]. *Katsudo no Sekai* 1.5 (May 1916): 22–23.

Veblen, Thorstein. *The Theory of the Leisure Class*. New York: Macmillan, 1899.

Walker, Alexander. *Rudolph Valentino*. New York: Penguin, 1976.

Waller, Gregory. "Historicizing, a Test Case: Japan on American Screens, 1909–1915." Unpublished manuscript obtained from Sumiko Higashi.

Watanabe, Masao. "Meiji shoki no Dawinizumu" [Darwinism in the early Meiji period]. In *Seiyo no shogeki to nihon* [Impact of the West and Japan], ed. Haga Toru, Sukehiro Hirakawa, Shunsuke Kamei, and Keiichiro Kobori, 83–107. Tokyo: Tokyo daigaku shuppan kai, 1973.

Watkins, Fred. "Sessue Hayakawa Today." *Films in Review* 17.6 (June/July 1966): 391–92.

Welsh, Jim. "DeMille's Sensation Restored: Kino on Video's *The Cheat*." *Literature/Film Quarterly* 24.4 (1996): 452–53.

Whissel, Kristen. "The Gender of Empire: American Modernity, Masculinity, and Edison's War Actualities." In *A Feminist Reader in Early Cinema*, ed. Jennifer M. Bean and Diane Negra, 141–65. Durham, N.C.: Duke University Press, 2002.

Williams, Linda. "Melodrama Revised." In *Refiguring American Film Genres: Theory and History*, ed. Nick Browne, 42–88. Berkeley: University of California Press, 1998.

———. *Playing the Race Card: Melodramas of Black and White from Uncle Tom to O. J. Simpson*. Princeton, N.J.: Princeton University Press, 2001.

Willis, Betty. "Famous Oriental Stars Return to the Screen." *Motion Picture Magazine* 42 (October 1931): 44–45, 90.

Winokur, Mark. "Improbable Ethnic Hero: William Powell and the Transformation of Ethnic Hollywood." *Cinema Journal* 27.1 (fall 1987): 5–22.

Wolfe, Charles. "The Return of Jimmy Stewart: The Publicity Photograph as Text." In *Stardom: Industry of Desire*, ed. Christine Gledhill, 92–106. London: Routledge, 1991.

Wong, Eugene Franklin. *On Visual Media Racism: Asians in the American Motion Pictures*. New York: Arno, 1978.

"Ya konnichiwa: Hayakawa Sesshu shi" [Hi, hello: Mr. Sessue Hayakawa]. *Shukan Yomiuri* (20 September 1959): 30–34.

Yamaguchi, Hikotaro. "Okina Rokkei ni kuyu" [I regret about Okina]. *Rafu Shimpo* 3719 (23 January 1916): 7.

Yamaguchi, Reiko. *Joyu Sadayakko* [The actress Sadayakko]. Tokyo: Asahi shinbun sha, 1993.

Yamamoto, Togo. "Beikoku seigeki tsushin" [News about American silent films]. *Katsudo Gaho* 6.9 (September 1922): 62–65.

———. "Renai geki ni akita beikoku eiga kai" [The American motion picture world got tired of love stories]. *Katsudo Gaho* 5.2 (February 1921): 42–43.

Yamanaka, Fujiko. "Hayakawa Sesshu 'onna' o kataru" [Sessue Hayakawa talks about "women"]. *Fujin Saron* 2.10 (October 1930): 118–21.

Yamanaka, Toshio. "Umi no kanata yori" [From overseas]. *Katsudo Zasshi* 11.12 (December 1925): 91.

Yamauchi, Uichi. "Sesshu san!" [Mr. Sessue!] *Katsudo Kurabu* 6.4 (April 1923): 108.

Yanagawa, Shunyo. "Bunsei rekiho roku" [Records of visiting famous writers]. *Katsudo Shashin Kai* 12 (August 1910): 3.

Yanaihara, Tadao. "Jinko mondai to imin" [Problems of population and immigration]. In *Ishokumin mondai koshukai koenshu* [Anthology of lectures on the problems of immigration], ed. Shakai kyoku shakai bu, 75–112. Tokyo: Shakai kyoku shakai bu, 1927.

Yano, Seiichi, ed. *Miyako Shinbun geino shiryo shusei: Taisho hen* [Compilation of materials on entertainment in the Miyako Shinbun: Taisho edition]. Tokyo: Hakusuisha, 1991.

Yokoyama, Toshio. *Japan in the Victorian Mind: A Study of Stereotyped Images of a Nation, 1850–1880.* London: Macmillan, 1987.

Yomota, Inuhiko. *Nihon no joyu* [Actresses of Japan]. Tokyo: Iwanami, 2000.

Yoneyama, Hiroshi, ed. "Rafu Nihonjin kai kiroku" [Record of Rafu Nihonjin kai]. Unpublished document, 1994.

Yoshihara, Mari. *Embracing the East: White Women and American Orientalism.* New York: Oxford University Press, 2003.

———. "Women's Asia: American Women and the Gendering of American Orientalism, 1870–WWII." Ph.D. diss., Brown University, 1997.

Yoshimoto, Mitsuhiro. *Kurosawa: Film Studies and Japanese Cinema.* Durham: Duke University Press, 2000.

———. "Logic of Sentiment: The Postwar Japanese Cinema and Questions of Modernity." Ph.D. diss., University of California, San Diego, 1993.

Yoshiyama, Kyokuko. *Nihon eiga kai jibutsu kigen* [Origin of things in Japanese cinema world]. Tokyo: Shinema to engei sha, 1933.

Yoshiyuki, Junnosuke. "Sekai ni kakeru Nihon no hashi: Hayakawa Sesshu" [The Japanese bridge over the world: Sessue Hayakawa]. *Shukan Gendai* [Weekly modern] 50 (19 December 1963): 46–49.

Yutkevich, Sergei, and Sergei Eisenstein. "The Eighth Art: On Expressionism, America and, of course, Chaplin." In *S. M. Eisenstein: Selected Works*, vol. 1, *Writings, 1922–34*, ed. and trans. Richard Taylor, 29–32. London: BFI, 1988.

Zhang, Zhen. "'An Amorous History of the Silver Screen': Film Culture, Urban Modernity, and the Vernacular Experience in China, 1896–1937." Ph.D. diss. University of Chicago, 1998.

Zito, Stephen F. "Thomas Harper Ince: The Creative Years (1910–1915)." Unpublished paper, 7 May 1969.

INDEX

Makeup, 34, 57, 61, 65, 83, 93–94, 164, 179, 181–84, 189, 198, 201, 256; of *kumadori*, 40, 55, 209

Man Beneath, The, 162, 170, 174–76

Manchuria, 67–68, 263, 267–68

Manifest destiny, 78

Man's Name, A, 224–25

Man Who Laughs Last, The (aka *The Man Who Laughed*), 263, 266

Man Who Turned White, The, 229

Marion, Frances, 173, 292 n. 12

Mark of Zorro, The, 190

Martin, Vivian, 113, 116, 183, 310 n. 13

Masculinity, 3, 41–42, 65, 108, 110, 191–93, 204, 278

Masks, 34, 200–213, 230, 282

Masochism, 3

Masquerade, race and, 15, 111–12, 120, 166–67, 175, 183, 190, 211

Mass culture, 242–43

Matinee idol, 1–3, 193, 239, 241, 275

McClatchy, Valentine Stuart, 33, 216

Meiji Reconstruction (1868), 50

Melodrama, 14–16, 265; acting style and, 196–97; American popular culture and, 106; *An Arabian Knight* and, 189–90, 193; *Broken Blossoms* and, 183–84; *The Call of the East* and, 121–24; *The Cheat* and, 38–44, 204–6; *Death Mask* and, 78–81; family and, 82–83; *Forbidden Paths* and, 108–16, 208–9; gender and, 106; general magazines and, 144; *Hashimura Togo* and, 103; *The Honorable Friend* and, 92–94; *The Honor of His House* and, 125–26; "Indian films" and, 77–78; race and, 106; *The Secret Game* and, 129; self-sacrifice as motif in, 2, 12, 15–16, 64, 82, 103–35, 142, 173, 180, 189, 193, 208, 210, 225–27, 243, 263; *The Swamp* and, 185–86; theater and, 196–97, 201–2; *The Tong Man* and, 182–83; *The Typhoon* and, 69–75, 203; *The Vermilion Pencil* and, 226; *Where Lights Are Low* and, 225;

The Wrath of the Gods and, 14, 57–65, 202

"Melting pot," 2, 89, 143

Mexico, 82, 84, 109–13, 116, 155, 174, 253, 299 n. 3

Michaels, Walter Benn, 215

Michelangelo, 5

Middle class, 7, 12–16, 140, 284 n. 27; Americanization Movement and, 89–90; as audience, 9–15, 53–54, 59, 87–88, 107, 156, 165, 187, 191, 203, 207; *The Cheat* and, 21, 29–49, 206; discourse of domesticity, family, and home and, 30–37, 44, 77, 88, 97, 123, 142; *Forbidden Paths* and, 109–10; genteel tradition and, 107, 118; *Hashimura Togo* and, 100–105; Japan and, 146–47, 239; morality and, 117, 146, 149; *O Mimi San* and, 52; *The Wrath of the Gods* and, 59–65

Mie (glaring), 39, 65, 74, 80–81, 198, 200–201, 203, 206, 209

Mikado, or The Town of Titipu, The, 14, 52–56

Militarism, 6–7, 9, 33, 217, 267–76, 279

Milliet, Paul, 25

Mimicry, 80, 158, 176, 245

Ministry of Education, 147

Ministry of Foreign Affairs, 225, 265

Ministry of Navy, 265

Miscegenation, 38–39, 72, 88, 107, 110–11, 116, 122–25, 134, 184–87, 190, 193, 207, 236, 263–65

Mise-en-scène, 71–72, 131

Misérables, Les, 274

Miura, Tamaki, 221, 304 n. 13

Miyatake, Toyo, 1

Model minority, 2, 12, 14, 193, 203, 207–8. *See also* Americanization; Assimilation

Modernity, 8, 13, 32, 108, 242, 254, 268

Modernization, 83; cinema and, 18, 146, 242–60, 266–67; Japan and, 7, 9–13, 17–18, 32–33, 50–51, 67–68, 73–75,

Race, 8, 17, 29–31, 38, 44, 53, 62, 88,
    97, 102, 187, 215, 220, 223, 225–26,
    250, 254, 302 n. 45; Asia and, 11–12,
    44, 112, 211; child discourse and, 164;
    masquerade and, 15, 111–12, 120, 166–
    67, 175, 183, 190, 211; melodrama and,
    106; morality and, 106–8
Racial difference, 33, 112, 122, 142, 164,
    167, 215, 218, 230, 264
Racial Equality Clause, 216, 250
Racial hierarchy, 11, 58–59, 68, 72, 77,
    88, 102–16, 124, 140, 164, 178–79,
    188, 215, 236, 239, 249–50, 262, 299
    n. 15; movable middle-ground posi-
    tion in, 9–12, 15, 67, 70, 88, 162–63,
    167, 179, 187–88, 203–4, 215, 219–20,
    227–29, 235, 271, 275, 279
Racism, 3–5, 68, 73–74, 102, 112, 115,
    118, 123–25, 174, 215–17, 225–26, 236,
    249, 281
Radio, 254
Rafu Nihonjin-kai (Japanese association
    of Los Angeles), 154
Rafu Shimpo, 26–30, 153, 166, 185, 219,
    221, 225, 235–39. See also Japanese
    American press
Rashomon, 275, 330 n. 84
Ray, Charles, 241
Realism, 16–17, 24, 52, 154–58, 167, 172–
    75, 180–81, 187, 196–97, 238, 242
Reception, 8, 13, 16–18, 23–28, 117–18,
    135, 153–54, 167, 172–73, 176, 180,
    191–93, 214, 220–22, 224, 235–60,
    265–70, 272, 278
Red Cross, 21, 35–41, 204–5, 276
Reid, Wallace, 88
Reiko no chimata ni [At the top of sacred
    light], 256
Relic of Old Japan, A, 294 n. 22
Re Mizeraburu [Les Misérables], 274
Representation, 15, 136, 191, 213; Japan
    and, 8, 154–80, 222, 243–47, 269–70,
    281

Restrained style, 97; acting and, 196–
    213, 251, 329 n. 71
Ri Koran, 328 n. 56
Rimmon-Kenan, Shlomith, 297 n. 12
RKO Radio Pictures, 315 n. 55
Robbins, Marc, 183, 185
Robertson-Cole Distributing Corpora-
    tion, 16–17, 168–78, 191, 214, 219–30,
    255, 261–62, 303 n. 1
Robinson, Edward G., 327 n. 41
Rodin, Auguste, 24
Rohmer, Sax (aka Arthur Sarsfield
    Ward), 263, 288 n. 66
Rojo no reikon (Souls on the Road), 256
Romeo and Juliet, 182–83, 211
Roosevelt, Theodore, 33
Russia, 66–68, 216, 285 n. 12
Russo-Japanese War, 9, 33, 66–67, 265

Sadayakko (aka Madame Yacco), 24–25,
    137, 139
Sakura-Jima, 57–58
Samurai (play), 262
Scher, Louise, 25
Screen persona, of Hayakawa, 49, 97,
    139, 220
Sea Is Boiling Hot, The, 279
Second World War. See World War II
Secret Game, The, 128–35, 139, 162,
    209–10
Secret Sin, The, 46
Seed of the Sun, 216
Sei no kagayaki [Radiance of life], 257
Self-sacrifice. See Melodrama: self-sacri-
    fice as motif in
Sennett, Mack, 76, 290 n. 4
Sensuality, 110–11, 114–15, 132, 190, 227–
    28. See also Eroticism
Sen Yan's Devotion, 262
Sessue Hayakawa Feature Play Company,
    223–24
Seventh Heaven, 266, 268
Sexuality, 8, 29, 88, 94, 107, 109–11,

DAISUKE MIYAO is an assistant professor of Japanese literature and film at the University of Oregon. He is a coeditor of Casio Abe's *Beat Takeshi vs. Takeshi Kitano*.

Library of Congress Cataloging-in-Publication Data
Miyao, Daisuke.
Sessue Hayakawa : silent cinema and transnational stardom / Daisuke Miyao.
p. cm.
Filmography: p.
Includes bibliographical references and index.
ISBN-13: 978-0-8223-3958-8 (cloth : alk. paper)
ISBN-13: 978-0-8223-3969-4 (pbk. : alk. paper)
1. Hayakawa, Sesshu, 1889–1973. I. Title.
PN2928.H35M59 2007
791.4302′8092—dc22
[B] 2006027824